Theological Issues
in the
Letters of Paul

FOR DOROTHY

with thanksgiving
at the half-century mark

Theological Issues in the Letters of Paul

J. LOUIS MARTYN

ABINGDON PRESS
NASHVILLE

Library of Congress Cataloging-in-Publication Data

Martyn, J. Louis (James Louis), 1925-
    Theological issues in the letters of Paul/J. Louis Martyn.
        p.   cm.
    Includes bibliographical references and indexes.
    ISBN 0-687-05622-5 (alk. paper)
    ISBN 0-687-02704-7 (pbk.)
    1. Bible. N.T. Epistles of Paul—Theology.   I. Title.
BS2651.M38   1997
227'.06—dc21   97-15082
                                                                              CIP

02-03-04-05-06 — 10 9 8 7 6 5 4 3

Typeset by Waverley Typesetters, Galashiels
Printed and bound in Great Britain by Bookcraft, Avon

Contents

Preface

My initial and happily acknowledged debt is to Martinus C. de Boer. It was he who generously suggested drawing on a number of my essays in order to produce a coherent volume on Pauline theology. Written in a period stretching over more than three decades, the essays have been extensively edited, in several cases thoroughly rewritten. In numerous studies of Paul, the apostle's letter to the Romans has been allowed to serve as the primary lens through which the other letters are read. Here primacy has been granted to Galatians, but I trust that the resulting angle of vision can help us to sense major issues in the other letters as well.

For including the volume in the series *Studies of the New Testament and Its World* my thanks go to John Barclay, Joel Marcus and John Riches; also to the gracious publishers at T&T Clark Ltd. Similarly, for the Abingdon Press edition I am indebted to the courteous professionals at that house.

Acknowledgements

With permission from the respective publishers, the chapters in this volume include, often in greatly revised form, material that appeared earlier in various settings:

Chapter 1: A Law-Observant Mission to Gentiles
'A Law-Observant Mission to Gentiles: The Background of Galatians,' *SJT* 38 (1985) 307–324; cf. Martyn, *Galatians*, Comments 6 and 33.

Chapter 2: A Tale of Two Churches
Written both for the present volume and, in a different form, for Martyn, *Galatians*, Comment 46.

Chapter 3: Romans as One of the Earliest Interpretations of Galatians
'Paul and His Jewish-Christian Interpreters,' *USQR* 42 (1988) 1–15; cf. Martyn, *Galatians*, Introduction §§11–13.

Chapter 4: Leo Baeck's Reading of Paul
'Introduction to Leo Baeck,' *Jewish Perspectives on Christianity* (ed. F. A. Rothschild; New York: Crossroad, 1990; New York: Continuum, 1996) 21–41. The German edition (Neukirchen: Neukirchener, 1997) has some supplementary footnotes. Appendix: A Review of *The Mythmaker: Paul and the Invention of Christianity* by Hyam Maccoby (New York: Harper & Row, 1986). *New York Times*, July 20, 1986. Copyright © 1986 by The New York Times Co. Reprinted by Permission.

Chapter 5: Galatians, An Anti-Judaic Document?
Written both for the present volume and, in a different form, for Martyn, *Galatians*, Introduction §17.

Chapter 6: Epistemology at the Turn of the Ages

'Epistemology at the Turn of the Ages: 2 Corinthians 5:16,' *Christian History and Interpretation: Studies Presented to John Knox* (ed. W. R. Farmer, et al.; Cambridge: Cambridge University Press, 1967) 269–287.

Chapter 7: Apocalyptic Antinomies

'Apocalyptic Antinomies in Paul's Letter to the Galatians,' *NTS* 31 (Cambridge: Cambridge University Press, 1985) 410–424.

Chapter 8: Christ and the Elements of the Cosmos

'Christ, the Elements of the Cosmos, and the Law in Galatians,' reprinted by permission from *The Social World of the First Christians: Essays in Honor of Wayne A. Meeks* (eds L. M. White and O. L. Yarbrough, copyright © 1995 Augsburg Fortress) 16–39; cf. Martyn, *Galatians*, Comment 41.

Chapter 9: God's Way of Making Right What Is Wrong

'On Hearing the Gospel Both in the Silence of the Tradition and in Its Eloquence,' *From Jesus to John: Essays on Jesus and New Testament Christology in Honour of Marinus de Jonge* (ed. M. C. de Boer; Sheffield: Sheffield Academic Press, 1993) 129–147; cf. Martyn, *Galatians*, Comment 28.

Chapter 10: The Abrahamic Covenant, Christ, and the Church

'Covenant, Christ, and Church in Galatians,' reprinted by permission from *The Future of Christology: Essays in Honor of Leander E. Keck* (eds A. J. Malherbe and W. A. Meeks, copyright © 1993 Augsburg Fortress) 137–151; cf. Martyn, *Galatians*, Comment 37. Appendix: A Review of *Paul the Apostle: The Triumph of God in Life and Thought*, by J. Christiaan Beker (Philadelphia: Fortress, 1980): *WW* 2 (1982) 194–198. Copyright © 1982 Word & World, Luther Seminary. Reprinted with permission.

Chapter 11: The Textual Contradiction Between Habakkuk 2:4 and Leviticus 18:5

'Paul's Understanding of the Textual Contradiction Between Habakkuk 2:4 and Leviticus 18:5,' *From Tradition to Inter-*

pretation: Studies in Biblical Intertextuality in Honor of James A. Sanders (eds C. A. Evans and S. Talmon; Leiden: Brill, 1997) 345–353; cf. Martyn, *Galatians*, Comment 35).

Chapter 12: The Covenants of Hagar and Sarah
'The Covenants of Hagar and Sarah,' *Faith and History: Essays in Honor of Paul W. Meyer* (ed. J. T. Carroll et al.; Atlanta: Scholars Press, 1990) 160–192; cf. Martyn, *Galatians*, Comment 45.

Chapter 13: John and Paul on the Subject of Gospel and Scripture
'Listening to John and Paul on the Subject of Gospel and Scripture,' (with B. R. Gaventa, and P. W. Meyer) *WW* 12 (1992) 68–81. Copyright © 1992 Word & World, Luther Seminary. Reprinted with permission.

Chapter 14: The Crucial Event in the History of the Law
'The Crucial Event in the History of the Law (Gal 5:14),' *Theology and Ethics in Paul and His Modern Interpreters: Essays in Honor of Victor Paul Furnish* (eds E. H. Lovering, Jr. and J. L. Sumney; Nashville: Abingdon, 1996) 48–61; cf. Martyn, *Galatians*, Comment 48.

Chapter 15: The Daily Life of the Church in the War Between the Spirit and the Flesh
Written both for the present volume and, in a different form, for Martyn, *Galatians*, Comment 49.

Chapter 16: A Formula for Communal Discord!
'A Formula for Communal Discord as a Clue to the Nature of Pastoral Guidance,' *Putting Body and Soul Together: Essays in Honor of Robin Scroggs* (eds A. Brown, G. F. Snyder, and V. Wiles; Valley Forge: Trinity, 1997) 203–216.

Chapter 17: From Paul to Flannery O'Connor with the Power of Grace
'From Paul to Flannery O'Connor with the Power of Grace,' *Katallagete* (Winter, 1981) 10–17. The essence of O'Connor's story 'Revelation' is taken with permission from Alexandra Brown 'The Word of the Cross, Pattern for Moral Discernment: From Paul to Flannery O'Connor,' *Doctrine and Life* 47 (1997).

Abbreviations, Texts, and Translations

Biblical Books (with the Apocrypha)

The text of the New Testament is K. Aland, et al., *Novum Testamentum Graece* (27th edition; Stuttgart: Deutsche Bibelgesellschaft, 1993). *Abbreviations* are those used by the Society of Biblical Literature. Quotations are sometimes drawn from NEB, RSV and NRSV; where there is no notation, the *translations* are those of the author.

Pseudepigrapha of the Old Testament

Abbreviations are those used by the SBL (plus *JosAs* for *Joseph and Asenath*). Quotations are drawn from *OTP*, occasionally with minor changes made from the original texts.

The Writings of Philo

Texts: *LCL*, from which English quotations are drawn, sometimes altered slightly on the basis of the Greek.

Abbreviations:

de Abr.	On Abraham
de Agric.	On Husbandry
de Deo	(see in Bibliography F. Siegert, *Philon*)
de Fuga	On Flight and Finding
de Gig.	On the Giants
Heres	Who is the Heir
de Migr. Abr.	On the Migration of Abraham
de Op. Mundi	On the Creation
de Post. Caini	On the Posterity and Exile of Cain
de Somn.	On Dreams
de Spec. Leg.	On the Special Laws

de Virt.	On the Virtues
de Vita Cont.	On the Contemplative Life
de Vita Mos.	On Moses
Leg. Alleg.	Allegorical Interpretation
Quest. Exod.	Questions and Answers on Exodus
Quod Deus Imm.	On the Unchangeableness of God
Quod Omn.	Every Good Man is Free

The Writings of Josephus

Texts: *LCL*, from which English quotations are drawn, sometimes altered slightly on the basis of the Greek.

Abbreviations:

| Ant. | *Jewish Antiquities* |
| Ap. | *Against Apion* |

Dead Sea Scrolls

Texts: Usually E. Lohse (ed.), *Die Texte aus Qumran* (Darmstadt: Wissenschaftliche Buchgesellschaft, 1971); English quotations are drawn sometimes from G. Vermes, *The Dead Sea Scrolls in English* (3rd ed.; London: Penguin, 1987) and sometimes from F. G. Martinez, *The Dead Sea Scrolls Translated* (Leiden: Brill, 1994), occasionally altered slightly.

Abbreviations:

CD	*Covenant of Damascus*
1QS	*Rule of the Community*
1QH	*Thanksgiving Hymns*
1QpHab	*Pesher on Habakkuk*

Rabbinic Literature

Abbreviations are those of the Society of Biblical Literature (similar to those given in M. Jastrow, *A Dictionary of the Targumim, the Talmud Babli and Yerushalmi, and the Midrashic Literature* [2 vols; New York: Pardes, 1950]).

Non-Canonical Early Christian Literature

Ascents of James	*The Ascents of James* (cited by book, chapter, and verse in Clementine *Recognitions* and by page numbers in Van Voorst, *Ascents*, and Jones, *Source*)
Clementine *Hom.*	
Clementine *Recog.*	Pseudo-Clementine *Homilies* and *Recognitions* (see B. Rehm in Bibliography)
Ep. Pet. Jas.	*The Epistle of Peter to James* (cited by chapter and verse, and by page numbers in HS)
Eusebius *EH*	Eusebius *Ecclesiastical History*
Herm. Man.	*Hermas Mandates*
Herm. Vis.	*Hermas Visions*
Ign. *Magn.*	Ignatius *Letter to the Magnesians*

Greek and Latin Literature

(Neither Jewish nor Christian; the works are sometimes abbreviated in obvious ways)

Aristotle *Metaphysics*
     Rhetoric
Cicero *Topica*
Empedocles
Epictetus *Discourses*
     Enchiridion
Heraclitus
Homer *Iliad*
     Odyssey
Quintilian *Institutio Oratoria*

General Abbreviations

AB	*Anchor Bible*
ABD	*Anchor Bible Dictionary* (ed. D. N. Freedman; New York: Doubleday, 1992)
ANRW	*Aufstieg und Niedergang der Römischen Welt* (eds H. Temporini and W. Haase; Berlin: de Gruyter, 1971–)

BAGD	W. Bauer, W. F. Arndt, F. W. Gingrich, and F. W. Danker, *A Greek-English Lexicon of the New Testament and Other Early Christian Literature* (Chicago: University of Chicago Press, 1979)
BDF	F. Blass and A. Debrunner, *A Greek Grammar of the New Testament and Other Early Christian Literature* (trans. and rev. R. W. Funk; Chicago: University of Chicago Press, 1961)
Billerbeck	H. Strack and P. Billerbeck, *Kommentar zum Neuen Testament aus Talmud und Midrash* (6 vols; Munich: Beck, 1926–63)
BJRL	*Bulletin of the John Rylands Library*
CBQ	*Catholic Biblical Quarterly*
DK	H. Diels and W. Kranz, *Die Fragmenta der Vorsokratiker* (3 vols; Berlin: Weidmann, 1951 1952).
ETL	*Ephemerides theologicae lovanienses*
EvT	*Evangelische Theologie*
ExpTim	*Expository Times*
HS	E. Hennecke, *New Testament Apocrypha* (2 vols; ed. W. Schneemelcher; Philadelphia: Westminster, 1963–65)
HTR	*Harvard Theological Review*
IBS	*Irish Biblical Studies*
Int	*Interpretation*
JBL	*Journal of Biblical Literature*
JSHRZ	*Jüdische Schriften aus hellenistisch-römischer Zeit* (ed. W. G. Kümmel; Gütersloh: Mohn, 1973)
JSNT	*Journal for the Study of the New Testament*
LCL	*Loeb Classical Library*
lit.	literally
LSJ	H. G. Liddell and R. Scott, *A Greek-English Lexicon* (rev. and aug. H. S. Jones; 2 vols; Oxford: Clarendon, 1951)
MGWJ	*Monatschrift für Geschichte und Wissenschaft des Judentums*
MH	J. H. Moulton and W. F. Howard, *A Grammar of New Testament Greek* (vol. 2; Edinburgh: T&T Clark, 1928)

MM	J. H. Moulton and G. Milligan, *The Vocabulary of the Greek Testament Illustrated from the Papyri* (London: Hodder & Stoughton, 1930)
MT	J. H. Moulton and N. Turner, *A Grammar of New Testament Greek* (vol. 3; Edinburgh: T&T Clark, 1963)
NedTTs	*Nederlands theologisch tijdschrift*
NTS	*New Testament Studies*
OTP	*The Old Testament Pseudepigrapha* (2 vols; ed. J. H. Charlesworth; New York: Doubleday, 1985)
PG	Migne, *Patrologia Latina*
RB	*Revue Biblique*
RSR	*Religious Studies Review*
SJT	*Scottish Journal of Theology*
ST	*Studia theologica*
TAPA	*Transactions of the American Philological Association*
TDNT	*Theological Dictionary of the New Testament* (10 vols; eds G. Kittel and G. Friedrich; Grand Rapids: Eerdmans, 1964–1976 [German volumes began in 1933])
TLZ	*Theologische Literaturzeitung*
TS	*Theological Studies*
TTZ	*Trierer theologische Zeitschrift*
USQR	*Union Seminary Quarterly Review*
WW	*Word and World*
ZBG	M. Zerwick, *Biblical Greek* (Rome: Biblical Institute, 1963)
ZNW	*Zeitschrift für die neutestamentliche Wissenschaft*
ZTK	*Zeitschrift für Theologie und Kirche*

Translations of the Bible

NEB	*New English Bible*
REB	*Revised English Bible*
RSV	*Revised Standard Version*
NRSV	*New Revised Standard Version*
JB	*Jerusalem Bible*
NJB	*New Jerusalem Bible*

Part I

Paul and Christian Judaism

Part I
Paul and Christian Judaism

There have been numerous studies of Paul and Judaism, and for very good reasons. Writing to his church in Philippi, for example, Paul identified himself as a 'Hebrew born of Hebrews . . . as to righteousness under the Law, blameless' (Phil 3:5–6). Judaism – notably the significantly Hellenized forms found in the Diaspora – played a very weighty role in the formation of Paul's identity.[1]

Yet there are in his letters – often in the same passages that reflect his Jewish heritage – references that seem to express a negative stance toward Judaism. After saying that, as to righteousness under the Law, he was blameless, Paul continued, 'Yet whatever gains I had, these I have come to regard as loss because of Christ' (Phil 3:7; cf. Gal 1:13–16). One is not surprised to find interpreters speaking of Paul's break with Judaism. Here, however, two caveats are essential, one with regard to the word 'break,' one with respect to the term 'Judaism.'

Break. (*a*) Whereas the use of this term could lead us to think of something Paul himself did – he decided one day to break away from his religious heritage – in the passage in Philippians Paul refers essentially to the effect of a deed of God. Something about the nature of God's act in Christ took from Paul *against his will* significant aspects of his Jewish heritage (cf. Gal 2:19–20; 1 Cor 1:23). To speak in a simplistic manner of Paul's break with Judaism could easily cause us to attribute to Paul what he himself attributed to God's new-creative act in Christ. But there is more. (*b*) To speak simply of a break could also blind us to Paul's certainty that the God and Father of Jesus Christ was the same God who centuries earlier had made an indelible promise to Abraham. Thus, in the disruptive action of God in Christ, Paul found that crucial aspects of his Jewish heritage were also given back to him, re-minted into non-religious currency, but, if anything,

---

[1] See especially Barclay, 'The Jews of the Diaspora;' idem, *Diaspora.*

with heightened significance: 'God is one' (Gal 3:20; Rom 3:30); Abraham is 'the father of us all' (Rom 4:16; cf. Gal 3:29).[2]

Judaism. Studying Paul's letters, we can gain even greater precision in our use of this term if we pose two further questions. What are we to say about Paul and Judaism when we think, first, of his oral evangelism and, second, of his letter writing? Genuine answers are forthcoming if we attend to the identity of flesh-and-blood persons with whom Paul was actually in contact. (*a*) On the one hand, almost without exception, Paul stood face to face in his oral proclamation not with Jews (and thus with Judaism), but rather with the Gentiles to whom he was sent by God (e.g. Gal 1:16; 2:7, 9; Rom 11:13).[3] Hence, in city after city, while Paul must have been initially sensed by his Gentile hearers as a Jew given to numerous expressions drawn from the Jewish scriptures, he himself included in his inaugural preaching neither positive references to Judaism itself nor the negative notes about matters Jewish that characterize Phil 3:7 and other passages (see, e.g. 1 Thess 1:9–10; Gal 3:1; 4:13–14; 1 Cor 2:2). (*b*) On the other hand, Paul's letters do contain those surprisingly negative notes, and most of them are sounded in passages in which the apostle *is* dealing with Jews, *but* Jews of a special sort. That is to say, the tensile elements vis-à-vis Jewish motifs reflect in the main Paul's ferocious conflicts with identifiable persons who prove to have been *Christian* Jews, active among Gentiles in the Diaspora, while being closely related to the 'mother' church in Jerusalem.[4] The point bears emphasizing: Most of

---

[2] On Abraham and Christ as non-religious figures, see chapters 5 and 10 below.

[3] Working in accordance with the Jerusalem agreement – 'they saw clearly that I had been entrusted by God with the gospel as it is directed to those who are not circumcised, just as Peter had been entrusted with the gospel to those who are circumcised' (Gal 2:7) – Paul did not commence his evangelistic labors in the local synagogue (so Acts), but rather in conversations and discourses held in tentmaker's shops, in the street, in private homes, among groups gathered by the riverside, etc. See Hock, *Tentmaking.* In light of 2 Cor 11:24, Barclay is right to say that 'at least in his defence [prior to receiving the thirty nine lashes], *if at no other time,* [Paul] must have given some account of his convictions to an audience of Jews' ('Diaspora Jews,' 116 n. 53; emphasis added). As the pertinent data in Paul's letters show, however, those occasions were in fact exceptions that prove the rule (was it on one of those exceptional occasions that Crispus was converted [1 Cor 1:14; cf. Acts 18:8; 1 Cor 7:18]?). See Meeks, *Urban,* 25–32; Downing, 'Preparation.'

[4] Especially for our understanding of these Christian Jews active among Gentiles in the Diaspora, significant help is to be found in the works of Barclay, mentioned in note 1 above; cf. also B. W. Winter and A. D. Clark, *Acts.* And the better we understand these opponents of Paul, the more fully will comprehend the apostle himself.

the passages that seem to reflect on Paul's part a sustained and critical consideration of Jewish matters – and Jews – show us, when carefully examined, a theologian in heated combat with certain circles of Christian Jews, not with Judaism itself (whether Palestinian or Diaspora).[5] This proves to be a matter of considerable importance for the history of early Christianity (Part I). It is also a point closely related, as we should expect, to Paul's understanding of God's way of making right what is wrong (Part II), to his interpretation of scripture (Part III) and, not least, to his perception of the church's daily life (Part IV).

Regarding the Jerusalem church's standing in the background of the anti-Pauline, Christian Jewish groups reflected in Galatians and 2 Corinthians, see chapters 2 and 6 below. And if the 'evil workers' who 'mutilate the flesh' (Phil 3:2) are very nearly the same as the pseudo-apostles of 2 Corinthians (e.g. Gnilka, *Philipperbrief,* 218), their being in some measure related to the Jerusalem church is certainly possible.

[5] Parts of Romans constitute an exception of true significance, but an exception nonetheless (e.g. Rom 2:17–3:20; 9:1–11:36). In that letter, that is to say, Paul brings Jews and Judaism within his purview for two major reasons, neither of which requires us to modify the point made in the text above. (*a*) First, Jews and Judaism were important to the church in Rome, a mixed and complex congregation not founded by Paul, but from which he planned to launch a mission to Gentiles in Spain. (*b*) Second, and at least equally important, Jews and Judaism were significant to the church in Jerusalem; and in writing Romans, Paul was anxiously aware that, temporarily leaving his Gentile mission field, he would shortly have to deal directly with that church, and thus with its members who were still active in the mission to the Jews (Rom 15:25; 15:8). Moreover, and a source of even greater anxiety, Paul seems to have thought that these evangelists to the Jews held him to some degree responsible for the slim results of labors they had undertaken at God's direction (Rom 9:1–3; 10:1; cf. Acts 21:20–21 and chapter 2 below). Influential members of the Jerusalem church may even have feared that Paul intended to found in Spain purely Gentile congregations in which Jewish traditions would play virtually no role at all (cf. Keck, 'Judgments'). Thus, contemplating developments in Rome and Jerusalem, Paul found necessary a comprehensive vision that takes explicit account of Jews and Judaism.

1

A Law-Observant Mission to Gentiles

A Widely Accepted Portrait of Early Christian Missions

That the early church was passionately evangelistic is clear to every reader of the New Testament. Equally clear, or so it would seem, is the scholarly consensus that when Christian evangelists – notably Paul and his co-workers – took the step of reaching beyond the borders of the Jewish people, they did so without requiring observance of the Jewish Law. The work of these evangelists, in turn, is said to have sparked a reaction on the part of firmly observant Christian Jews, who, seeing the growth of the Gentile mission, sought to require observance of the Law by its converts. Struggles ensued, and the outcome, to put the matter briefly, was victory for the mission to the Gentiles, for the Law-free theology characteristic of that mission, and for the churches produced by it.[1] In broad terms such is the standard portrait of early Christian missions. That portrait was codified at the beginning of the twentieth century by the great historian Adolf von Harnack (1851–1930).[2] However varied the Gentile mission may have been in minor regards, in respect to the Jewish Law all *primary, evangelistic* efforts toward Gentiles were the same: *The* Gentile mission was the mission loosed from observance of the Law.

This portrait is not arbitrary. Harnack and his successors drew it on the basis of primary evidence in the letters of Paul, traditions and editorial material in the Acts of the Apostles, and other traditions scattered throughout the New Testament, notably in the gospels.[3] The

---

[1] Instructed by my friend Paul Meyer, I have learned in the final analysis to refer to the theology characteristic of the Pauline churches as circumcision free rather than as Law free; see chapter 14 below. In the present context, however, I will stay with the standard nomenclature.

[2] Harnack, *Mission*.

[3] Regarding the testimony of Luke and the other synoptists, see Martyn, 'Mission to Gentiles,' 308–309.

evidence in Paul's letters is basic, because those letters were written during the sixth decade of the first century, in the midst of what is termed the Gentile mission. Most influential is a paragraph in Paul's letter to the churches of Galatia, in which, speaking of the leaders of the Jewish-Christian church in Jerusalem Paul says, '. . . they saw clearly that I had been entrusted by God with the gospel as it is directed to those who are not circumcised, just as Peter had been entrusted with the gospel to those who are circumcised' (Gal 2:7). From Paul's own mouth, therefore, we have a picture that presents two distinguishable missions proceeding along two parallel lines. The context of the quotation makes it clear that one of the lines is Law observant, while the other is not: Peter pursues *the* mission to the Jews (Law observant); Paul pursues *the* mission to the Gentiles (Law free). Thus, the standard portrait of *the* unified, Law-free mission to the Gentiles is drawn on the basis of primary evidence stemming from that mission itself.

Doubt

Is that portrait also fully accurate? Reading between the lines of Paul's letters, we may be assailed by doubt. Here and there, we find hints that at least some early Christian preachers directed their evangelistic message to Gentiles without surrendering observance of the Law. Could it be, in fact, that Galatians, the major witness to the existence of a single, Pauline Law-free mission to Gentiles, proves, upon inspection, to reflect a picture rather more complex than is customarily assumed?

We have only to consider the persons whose coming into Paul's Galatian churches compelled him to write the letter. Is their work entirely secondary to Paul's labors, in the sense that they have no Gentile mission of their own? An affirmative answer is reflected in the custom of referring to these persons as Paul's 'opponents,' for in that usage we imply that their identity is given in their opposition to Paul.[4] True, Paul makes it clear that he views them as opponents, and there are indications that to a considerable extent they view him in the same manner. There is, however, one good reason for considering that nomenclature somewhat reductionistic. As Paul himself makes clear, he is certain that, in their basic identity, these persons are opponents of *God*, not merely of himself (Gal 1:6–9). Could he be implying that they oppose God

---

[4] E.g. Luedemann, *Paulus*, 2.144–152.

quite fundamentally by carrying out their own Law-observant mission to Gentiles? As we focus our attention on that question, we will avoid a premature answer by referring to these persons neutrally as 'the Teachers,' thus taking care not to identify them solely on the basis of their relationship with Paul.[5]

Do the data available to us offer clues sufficient in number and clarity to enable us to draw a reliable picture of the Teachers? There are solid grounds for confidence, even though we have nothing from the hands of the Teachers themselves.

Data in Galatians Itself

Most important are several explicit and highly revealing references to the Teachers in Galatians itself: 1:6–9; 3:1–2, 5; 4:17; 5:7–12; 6:12–14. From these passages alone we can arrive at a sensible portrait. But there is also the helpful fact that, because Paul composes no sentence of the letter without thinking of the Teachers, his explicit references to them are accompanied by numerous allusions to them and to their work. As we will see below, carefully interpreted, these allusions fill out in important ways Paul's explicit references.

Pertinent Jewish and Christian-Jewish Traditions[6]

Data in Galatians show the Teachers to have connections both with Diaspora Judaism and with Palestinian, Christian Judaism. Whatever their birthplace and locale of education, the Teachers are messianic Jews, at home among Gentiles, in the sense of being able not only to live

---

[5] We will deal below (and especially in chapter 2) with the probability that the Teachers were in touch with the False Brothers and their circumcision party in the Jerusalem church, even being to some degree sponsored by that wing of the 'mother' congregation. Thus, we can assume that the Teachers were well acquainted with stories about Paul's activities, both at the Jerusalem meeting and in the Antioch incident (Gal 2:1–14). It is therefore possible that, in part, they came to Galatia in order to counter Paul's work. As we will see, however, they seem also to have had their own Law-observant mission to Gentiles, apart from their concern to correct what they took to be Paul's errors (cf. chapters 10 and 12 below).

[6] Here and elsewhere I intend some degree of distinction between the adjectival expressions 'Jewish-Christian' and 'Christian-Jewish' (and their corresponding nouns), the second word being the dominant one (see Glossary). Churches, for example, that were essentially Jewish sects would be groups of Christian Jews, rather than groups of Jewish Christians.

among them, but also to make effective, apologetic contact with them. Several motifs that Paul connects with the Teachers – the view that Gentiles worship the elements of the cosmos, for example – find significant parallels in the apologetic literature of Diaspora Judaism (chapter 8 below). We can enrich our portrait of the Teachers, therefore, by relating some aspects of their message, as reflected in Galatians, to passages in some of the literature of Diaspora Judaism, such as Wisdom, the writings of Philo and Josephus, *Aristobulus*, and *Joseph and Asenath*.[7]

From Galatians itself, we can also see that the Teachers are in touch with – indeed understand themselves to represent – a powerful circle of

[7] On Wisdom, Philo, Josephus, *Aristobulus* and *Joseph and Asenath*, see the articles, with bibliographies, of Winston, Borgen, Feldman, Holladay, and Chesnutt in *ABD*. On the literature of Diaspora Judaism, as it is important for our understanding of early Christian theology and history, one can still learn by reading with care such older works as those of Dalbert, *Theologie*, Bussmann, *Missionspredigt*, and Georgi, *Opponents*. But see notably the corrective and enriching dimensions of more recent contributions: Borgen, 'Judaism (Egypt),' *ABD*; Applebaum, 'Judaism (North Africa),' *ABD*; Walter, 'Diaspora-Juden;' Barclay, 'Diaspora Jews;' idem, *Diaspora*. Older theories about a unified and organized Jewish *mission* to Gentiles in the first century – sometimes formulated in part by taking at face value Matt 23:15 – cannot be sustained. See, e.g. Walter, 'Diaspora-Juden,' 50–51; McKnight, *Jewish Missionary Activity* (but also the tempering review by Westerholm, *JBL* 113 [1994] 330–332); Goodman, 'Jewish Proselytizing;' Feldman, *Jew and Gentile*. But the rejection of the theory of an organized Jewish mission to Gentiles does not tell us that the motif of hoped-for conversions is wholly absent from the literature of Diaspora Judaism. We can take *Joseph and Asenath* as an example. Burchard is right both to reject the characterization of *JosAs* as a missionary tract – a document having no theme other than the conversion of a Gentile – and to affirm that it was written for Jews, born and converted (*OTP* 2.194–195). He is also right, however, (*a*) to identify Gentile conversion to Judaism as the author's main focus ('Importance,' 104), (*b*) to speak of Asenath's re-creative transformation as 'a pattern which conversion often followed' (*OTP* 2.192; note especially Joseph's prayer for Asenath; *JosAs* 8:9), and thus (*c*) to characterize conversion as the subject by which the author can remind converts 'of what they, or their forefathers, gained by crossing over to Judaism' (*OTP* 2.195). Thus, as regards our attempts to portray the Teachers in Paul's Galatian churches, *JosAs* – and other Diaspora literature as well – is helpful in a role secondary to data in Galatians itself (in spite of the fact that most of this literature is Alexandrian). In the study of Diaspora literature, it is important to note two apologetic stances, and to note also their combination. *First*, there is the apologetic stance that reflects an enormous cultural and religious distance from Gentiles (see notably Barclay, 'Diaspora Jews'). Jewish authors express horror, for example, at their Gentile neighbors' idolatry and sexual practices, insisting on what one might call the absolute superiority of Judaism (e.g. *JosAs* 8:5). *Second*, there is also the apologetic stance that can express a loathing for polytheism and insist on the superiority of Judaism, precisely in order to extol Gentile conversion. In *JosAs*, insistence on the maintenance of an absolute religious distance from Gentiles serves the climactic presentation of Asenath as the prototypical proselyte, whose conversion is dramatized – indeed

Christian Jews in the Jerusalem church, a group utterly zealous for the observance of the Law (chapters 2 and 12 below). Seeking to reconstruct the Teachers' message, then, we will find pertinent data in such Palestinian Jewish traditions as those preserved in Sirach and the Dead Sea Scrolls. There are even good reasons for thinking that certain traditions current in the Jerusalem church of the first century were in fact preserved and shaped in two second-century communities of Christian Jews, known to us from the *Epistle of Peter to James* and the *Ascents of James*, not to mention Christian-Jewish traditions in the canonical epistle of James and in the gospel of Matthew.[8] With caution, then, we can further enrich our portrait of the Teachers by noting certain passages in these Christian-Jewish sources.[9]

In short, then, the picture that emerges from Paul's own references to the Teachers' work shows considerable internal coherence *and* a number of motifs for which there are significant parallels in traditions connected with Diaspora Jews, Palestinian Jews, and Christian Jews of various locales. We have reason, then, to think that a trustworthy picture can be drawn.[10]

---

celebrated – in fine detail, and who leads her entire family to embrace Judaism (*JosAs* 20:7–8; cf. Asenath as a City of Refuge for all Gentiles who repent, 15:7; 16:16; 19:5). As we will see, an analogous combination of these two apologetic stances proves to be characteristic of the Teachers who invaded Paul's Galatian churches. Their horror at the Godless life of Gentiles does nothing other than serve their major motif: that of recommending the path of conversion to the God of Abraham.

[8] The history of the study of *Ep. Pet. Jas.* and of *Ascents* is complex and the critical literature extensive. See notably F. S. Jones, who has recently expressed doubt about the theory of a source called *The Preachings of Peter*, of which *Ep. Pet. Jas.* has been thought to be the first element (*Source*, xii). The source-critical issues will never be altogether settled. See Strecker, 'The Kerygmata Petrou;' Klijn and Reinink, *Evidence*, 31–32, 37, 69; J. L. Martyn, 'Clementine Recognitions;' H. D. Betz, *Galatians*, 9, 331–332. On James, see L. T. Johnson, *James*; on Matthew, Davies and Allison, *Matthew*; and Luz, *Matthew* (especially, 79–95); idem, *Theology*.

[9] On occasion I will even cite late rabbinic traditions, but only to amplify a point secured by other sources, or to suggest a possibility not essential to the exegetical argument.

[10] The integrity of the picture that will emerge below, added to the points of similarity with certain motifs in Jewish and Christian-Jewish traditions, suggests that Paul was himself well informed about the Teachers and their labors. In our own effort to reconstruct a picture of the Teachers, two extremes are to be avoided. On the one side, lies the temptation to be overly bold in our detective work, falling unawares into massive speculation, reconstructing an entire face, so to speak, on the basis of the cut of the mustache. Some of Paul's polemical statements were doubtless formulated by him solely for the sake of rhetorical emphasis. On the other side, lies the temptation to be too modest, limiting ourselves to points which can be scientifically demonstrated beyond

A Sketch of the Teachers and Their Message

1. Outsiders

Paul consistently differentiates the Teachers from the members of his Galatian congregations. He addresses the Galatians quite directly as 'you,' whereas he always refers to the Teachers by such terms as 'some persons,' 'they,' 'these people.' The Teachers are outsiders who have only recently come into the Galatian churches.[11]

2. Jews

Paul almost certainly knows the Teachers' names, or at least some of the epithets by which they identify themselves (cf. 2 Cor 11:22–23). We can conclude, then, that, instead of using their names and epithets, he employs such colorless expressions as 'some persons' in order to indicate disdain. We also note, however, that he does employ three descriptive terms in his direct references:

(*a*) those who are frightening you (1:7, cf. 5:10);
(*b*) those who are troubling your minds (5:12);
(*c*) those who are circumcised (6:13).

We shall return to the first two of these below. The third almost certainly tells us that the Teachers are Jews. We thus have a group of Jews who have come into the Galatian churches from somewhere else.[12]

---

doubt. Exegesis is more an art than a science, although it partakes of both. It is by asking at crucial points how the Galatians are likely to have understood the text in front of us that we shall acquire both the scientific control and the poetic imagination needed for our own understanding of the text. Note the cautions offered by Barclay, 'Mirror Reading;' Sumney, *Opponents*.

[11] *Pace*, e.g. Munck, *Paul*, 87–90. See Hawkins, 'Opponents.' As we will see, the Teachers are outsiders to the Gentile communities of the Galatians, somewhat as Joseph is an outsider to the Egyptian family of Asenath in *JosAs*.

[12] Both in 'Gegner' and in 'Diaspora-Juden,' Walter argues that the Teachers were some of the *non-Christian* Jews who, like the pre-Christian Paul himself, persecuted the church (for Walter, they were intent on abolishing the circumcision-free Christian mission). Before making the case for his hypothesis by analyzing data in Galatians, Walter refers to Acts 20:3; 21:27–29; 22:22; 23:12–15 and Matt 23:15 ('Gegner,' 351). The final result is a reading of the data that is at once provocative and productive. Had one asked the Teachers whether they were Jews, the response would almost certainly have been in the affirmative. As I will argue below, however, they were surely Christian Jews, in the sense that, employing the term 'gospel' in their own mission, they confessed Jesus to have been the Messiah, whose death atoned for the sins of all peoples, thus opening the way for the taking of the Law to the Gentiles.

3. Christian-Jewish Evangelists

What, precisely, are they doing in these congregations? In his initial reference to the Teachers (1:6–9), Paul says that, under their influence, the Galatians are turning their allegiance to 'another *gospel.*' Then, having said that, he corrects himself by insisting that in reality there is no 'other gospel.' Does Paul take the route that requires self-correction only for the sake of rhetorical emphasis? Probably not. It would have been easier to avoid associating the Teachers with the term 'gospel,' by saying that, under their influence, the Galatians are turning *away from* the gospel, in that they are giving their allegiance to a *false teaching* (cf. 'the teaching of Balaam' in Rev 2:14) or to an *impotent philosophy* (cf. 'philosophy . . . according to human tradition' in Col 2:8). It seems highly probable that Paul takes the path requiring self-correction because he knows that the Teachers are in fact referring to their message as 'the gospel.' It follows that, no less than the Apostle himself, the Teachers are in the proper sense of the term evangelists, probably finding their basic identity not as persons who struggle against Paul, but rather as those who preach 'the good news of God's Messiah.' They are, then, Jews who have come into Galatia proclaiming what they call the gospel, God's good news. And what do they consider that good news to be?

4. The Law as the Good News

Although they themselves speak of the good news as the gospel of Christ, Paul repeatedly portrays them as those who find in the Law the absolute point of departure for their theology (e.g. 5:3–4). Whatever they may be saying about Christ (see below), the Law is itself both the foundation and the essence of their good news.

5. The Law as the Good News for Gentiles

For whom is the Law good news? In the Teachers' view, the Law is good news for the whole of the world, and specifically for Gentiles.[13] For that reason the Teachers' evangelistic vision is, in its scope, no less univer-

---

[13] Cf. Acts 21:20–21; *Ep. Pet. Jas.* 2:3 (HS 2.112). The Teachers are thus first cousins, so to speak, of various Diaspora Jews who dramatically portrayed and even facilitated Gentile conversions to Judaism. See, e.g. *JosAs* and Wisdom, and note that in *JosAs* nomistic salvation 'is a "necessity" appropriate only for non-Jews' (Burchard, *OTP* 2.192).

salistic than that of Paul (3:8).[14] Just as we do well not to speak of the Teachers simply as Paul's opponents, so we shall not refer to them as 'Judaizers,' as has so frequently been done. For in modern parlance the term 'Judaizer' usually refers to someone who wishes to hem in Gentile Christians by requiring them to live according to 'narrow' Jewish practices.[15] In their own time and place, the Teachers are embarked on an ecumenical mission. They are Christian Jews active in the Diaspora, who preach their nomistic gospel in Greek, quote the Law in Greek, and interpret the Law in ways understandable to persons of Greek culture.[16] Moreover, the Teachers carry out their mission under the genuine conviction – shared, for example, by the author of Wisdom – that the Law of Moses is the cosmic Law, in the sense that it is the divine wisdom for *all* human beings.[17] From the vocabulary employed by Paul in Gal 4:24–25, we can surmise that, in issuing their evangelistic invitation, the Teachers spoke explicitly of 'the covenantal Law of Sinai.'

6. The Motivation for a Law-Observant Mission to Gentiles

Beyond indicating that the Teachers are greatly concerned to correct what they see as the Law-less evangelism of Paul, the letter shows that they are carrying out their Law-observant mission to Gentiles in order to keep on good terms with some persons of considerable power (Gal 6:12). But their concentration on the expression 'descendants of Abraham' (see below) raises the additional possibility that they see their mission in thoroughly positive terms, perhaps understanding it to be the means by which God is filling out the infinite number of progeny he had promised to the patriarch. One notes the motivation for the Law-observant mission to Gentiles portrayed in the *Ascents of James*:

---

[14] On the motif of universalism in some Jewish traditions, cf. e.g. Urbach, 'The hope for conversion did not cease as long as the belief in Israel's election and in the power of the Torah was a living and dynamic faith that deemed its purpose to be the perfection and renewal *of the world*' (*Sages*, 552, emphasis added).

[15] See Ign. *Magn.* 10:3; Burton, *Galatians*, liii-lxv; and note the motif of Jewish universalism in chapter 4 below.

[16] Note especially the Teachers' Pythagorean-like, columnar interpretation of Genesis 15–21 (chapter 12 below).

[17] Cf. Georgi, 'Weisheit Salomos;' Walter, 'Diaspora Juden,' 49. Note the claim, widespread in Diaspora Judaism, that the whole of Greek philosophy is dependent on Moses; see, e.g. Walter, *Aristobulos*, 43–51; Philo *de Vita Mos.* 2.12–44.

It was necessary, then, that the Gentiles be called . . . so that the number [of descendants] which was shown to Abraham would be satisfied; thus the preaching of the kingdom of God has been sent into all the world.[18]

7. The Law as the Source of the Spirit

God's readiness to invite Gentiles into his own people is marked by the fact that God bestows his Spirit even on communities of Gentiles, if their communal life is ordered by correct exegesis of scripture and thus by true observance of his Law.[19] In Gal 3:1–5 there are several hints that Paul is contrasting the type of worship service the Galatians first knew under his direction with the type of worship service they are now experiencing at the hands of the Teachers. Both services have about them certain aspects of the theater. In his preaching, Paul clearly portrayed before the Galatians' eyes the dramatic picture of Christ, as he suffered crucifixion (3:1). Presented with this theater, the Galatians found that the message of the cross elicited their faith, and that the Spirit fell upon them.

Now a new acting company has arrived on the scene, presenting a novel and highly effective drama.[20] In the services of worship conducted by the Teachers, the Galatians see extraordinarily masterful exegetes who quote and interpret the Scriptures with the firm conviction that out of true exegesis will flow mighty manifestations of the Spirit (Gal 3:5).[21] And, indeed, developments in Galatia seem to confirm this conviction. In their dramatic services, the Teachers somehow manage to demonstrate to the Galatians the impressive connection between their

---

[18] The Latin text of Clementine *Recognitions* 1.42.1 (for both Latin and Syriac, see Van Voorst, *Ascents*, 57; F. S. Jones, *Source*, 72). Here and elsewhere, I cite the *Ascents of James* both by the numbering in the Clementine *Recognitions* and by the pages in Van Voorst, *Ascents* and F. S. Jones, *Source*. Cf. Philo *de Somn.* 1.173–176.

[19] Note several of the motifs in Joseph's prayer for Asenath prior to her conversion to Judaism: 'Lord God of my father Israel . . . renew her by your spirit . . . and number her among your people that you have chosen . . .' (*JosAs* 8:9); and cf. Joseph's later giving to the new convert 'spirit of life,' 'spirit of wisdom,' and 'spirit of truth' (*JosAs* 19:11).

[20] Cf. the *Exagoge* of Ezekiel the Tragedian (*OTP* 2.803–819).

[21] See Sir 39:1–8; Philo *de Spec. Leg.* 1.8; 3.178 (exegetes who are more than human [*thespesioi andres*]). Cf. Georgi, *Opponents*, 112–117, 258–271; according to some Jewish traditions 'the spirit portrayed and communicated itself essentially in the interpretation of the scriptures' (114); Fishbane on mantic oracles (*Biblical Interpretation*, 268–269). Note also that the dirge of *m. Sota* 9:15 – 'When ben Zoma died, there were no more interpreters', etc. – reflects the assumption of an earlier connection between exegesis and the glory of the Law (*kabōd hattorah*).

interpretation of the Law and the miraculous dispensation of the Spirit.[22] It follows that God is to be known as the one who supplies the Spirit to those who are both true exegetes of his Law and faithful observers of it.

8. The Threat of Exclusion

This laying down of a strict condition for the dependable granting of the Spirit is a token for the conditional nature of the whole of the Teachers' good news. We return, then, to the fact that Paul twice characterizes the Teachers as persons who frighten the Galatians (1:7; 5:10). How are we to understand these two references? Help comes from Paul's comment in Gal 4:17, where, employing the image of a gate, he says that the Teachers threaten to shut the Galatians out of salvation. Encountering Gentiles they consider to have been badly misled by Paul, the Teachers feel they must issue a sharp warning: '*Only if* you pass through the gate of repentance into the genuine observance of God's Law, will you be included in God's people Israel, thus being saved on the day of judgment.'[23]

9. The Necessity of Circumcision as the Commencement of Law Observance

How is a Gentile to pass through the gate to salvation? One of the major foci of the Teachers' preaching is the subject of circumcision (e.g. Gal 6:12). It is a subject that properly belongs to proselytizing, for, in most cases, a Gentile passes into the people of the Law by belonging to a family, the males of which submit to circumcision.[24] Circumcision is the commandment par excellence, the commandment which signifies full participation in the people of God. The Teachers, then, are circumcised, Christian Jews who preach circumcision to Gentiles as the act appropriate to the universal good news of God's

---

[22] The Teachers' success may have been similar to that achieved somewhat later in the Corinthian church by the pseudo-apostles. Note the portrait of Abraham in Philo *de Virt.* 217; and cf. chapter 6 below.

[23] Like the other pictures Paul paints of the Teachers, this one is decidedly negative. But the Teachers' own view of their threat was probably analogous to the harshly strict words of Joseph to Asenath (*JosAs* 8:5). When the Teachers were not dealing with Gentiles they considered to have been misled by Paul, they may have employed the image of the gate in an essentially positive way, understanding themselves to be gatekeepers intent on ushering Gentiles through the gate into full participation in the people of God, Israel. See Joseph's prayer for Asenath (*JosAs* 8:9).

[24] Cohen, 'Crossing;' Lieu, 'Circumcision.'

Law, the observance of which is the condition for God's pouring out his Holy Spirit. They also preach the necessity of the observance of holy times (Gal 4:10) and the keeping of dietary regulations (2:11– 14).

10. *The Christ of the Law*

We may further summarize the motifs we have mentioned thus far by asking what the Teachers say about Christ, the Messiah. However difficult it may be to answer this question with the detail we would desire, and however uncertain we remain as to how the Teachers are successfully communicating their christology to the Galatian Gentiles, five points can be stated with some degree of confidence.[25] (*a*) The Teachers view Christ much as do the members of the strictly observant circumcision party in the Jerusalem church, perhaps seeing him as the savior who brought to completion the ministry of Moses.[26] (*b*) In any case, they view God's Christ in the light of God's Law, rather than the Law in the light of Christ. This means that, in their christology, Christ is secondary to the Law. (*c*) Paul is emphatic, when he says that the Teachers avoid taking their theological bearings from the cross (e.g. Gal 6:12). They must be including references to Christ's death, however, presumably understanding it to have been a sacrifice for sins, perhaps emphatically for the sins of Gentiles. In short, the Teachers must see Christ's death as a redemptive sacrifice enacted in harmony with God's Law (chapter 9 below). (*d*) We can be sure, above all, that they consistently avoid every suggestion that God's Law and God's Christ could be even partially in conflict with one another.[27] (*e*) In their own terms, they are presumably certain that Christ came in order to fulfill the Law and the prophets (cf. Matt 5:17–18), perhaps even to complete Moses' ministry by bringing the Law to the Gentiles.[28] For them, the Messiah is the Messiah of the Law, deriving his identity from the fact that he confirms – and perhaps normatively interprets – the Law.[29]

---

[25] Absent from these five points is the suggestion that the Teachers' christology included dimensions of the this-worldly, political, anti-Gentile messianism we find in some of the traditions of Diaspora Judaism. See, e.g. *Sybilline Oracles* 3, and cf. Amir, 'Die messianische Idee:' J. J. Collins, 'Sybilline Oracles;' idem, 'Messiahs.'

[26] Cf. Van Voorst, *Ascents*, 163, F. S. Jones, *Source*, 160.

[27] Cf. Jas 1:22–25; *Ep. Pet. Jas.* 2:3 (HS 2.112).

[28] On the expectation that the Messiah will bring the Law to the Gentiles, see later rabbinic references, such as *Gen. Rab.* 98:9.

[29] For the Christian-Jewish conviction that Christ permanently confirmed the Law, see Matt 5:17–19; *Ep. Pet. Jas.* 2:5 (HS 2.112).

17

If Christ is explicitly involved in the Teachers' commission to preach to the Gentiles, that must be so because he has deepened their passion to take to the nations God's gift of gifts, the Spirit-dispensing Law that will guide them in their daily life.

These ten points would seem to encapsulate most of what Paul reveals about the Teachers and their gospel in his direct references. As noted earlier, however, there are other data quite revealing of the Teachers' gospel, allusions which, carefully interpreted, fill out in important ways the picture we receive of these evangelists, and especially of their gospel.

11. The Descendants of Abraham; the Blessing of Abraham

The character of Paul's argument in Gal 3:6–29 shows that he refers to 'the descendants of Abraham' because the Teachers are already doing that in their own way (chapter 10 below). Specifically, the Teachers are designating themselves as Abraham's descendants, and they are telling the Galatians that they can claim that identity for themselves if they submit to circumcision.[30] Indeed, the Teachers seem also to be speaking at some length about 'the blessing of Abraham,' indicating that when God blessed the patriarch, he did so in such a way as eventually to bless those Gentiles who, by circumcision and Law observance, become 'Abraham's true descendants.'[31] We thus find solid confirmation of the suggestion of Holtzmann that 'descendants of Abraham' is one of the Teachers' favorite catchwords.[32]

---

[30] We know that the expression 'descendants of Abraham,' was a significant self-designation among Christian Jews of the first century (2 Cor 11:22; John 8:33, 37). Jewish references to the proselyte as a descendant of Abraham are very numerous; see, e.g. *Tanh.*, Lekh Lekha 32a; cf. Philo *de Virt.* 219.

[31] It is worth noting that the Christian Jew who authored the second-century *Ascents of James* portrayed true religion as the line extending from Abraham to his descendants. Similarly, as noted above, in the *Ascents*, God's blessing of Abraham provides the motivation for the Law-observant mission to Gentiles (1.42.1; Van Voorst, *Ascents*, 57; F. S. Jones, *Source*, 72).

[32] Holtzmann, *Einleitung*, 243. See now Brinsmead, *Dialogical Response*, 107–114. With regard to the history of early Christian missions, it is important that, concerning the link between Abraham and the impulse to evangelize the Gentiles, it is the author of Galatians who is doing the reacting, not the Teachers. There is no good evidence that they have developed their interpretations of the Abraham texts simply in order to counter the effects of Paul's circumcision-free mission. On the contrary, Paul takes up the traditions about Abraham – and especially the expression 'descendants of Abraham' – in his argument against the use the Teachers are already making of those traditions in their Law-observant mission.

12. 'Jerusalem Is Our Mother'

In chapter 2 below we will see good reason to think that, in addition to identifying themselves and their Law-observant Gentile converts as 'descendants of Abraham,' the Teachers speak of Jerusalem as their 'mother,' referring thereby to the Jerusalem church.[33] We cannot say with certainty that the Teachers have come to Galatia from Jerusalem, but there are grounds for thinking that they claim to be the true representatives of the Jerusalem church, and that, in making that claim, they are confident of the support of a powerful group in that church.[34]

13. Israel

The way in which Paul employs the word 'Israel' in his final blessing (Gal 6:16) suggests that, in inviting the Galatians to claim Abraham as their father and the Jerusalem church as their mother, the Teachers are promising the Galatians that they will thereby enter the company of God's people Israel.[35] It is even conceivable that the Teachers are emphasizing the antique superiority of Israel by noting – at least in effect – that Plato and Pythagoras imitated the Law of Moses.[36]

14. Victory Over the Impulsive Desire of the Flesh

Finally, horrified at the continuation of various Gentile patterns of life among the Galatian churches (cf. 5:20–21a), the Teachers are taking up the matter of the Galatians' daily behavior. Here, in addition to attacking Paul for leaving the Galatians without potent ethical guidance – an unfaithful student of the Jerusalem apostles, Paul does not teach his Gentile converts what the Law means for the church's daily life – they voice a crucial promise: 'If you Galatians will become observant of the Law, we can promise you that you will not fall prey to the Impulsive Desire of the Flesh' (cf. Gal 5:16; 4 Macc 1; chapter 15 below). In this regard, as in others, the Teachers are likely to have portrayed Abraham as the model to be emulated. For, by keeping God's commandments,

---

[33] Cf. again Holtzmann, who advanced the thesis that the agitators spoke of Jerusalem (presumably Holtzmann meant the city) as their mother (*Einleitung*, 243).

[34] See again chapter 2 below, and cf. the image of the Jerusalem church in the *Ascents of James*, Van Voorst, *Ascents*, 174–180. Note the argument of F. S. Jones for locating the *Ascents* in Judea or Jerusalem (*Source*, 157–167).

[35] Martyn, *Galatians*, Comment 52.

[36] See, e.g. *Aristobulus* Frag. 3.

the patriarch was said to have avoided walking in the path of the Impulsive Desire of the Flesh.[37]

Most of these motifs can be effectively brought together if, attempting to sense the reasons for the Teachers' remarkable success among the Galatians, we allow ourselves the disciplined freedom to imagine a sermon they might have preached on the subject of the identity and blessedness of Abraham's true descendants.

The Teachers' Sermon on Abraham[38]

Listen, now![39] It all began with Abraham. Looking beyond the fascinating movements of the heavenly bodies, he was the first to discern that there is but one God. Because of that perception, he turned from the service of dumb idols to the worship of that true God.[40] Therefore God made him the father of our great people Israel. But that was only the beginning, for God blessed Abraham in a way that is coming to its fulfillment only now in the messianic age. Speaking through a glorious angel, God said to Abraham:

> In you shall all nations of the world be blessed, for I shall multiply your descendants as the stars of heaven. Come outside, and look toward heaven, and number the stars, if you are able. So shall your descendants be, for I speak this blessing to you and to your descendants (cf. Gen 12:3; 15:5; 17:4; 18:18).

What is the meaning of this blessing which God gave to Abraham? Pay attention to these things: Abraham was the first proselyte. As we have said, he discerned the one true God and turned to him. God's blessing took the form, therefore, of an unshakable covenant with Abraham, and God defined the covenant as the commandment of circumcision.[41] He also revealed to Abraham the heavenly calendar, so

---

[37] CD 3:1–3; 16:4–6.

[38] On the role of Abraham in the Teachers' theology see Barrett, 'Allegory;' Brinsmead, *Dialogical Response*; Hansen, *Abraham*; Walter, 'Gegner.' Rabbinic references are given for some of the motifs included in the following sermon, but usually in addition to references of early date. Regarding the scheme for referring to passages in the *Ascents of James*, see note 18 above.

[39] At numerous points in Galatians (noted here in parentheses), Paul's words reflect the message of the Teachers.

[40] Philo *de Abr.* 69–70; Josephus *Ant.* 1.155–156; *Jub.* 11:16–17; *Hebrew Testament of Naphtali* 9; chapter 8 below.

[41] Gen 17:10.

that in his own lifetime our father was obedient to the Law, not only keeping the commandment of circumcision, but also observing the holy feasts on the correct days.[42] Later, when God handed down the Law on tablets of stone at Sinai, he spoke once again by the mouths of his glorious angels, for they passed the Law through the hand of the mediator, Moses (Gal 3:19).[43] And now the Messiah has come, confirming for eternity God's blessed Law, revealed to Abraham and spoken through Moses.[44]

And what does this mean for you Gentiles? Listen again to the scripture we have just quoted. When God said to Abraham that in him all nations of the world would be blessed, God spoke explicitly of blessing you Gentiles in Abraham. But this blessing will come to you only if you are included in the people of Israel via your legitimate incorporation into our father Abraham. For, in addition to being himself the first proselyte, Abraham was the great maker of proselytes.[45] You must become, therefore, Abraham's true descendants, his true seed, along with us.[46]

Listen yet again to scripture. It is written that Abraham had two sons: Isaac and Ishmael (Gal 4:22). On the day of the feast of the first fruits, Isaac was born of Sarah the freewoman, and through him have come we Jews, true descendants of Abraham.[47] Earlier, Ishmael was born of Hagar the slave girl, and through him have come you Gentiles. You are descendants of the patriarch! We are in fact brothers![48]

Offspring through Ishmael, however, you are descended through the son who was begotten by Abraham while, lacking in trust, he was yet ignorant of God.[49] Most important of all, you have come through the slave girl, and, failing to observe God's covenantal Law, you are enslaved to the power of the Impulsive Desire of the Flesh (Gal 5:16). In a word, you Gentiles are not yet *true* descendants of Abraham. You have not

---

[42] *Jub.* 16:12–28; Sir 44:19–20.

[43] Deut 33:12 (LXX); *Jub.* 1:29; Acts 7:38, 53; Davies, 'Josephus.'

[44] Matt 5:17–18; *Ep. Pet. Jas.* 2:5 (HS 2.112).

[45] CD 16:4–6; *Tanh.* Lekh Lekha 32a; '*Abot. Nat.* 12:27a (Goldin, *Rabbi Nathan*, 68); *Midr. Pss.* 110:1; *Gen. Rab.* 43,7.

[46] In both Jewish and Christian-Jewish tradition, it was held that proselytes enter corpus Israel as descendants of Abraham; see, e.g. *Tanh.* Lek Leka 32a; *p. Bik.* 64a (on *m. Bik.* 1:4); *Ascents of James* 1.42.1 (Van Voorst, *Ascents*, 57; F. S. Jones, *Source*, 72).

[47] *Jub.* 16:13.

[48] *Jub.* 16:17; 1 Macc 12:21; *Ascents of James* 1.33.3; 1.34.1 (Van Voorst, *Ascents*, 48–49; F. S. Jones, *Source*, 60–61); *b. Sanh.* 59b.

[49] *Ascents of James* as in preceding footnote.

been incorporated into Israel. In order to participate in God's blessing of Abraham, therefore, you are to make your descent legitimate.

Who are the genuine and therefore blessed descendants of Abraham, Abraham's true seed (Gal 3:7, 29)? Again the answer is given in scripture, for the Law makes clear that God has set Two Ways before human beings, the Way of death and the Way of life.[50] You can see this in the case of our father Abraham. He chose the Way of life. Turning from idols to the observance of the Law, he circumcised himself, thus avoiding walking in the deadly power of the Impulsive Desire of the Flesh.[51] It follows that Abraham's true descendants are those who choose the path of virtue, becoming faithfully obedient to the virtue-creating Law, along with faithful Abraham (Gal 3:6–9). Let us say yet again that transference to the path of true descent is precisely what we now offer to you. For, fulfilling the ancient blessing he pronounced over Abraham, God is pleased at the present holy time to extend this line of true descent to the Gentiles. To be specific, God is creating descendants of Abraham through the Law-observant mission to Gentiles approved by his church in Jerusalem, the community that lives by the Law confirmed to eternity by the Christ.[52] In our Lawful preaching to the Gentiles, we represent that church, the community of James, Cephas, and John (Gal 2:1–10).

What are you to do, therefore, as Abraham's descendants through Ishmael, the child of Hagar the slave-girl? The gate of conversion stands open (Gal 4:9, 17)![53] You are to cast off your enslavement to the Flesh by turning in repentance and conversion to God's righteous Law, as it is confirmed by his Christ.[54] Follow Abraham in the holy, liberating, and perfecting rite of circumcision (Gal 3:3; 6:13).[55] Observe the feasts at their appointed times (Gal 4:10). Keep the sacred dietary requirements (Gal 2:11–14). And abstain from idolatry and from the passions of the

---

[50] E.g. Deut 30:19; Jer 21:8.

[51] Gen 6:5; CD 3:1–3; 16:4–6; Jas 1:2–4, 12–15; 4:5–6. For the motif of turning from idols, cf. *JosAs*. On the Impulsive Desire of the Flesh, see chapter 15 below.

[52] *Ascents of James* 1.33.3–1.43.3 (Van Voorst, *Ascents*, 48–59; F. S. Jones, *Source*, 60–74); *Ep. Pet. Jas.* 2:5 (HS 2.112).

[53] Cf. Joseph's prayer for Asenath in *JosAs* 8:9.

[54] Cf. *JosAs* 15:7.

[55] Holding Gentiles to be Ishmaelite descendants of Abraham, in spite of their being uncircumcised, the Teachers may simply have ignored – or interpreted symbolically? – the scriptural tradition according to which Abraham circumcised Ishmael (Gen 17:23). For, being yet ignorant of God's true power, Abraham did not carry out that act on Ismael's eighth day.

Impulsive Flesh (Gal 5:19–21). Then you will be perfected as true descendants of Abraham, members of the covenant people of Israel, heirs of salvation according to the blessing which God solemnly uttered to Abraham and to his descendants (Gal 3:7, 8, 16).[56] Indeed, by entering the people of Israel, you will fill up the vast number of descendants God promised to Abraham.[57]

You say that you have already been converted by Paul? We say that you are still in a darkness similar to the darkness in which not long ago you were serving the elements of the cosmos, supposing them, as Abraham once did, to be gods that rule the world (chapter 8 below). In fact, the fights and contentions in your communities show that you have not really been converted, that Paul did not give you the divinely ordained antidote to the Impulsive Desire of the Flesh, the guidance of God's holy Law, the perfecting observance of which is commenced in the circumcision of the flesh (Gal 5:15). Being an unfaithful student of the Law-observant apostles in the mother church of Jerusalem, Paul has allowed you to remain a group of sailors on the treacherous high seas in nothing more than a small and poorly equipped boat. He gave you no provisions for the trip, no map, no rudder, and no anchor. In a word, he failed to pass on to you God's greatest gift, the Law.[58] But that is exactly the mission to which God has called us. Through our work, the good news of God's Law is invading the world of Gentile sin.

We adjure you, therefore, to claim the inheritance of the blessing of Abraham, and thus to escape the curse of the Impulsive Desire of the Flesh and sin (Gal 1:4a; 3:18; 5:16). For, be assured, those who follow the path of the Flesh and sin will not inherit the Kingdom of God, lacking the perfection of virtue given by the Law (Gal 3:3). It is entirely possible for you to be shut out (Gal 4:17). You will do well to consider this possibility and to tremble with fear.[59] For you will certainly be shut

---

[56] As the Teachers offered the Galatians a religious process that leads to perfection (Gal 3:3), one may note the motif of re-creation in *JosAs*. In praying for Asenath's conversion, Joseph links the image of God the creator to that of God the new creator: 'Lord God . . . who gave life to all things and called them from the darkness to the light, and from the error to the truth, and from the death to the life, you, Lord, bless this virgin, and renew her by your spirit, and form her anew by your hidden hand, and make her alive again by your life . . .' (8:9; cf. Stuhlmacher, 'Erwägungen'). See also *JosAs* 15:5 ('renewed and formed anew and made alive again'); cf. 16:16; 18:9.

[57] *Ascents of James* 1.42.1 (Van Voorst, *Ascents*, 57; F. S. Jones, *Source*, 72).

[58] *Ep. Pet. Jas.* 2:3 (HS 2.112).

[59] Cf. *JosAs* 10:1–3.

out unless you are truly incorporated into Abraham by observing God's glorious and angelic law. Turn therefore in true repentance, and come under the wings of the Divine Presence, so that with us you shall be saved as true descendants of father Abraham.

2

A Tale of Two Churches

Interpreting Genesis 16–21 in Gal 4:21–5:1, Paul finds in the figures of Hagar and Sarah a pair of opposites, slave and free. Indeed under their headings, he sees other oppositional pairs, constituting two columns of opposites that refer respectively to the Law-observant mission of the Teachers and the circumcision-free mission pursued by himself (note in Gal 4:25 the technical term *systoicheō*, 'to stand in the same oppositional column with'):

Hagar	*Sarah*
slave	free
Ishmael	Isaac
the son begotten by the power of the flesh, that is by circumcision	the son begotten by the power of God's promise/the Spirit
begetting father: circumcision of the flesh	begetting father: the promissory Spirit
bearing mother: the covenant from Mount Sinai	bearing mother: the covenant of God's promise
the nomistic covenant, represented by Hagar and by Sinai, is bearing children – that is to say Gentile churches, small in number (4:27) – into the state of slavery via the Law-observant mission to the Gentiles[1]	the promissory covenant, represented by Sarah, is mother to those who escape from slavery, being the churches, large in number (4:27), that are resulting from the circumcision-free mission to the Gentiles

Paul's view of these oppositional pairs seems clear. How are we to understand, however, his references in Gal 4:25–26 to two Jerusalems? We can be sure that he sees them as yet another pair of opposites, but to what do they refer in the present setting? That is a question of considerable importance, for in the dominant interpretation, Paul's

[1] See chapter 12 below.

25

reference to the enslaved and enslaving Jerusalem in Gal 4:25, like that
to the Sinai covenant in 4:24, is taken to mean 'the political and
religious institution of Judaism.' The passage is then read as a polemic
against Judaism as such.[2] A brief consideration of Paul's references to
Jerusalem in his other letters will facilitate our analysis of the references
in Galatians.

Jerusalem in 1 Corinthians and Romans

Half of Paul's ten references to Jerusalem fall in these two letters, the
other five being in Galatians.

1 Corinthians

16:3–4. And when I arrive in Corinth, I will send those whom you accredit
by letter to carry your gift to *Jerusalem*. If it seems advisable that I should
also go, they will accompany me.

Romans

15:19. . . . so that from *Jerusalem* and as far around as Illyricum I have fully
preached the gospel of Christ.

15:24–26. I hope to see you in passing as I go to Spain . . . At present,
however, I am going to *Jerusalem* with aid for the saints. For Macedonia and
Achaia have been pleased to make some contributions for the poor among
the saints in *Jerusalem*.

15:30–31. I appeal to you, brothers and sisters . . . to strive together
with me in your prayers . . . that I may be delivered from the unbelievers
in Judea, and that my service for *Jerusalem* may be acceptable to the
saints.

From these passages, it is obvious that Paul can use the word 'Jerusalem'
as a geographical term, coordinate with the terms Illyricum and Spain.
It is equally clear, however, that Paul's interest in geography is
thoroughly ecclesiological. Jerusalem is the place from which the gospel
has commenced its march into the rest of the world, and that is in itself
a strong hint that, when he uses the word Jerusalem, Paul thinks in the
first instance of the Jerusalem church, not of the city as such, and
certainly not of the Jewish cultus with its temple, its priests, and its
traditions.

---

[2] H. D. Betz, *Galatians*, 246. Betz's conclusion: 'According to Galatians, Judaism is
excluded from salvation altogether . . .' (251).

This reading receives support, furthermore, from the fact that Paul employs other place names as metonyms for the churches in those locales. It is not Macedonia and Achaia, but rather the churches in those areas, that have assembled funds for the Jerusalem church. And the service those churches are thus performing is being rendered not to the city of Jerusalem, but rather to the church there. Worth particular note is the fact that in Rom 15:31 Paul uses the word 'Jerusalem' as a metonym for the Jerusalem church.

The same ecclesiological geography is evident in 1 Cor 16. The gift of the Corinthian church is to be carried to the city of Jerusalem in order that it may be handed over to the Jerusalem church. From Romans and 1 Corinthians, then, we see Paul using the term 'Jerusalem' both literally to refer to the city *as the locale of the Jerusalem church* and as a metonym to speak of *that church itself.* Is that pattern also characteristic of Galatians?

The Word Jerusalem in Galatians

1:17. . . . nor did I make a trip up to *Jerusalem*, to those who were already apostles before I became one.

1:18. Then after three years had passed, I did go up to *Jerusalem*, to visit Cephas.

2:1–2. Then, fourteen years later, I went up to *Jerusalem* again, accompanied by Barnabas; and I also took along Titus . . . and I communicated to them (the Jerusalem church) the gospel that I preach among the Gentiles.

4:25. . . . and Hagar stands in the same oppositional column with *the present Jerusalem*, for like Hagar the present Jerusalem is in slavery together with her children.

4:26. But, in contrast, *the Jerusalem that is above* is free; she, not the present Jerusalem, is our mother.

In the first three of these references, we find exactly what we found in 1 Corinthians and Romans. To put the matter negatively, in 1 Corinthians, Romans, and Gal 1:17–2:2, Paul never uses the word 'Jerusalem' to refer to the Jewish religion. It is true that the two instances in the first chapter of Galatians are geographical, but Jerusalem is there nothing other than the locale of the Jerusalem church. And in Gal 2:1–2, Paul employs the term Jerusalem both to refer to the city and – emphatically – as a metonym for the Jerusalem church (the antecedent of *autois* in Gal 2:2; cf. Rom 15:31). When, then, the Galatians hear Paul's reference to Jerusalem in Gal 4:25, their ears are already tuned to expect a metonym in which 'Jerusalem' is the Jerusalem church, and Paul takes no step to discourage that interpretation.[3]

Paul's View of the Jerusalem Church in Galatians[4]

That Paul intends the Galatians to hear in 4:25 a reference to the Jerusalem church becomes highly probable when we note that he includes in his letter a series of four vignettes of that older congregation. Each of these is painted against the background of statements about the Jerusalem church being made to the Galatians by the Teachers. And each – from the second through the fourth – shows an increased level of tension and distrust between Paul and that church.

The First Vignette: Paul's Respectful Distance From the Jerusalem Church (Gal 1:17–18)

In his preaching to the Galatians, Paul may have mentioned Jerusalem as the site of the crucifixion of Jesus, but there is no compelling reason to think that, in any substantive way, he referred to the Jerusalem church.[5] The Teachers, however, are certainly speaking at length about the church in Jerusalem, very probably using the word Jerusalem metonymically, as we will see below.[6] Behind Paul's references in 1:17–18 lies the Teachers' depiction of themselves as the only true representatives of the Jerusalem gospel who are active among the Gentiles. They charge

---

[3] Cf. Mussner: 'One would first think of the city of Jerusalem as the spiritual center of Judaism . . . It is also possible, however – indeed probable – that in speaking of 'the present Jerusalem,' Paul refers not to the city as the spiritual center of Judaism, but rather to *the city of Jewish Christianity*, whose radical exponents speak of *Jerusalem* as the repository of the true gospel. For them, therefore, Jerusalem is the decisive base of Christianity that authorizes them to preach a message contrary to that of Paul. In this regard, they may even have employed the slogan 'Jerusalem is our mother,' as H. J. Holtzmann suggested' (*Galaterbrief,* 325).

[4] Cf. now Vouga, 'Der Galaterbrief,' 248–250.

[5] Paul obviously spoke to the Galatians about the Jerusalem church when he told them of his collection and of the way in which they were to assemble funds in their own churches (1 Cor 16:1). He did that, however, after writing Galatians (Martyn, *Galatians,* Comment 24).

[6] Similar ecclesiological metonyms are easy to find in modern usage. In the Church of England one would hear references to 'Canterbury,' meaning the authority of the cathedral there. Among Roman Catholic clerics 'Rome' often means the ecclesiastical authorities in that city.

that, although Paul himself got his gospel from the Jerusalem apostles, he has now deviated from that instruction in fundamental regards.[7]

Given this charge, Paul is compelled to speak of the Jerusalem church, but in the earliest of his pictures (1:17–18), that church is barely visible in the distance. He got his gospel directly from God, not from the church in Jerusalem. Given his certainty of that fact, he is equally sure that his gospel cannot be measured by any ecclesiastical authority, including the one in Jerusalem.

The Second Vignette: The Meeting in the Jerusalem Church (Gal 2:1–10)

Marked ambivalence toward the Jerusalem church emerges in Paul's account of the meeting that took place when the Antioch church sent messengers to confer with the older congregation. Referring to the Jerusalem church by the metonym 'Jerusalem' (2:2), he indicates that that congregation housed at least two distinct groups. One consisted of the recognized leaders, James, Peter, and John. A second was made up of persons Paul calls the False Brothers, a circle intent on compelling the Gentile churches, daughters of the Antioch church, to observe the Law of circumcision. It is this group that causes Paul to exercise tactical care in his approach to the Jerusalem church (2:2b). Thus, the presence of the False Brothers in that community and the leeway apparently given them by the Jerusalem apostles lead Paul to have distinctly ambivalent feelings about the Jerusalem church itself.

On the one hand, he is able to end his account of the meeting with a reference to a victory for the truth of the gospel (Gal 2:9–10). The leaders perceived God's hand in his circumcision-free mission to the Gentiles no less than in Peter's mission to the Jews. Moreover, with Barnabas, Paul is more than ready to collect funds in the Antioch church for the poor in the Jerusalem church, thus reflecting his certainty that the apostolic gospel was active in and through that church no less than in and through the church in Antioch.

On the other hand, there is the simple, but significant, fact that Paul says nothing about the way in which the leaders of the Jerusalem church related themselves to the False Brothers. One wonders, for example, why he does not say that in a climactic confrontation, witnessed by the

---

[7] Chapter 1 above. In addition to charging that Paul was an unfaithful student of the Jerusalem apostles, the Teachers may have told the Galatians that he had proven himself to be callous about the financial suffering in the Jerusalem church (Martyn, *Galatians*, Comment 24).

whole of the Jerusalem church, the leaders firmly withstood the False Brothers' attempt to require circumcision of Gentile converts. Why does he have to say, instead, that the task of withstanding the False Brothers fell to him and Barnabas (2:5)? Obviously the leaders did not directly confront and ultimately vanquish their colleagues. Nor does Paul say that, after the leaders recognized his mission, they instructed the False Brothers henceforth to leave him in peace. Clearly the acknowledged leaders in Jerusalem did no such thing.[8] Much to Paul's displeasure, then, the False Brothers remained after the meeting what they had been before it: respected and influential members of the Jerusalem church belonging to or constituting a party within that church that was – or in any case could prove to be – supportive of the Law-observant mission to Gentiles (note also Acts 21:20).

The Third Vignette: Messengers From the Jerusalem Church Come To the Church in Antioch (Gal 2:11–14)

The continued existence of that party within the Jerusalem church is a presupposition of Paul's account of what is usually termed 'the incident in Antioch,' a turn of events, however, as revealing of developments in Jerusalem as it is of developments in Antioch. After the Jerusalem meeting, the False Brothers simply licked their wounds and waited for a better opportunity to assail the Antioch church's circumcision-free mission. That opportunity apparently came with the departure of Peter from the Jerusalem church and with the increased authority of James.[9]

Forming the nucleus of 'the circumcision party,' the False Brothers seem now to have approached James, astutely scaling down their appeal: 'If for Gentile converts circumcision is to be left aside, let us require at least the observance of the food laws.' It was a clever move. Given the fact that this group was known under the name 'the circumcision party,' they may have intended to leave aside the demand of circumcision only for the moment. In any case, persuading James to dispatch messengers to the Antioch church, the False Brothers may have entertained the hope of provoking a confrontation with the man who had successfully

---

[8] One might ask speculatively whether the False Brothers may have repented of their circumcision attempt, thus agreeing to abandon their opposition to the Antioch church's circumcision-free work among Gentiles. As that would have been a magnificent victory for 'the truth of the gospel,' Paul would surely have reported it, had it happened.

[9] James is named first among the 'pillars' (2:9). See R. E. Brown, et al. *Peter*, 30.

antagonized them at the conference, the man who was now standing in the forefront of the Antioch church's Gentile mission, Paul.

James's motives and expectations may have been less concerned with Paul and more tightly focused on the future of Peter's mission to the Jews.[10] In any case, James agreed to send messengers to Antioch. Thus, having formed their own party in the Jerusalem church, the False Brothers had now acquired greater influence there, and, with the cooperation of James, their influence continued to radiate out from that church.

If the False Brothers, now leaders of the circumcision party, hoped that the sending of the delegation to the Antioch church would draw their old enemy into a confrontation in which he would suffer defeat, they shortly saw their hope fulfilled in dramatic fashion. For Paul suffered a painful breach with his co-worker Barnabas, with Peter, and indeed with what had been for some time his home church, the one in Antioch.[11] For our present concerns, the important point is that Paul must also have come away from this political defeat with heightened distrust of the Jerusalem church itself. Certainly there is no indication that he considered returning to Jerusalem with James's messengers, hoping by direct argument to lead the Jerusalem church to recognize 'the truth of the gospel' in the matter of the food laws.

His political defeat and the shaking of his confidence in the Jerusalem church were not the end of the matter. We can be sure that James's messengers carried back to the Jerusalem church a full report, and we can be confident that this report brought about at least five further developments of consequence. (1) The messengers' report must have pleased the False Brothers considerably, showing them that Paul was far from invincible, and encouraging them to look for further ways to put an absolute end to his work. (2) The report must have added yet more strength to the position of the False Brothers in the Jerusalem church, solidifying in the minds of other members their portrait of Paul as an intransigent maverick, caring more for his private views than for the unity and health of God's church. (3) The report probably enabled the False Brothers to portray Paul as utterly undependable. That is to say, they are likely to have pointed out that, by withdrawing from the Antioch church, Paul had also terminated his participation in that

[10] See E. P. Sanders, 'Gal 2:11–14.'
[11] That the breach with Peter and Barnabas was not permanent is suggested by 1 Cor 1:12; 9:5–6.

church's collection for the relief of the church in Jerusalem.[12] (4) The report will have pleased James himself, to the degree that it included an assurance of Peter's compliance with the request that he not enter into close association with persons failing to keep the food laws. James may very well have regretted the breach with Paul, but we may suppose that, like Peter and the Jewish members of the Antioch church, he held Paul responsible for it.

Again, moreover, there is no indication that James did anything to curb the False Brothers. On the contrary, having complied with their request that he send messengers to the Antioch church, he may have been open to further suggestions from them. (5) Finally, the report of the Antioch incident seems to have made its way in some form to the Teachers, whether by their being themselves resident in the Jerusalem church at that time, or by their being in communication with persons belonging to the circumcision party in that church, perhaps the False Brothers themselves. And, drawing on the report, the Teachers apparently gave to the Galatians their account of the Antioch incident, perhaps emphasizing both Paul's intransigence and the powerful role played in Antioch's future work by the elder church in Jerusalem.

In whatever form we are to think of them, these five developments must have influenced the way in which Paul subsequently thought of the Jerusalem church. He had now to take into account the ability of the False Brothers, via James, to reach out into the life of other churches, even changing the nature of the Antioch church's Gentile mission. And with the developments in Galatia, he had to take into consideration some kind of positive connection between the Teachers and the Jerusalem church, insofar as it had fallen under the influence of the False Brothers. We have to imagine in Paul the sort of distrust that can grow into theological fury.

The Fourth Vignette: The Jerusalem Church is Mother to the Teachers, and is to That Degree Supporting a Mission That is Giving Birth to Churches Enslaved to the Law (Gal 4:25)

We have already seen that Paul's metonymic reference to the Jerusalem church in Gal 2:1 will have tuned the Galatians' ears to hear the same reference in 4:25. When, now, two observations about 4:25 are added to the sequence of historical vignettes sketched above, we see that a

---

[12] Martyn, *Galatians*, Comment 24.

metonymic reference to the Jerusalem church in 4:25 is indeed Paul's intention.

(1) There is, first, the polemical tone to Paul's assertion in 4:26. Between the final clause of 4:25 and the sentence of v. 26 Paul draws a sharp and emphatic contrast (adversative *de*), saying in effect,

> It is not the present Jerusalem – the Jerusalem that is in slavery together with her children – that is our mother. On the contrary, our mother is the Jerusalem above, the Jerusalem that is free.

Paul's polemic suggests not only that the Teachers are employing the term 'Jerusalem' as a metonym for the Jerusalem church, but also that they are using the word 'mother,' claiming authorization from that church for their mission, when they say 'Jerusalem is our mother.'[13] It is striking that Paul does not dispute this claim. If he had had secure confidence that, under the leadership of James, the Jerusalem church would have disowned the Teachers, falsifying their claim to be mothered by that congregation, he could easily have said so. The Teachers are apparently able, at least partially, to substantiate their claim.

To assess the hypothesis that the Teachers were able to make such a claim, we need only to recall the first three vignettes sketched above. At the time of the Jerusalem meeting, the False Brothers passionately favored giving the support of the Jerusalem church to a Law-observant mission to the Gentiles. We have seen no good reason to think that the final result of the meeting caused them to abandon that passion. On the contrary, the subsequent dispatching of messengers to Antioch is best understood – insofar as the False Brothers were concerned – as the first step in a renewed attempt to establish such a mission. And the work of the Teachers is exactly the Law-observant mission to the Gentiles desired by the False Brothers. The remarkable success the Teachers are having among the Galatians may itself testify to the connections they have in

---

[13] As we have noted in chapter 1 above, this hypothesis was advanced in a different form by Holtzmann in 1886 (*Einleitung*, 243; cf. Mussner, *Galaterbrief*; Lührmann, *Galater*). On the basis of the four vignettes, we can even offer a suggestion regarding an important development in the Galatians' vocabulary. There is no good reason to think that these ethnic Galatians ever used the term 'Jerusalem' as a way of referring to the Jewish cultus focused on the temple. Considering the probability, however, that, in the manner indicated above, the Teachers spoke of 'Jerusalem' as their 'mother,' there is reason to think (*a*) that, prior to receiving Paul's letter, the Galatians had learned to refer to the mothering Jerusalem church simply as 'Jerusalem,' and (*b*) that Paul knew of that development in their vocabulary as he wrote his letter.

the mother church.[14] It follows that in Gal 4:25 Paul himself adopts one of the Teachers' locutions, using the word 'Jerusalem' as a metonym for the Jerusalem church.

(2) The metonymic reading of 'Jerusalem' in 4:25 is further supported when we note that in Gal 4:21–5:1 Paul coordinates three motifs: (*a*) 'begetting by the power of the flesh' (begetting by circumcision), (*b*) 'bearing children into slavery,' and (*c*) 'the present Jerusalem.' For in his account of the meeting in the church of Jerusalem (second vignette above) Paul coordinated these same three motifs: (*a*) the False Brothers' demand that Gentile converts be circumcised, (*b*) Paul's assessment of this demand as an attempt at enslavement, and (*c*) the locus in which that demand was lodged, the Jerusalem church. It is indeed in his comment about the False Brothers' demand for the circumcision of Gentiles – a demand voiced *in* the Jerusalem church – that Paul first mentions freedom and enslavement as a pair of opposites (2:4). When, then, in 4:22–25 Paul says that 'the present Jerusalem' is begetting children by circumcision, thus bearing them into the state of slavery, he is surely using the Teachers' metonym for the Jerusalem church, modifying that metonym by the limiting word *present*.

To the degree that it affords hospitality to the False Brothers and their circumcision party, thus in some manner mothering the Law-observant mission to the Gentiles pursued by the Teachers, the Jerusalem church is nothing more than an earthly entity, limited to the *present* time and even analogous to the *present* evil age, painful as it doubtless is for Paul to harbor such a thought.[15] In this fourth vignette, then, the ambivalence shown in the second and the distrust reflected in the third have ripened into theological fury. In that state of anger, Paul is not at all concerned to provide a complete and balanced portrait of the church in Jerusalem. On the contrary, he refers in Gal 4:25 to *the Jerusalem church that is being made present in Galatia* by the Teachers' claims (and probably on the basis of their relationship with the False Brothers). Thus, *to the degree* that, under the sway of the False Brothers,

---

[14] Cf. Käsemann: 'Only the authority of the church in Jerusalem could shake the authority Paul had in his own churches . . .' ('Legitimität,' 490).

[15] Did the idea of assembling his own collection for the Jerusalem church arise in Paul's mind partly as a result of his portraits of that community in Galatians? Did he see in his collection and in its delivery, that is to say, a way of differentiating the Jerusalem church – as a highly valued community with which God continued to bind the Gentile churches – from the False Brothers and their allies? See chapter 3 below.

the Jerusalem church is offering support to the Teachers' work – thus reaching out into the life of his churches as it earlier reached out into the life of the Antioch church – Paul is sure that the Jerusalem congregation is itself producing Gentile churches that are enslaved.[16] From 2 Corinthians and Romans we know that this was far from Paul's final portrait of the elder church.[17] It is, however, the climactic one in his extraordinarily angry letter to the Galatians.[18]

But by adding the word 'present,' thus anticipating the contrasting word 'above,' and in effect preparing the way for placing two Jerusalems in the columns of opposites, Paul continues to speak not only of the Law-observant mission, but also of the mission God has entrusted to him.[19] Just as, in the cross of Christ, God has provided a fully potent

[16] On the motif of persecution in Gal 4:29 and its possible connection with the False Brothers, see Martyn, *Galatians*, ad loc, and 2 Cor 11:26.

[17] Further Jerusalem vignettes could be sketched, therefore, from those two later letters. Regarding the picture of the Jerusalem church that may be reflected in 2 Corinthians, see the exegetical arguments of Käsemann, 'Legitimität,' and Barrett, 'Opponents.' Note particularly the thesis (as early as F. C. Baur) that the 'super-apostles' of 2 Cor 11:5 and 12:11 were the primal apostles in the Jerusalem church, being therefore distinct from the 'pseudo-apostles' who actually invaded Paul's Corinthian church, the latter claiming to be sponsored by the former (2 Cor 11:13). In Käsemann's hands this thesis continues with the observation that Paul did not feel compelled to attack the Jerusalem apostles themselves. He says only that he is not inferior to them. And by giving them the ironic sobriquet 'super-apostles,' he recognizes their possession of a certain kind of priority, while at the same time suggesting that he himself does not stand in awe of them (cf. Gal 2:6). Käsemann's summary: In 2 Cor 10–13 Paul is concerned to deal ruthlessly with the invaders of his Corinthian church (the 'pseudo-apostles'), without getting caught in a direct conflict with the Jerusalem apostles ('Legitimität,' 493). This reading is not universally accepted (see, e.g. Furnish, *II Corinthians*, 49, 502–505; Luedemann, *Paulus*, 134). The series of vignettes in Galatians, however, not to mention the anxiety expressed in Rom 15:25–32, can be offered in secondary support of it.

[18] Cf. now Trobisch, *Letter Collection*, where the thesis is advanced that Paul himself assembled and edited Galatians, 1 and 2 Corinthians, and Romans, sending the result, with a cover letter (Rom 16) to the church in Ephesus, hoping that this epistolary collection would be of service in presenting his side in a long dispute with the authorities of the Jerusalem church. Trobisch thinks that, in this letter collection, Galatians, having the literary form not of a private letter, but rather of an authorized document comparable to an affidavit (Gal 6:11–18), 'should be used by [Paul's] friends to prove his case against the saints in Jerusalem' (*Letter Collection*, 94). The thesis is illuminating with respect to ancient letter collections, and suggestive as regards the history of Paul's relationship with the Jerusalem church. In some other regards, however, the thesis creates more problems than it solves – especially in connection with Paul's collection of money (see Martyn, *Galatians*, Comment 24) – and the forensic analysis of Galatians itself is untenable. See further Vouga, 'Der Galaterbrief.'

[19] For rabbinic patterns of contrasting 'the Jerusalem of this world (or age)' with 'the Jerusalem of the future world (or age)' see Billerbeck 1.573; Neusner, 'Really "Ethnic"?'

antidote to the present evil age (Gal 1:4), so over against the present misled and misleading church of Jerusalem, God has provided the church in heaven, 'the Jerusalem above.' And this true mother, although lacking earthly authorization, is nevertheless producing far more children than those being born in the Law-observant mission (Paul's interpretation of Isa 54:1 in Gal 4:27). For the heavenly Jerusalem guides the true church below, divorcing it, precisely in its expansion, from an earth that is closed in on itself.[20] In this way, the heavenly Jerusalem is God's servant, calling the church into existence as the new creation, in which religious differentiations and ossifying traditions are obliterated. Certain that this Jerusalem above, not the time-bound church in Jerusalem, is the mother of the Galatians, Paul completes his columns of opposites, by referring to the two Jerusalems:

The present Jerusalem	*The Jerusalem above*
that is to say, the Jerusalem church insofar as it allows the False Brothers to sponsor the Law-observant mission to the Gentiles, while blocking official support for the circumcision-free Gentile mission	that is to say, the mother of the churches born in the circumcision-free mission to Gentiles, their lacking official support from the Jerusalem church
the child begotten by the power of the flesh, engaging in persecutory activity, that is the Teachers and their totally loyal followers who oust the catechetical instructors left by Paul as leaders in the Galatian churches (Gal 6:6)	the child begotten by the power of the Spirit, suffering persecution at the hands of the child begotten by the power of the flesh, that is the catechetical leaders who form the nucleus of the Galatian churches and who are being ousted by the circumcising Teachers and their totally loyal followers
the slave girl and her son who are to be thrown out, that is the Teachers and their totally loyal colleagues who are to be expelled from the Galatian churches (Gal 4:30).	the Galatian churches as those addressed by God in the words of Gen 21:10 – 'Throw out the slave girl and her son. For the son of the slave girl will certainly not come into the inheritance along with the son of the free woman.'

[20] I have drawn elements of this sentence from Käsemann, 'Leiblichkeit,' 8.

3

Romans as One of the Earliest Interpretations of Galatians

The earliest interpretation of Galatians was carried out by the Galatians themselves. We have no sources by which in the proper sense to reconstruct that interpretation, but we are not wholly in the dark. From the letter itself, we can surmise that in the Galatian churches, there will have been two major interpretations.

Interpretation by the Teachers and Their Followers

As Paul wrote his letter, he assumed that the Teachers, being still active in his Galatian churches, would be present when the letter was read aloud; and there is no reason to think that his assumption was incorrect. Indeed, we can match it with one of our own: The Teachers will have assured the Galatians that they were more than competent to offer their help in the interpretation of the volatile letter. We can first imagine, then, certain aspects of the interpretation of the document by the Teachers and their enthusiastic followers. Three matters in particular will have seized their attention: Paul's sharply critical reference to the Jerusalem church (Gal 4:25–27; chapter 2 above), his outrageous comments about the Law (notably 3:19–20), and his less-than-satisfactory reference to Israel (6:16).[1]

Jerusalem

The Teachers will not have failed to note Paul's references to the Jerusalem church in Gal 4:25. For there, as we have seen, Paul says that, insofar as the Jerusalem congregation is lending its sponsorship to the Teachers' Law-observant Gentile mission, it is in slavery and is begetting children into slavery (spawning Law-observant churches, that is, among

---

[1] The Teachers may also have shown the Galatians that Paul's interpretation of Gen 17:8 as a reference to a singular seed (Gal 3:16) is contradicted by the whole of Genesis 17 itself.

the Gentiles). If the Teachers themselves considered the Jerusalem church to be their 'mother,' as seems very likely, we can easily imagine the depth of their anger at Paul's words.

The Law

Even the followers of the Teachers may have been momentarily inclined to applaud some elements in Paul's exegetical demonstration that the Law bears witness to the birth of their own churches (Gal 4:21–5:1). And they will surely have been pleased – on the first reading – to hear his positive reference to the Law in 5:14. The picture he draws of the Law's genesis, however – it was instituted by angels acting in God's absence – must have struck followers of the Teachers as outrageous.[2] And his charge that the Law is one of the cosmic powers that enslave human beings (3:23, 4:3–5; chapter 8 below), will certainly have been considered monstrous.

Israel

Similarly, both the Teachers and their followers will have been offended by the way in which Paul refers in closing to 'the Israel of God' (Gal 6:16). For with that expression, he says that the God of Israel is first of all the Father of Jesus Christ, and thus that Israel is the people whom God is calling into existence in Christ (1:6, 13). The Teachers' followers will also have noticed that, although Paul refers to Abraham, to Sarah (the 'free woman' of 4:22), and to Isaac, he nowhere mentions the long history of God's dealings with the people of Israel.[3] Indeed, whereas the Teachers are inviting all of the Galatians to enter the company of Law-observant Israel, referring to this holy and elect people of God as 'the (plural) seed of Abraham,' Paul speaks of Christ as the singular seed of Abraham, thus seeming to eclipse the sacred history of Israel (chapter 10 below).

We cannot be greatly surprised, then, to find in Paul's later letter to the Romans evidence suggesting that, under the influence of the Teachers, the Galatian churches refused to participate in the collection Paul proposed to assemble from his churches for delivery to the church in Jerusalem (Rom 15:26; Martyn, *Galatians*, Comment 24). Politically, the interpretation of Galatians by the Teachers and their followers

---

[2] Martyn, *Galatians*, Comment 38.

[3] Paul's use of the prophetic call traditions in Gal 1:15 is as punctiliar as are his references to Abraham in 3:6–29.

seems to have won the day. Greatly offended by the letter, these persons apparently persuaded almost all of their colleagues in the Galatian churches to distance themselves from Paul, taking care, in fact, not to be perceived in Jerusalem as belonging to the orb of Paul's circumcision-free mission. In the end, that is, the Teachers were probably as successful in their hostile interpretation of Paul's letter as they were in their initial mission among the Galatians. Had they brought to their side *every* member of the Galatian churches, however, we could very well lack the letter itself.

Interpretation by the Pauline Catechetical Instructors

The preservation of the letter strongly suggests that the Teachers' success was less than total. It is easy to imagine that at least some of the Pauline catechetical instructors heard the letter as Paul intended. They may well have had to leave their Galatian cities in order to find themselves in a truly Pauline congregation, perhaps moving as far as Ephesus or another of the Aegean cities. In that case they would have taken at least one copy of the letter with them, and their doing that would be one explanation of the document's being preserved and eventually placed in a collection of Paul's letters.[4]

Interpretation by Paul Himself

It is virtually inconceivable that the readings given his letter in Galatia – especially its interpretation by the followers of the Teachers – remained unknown to Paul. We are to imagine the apostle receiving a discouraging report from the messenger whom he had trusted to deliver the letter.[5] Indeed, there is reason to think that Paul not only learned of the hostile interpretation, but also that, after learning of it, he took measures to correct it, with regard to all three of the matters so offensive to the Teachers: the linking of the Jerusalem church to slavery (Gal 4:25), the absence of God in the portrait of the Law's genesis (3:19–20), and the apparently un-Jewish reference to the Israel of God (6:16).

---

[4] For the thesis that Paul himself is responsible for the initial collection of his letters, see Trobisch, *Letter Collection*.

[5] Contrast *1 Clement* 65:1: 'Send back quickly to us our messengers . . . in peace with gladness . . . so that we may speedily rejoice in your good order.'

A Second Letter to the Galatian Churches

The messenger may have told Paul that, after hearing his highly critical reference to the Jerusalem church, the Teachers intensified their efforts to portray him as a man who has no genuine respect for that oldest of the congregations, and who thinks unimportant the relation of his own Gentile churches to that Jewish church in Palestine.[6] That would have been a view that required fundamental correction. At the conference in Jerusalem (Gal 2:1–10), Paul had been the participant most energized by the vision of one world-wide church drawn both from Jews and from Gentiles.[7] Even after the nefarious activity of the False Brothers and the Teachers, to contemplate a genuine divorce between his churches and the church in Jerusalem would have seemed to Paul the same as suggesting that the word of God had failed (cf. Rom 9:6). His first interpretive step seems, then, to have been a corrective supplement to his Galatian letter, in part a guide to its interpretation. That interpretive supplement lay in the conception of a plan to assemble a collection from his Gentile churches for delivery to the church in Jerusalem, thus clearly expressing his own concern for the unity of God's church throughout the whole of the world. He wrote a second letter to the Galatians (subsequently lost), placing before them his determination to collect funds for the Jerusalem church, and even suggesting a way by which they could assemble the money that would represent them (1 Cor 16:1–2).

A Letter to the Church in Rome

Later, he wrote to the church in the capital of the empire. Here he made use of his letter to the Galatians, and part of his reason for doing so may have been to guard that earlier letter from interpretations he considered misleading.

Why would it be in a letter to the Roman church that Paul should be concerned to correct misinterpretations of his earlier letter to the Galatians? The reason is complex: As he wrote the Roman letter, Paul was surely thinking of several weighty matters. He was contemplating the Spanish mission he planned to launch from that church. With that

---

[6] In Gal 2:10 Paul had already begun to correct an earlier form of the Teachers' charge that he cared nothing for the Jerusalem church, for he says that, prior to his divorce from the Antioch church, he participated *enthusiastically* in its periodic dispatching of funds to Jerusalem.

[7] Cf. Achtemeier, *Quest*; Dunn, *Unity*.

mission in mind, he was determined that the Roman church have an accurate grasp of his gospel, being thereby able enthusiastically to support his work in Spain. He was thus concerned that his Spanish mission not be seen as an attempt to make the world-wide church a purely Gentile affair.[8]

For that reason alone, his thoughts also went to the East, to the Jewish Christian church in Jerusalem, and specifically to the trip he had momentarily to make to that church, in order to deliver to it his collection. For the collection was Paul's crucial witness to the grand unity of the church of God in the whole of the world.[9]

There was in the Jerusalem church, however, a group of persons who did not at all share Paul's conviction that the unified church included circumcision-free Gentile congregations. These persons were the False Brothers, leaders by now of the circumcision party that had caused Paul great difficulties in Jerusalem itself (Gal 2:4–5), in Antioch (2:12), and in Galatia (see chapter 2 above). Paul's plan to journey to Jerusalem thus brought to him the prospect of a renewed confrontation with a group that was both intensely hostile to him and greatly influential in Judea and beyond.[10] This prospect created in Paul a considerable amount of anxiety (Rom 15:30–33).

There is, moreover, reason to think that Paul's anxiety was related both to the Galatians and to the letter he had written to them. The False Brothers' circumcision party in the Jerusalem church was almost certainly in touch with the Teachers, both before and after the latter's work in Paul's Galatian congregations. We have already noted the probability that, under the influence of the Teachers, the Galatian churches had refused to participate in Paul's collection. We must add that this step had very serious consequences for Paul's trip to Jerusalem. The apostle had now to consider the possibility that, when the Jerusalem church debated within its own ranks whether to accept his collection, some of those in the circumcision party – already knowing the answer – would ask him whether any of the funds were coming from the Galatian

---

[8] So Keck, 'Judgments.' The literature on the purpose of Romans is extensive. Beyond the commentaries, see notably Donfried, *Debate* (especially, with minor reservations, the chapter by Jervell); Jewett, 'Mission;' Sampley, 'Different Light;' Barclay, 'Romans 14.1–15.6,' 288–289.

[9] See especially Georgi, *Remembering.*

[10] Note Paul's references to difficulties in Philippi and Corinth. See Gnilka, *Philipperbrief;* Georgi, *Remembering;* Käsemann, 'Legitimität;' Barrett, 'Opponents;' Furnish, *II Corinthians;* Sumney, *Opponents.*

churches. Should that question be posed, he would have to admit that the Galatians had withdrawn from the circle of his churches. Paul may even have had to consider the possibility that Jewish Christians in the Jerusalem church who knew enough to ask that embarrassing question might also know something of his Galatian letter, such as the three crucial matters mentioned earlier (the Jerusalem church; the Law; Israel; cf. Acts 21:21).

We have no indication, to be sure, that Paul ever regretted writing the Galatian letter, but one can easily imagine that, on the eve of his last trip to Jerusalem, he regretted the harsh interpretation that had been placed upon the letter by the Teachers and their followers. Such regret, in any case, is consonant with the fact that, in writing to the Romans, Paul clarified, supplemented – perhaps one should even say modified – some of the things he had said to the Galatians about the Law and about Israel.[11]

Seen in this way, parts of Romans constitute an interpretation of Galatians made by Paul himself. Because Galatians has sometimes seemed to give the Christian church permission to adopt an anti-Judaic stance (see chapter 5 below), Paul's own interpretation of that letter is truly important. By attending briefly to the ways in which Paul spoke in Romans about the Law and about Israel, we may be able to see more clearly what he intended when he referred to the Law and to Israel in the earlier letter to the Galatians.[12]

The Law

Writing to the Gentile Christians in Galatia and being concerned about their incipient adherence to the Law as the means of salvation, Paul portrayed the Law itself as an enslaving tyrant, thus expressing a view of the Law foreign to all strains of Jewish and (first-century) Jewish-Christian thought known to us.[13]

---

[11] The third problem – Paul's linking the Jerusalem church with slavery in Gal 4:25 – also receives attention in Romans. For, with his positive references to 'the saints in Jerusalem' and with his statement that his Gentile churches are in debt to the Jerusalem church (Rom 15:25–27), Paul demonstrates his fundamental affirmation of the initial congregation, insofar as it is not dominated by the False Brothers and their circumcision party.

[12] An unsophisticated interpretation of Galatians on the basis of Romans is to be avoided (cf. Häbner, *Law*, 36). With care, however, and within definite limits, that route can be helpful. See, e.g., chapter 16 below.

[13] Both gnostic and orthodox Christians of later centuries drew distinctions between enslaving and liberating parts of the Law. See note 11 in chapter 14 below.

When he writes to the Romans, Paul does not reverse himself as regards there being a connection between the Sinaitic Law and tyranny; but his concern that he be accurately understood by Law-observant Jewish Christians (both in Rome and in Jerusalem) does lead him to a carefully nuanced formulation of that connection. Thus in Romans he says that the Law itself is holy and even spiritual (Rom 7:12, 14), an affirmation that would surely have been misunderstood had he directed it to the Gentile Christians in Galatia. He still insists, however, that when this holy and spiritual Law is faced with the overwhelming and malignant power of Sin, it proves to be impotent to bring Sin under control (Gal 3:21, 5:16; Rom 8:3). That controlling task is accomplished by God's sending of his Son, not by the Law. In the light, then, of God's act in Christ, Paul sees that the Law, being impotent, has fallen into the hands of Sin, and Sin has been able to use the Law to kill human beings (Rom 7:7–11). From Galatians to Romans, therefore, Paul is fundamentally consistent in drawing a connection between the Law and tyranny, but in Romans he clarifies – to some extent modifies – what he had said in Galatians. The Law is connected with tyranny, but only by way of Sin. For the tyrant itself is Sin, whereas the holy and spiritual Law is only an instrument in Sin's hands, and, in that sense, Sin's effective power (cf. 1 Cor 15:56).[14]

Israel

Focusing his Galatian letter tightly on the difference between two *Gentile missions* – the Teachers' and his own (chapter 2 above and chapter 12 below) – and thus referring nowhere to non-Christian Jews, Paul had spoken of the churches born in his mission as 'the Israel of God' (Gal 6:16). It was a locution subject to possible misunderstanding, not least if reported to the Jerusalem church. In Romans, then, Paul clarifies and supplements his use of the word 'Israel,' composing three long and complex chapters on the subject of God's faithful relationship to Israel (Rom 9–11).[15] He is aware that some have charged him with a callous apostasy from this special people of God, the people to whom the proper mission of the Jerusalem church was directed.

Significantly he does not defend himself by speaking immediately of his high regard for Israel's lengthy history. He begins, rather, with the

---

[14] See Meyer, 'Worm.'
[15] See also the final sections of chapter 10 below.

history of the gospel, referring to his deep pain and profound grief at one aspect of that history: most of Israel is now rejecting the gospel. As a world traveler, Paul is well acquainted with universal human disobedience to God (Rom 1:18–32). The disobedience of Israel, however, has about it something special. It is the great contradiction: the very people specially blessed by God is now largely disobeying God's gospel. This development is necessarily the great contradiction, because Paul can deny neither God's ancient election of Israel nor God's present, elective utterance of the gospel. Squarely facing this paradox, Paul necessarily sees that Israel is now standing 'between God and God' (cf. Rom 11:28).[16] In the final analysis, the great contradiction, incomprehensible to human reason, points, then, to God's own mystery, about which Paul has to speak in parables (Rom 11:16–24) and in the mysterious language of apocalyptic (Rom 11:25–36), in order to affirm God's sovereign election, God's faithfulness to Israel, and God's invincible power.

There are elements of this discussion that clarify and explicate what Paul had said about Israel in Galatians. The author of Galatians had said explicitly that Christ was the seed of Abraham (Gal 3:16), but he had also denied a line of physical descent in the many generations between the patriarch and Christ (chapter 10 below). Now, preparing for his trip to the Jewish Christian church in Jerusalem, Paul speaks explicitly of Abraham, Sarah, Isaac, Rebecca, and Jacob. He also makes clear that the patriarchs, being the first embodiment of God's gracious election, form the first fruits (Rom 11:16). Thus, by considering the patriarchal generations, he demonstrates that God is true to his word of elective grace (Rom 9:6–13).[17] Indeed, because God's word is both invincible and indelible, the ancient election of Israel remains a paradigm for God's dealing with all of humanity.

However different these affirmations may seem from those in Galatians, the basis on which Paul states them is precisely the basis of everything he had said in Galatians: the gospel of Christ. That God is true to his gospel-word of elective grace means, as Paul had said in Galatians, that the true Israel is the Israel *of God*. Far from rescinding this earlier reference, Paul now explicates it by speaking of a distinction between Israel and physical descent from the patriarch: 'not all who are

---

[16] This is a perceptive expression coined by Gerhard Ebeling and quoted by Luz, *Geschichtsverständnis* 296.
[17] Cf. Walter, 'Römer 9–11;' Meeks, 'Trusting;' E. E. Johnson, *Romans 9–11*.

descended from Israel belong to Israel' (Rom 9:6b). Profoundly hesitant to separate the word 'Israel' from those who bear that name because of their ethnic identity, Paul is nevertheless certain that genuine descent happens solely by God's election. That is true today, Paul claims, as one sees in the history of the gospel; it was also true in every patriarchal generation (Rom 9:6–13).

In this elective gospel Paul also sees, however, the invincibility of God's graceful word. This word tells Paul that Israel stands not between God and Satan – the dualistic motifs of Rom 8:38–39 are not continued in Romans 9–11 – but, as we have already said, between God and God. Thus, it is both true and of crucial importance that Paul now makes explicit the salvation of 'all Israel' (Rom 11:26). It is equally important to notice the grounds for that eschatological confidence. All Israel will be saved because, being the God who rectifies the ungodly, God is also the one whose capacity to show mercy is more powerful than the capacity of human beings to be disobedient (Rom 11:30–31). Paul was surely familiar with the classic view of Israel's eschatological relation to all other human beings: at the End, the Gentiles will flow up to Jerusalem, being saved by absorption into Israel (as the Teachers in Galatia had probably claimed; e.g., Isa 2:2–3; *Pss. Sol.* 17:30–32). In Romans Paul reverses that view, affirming *Israel's* ultimate salvation because he knows of God's ultimate purpose for *all* human beings: 'God has shut up all into disobedience, in order that he might have mercy on all' (Rom 11:32; an interpretation of Gal 3:22).[18]

Surprisingly, in this climactic sentence of his discussion of Israel, Paul does not mention Israel! He speaks rather of God's powerful mercy being shown to all human beings, and he bases his argument on that comprehensive mercy. It is clear, therefore, that in Romans Paul basically derives his theology of Israel from the universality of the gospel, about which he had already spoken in Galatians. Far from laying a foundation for the view that the church has replaced Israel, this theology is free of anti-Judaic cant (cf. chapter 5 below). It is a theology drawn from the gospel, and fundamentally it is Paul's theology both in Galatians and in Romans.

---

[18] See Bassler, *Impartiality.*

Luther reverted to pure Paulinism, and thus to a thorough antithesis with Judaism (Baeck cites Troeltsch, Dilthey, Wundt). Faith once again eclipses works, doctrinal religion triumphs over active ethics, and grace obliterates the human will.

There is, moreover, the truly hazardous alliance with the state, an alliance in which the responsibility for morality, being viewed, at best, as an appendix to religion, is handed over to the civil authorities. Abdicating the task of creating its own system of ethics, the religion of Luther granted unlimited power to the state.

(5) With Calvin and with the Baptist movement things developed quite differently. There is a significant return from the unhealthy weakness of Paulinism to the healthy strength of Judaism. Indeed one may speak here of a genuine revolution brought about by that which is Jewish in the church. Faith no longer has its purpose in itself. The Pauline, Augustinian, Lutheran passivity is left behind, as one realizes that faith is directed toward moral effectiveness. Connections with the state are refused, as legal piety is once again given a place internal to religion. And the positive role given to the Jewish heritage even sets question marks to the sacraments and to the doctrines of original sin and of Christ's divinity, thus suggesting the possibility of a return to Jewish monotheism.

This overview of twenty centuries of Christian history shows something of fundamental importance. Judaism has its indestructible life inside the church as well as outside it. True enough, Judaism can be strenuously opposed and even driven underground, but it always reemerges to find new forms of life, not only in its own proper stream, but also in that of the church.

Conclusion

Baeck's picture of Christianity, drawn by analyzing both its essence and its history, leaves us with two tones, one sharply negative, one affirmatively positive. As regards the former, the essays identify three major mistakes made by Christianity: First, it came into being when Paul mixed together things that cannot rightly be combined, the Jewish and non-Jewish elements mentioned above. Second, time and again Christianity turned its back on Judaism, giving its primary allegiance to the non-Jewish, romantic element, thus pretending that it could have God's mystery without God's commandment. And third, Christianity repeatedly failed to acknowledge the locus of its only true power, the stream of Judaism, which, in spite of all counterforces, coursed through its own history.

The positive side of the picture begins to come into view when one notes that, however fascinated Baeck may have been with the question of essence, in the end that question had to give way to the question of history. Baeck could not speak finally in timeless categories. He had rather to refer to Judaism and Paulinism as two historical antagonists, warring against one another within the mind and heart of Christianity over the span of centuries. Something, moreover, kept Baeck from viewing this war as a struggle that would end in a victory for the romantic antagonist, or even in a stalemate between the two.

True enough, the realism of 'Judaism in the Church' brings Baeck to a lamentation of the numerous points in church history at which Pauline theology (as he understood it) achieved periodic victories. As the final paragraph shows, however, that essay is, in the main, one of Baeck's most confident celebrations of the indomitable power of Judaism ultimately to triumph; and it is clear that Baeck is confident of that triumph not only in Judaism's own proper stream, quite apart from Christianity (so in the closing paragraphs of 'Mystery and Commandment' and 'Romantic Religion'), but also in the stream of Judaism that flows and always will flow in the church. Thus, when his final word announces the victory of Judaism, it speaks not of a victory over the church but rather of a victory within it: '*Et inclinata resurget.*' And it is, presumably, his confidence in this victory that made it possible for the one who, years later, had experienced the horrors of the Holocaust to change the angelic announcement from:

. . . peace among men of good will

to:

peace among men of bad will.[22]

IV

Baeck's sketch of the teaching of Jesus, his analysis of the essence of Christianity, and his account of its history constitute an impressive

---

[22] Cited in Th. Bovet, *Angst-Sicherung-Geborgenheit* (1975), Baeck's words are surely a conscious reversal of one of the traditional translations of Luke 2:14, a translation now generally replaced by 'peace among those with whom he [God] is pleased.'

accomplishment, truly helpful to genuine communication between Jews and Christians. We will turn in a moment to speak of the challenge to Christians. Before that, however, there is need for a brief critique, offered, one may hope, in the same candid spirit in which Baeck offered his critique of the work of Harnack. We focus our attention on two major flaws, both of which, because of Baeck's obvious fascination with Paul, have primarily to do with the apostle to the Gentiles.

The first flaw arises from Baeck's tendency to credit first-century authors with views that emerged only much later in the church's history. We notice, for example, that in 'Romantic Religion' he begins with an extensive definition of romanticism crafted on the basis of authors who lived in the nineteenth century. He thus allows Schleiermacher to speak of 'the feeling of absolute dependence' before he brings his reader to the letters of Paul. One is not wholly surprised, then, to find him shortly employing this very expression to encapsulate the faith of Paul himself and the result is his charge that Paul is the father of the romantic passivity of Christianity.[23] It is true that on occasion Paul can speak in terms that are distinctly enthusiastic (e.g. the refrain 'but now . . .'). He also speaks, however, of a faith that is active in love, and specifically in love directed toward the neighbor, in accordance with Lev 19:18 (e.g. Gal 5:6 and 5:14). Paul also knows that the Spirit, far from transporting the individual into a passive and egoistic state of romantic dreaminess, leads the community into an active and communal life of love, joy, peace, compassion, and the selfless service of one another (Gal 5:22; Phil 2:2–4).

That anachronistic flaw is then deepened by Baeck's consistent failure – together with many of his contemporaries who were professional New Testament scholars – to listen to Paul's voice in the context of the apostle's battles with various other teachers in his churches.[24]

Baeck does not see, therefore, that the true analogue to nineteenth-century romanticism is to be found not in Paul, but rather in some of the members of his Corinthian church, who, much to Paul's dismay, said that they were already filled, had already become rich, and were already ruling as kings (1 Cor 4:8). It is true, as we have noted above, that there is a strain of such enthusiasm in Paul's own theology, but it is

---

[23] 'Romantic Religion,' 213 and passim.

[24] Baeck occasionally cites F. C. Baur, but the major insights of the Tübingen giant seem to have escaped him as readily as they escaped many of the New Testament scholars of the first half of the twentieth century. Regarding Baur, see chapter 13 below.

always held in check by his insistence – often expressed in sharply polemical tones – that the church lived in the earthy (and earthly) cross of Christ and in the hope of Christ's parousia. Thus, when the Corinthian enthusiasts perceived the Eucharist to be a sort of medicine of guaranteed immortality, to be consumed by individuals at their own convenience and for its own sake, Paul said: '. . . let anyone who thinks that he stands [by consuming the Eucharist as though it were magic food and drink], take heed lest he fall' (1 Cor 10:12).

For Paul the Eucharist is by no means a possession of the 'perfected man.' On the contrary, it stands precisely as a sign of the fact that the church lives in an uncompleted interim, for in celebrating the Lord's supper, 'you proclaim the Lord's death until he comes' (1 Cor 11:26). No one in the early Christian church understood better than Paul the distinction between the faith that is active in love and the mystical superstition that longs to hug itself to sleep. And no one fought for that distinction more vigorously.

The second major flaw in Baeck's treatment of Paul is closely related to the first, and again, to a degree, it corresponds to a deficiency characteristic of the Pauline studies of Baeck's time. Just as he does not see that Paul fought one of his major battles against the emergence of magical enthusiasm in his churches, so he fails to see that Paul's own position is not at all romantic, but rather apocalyptic. Indeed, Baeck's preoccupation with nineteenth-century romanticism leads him to make three unfortunate errors with regard to Paul's apocalyptic perspective, the first pertaining to Paul's understanding of the present, the second having to do with his perception of the future, the third being focused on his view of the human being.

(a) Given the provisional dualism of Paul's apocalyptic theology, Baeck is altogether correct to say that Paul sees history as 'a theatrical drama being played out between the below and the above;' it is 'a struggle.'[25] One cannot say in Paul's name, however, that this historical struggle 'really takes place beyond the human sphere.'[26] On the contrary, the apocalyptic drama, having been inaugurated by the coming of Christ, has already begun, and it is occurring in the world into which Christ came. True enough, being a genuine apocalyptic drama, it includes suprahuman actors (it was, e.g., the *archontes*, the rulers of this

---

[25] 'Romantic Religion,' 220; slightly changed; see *Jahrtausenden*, 65 ('Schauspiel').
[26] Ibid.

present evil age, who 'crucified the Lord of Glory'; 1 Cor 2:8), but they do not at all drive the human actors off the stage (1 Thess 2:14–15). Daniel, one must recall, was sure that developments on the earthly stage – dominantly the machinations of Antiochus IV – were hopelessly enigmatic and enigmatically hopeless apart from the bi-focal vision of apocalyptic, a vision in which one sees not only those earthly developments, but also and simultaneously the corresponding (and revealing) developments on the heavenly stage.[27] In Paul we find something similar, even though the *archontes* are not pictured as beasts with horns.

What demands emphasis is that Paul's everyday vision is genuinely bi-focal, and therefore not otherworldly. Paul's apocalyptic is emphatically not a form of romanticism but rather the truly powerful antidote to that virus.[28] One can see what is involved if one will patiently interview Paul on the subject of history as a *struggle*. For while he does indeed speak of the involvement of suprahuman powers, he also knows that human beings are themselves genuine actors in the struggle of history. One will look in vain for a passage in which Paul tells the community of active faith to sit passively by, as the forces of evil have a field day.[29]

Precisely the opposite! The community is summoned now into the thick of the apocalyptic battle by an apostle who is himself thoroughly identified with the struggle of those who are weak and stumbling (2 Cor 11:29), and who, for that reason, bears the marks of battle 'through great endurance, in afflictions, hardships, calamities, beatings, imprisonments . . . hunger . . .' (2 Cor 6:4–5). The present is not a timeless time in which one is encouraged to run away from real life into a dreamy romanticism. It is, on the contrary, the time of the most vigorous struggle (*agōn*) for the extension of God's rectifying justice to the whole of the world.

This understanding of the present as the time of apocalyptic war is derived, in Paul's case, from the event of Christ's crucifixion, the head-

---

[27] See chapter 17 below.

[28] It is misleadingly partial and thus quite incorrect to say that Paul's vision 'disclosed the "above," the celestial' ('The Faith of Paul,' 151).

[29] Baeck rightly points to the disastrous effects of the dominant interpretation accorded to Rom 13:1 in the history of the church ('Let every person be subject to the governing authorities . . .'). Paul's own intention was probably to combat a tendency of the enthusiasts to withdraw into a kind of privitistic individualism. See Käsemann, 'Romans 13.'

on collision between the powers of evil and the power of God (see again 1 Cor 2:8).[30] It involves, therefore, a profoundly serious view of evil. One notes, by contrast, that Baeck's view of evil was fundamentally influenced by the easy optimism characteristic of the European scene at the end of the nineteenth century rather than by the apocalyptic Hasidim whose understanding of evil is enshrined in the book of Daniel. As a result, Baeck did not grasp Paul's apocalyptically realistic portrait of evil and sin.[31]

The *centrum Paulinum* is not Paul's own vision of the resurrected Christ, in the sense Baeck accords to that expression, but rather what Paul himself calls 'the word of the cross.'[32] Paul sees simultaneously, as it were, the crucified Christ and the resurrected one, and it is this simultaneity that causes his apocalyptic vision of life to be truly bi-focal and thus altogether antithetical to romantic religion. The real world emerges in the cross/resurrection, the world of God's decisive battle for the rectification of the world, the battle into which human beings are called by being 'crucified *with* Christ' (Gal 2:19).

(*b*) For Paul the nature of this present battle is determined, however, not only by the past event of Christ's death/resurrection, but also by the future event of his parousia. The apocalyptic drama encompasses, therefore, not only the real and present warfare, but also the confidently hoped-for consummation of that warfare in the future. Here we have simply to say that Baeck allowed his own view of Paul to determine which texts received his attention. Knowing ahead of time, so to speak, that Paul was a consistent romantic, Baeck also knew that the structure of Paul's faith can scarcely have been characterized by genuine hope. One notes that Baeck ignores the lengthy apocalyptic discourse Paul gave to the Thessalonian church on the sure hope of the victorious

[30] See chapter 15 below.

[31] Baeck's view of evil and his understanding of the human will are, of course, inextricably intertwined. One notes with some degree of astonishment that the rightly venerated survivor of Theresienstadt – having come face to face with one of evil's most massive attacks in the Holocaust – maintained his earlier views essentially intact. Human beings are able to decide to be obedient. Contemplating the Nazi madness, one might rather think of Hosea's picture of an enslaved will, for which a mere call to repentance (*teshuvah*) is impotent: 'Their deeds do not allow them to return (*lashuv*) to their God' (Hos 5:4). See D. W. Martyn, 'A Child and Adam: A Parable of the Two Ages,' *Apocalyptic and the New Testament* (eds J. Marcus and M. L. Soards; Sheffield, 1989), 317–333.

[32] Baeck is not speaking for Paul when he says, 'the resurrection is the gospel and nothing else. . . . This [the resurrection] is the sole theme' ('The Faith of Paul,' 151).

parousia (1 Thess 4:13–5:11). Disquiet at this instance of procrustean interpretations grows into amazed disbelief when one sees that in 'The Faith of Paul' Baeck excises the apocalyptic paragraph of 1 Cor 15:23–28, confidently declaring it to be a post-Pauline interpolation, although there is no manuscript of the letter that lacks it.[33] The net result is that Baeck does not give due attention to either focus of Paul's apocalyptic christology: Christ's death and Christ's future parousia!

The better route is to recognize that one of Paul's most important concerns was focused on his struggle on behalf of the not-yet-realized hope of the parousia, and thus of the view that Christian life is essentially oriented to the future, being determined by Christ's future no less than by his past.[34]

(c) How, then, is this hope-filled view of the future related to Paul's understanding of the human being? We recall that Baeck's Paul is one who believes that the Christian vision severs human beings from their will, making them the object of a predetermined (and thus non-genuine) history, rather than the will-endowed agents of history, responsible for the future.

Again, Baeck goes astray because he does not see Paul's particular form of apocalyptic. It is true that for Paul there is no general freedom of the will, but the apocalyptic drama of Jesus Christ is in no way responsible for that state of affairs. On the contrary, it is in that drama that God is actively freeing the will, thus creating among the Gentiles a liberated community that is able to be addressed by the commandment (1 Cor 7:19).[35] And it is this newly addressable community that is called by God into the apocalyptic warfare for the glorious future of the whole of humanity. The members of this community are scarcely will-less romantics, hopeless subjects of history with no task and no genuine future. They are newly enrolled soldiers called into the obedience of faith and sent into the warfare in which God is regrasping the world for himself.[36]

---

[33] 'The Faith of Paul,' 152, n. 26.

[34] See Käsemann, 'Apocalyptic;' Moltmann, *Hope* (1967); Morse, *Logic*; Beker, *Paul.* We will have occasion below to applaud Baeck's challenge that modern Christians learn to speak of the future. In issuing that challenge, Baeck was far closer to Paul than he realized.

[35] See chapters 14 and 15 below.

[36] For this picture of an apocalyptic Paul we are indebted above all to the works of Käsemann. See Riches, *Study*, 125–133.

V

Does this critique tell us that the strong link Baeck discerns between Christianity and romanticism (as he defined the latter; see note 17 above) is entirely beside the point? Hardly! Baeck's perception and analysis of that link yield one of the major challenges put to Christianity in the twentieth century. The full hearing of that challenge is essential to a genuine dialogue between Jews and Christians and, for that reason, to the health and integrity of Christianity itself.

There is, first, the striking question Baeck has directed to the professional church historians. Is there one major key to the highly complex history of the church, and if so, what is it? Especially since the Reformation one can easily find numerous works in which that key is identified (however implicitly) as the relation of Christianity to Judaism. Thus the grand sweep of the history of Christianity has been presented as an alternation between, first, noble and healthy surges into ground that is new and distinctively Christian, and, second, timid and unhealthy relapses into modified forms of Judaism.[37] Baeck, agreeing that the key to church history lies in the relations of Christianity to Judaism, turns this historical sketch precisely on its head. For him the periods of health and strength have been the Jewish ones; the periods of unhealth and weakness have been those marked by relapses into non-Jewish romanticism.

This is a sketch of church history that can and must alert the church to the ever-present danger presented by the ghost of Marcion. One of the current forms of the Marcionite danger can be seen in the call of some third-world theologians for the building of Christianity on the basis of various native religions rather than on the basis of the Old Testament. It is precisely at such a juncture as this that Christians need to hear the voice of Baeck as a man concerned about the future of the entire human race. For severance from the Old Testament has always thrown the church into some form of ethical chaos, dangerous both to itself and to others.

Baeck's ethical challenge is extraordinarily perceptive. He sees that what is commonly called ethics has had a very hard time finding a recognized and stable home in Christianity.[38] Indeed, over the span of

---

[37] To some degree this pattern is found, one scarcely needs to say, in the work of Baeck's early antagonist, Harnack. Cf. note 4 in chapter 12 below.

[38] See Part IV in the present volume.

centuries, the dominant picture – and the one to which Baeck gives repeated attention – is the one in which ethics is excluded from the sphere considered proper to Christianity, either by being banned to live in a sort of shabby lean-to, having no organic relation to the main house of faith, or by being handed over entirely to the state. Not infrequently ethics has thus become, at worst, the sanctification of a tyrannical government and, at best, 'a message that is perceived dimly, as if from a vast distance, a message that can mean everything while demanding nothing . . .'[39] From such ethics one learns to be prudent, to find the *modus vivendi*; and thus, in the end, one falls into the kind of casuistry that can be comfortable with the neighbor's suffering.[40] About this part of Baeck's charge there can be no argument. Christian history provides more examples than one wishes to enumerate.

The full profundity of Baeck's analysis of Christian ethics ensues, however, from his recognition that the organic relationship between faith and ethics is equally compromised when ethics moves in from the lean-to and takes over the house, pretending to be the whole of Christianity, thus rendering unnecessary and, in fact, useless, everything having to do with the mystery of God's transcendent and prevenient activity. Here we have the pattern Baeck identifies as 'the commandment without the mystery.' In making this point, Baeck speaks, to be sure, of Judaism, but the implications for Christianity are altogether clear, perhaps indeed clearer to us than they were to Baeck. First, re-capitulating the earlier warning about the eclipse of the activity of ethics by the passivity of faith, Baeck says: 'This religion of mere passivity, devoid of commandments, is no longer Judaism [in his opinion, it is, of course, Christianity].'

Then he adds:

> Nor is Judaism to be found where the commandment is content with itself and is nothing but commandment; where the whole sphere of life is supposed to be embraced by commandments, and only that which lies under the rays of their cold light is presumed to be the meaning of life . . . The very ground on which Judaism rests is abandoned when . . . it is assumed to be merely an ethic or the support for an ethic; when it becomes a mere edifice

---

[39] 'Romantic Religion,' 265; slightly changed, *Jahrtausenden*, 101.

[40] The vast distance separating casuistry from an ethics that, with integrity, permeates every corner of daily life is powerfully presented in 'Mystery and Commandment' 182, a passage containing a much-needed corrective to Christian caricatures of 'Jewish legalism.' One will find it an instructive exercise to compare that passage with some remarkably similar comments of Käsemann, 'Worship.'

> of ideas . . . or when that which the mystery intimates is no longer supposed to be the foundation of man's life . . . There is no such thing as a Judaism . . . in which the idea of God is merely a decorative embellishment or a crowning pinnacle.[41]

Again, from the Christian side, a genuine response involves basic agreement. It is, as we have said, precisely the integrity of devotion and deed, of theology and ethics, that has been so often absent in the history of the church. There are, however, two groups who have lost that integrity: those thinking it possible to have the roots without the branches, and those thinking they can have the branches without the roots. To both groups Baeck's voice comes as that of the physician who is truly concerned with the patient's recovery: 'The world of Judaism [and thus of health] is to be found only where faith has its commandment, and the commandment its faith.'[42]

Read together with the essays on romantic religion and Judaism in the church, 'Mystery and Commandment' is one of the most important words spoken to the church in the twentieth century. The future of humanity demands that Christians pay very close attention to the witness of Judaism, and specifically to the Jewish prescription offered by Leo Baeck.

For many Christians, however, the medicine cannot be swallowed precisely in the form prescribed, as though a return to Judaism, as such, were the effective answer to the probing challenge.[43] We must, rather, honor the integrity of Leo Baeck by taking our bearings both from his challenge and from the Christian critique of it; in this way, at least the beginning of a creditable response may be possible. The periods in the history of the church at which romanticism (again as defined by Baeck) has raised its head are indeed periods of abysmal failure; and exactly the

---

[41] 'Mystery and Commandment,' 176–178.

[42] Ibid., 177.

[43] The question whether the church is to be perceived as a sect within Judaism was posed very clearly in the first century. The dominant answer – and ultimately the victorious one – was in the negative, as we can see, for example, in reading Paul's letter to the Galatians. Some of the theologians who are currently attempting to formulate post-Holocaust statements on the relations between Jews and Christians – a desideratum – seem partially to have forgotten such early Christian documents as Galatians. Klappert, for example, thinks he can call on the name of Baeck in order to fight against 'something new in contrast with Judaism' in favor of 'something new *in* Judaism' ('Brücken,' 296–297). No issue facing the church is more crucial to its own health than that of a theologically mature relationship with Judaism, but that relationship places demands on both parties. See note 27 in chapter 12 below.

same is to be said of the periods marked by what Baeck called the ethics of the surface.

None of these periods, however, is accurately identified as a re-emergence of Paulinism. On the contrary, each is characterized by the domestication of the bi-focal vision that characterized early Christian theology, not least that of Paul. The romantics have repeatedly domesticated that apocalyptic theology by turning it into a uni-focal form of otherworldliness. Enraptured, they have gazed into heaven, with no concern for this world (Acts 1:11). The surface ethicists, equally uni-focal, have carried out their domestication by eclipsing (from their own eyes!) the mystery of God's activity, turning their attention only to the earth (Col 2:23). The antidote to both of these retreats presents itself in the bi-focal theology of Christ's cross and Christ's parousia, a theology derived from the bi-focal nature of Jewish apocalyptic, but also reformed by being focused on the past, present, and future of Jesus Christ, the one who frees the human will for obedience.

Taken in this way, Baeck's challenge is a call to Christians to turn from the weak and ineffective – and ultimately dehumanizing – forms of both romantic passivity and shallow activity. It is also a call to return to the God of Abraham, Isaac, and Jacob by means of the Christian *Shema*, that is to say, by an active hearing of the original gospel preached by Jesus of Nazareth (so Baeck) as part of the fully apocalyptic gospel of Jesus Christ preached by Paul.

Appendix to Chapter 4

A Review of
The Mythmaker:
Paul and the Invention of Christianity
by Hyam Maccoby
(New York: Harper & Row, 1986)

The line of Hyam Maccoby's argument in this book is clear: Jesus was a Pharisee who regarded himself as the Jewish Messiah, a human leader who would restore the Jewish monarchy by calling on God to drive out the Roman invaders and establish an independent Jewish state. Believing that God would perform this liberating miracle on the Mount of Olives (as foretold by Zechariah), Jesus went to Jerusalem, only to find that his utopian dream was not fulfilled. The Romans perceived his plan, arrested him and tried and executed him. They had already done this to other leaders of Jewish liberation movements, as Mr Maccoby points out in his earlier book, *Revolution in Judea*.

After Jesus' death, the argument runs, his immediate followers, all of them Pharisees, founded the Jerusalem church. Members of this community were indistinguishable from other Pharisees in all regards except their belief that Jesus, having been raised from the dead, would soon return to resume successfully his mission of overthrowing the Romans and restoring the Jewish state. Altogether observant of the Jewish law, these Nazarenes, as they were called, constituted in fact a branch of Judaism; they continued to practice circumcision, keep the food laws and reverence the Temple. Being opposed to the quisling High Priest and to all other Roman collaborators, they proved themselves true Jews by remaining in Jerusalem during the war of 66–70, loyally playing their part in the fight against Rome.

With the fall of the holy city, they were scattered to other places. These authentic successors of Jesus, woefully impoverished and dispersed, came in time to be known as the Ebionites (the poor ones). Faithfully preserving the views of Jesus himself, the Ebionites correctly taught that Jesus was a human being concerned with inaugurating a new age on earth. They too observed the law and regarded themselves as Jews, not as adherents of a new and separate religion called Christianity.

Thus far the picture of the 'Jesus movement' is intelligible, thoroughly Jewish, and marked by law-observant continuity. The people in this picture are also eminently admirable. From Jesus onward they are all Pharisees, realistic activists, engaged in resistance against Roman occupation, determined to make the world a better place in which to live and not to escape from it into some otherworldly form of romanticism.

In Mr Maccoby's view, within a few years Paul enters this engaging picture as a strange, foreign and unsavory figure with motives considerably less than honorable. Indeed, although in his own writings he hid the facts surrounding his birth and youth, the true picture can be gleaned from the traditions of the Ebionites. Contrary to his own claims, Paul was born a Gentile and never became a Pharisee. From Tarsus he went to Jerusalem with the keen desire to become a Jew. He attached himself, however, to the quisling High Priest (a Sadducee) and became one of his hired thugs, bent on persecuting the Nazarenes. Somehow the love affair with Judaism went sour and Paul, now agonizingly estranged from both the collaborationist High Priest and the nationalistic Nazarenes, set about to create a new religion.

Corresponding to the agony of his own psyche, Paul posited from gnosticism a cosmic agony, a world held in darkness and yearning for the salvific light. From the same source he drew the picture of a heavenly visitor, a god who comes to earth to impart true knowledge (gnosis) and save humanity from the powers of darkness. From the sado-masochistic elements of the mystery religions (Mr Maccoby says Paul had youthful experience in the horrible cult of Attis) Paul gave specific content to the saving knowledge imparted by the divine visitor: The visitor caused human beings to know that his own death had been the sacrificial atonement necessary to rescue humanity from a dark world that is itself a hell. Finally, from Judaism this tormented and confused Gentile borrowed the concept of a history stretching from Adam to Abraham, and finally to the church, a wholly new community, which he boldly declared to be the heir of the promises made by God to Abraham. The net result is that Paul, departing entirely from the Pharisee traditions of Jesus, invented out of his own agony and despair the essentially gnostic myth of Christianity, a world-weary religion attractive to those intent on escaping the universal human responsibility to work for a better world. It was also a religion that, ominously, shared with gnosticism an inherent anti-Semitism.

It is important to bring Mr Maccoby's conclusion clearly into focus. He is not saying merely that Paul, rather than Jesus, was the founder of Christianity. That thesis was developed more than 100 years ago by the Jewish historian Heinrich Graetz, and it has been many times repeated. The issue Mr Maccoby wishes to address is not the invention of a legitimate religion called Christianity. The issue is anti-Semitism, and here further precision is imperative. Mr Maccoby is not suggesting that Paul played a peripheral role in the gradual and complex development of Christian anti-Semitism. Nor is he saying that over the centuries unscrupulous interpreters have twisted Paul's words into expressions of anti-Semitism altogether at variance with Paul's own intentions. He is saying, rather, that Paul is himself the originator of the Christian myth and thus of anti-Semitism among Christians. If this charge can be sustained, one must ask whether it would be extravagant to remove Paul's letters from the Christian Bible.

That Mr Maccoby's book should drive one to pose such a question is indication enough that it is not a series of casual comments over afternoon tea. It is a thoughtfully constructed treatise addressing matters the author considers pertinent to the study of one of the most lethal viruses known to the human race, anti-Semitism among Christians. Concerning that virus three questions are of paramount importance. How did it get its start? What factors have facilitated its development? Can Jews and Christians work together to locate antidotes that are truly effective?

To the second of these questions Mr Maccoby has made an earlier and significant contribution by translating and annotating the primary documents of the three well-recorded Jewish-Christian disputations of the Middle Ages. His book *Judaism on Trial* (1982) is a fascinating treatment celebrating the figure of Nahmanides, one of the most impressive Spanish medieval rabbis. In *The Mythmaker* he turns directly to the question of how anti-Semitism began among Christians, and he seems to intend, at least indirectly, to make a contribution to answering the third question. He hopes that thoughtful Christians will put some distance between themselves and the father of anti-Semitism. A serious response thus requires an inquiry into the adequacy of the author's account of Paul's role in Christian origins as an explanation of the genesis of anti-Semitism. It also requires consideration of whether the author's publication of this account can serve as an effective antidote to anti-Semitism among people who call themselves Christians.

Especially since the Enlightenment, a number of Jewish scholars have been teachers to Christians. One thinks gratefully of Moses Mendelssohn, Graetz (who, as I hinted above, set much of the agenda for subsequent Jewish interpretations of Paul), Hermann Cohen, Leo Baeck, Joseph Klausner, Martin Buber, H. J. Schoeps, David Daube, Paul Winter, Abraham Joshua Heschel, Shalom Ben Chorin, Pinchas Lapide, and others. A great deal of their teaching has been focused on the study of Jesus and, although attended by some disagreements (notably regarding Jesus' trial), it has often had its salutary effect on the work of Christian scholars. Our understanding of Jesus' parables, for example, has been enriched by the labors of Jewish interpreters. Jewish scholars have also written on broad issues of Christian origins, including the study of Paul. And, while this part of the ecumenical conversation has sometimes been difficult indeed, wherever Jewish interpreters have taken Paul seriously (in this regard Leo Baeck is exemplary), Christians have had an opportunity to learn.

From the company of these Jewish scholars one turns to Mr Maccoby with high expectations, only to be largely disappointed. Apparently the passionate need to charge Paul with fathering anti-Semitism has taken a great toll on the author's gifts as a historian, causing his labors to stand at some remove from those of the company mentioned above. Mr Maccoby's case against Paul rests on two main pillars, neither of which is able to bear the weight he places upon it.

First, there is the argument from comparative religion. Paul is said to have drawn the core of his theology from gnosticism, a religion characterized by Mr Maccoby as inherently anti-Semitic. Nowhere, however, does Mr Maccoby identify gnostic sources that can be dated as early as Paul's letters. Moreover, again and again, where Mr Maccoby turns to gnosticism to explain a Pauline motif, the data in Paul's letters themselves call instead for comparison with Jewish apocalyptic writings, notably the type of apocalyptic we know from the Dead Sea Scrolls.

In the letter to the Galatians, for example, Paul interprets Jesus' crucifixion by citing a verse from Deuteronomy, 'Cursed is everyone who is hanged on a tree,' a pronouncement having originally nothing to do with crucifixion. Our understanding of Paul's exegesis of this verse has been greatly improved since the discovery of the Dead Sea Scrolls, for in two of them, not mentioned by Mr Maccoby, we find the same text from Deuteronomy interpreted as a reference to crucifixion. This shows that Paul's interpretation is scarcely a piece of pagan thought that is 'alien to Jewish thinking,' as Mr Maccoby says. In sum, the argument that Paul developed the core of his theology from pagan, anti-Semitic forms of religion is without foundation.

The second major pillar of Mr Maccoby's case is what he calls 'the evidence of the Ebionites.' This is a turn in the argument that brings us to the question of the sources from which we gain our knowledge of Paul. Profound uneasiness as to the author's use of sources begins, however, in his section on Jesus, and a word about that is in order as an introduction to his interpretation of the Pauline sources. For Mr Maccoby, as for others, from the theologian Robert Eisler to the historian S. G. F. Brandon, Jesus must have been a nationalistic political figure who was threatening to the Romans, not an extraordinary religious teacher who was odious to some of the Jewish authorities. The Gospels consistently report, however, that Jesus' disciples were not arrested along with him, and that development is altogether unlikely for members of a seditious movement. Never mind, says Mr Maccoby. The Gospel writers, intent on depoliticizing Jesus, omitted to mention the 'details of the arrest of Jesus' followers.' Which details? The non-existent ones required by the presupposed portrait of Jesus.

Do things improve when Mr Maccoby takes us to the Pauline documents? Not very much. Those who wish to make Paul's acquaintance have at their disposal sources that fall into three categories: (*a*) seven letters written by Paul himself in the sixth decade of the first century; (*b*) Luke's account in the Acts of the Apostles, penned at the end of the century, along with several letters written by Paul's followers; and finally, (*c*) references to Paul in the traditions of Jewish-Christian groups, such as the Ebionites and their like, ranging in date from the late second century into the fourth. All of the items in this third category (mainly the *Ascents of James*, the *Preachings of Peter*, and a brief paragraph in the fourth-century ramblings about the Ebionites in the major work of the church father Epiphanius) have been meticulously studied since the seminal labors of F. C. Baur (1792–1860). It is widely known that the least reliable of them is the brief paragraph in Epiphanius. From this paragraph, clearly a mixture of fable and slander, Mr Maccoby draws the major dimensions of his portrait of Paul, using it to correct Paul's own letters and Luke's account. Little cause for wonder, then, that the slander continues. In Mr Maccoby's picture Paul, a man of doubtful antecedents, lacking in logical ability because of a feeble educational base, having failed in his attempt to become a genuine Jew, threaded his way by guile through a series of stormy episodes and, in short, told lies.

That descendants of those who for centuries were charged with deicide, descendants of those who were peremptorily summoned to the so-called Jewish-Christian disputations in the Middle Ages, descendants of those who were told in the nineteenth century to assimilate or suffer the consequences, descendants of those who were taken by the millions to the gas chambers, assimilated or not – that these descendants should find it difficult to trust what is said by a Christian, modern or ancient, calls for no explanation and should receive none. More than distrust, however, is required of the historian.

We are left, then, with the unwanted conclusion that historical tendentiousness precludes Mr Maccoby's book on Paul from serving as a potent antidote to the virus of anti-Semitism among Christians. The conclusion is doubly unfortunate, first because the author has put a good deal of work and sincerely held passion into the book, and second (and much more important) because there is in fact a connection between Paul and anti-Semitism that demands serious attention: Anti-Semites have been able to employ unconscionably some of Paul's utterances to their own ends. Indeed Paul said things that – torn from the literary, historical and theological contexts in which he said them – have been used to dehumanize Jews, women and, not least, black slaves and their descendants. Such statements call, however not for superficial castigation of Paul, but rather for contextual interpretation. And whoever engages in such interpretation will discern that Paul was not a romantic dreamer but rather a warrior in both worlds who was active against all forms of enslavement to the status quo.

From Mr Maccoby's book where is one to turn, then? To that extraordinary combination of learning and humility that enabled Leo Baeck, Abraham Heschel and others to read rather than raid the letters of Paul, and thus genuinely to hear the voice not of a charlatan, but of a thoroughly human being, whose concern for Israel led him both to moments of intense anguish ('I could wish that I myself were accursed and cut off from Christ for the sake of my brethren, my kinsmen by race' – Rom 9:3) and to moments of graceful certainty ('as regards election they are beloved for the sake of their forefathers. For the gifts and the call of God are irrevocable' – Rom 11:28–29).

5

Galatians, An Anti-Judaic Document?

Significant advances have been made in the reading of Paul's letters – not least the one to the Galatians – as the result of an ecumenical development: Since the middle of the nineteenth century a number of Jewish scholars have added their own learning and talents to the common attempt to understand the apostle. Begun in the work of the historian Heinrich Graetz (1817–91), modern Jewish study of Paul includes the labors of Leo Baeck, Joseph Klausner, H. J. Schoeps, David Daube, Samuel Sandmel, Shalom Ben Chorin, Pinchas Lapide, Hyam Maccoby, Alan Segal, Jacob Taubes, and, recently, Daniel Boyarin.[1] The most theologically profound contribution is that of Baeck; the most directly pertinent to the study of Galatians, that of Boyarin.[2]

From this welcome development, both Christians and Jews find it easier to distinguish peripheral issues from ones that are of true import. One of the latter – certainly more important since the Holocaust – is the question whether at least some of the anti-Judaic accents in the interpretations of Paul by Marcion, Luther, and others, are justified. Specifically, has Paul's Galatian letter received anti-Judaic interpretations because it is itself – at least in part – an anti-Judaic document, in the sense that, in writing it, Paul intended to pit himself against the religion of Judaism as such? Maccoby, for example, is almost certainly correct in his interpretation of Gal 3:19–20: In that passage, Paul portrays the genesis of the Sinaitic Law as an event in which God played

---

[1] Baeck, 'Romantic Religion;' Klausner, *Paul*; Schoeps, *Paul*; Daube, *New Testament*; Sandmel, *Genius*; Ben Chorin, *Paulus*; Lapide (with P. Stuhlmacher), *Paul*; Maccoby, *Mythmaker*; Segal, *Convert*; Taubes, *Paulus*; Boyarin, *Politics*. Published too late to be taken into account here is Nanos, *Mystery*.

[2] On Leo Baeck as a theological interpreter of Christianity, see chapter 4 above. Boyarin takes into account 'the entire context of the Pauline corpus,' but the fascinating character of his book arises to a large extent from the fact that it is conceived as 'a reading of Paul centered on Galatians' (*Politics*, 6).

no role.[3] What more could one need, in order to conclude that the document reflects an anti-Judaic intention?

Several other passages could also be cited as anti-Judaic, not least because, beginning with Marcion and Tertullian in the second century, some of these texts have seemed to be nothing other than Pauline attacks on the synagogue.[4] Moreover, Boyarin is right to point out that, after the political and cultural ascendancy of Christianity in the west, numerous Christians have used these Galatians texts in forming systems designed to coerce non-Christians into a nominally Christian, religious universality.[5] In addition to Gal 3:19–20, one could list especially 1:13–16 (note *Ioudaïsmos,* 'Judaism,' in 1:14); 2:13–16 (note *Ioudaioi,* 'Jews,' in 2:13 and the expressions *Ioudaïkōs zēn* and *Ioudaïzein,* 'to live in the Jewish manner,' in 2:14); 3:16; 3:28; and 4:21–5:1.

Detailed exegesis of these passages, however, fails to reveal an anti-Judaic intention on Paul's part (Martyn, *Galatians*), a conclusion that now finds welcome agreement in the study of Boyarin.[6] For without exception, in the passages listed, as in others, the ruling polarity is not that of Christianity versus Judaism, church versus synagogue. On the contrary, taking care to formulate a strict definition of religion, we can see that that ruling polarity has to do with God's apocalyptic act in Christ, on the one hand, and with religion, on the other.[7]

---

[3] Maccoby, *Mythmaker,* 188–189; Martyn, *Galatians,* Comment 38. See also, however, my cautionary review of *Mythmaker.* Appendix to chapter 4 above.

[4] The *locus classicus* for this reading of Galatians is 4:21–5:1, a passage in connection with which a major modern interpreter of Galatians says, 'According to Galatians, Judaism is excluded from salvation altogether . . .' (H. D. Betz, *Galatians,* 251). Glimpses into the history of the interpretation of this passage are provided in Martyn, 'Hagar and Sarah;' and in briefer form in chapter 12 below.

[5] Boyarin's justified charge against the history of Christian coercion runs throughout his book *Politics.* When he says, however, that Paul's universalism 'seems to *conduce* to coercive politico-cultural systems that engage in more or less violent projects of the *absorption* of cultural specificities into the dominant one' (228, emphasis added), he fails to reckon adequately with the difference between Paul's intentions and those of later interpreters, such as Marcion and his heirs. Note, e.g. the *way* in which Paul reverses the ancient Israelite hope of absorbing the Gentiles into herself (chapter 3 above).

[6] Boyarin, *Politics,* 136–157. One must note, however, that we have here an instance in which a common conclusion is reached by different, partially contradictory routes. Boyarin's discussion is somewhat complex: 'I argue that while Galatians is not an anti-Judaic text, its theory of the Jews nevertheless is one that is inimical to Jewish difference, indeed to all difference as such' (*Politics,* 156). As we will see below, one of the clearest indications that Galatians is not an anti-Judaic text lies in the letter's failure to contain a theory of the Jews, properly speaking.

[7] Martyn, *Galatians,* Comments 10, 13 and 43; and chapter 7 below.

Religion, that is to say, is the various communal, cultic means – always involving the distinction of sacred from profane – by which human beings seek to know and to be happily related to the gods or God (e.g., *eusebeia*; Epictetus, *Ench.* 31:1; Paris Papyri 29:10; *religio* as respect for what is sacred: *religio, id est, cultus deorum* [Cicero]). In the sense in which I employ the word here, religion is a human enterprise. Thus, in Paul's view, religion is the polar opposite of God's apocalyptic act in Christ. It is patriarchal (i.e. human) tradition, by which one knows what is sacred and what is profane, instead of the apocalypse of God that effects the end of that distinction (*patrikē paradosis* instead of *apokalypsis*; Gal 1:13–16; cf. Gal 3:28; 5:6; Rom 14:14). Religion, therefore, provides the human being 'with his most thorough-going possibility of confusing an illusion with God.'[8]

In Paul's letters, the polarity between religion and apocalypse is also evident in the difference between superstition and faith. For Paul, religion is the human being's superstitious effort to come to know and to influence God, rather than the faith that is elicited by God's invasive grace and that is active in the love of neighbor (Gal 4:8–10; 5:6, 13–14; Rom 1:25). To be sure, the new community created by God's act in Christ engages in the thankful worship of God, indeed worship in everyday life (Rom 12). This community even has rites, such as baptism (Gal 3:26–28) and the eucharist (Gal 2:12; 1 Cor 11:23–26), and it knows that it is distinct from the world at large.[9]

The formula of Gal 3:28 shows, however, that, in the life of the church, worship of God is the corporate act in which the religious distinction of sacred from profane is confessed to have been abolished precisely by God's redemptive deed in Christ. The Christ who is confessed in the formula *solus Christus* is the Christ in whom there is neither Jew nor Gentile. Instead of being the holy community that stands apart from the profane orb of the world, then, the church is the beachhead God is planting *in* the world. In short, the distinction between church and world is in nature apocalyptic rather than religious.

It is thus in the birth and life of the church that Paul perceives the polarity between human religion and God's apocalypse; and for that reason, a significant commentary on Paul's letters can be found in a

---

[8] Käsemann, 'Paul and Israel,' 184; cf. 191 and idem, *Essays*, 78; idem, *Romans*, 375. Religion involves the setting aside of sacred space, sacred time, sacred persons.

[9] See Gal 6:10, and note Paul's use of the term *hagioi* ('saints') in, e.g. Phil 1:1; cf. 'those outside [the church]' in 1 Cor 5:9–13.

remark of Dietrich Bonhoeffer: 'God has founded his church beyond religion . . .'[10] In considering the question whether Galatians is an anti-Judaic document, then, we may find help in four brief comments related to the cosmic antinomy between apocalypse and religion.[11]

The Practice of Judaism by Jews

Although the cosmic antinomy between apocalypse and religion plays a fundamental role in the whole of Galatians (chapter 7 below), Paul never presents it as an attack on the practice of Judaism by Jews. On the contrary, the issue he poses is without exception internal to the church. When Paul uses the term *Ioudaios*, 'Jew,' in Gal 2:13, 14, 15; 3:28, he refers to Jewish Christians, not to non-Christian Jews. And when he speaks of living in the Jewish manner (*Ioudaïkōs zēn* and *Ioudaïzein* in 2:14) he refers to a specific turn of events within the life of the Antioch church, Jewish Christians compelling Gentile Christians to accept the Jewish food laws (cf. Gal 2:3 and 6:12). None of these references suggests a critique of the synagogue.

Characteristic of Galatians is the sequence of four vignettes Paul provides of the church in Jerusalem (chapter 2 above). Not one of these vignettes has to do with the Temple cultus or the synagogue. All reveal the polarity between divine acts and religious acts *within* the church.

Are things not different, however, in Paul's reference to Judaism itself (*Ioudaïsmos*) in Gal 1:13–14? There, preparing to speak of the point at which God called him to preach Christ to the Gentiles, Paul refers to his earlier life as a zealously observant Jew (cf. Phil 3:5–6). And if we read that reference together with the affirmations of Gal 4:3–5, we must conclude that the letter does contain an *implication* with regard to Judaism: Paul's zealous observance of the Law failed to liberate him from enslavement to the elements of the old cosmos (cf. chapter 8 below). That liberation came through God's apocalypse of Jesus Christ, not through any religion, including that of Judaism.

Two qualifications are crucial, however. First, in referring to God's apocalypse of Jesus Christ (Gal 1:16), Paul is speaking of a deed of the God of Abraham, Isaiah, and Jeremiah. Second, he is offering the personal testimony of one Christian to other Christians who are tempted to commence observance of the Law *as* the means of salvation.

---

[10] Bonhoeffer, *Swords*, 118; cf. idem, *Letters*, 168. See Morse, 'Dialogue.'
[11] Cf. Käsemann, 'Worship;' Walter, 'Religiosität,' 436–441.

He is not formulating an attack on Jews who worship in the synagogue. Again, it is true that, to a great extent, the cosmic antinomy between religion and apocalypse is *the* issue of Galatians. It is also true that, in the final analysis, this cosmic antinomy cannot be anything less than comprehensive (note both Gal 3:22a and its rewording in Rom 11:32).[12] The fact remains, however, that in Galatians Paul always focuses this antinomy on issues that are internal to the church.

Opposition Among Religions

In Galatians the polarity between apocalypse and religion spells the end of all forms of opposition among religions. The apocalyptic, baptismal formula of Gal 3:28 – 'There is neither Jew nor Greek . . . in Christ Jesus' – expresses Paul's certainty that Christ is precisely not a religious figure at all, in the fundamental sense of playing a role in the distinction of sacred from profane. Of equal import is the resulting portrait of Abraham, the patriarch who finds in Christ his singular seed (Gal 3:16). From the two exegetical sections of the letter (Gal 3:6–4:7; 4:21–5:1), we sense that Paul understands Abraham in the light of Christ, Abraham's non-religious seed. True enough, the Teachers are presenting the patriarch as the quintessential religious figure, the paradigmatic proselyte who observed the Law even before Sinai (chapter 1 above). Seeing Abraham in the light of God's act in the Christ in whom there is neither Jew nor Gentile, Paul, however, finds in the patriarch himself a figure as far removed from the world of religion as is his seed.[13]

Like Christ, that is, Abraham plays no role in the distinction of sacred from profane. Just as the covenant God makes with him does not consist of commandments, so it involves neither sacred rites such as circumcision, nor sacred times, nor special foods. That covenant is God's promise, and nothing other than the promise (chapters 10 and 14 below). Abraham is located prior to the distinction of sacred from profane – Sinai – and the advent of Abraham's seed, Christ, far from being a sacred event in a religious history that includes Sinai, involves the termination of the sacred/profane distinction that was introduced (by angels) at Sinai.

---

[12] See again Boyarin, *Politics*, 136–157.

[13] Similarly, the prophetic figures of Isaiah and Jeremiah, whose shadows we sense behind Gal 1:15, bear their own witness, so to speak, to Paul's being called by God *out* of the realm of traditional religion.

With the advent of Christ, then, the antinomy between apocalypse and religion has been enacted by God once for all. Moreover, this antinomy is central to the way in which Paul does theology in Galatians, not least in connection with one of its major themes, rectification. As the antidote to what is wrong in the world does not lie in religion – religion being one of the major components of the wrong – so the point of departure from which there can be movement to set things right cannot be found in religion (chapter 9 below). Emphatically excluded in Galatians is the thought that, provided with a good religious foundation for a good religious ladder, the human being can ascend from the wrong to the right (cf. Deut 30:12). Things are the other way around. God has elected to invade the realm of the wrong – 'the present evil age' (Gal 1:4) – by sending his Son and the Spirit of his Son into it from outside it. This apocalyptic invasion thus shows that to take the Sinaitic Law to the Gentiles – as the Teachers are doing – is to engage in a mission that is marked at its center by the impotence of religion.

We sense, then, the reason for Paul's certainty that neither Christ nor Abraham is a religious figure, but we also see that, in Paul's view, the antinomy between apocalypse and religion militates against the emergence of religion *within* the church. And for that reason, the church is not a new religion set over against the old religion, Judaism.

Turning to Religion After the Apocalypse of Christ

The picture of religion in Galatians does not portray the service of worship in the synagogue. On the contrary, that picture is specifically focused on the issue that has been posed by the Teachers' work in the Galatian churches (chapter 1 above). When Gentiles turn to the observance of the Sinaitic Law after having been baptized into Christ, Paul tells them that they embrace a form of religion that is for them indistinguishable from the pagan religion into which they were born! For this step removes them from Christ (4:8–11; 5:4). Quite specifically, then, for Gentiles, Law observance is nothing other than a religion – as opposed to God's apocalypse in Christ – and therefore enslaving.

The Horizon of Galatians: Two Gentile Missions

Finally, there is the closely related matter of the letter's horizon. Just as there were no Jewish communities in the Galatian cities, and no former

Jews in the Galatian churches, so no Jews are addressed in the Galatian letter, and no Jews are being spoken about in the letter.[14] Paul had, in fact, no reason to think that the members of his Galatian churches would ever come into contact with non-Christian Jews.[15] Thus, the subject of church and synagogue lies beyond the letter's horizon.[16] We can return to the way in which the term 'Jew' is used in the formula of Gal 3:28, for it indicates what we might call the letter's theological topography:

> There is neither Jew nor Greek; there is neither slave nor free; there is no 'male and female;' for all of you are One in Christ Jesus.

With this formula, Paul speaks specifically and exclusively to those who are *in Christ Jesus*.[17]

Moreover, and of great importance, Paul's use of the formula has specifically to do with the difference between the Teachers' mission to the Gentiles and his own. Here his focus is entirely clear. Wherever the

[14] Anti-Judaic writings always speak *about* Jews (Gager, *Origins*, 35–112). Except for his testimony regarding his own past life, however, Paul includes among the dramatis personae of Galatians no non-Christian Jews, either in Judea or in the Diaspora. Thus, as noted above, we find no Jewish institutions, such as the Temple and the synagogue. A Christian interpreter is challenged by the willingness of a Jewish colleague to try the experiment of reading Galatians as a letter addressed to himself (Boyarin, *Politics*, 228–260). Indeed, truly instructive and deeply moving are Boyarin's percipient comments on coercive universalism and the joining of ethnic particularism with state power (259–260; see also footnotes). Beyond vigorously applauding those comments, however, I can scarcely say how a reading of Galatians as a letter addressed to a modern Jew should proceed. I can only confess both admiration and unease. For, removed from its original setting, Galatians can be made to say many things, as the history of its interpretation in the hands of the imperial church attests, and as Boyarin himself knows very well. See further Martyn, 'Hagar and Sarah.'

[15] Given this factor, it did not occur to Paul to include in his Galatian letter warnings against Gentile-Christian pride comparable to the warnings of Rom 11:13–36. Nor did he think to caution his readers against taunting Jews with the news that God played no part in the genesis of their Law. In Galatians Paul reveals a genuine horror at the spectacle of a Gentile church, cut off from the Jewish *churches* of Judea (Gal 2:2, 10).

[16] Paul was well acquainted with the institution of the synagogue, not only because of the role it played in his youth, but also because it was the setting in which, as an apostle, he was several times subjected to severe discipline for preaching the gospel to Gentiles without requiring their circumcision (1 Thess 2:15–16a; 2 Cor 11:24; cf. Fitzgerald, *Hardships*). We can also assume that before his call to be an apostle, he was accustomed to speaking in the synagogue setting (Gal 1:14; Phil 3:4–5). Everything in Galatians, however, shows that this letter is in no degree comparable to a sermon Paul might have conceived for a synagogue service.

[17] It is apparently Boyarin's tendency to omit this final phrase (e.g., *Politics*, 228) that leads him to find in Galatians a theory of the Jews (156).

Gentile mission is empowered *by God*, it does not continue the distinction between Jew and Gentile.[18] But this focus tells us that Paul is concerned with these two Gentile missions, not with two institutions, church and synagogue (chapter 12 below). The difference is monumental. For the letter's consumptive focus on the evangelization of Gentiles means that there is no Jewish horizon in Galatians.[19] For that, we must go to Romans 9–11 (chapter 3 above).

To be sure, taken out of its setting, placed, for example, in the hands of the imperial church that – leaving the message of Galatians far behind – came to see itself as the true religion, while viewing the synagogue as a false religion, Galatians can be made to say many things, some of them hideous. Read in its own setting, it is not an anti-Judaic text.[20]

---

[18] According to Gal 3:26–29, Gentiles become children of Abraham only by incorporation into the Christ who is beyond all religious differentiation.

[19] As we have noted above, Paul's reference to his early life in 1:13–14 causes Judaism to lie *just beyond* the letter's horizon. And the Teachers, not to mention their supporters in the Jerusalem church, will have sensed as much. Thus, later, anticipating his final trip to the Jerusalem church, Paul extends his horizon, so as to include all of Israel (Rom 9–11), although, as we have seen in chapter 3 above, even in Romans the redemption of all Israel is said to be the result of *God's faithfulness* to Israel, not the consequence of Israel's observance of the Law. The expanded picture in Romans serves only to emphasize by contrast, then, that Galatians itself does not contain a 'theory of the Jews' (*contra* Boyarin, *Politics*, 156). And the absence of such a theory is reason enough to say, *with* Boyarin, that Galatians is not an anti-Judaic text (ibid.).

[20] In light of the later emergence of the imperial church as the 'true religion,' we can pose the issue in a slightly different way, church and world: When Paul quotes the baptismal formula of Gal 3:28, with its accent on the newly created unity in Christ – 'for all of you are *One* in Christ Jesus' – does he himself employ the motif of unity in order to substitute a new form of anthropological polarity for an old one, the church *versus* the world? In short, in Paul's view, is the church nothing other than yet another pattern of 'us' versus 'them,' no longer Jew versus Gentile, or Gentile versus Jew, but rather Christian versus non-Christian, and thus, as Boyarin argues, a coercive universalism? And, if so, did Paul play a role in laying the foundation, on the basis of which a politically powerful church (certainly not existent in Paul's time) could coerce non-Christians into a nominally Christian, religious universality? For one major reason, these questions must be answered in the negative. For Paul, God's good news is marching into the whole of the world under the banner of the Christ who was crucified by the powers of the world (Gal 3:13; 1 Cor 2:8). True enough, in the cross power met power, God's power vanquishing the powers of the world (see chapter 17 below; and Cousar, *Cross*). But, God's victorious power is evident, not in the political might of an imperial church, but rather in the foolish weakness of this cross-centered gospel that brings its proclaimers into solidarity with those who are weak and stumbling (2 Cor 11:29; chapters 6 and 17 below). As God's new creation, the church lives *under* this cross, and for that reason the church is called to serve the world, not to stand aloof as a new 'us.'

Part II

Apocalyptic Rectification

Part II

Apocalyptic Rectification

Paul's letters reflect a keen awareness of the fact that in the human scene something is terribly wrong, and needs therefore to be set right. In Rom 1:18–32, for example, the apostle speaks at length about the ungodliness of those who by their wickedness suppress the truth. When we sense this ominously dark side to the human scene, as Paul perceives it, and when we note that Paul takes as his major theme the announcing of *good* news, we are not surprised to find him repeatedly referring to the setting right of that which has gone wrong.

We may be surprised, however, to find in Paul's letters virtually no use of certain words we often employ in connection with righting what is wrong. When he speaks to human beings of their wickedness, should he not call on them to *repent*? And should he not say that, after repenting, they can be assured of the peace and rightness that comes with *forgiveness*? Yet, in all of his references to the righting of what has gone wrong, Paul makes no significant reference to repentance and forgiveness.

Pondering the texts in question, we begin to see that Paul's view of wrong and right is thoroughly apocalyptic, in the sense that on the landscape of wrong and right there are, in addition to God and human beings, powerful actors that stand opposed to God and that enslave human beings. Setting right what is wrong proves, then, to be a drama that involves not only human beings and God, but also those enslaving powers. And since humans are fundamentally slaves, the drama in which wrong is set right does not begin with action on their part. It begins with God's militant action against all the powers that hold human beings in bondage.[1] Thus, that action of God, instead of con-

---

[1] The militant nature of God's rectifying act is reflected in the fact that Paul's doctrine of rectification is itself polemical. But its polemic is not focused on motifs central to Judaism (a common view; see, e.g., Becker, *Heil*). On the contrary, at its inception, and thus at its core, Paul's understanding of God's rectifying act in Christ was formed in a polemic with the views of certain Christian Jews (Part I above; chapter 9 below), not with Judaism itself.

sisting at its center of a call for the slaves to repent and seek forgiveness (!), proves to be the deed by which God frees human beings, thus producing a liberated community of mutual concern that is so radically novel as to be called the new creation.

6

Epistemology at the
Turn of the Ages[1]

2 Corinthians 5:16–17

(16) From now on, therefore, we regard no one from a human point of view; even though we once knew Christ from a human point of view, we know him no longer in that way. (17) So if anyone is in Christ, there is a new creation; everything old has passed away; see, everything has become new. (NRSV)

For a number of easily understood reasons 2 Cor 5:16 and 17 are among the most famous texts in the New Testament. The numberless comments on v. 16 have often been occasioned by the enticing hope that the verse can tell us something about Paul's relationship to Jesus of Nazareth.[2] And v. 17 is of such obvious theological importance that it has provided a base point not only for the work of New Testament interpreters,[3] but also for the construction of one of the twentieth century's theological systems.[4] Daily experience in the reading of Paul's letters teaches us, however, that the apostle's most important statements often present the greatest ambiguity; and that is nowhere more obviously true than in 2 Cor 5:16. In the present chapter, we will center our attention on this verse by reconsidering five of the numerous questions which it presents to us.

---

[1] Cf. the review of *Christian History and Interpretation* by Léon-Dufour, 'Bulletin,' 583–584; Boomershine, 'Epistemology;' Hall, 'All Things.'

[2] See, e.g. the comments by Bultmann in an article that is still a significant statement of the Jesus-Paul problem, 'Bedeutung.' Not discussed in either Wegenast, *Verständnis*, or Jüngel, *Paulus und Jesus*, 2 Cor 5:16 receives brief attention in Furnish, *Jesus*: '[the verse] does not help us to know whether Paul had ever heard or seen Jesus' (18). Cf. also Dunn, 'Jesus Tradition.'

[3] The careful reader of Bultmann's *Theology* perceives that 2 Cor 4–6 and the Fourth Gospel function as a canon within the canon, being two of the mountain peaks from whose heights all other early Christian literature is surveyed.

[4] Tillich, *Systematic Theology*.

Three Initial Questions

We begin with three questions that are tightly interrelated: (1) What interpretation is to be given to the expressions *mēketi* ('no longer;' v. 15), *apo tou nun* ('from now on;' v. 16), and *nun ouketi* ('no longer;' v. 16)? Obviously Paul refers to some turning point of earth-shaking proportions. Is it the death/resurrection of Jesus, Paul's own conversion, these two events superimposed on one another, or something to be distinguished from both of them?

(2) What role does v. 16 play in its context? It has been considered a digression between vv. 15 and 17.[5] Indeed, the thesis has been boldly advanced that the verse was inserted into its context by one of Paul's opponents in Corinth who wanted to make clear that the earthly form of Jesus (*Christos kata sarka*) was to be despised as the temporary dwelling place of the heavenly redeemer.[6]

(3) How are the two instances of the prepositional phrase *kata sarka* (lit. 'according to the flesh;' NRSV 'from a human point of view') to be syntactically construed?[7] If we take them to be adjectival, modifying *oudena* ('no one') and *Christon* ('Christ'), then Paul is saying that he now knows no fleshly person, and that, if he once knew the fleshly Christ, he knows that person no longer. If we take these phrases to be adverbial, modifying *oidamen* ('we know') and *egnōkamen* ('we knew'), then Paul is speaking about *ways* of knowing. He now knows no one in a fleshly way; if he once knew Christ in a fleshly way, he knows him in that manner no longer. Some interpreters believe they are speaking of the same alternative readings when they inquire whether the term *sarx* refers here to the flesh of the person being known or to that of the person who is the knower.[8]

Since the third of these questions is the most easily and clearly stated, we may profitably begin with it. Both alternatives have been elected

---

[5] E.g. Plummer, 'The verse is one of those parenthetical remarks which are so characteristic of St Paul' (*Second Epistle*, 175).

[6] Schmithals, 'Glossen;' cf. 1 Cor 12:3.

[7] Yet another issue is that of translating the phrase *kata sarka*. RSV and NRSV take the phrase with the verbs, arriving at the translation 'to regard (or know) someone from a human point of view.' Similarly NEB used the expression 'to take worldly standards into account is one's estimate (or understanding) of someone.' And NJB speaks of considering someone 'by human standards.' We will return to the translation question below.

[8] E.g. Plummer, *Second Epistle*.

and defended at length, and it is certainly true that Paul elsewhere uses the phrase *kata sarka* ('according to the flesh') sometimes adjectivally, sometimes adverbially.[9] Leaving aside the two occurrences in our verse, we can say with reasonable confidence that, of the remaining seventeen instances of this thoroughly Pauline expression,[10] only four are adjectival, while thirteen are adverbial.[11] It may also be worth noting that, when the two instances in our verse are subtracted from the six occurrences in 2 Corinthians, the remaining four are all in the adverbial column. Simple statistics could incline one to read the phrase adverbially.

But statistics of this sort can be misleading. They scarcely do away with the ambiguity. One is not entirely surprised to see that Bultmann came down first on one and then on the other side of this question. Indeed he was able to do so without having to alter his interpretation of the verse because he believed the adjectival and adverbial readings to be equivalent in meaning.[12] Georgi, however, has said with emphasis that to construe the phrase adverbially is to make the second half of the verse absurd.[13] On the basis of the arguments advanced by these two scholars alone, one must conclude that while the question is obvious, the solution is not.

A way forward lies, I think, in taking seriously into account the broad context which stretches from 2 Cor 2:14 to 6:10.[14] When that is done,

[9] The issue is weighed carefully by Windisch, *Der zweite Korintherbrief*, 184–189.

[10] Paul uses the phrase nineteen times, John once (8:15).

[11] I count the instances in 1 Cor 1:26 and Gal 4:29 as adverbial (see chapter 12 below).

[12] In 1929, electing the adjectival reading, Bultmann interpreted *Christos kata sarka* as an expression for the historical Jesus ('Bedeutung,' 208). In 1947 he softened his preference for the adjectival interpretation by saying that, while it is the better choice, in the final analysis the syntactical issue does not affect the meaning of the verse (*Probleme*, 16). A year later, in the first fascicle of the German edition of his *Theology* (234; English I.238–239), we find him opting for the adverbial reading, but still holding that the choice is interpretively irrelevant: 'A Christ known *kata sarka* is precisely what a Christ *kata sarka* is.' Windisch had reached essentially the same conclusion in his 1924 commentary (270).

[13] Georgi, *Gegner*, 291; *Opponents*, 277. Oepke, 'Irrwege,' used expressions equally emphatic against those who take the phrase adjectivally. Georgi seems to think that he and Bultmann stand more closely together than is actually the case. The sentence, 'Bultmann decides to associate *kata sarka* to the object' (*Gegner*, 291, n. 7; *Opponents*, 277 n. 297), is not entirely accurate. See preceding footnote.

[14] Bultmann was aware of the literary piece constituted by 2:14–6:10, and he correctly identified its major theme as that of the apostolic office (*Probleme*, 3). By the time he came to 5:16, however, the context he was bearing consciously in mind had shrunk to 5:11–6:10.

answers are readily at hand for all of our first three questions. For when we allow these chapters to speak as a unit, we are struck with two facts above all others: Paul defends his apostleship by various arguments, all of which refer to the turn of the ages.[15] And he mounts these arguments in a way which makes clear that only at that juncture is a person granted the new means of perception which enable one to distinguish true from false apostles. To put it in the prosaic language of scholarly investigation, Paul's statements establish an inextricable connexion between eschatology and epistemology.

2 Corinthians 2:14–17

The apostle stands where people are being saved and where people are perishing. He stands, that is, at the juncture of the ages. Evangelistically active at this point, he is to those on the one side a fragrance from death to death and to those on the other side a fragrance from life to life.

3:1–18

The true apostle needs no letters of recommendation. His children in the faith are his letter of recommendation, written not with material lying on the old-age side of the juncture (ink, tablets of stone), but rather with the power of the new age: the Spirit of the living God. It is God himself who qualifies the minister of the new covenant, and anyone who fails to recognize this has failed to grasp the transition from the dispensation of death and condemnation to the dispensation of the Spirit and of rectification. Does someone fail to perceive the far greater splendor of the latter? If so, he is like those over whose minds a veil lies. For one beholds the glory of the Lord and is changed into his image only when the veil is taken away.

4:1–5:10

Three paragraphs, each beginning, 'Therefore we do not lose heart . . .' or, 'Therefore we are of good courage . . .'

4:1–15

Therefore the true apostle does not lose heart. He carries out his task by the mercy of God. His gospel may be veiled as his opponents say. It is veiled, however, only to those whose allegiance to the old age (the god

---

[15] That should not surprise us in view of 1 Cor 4:8–13, a passage of unsurpassed lucidity with regard to Paul's understanding of his apostleship. See now Schrage, *Korinther*, Martyn, *Galatians*, Comment 1.

of this world) blinds them to the light which is streaming in from the glory of Christ, who is the 'image of God.'

It is true that our gospel appears unglorious! We ourselves are unglorious, persecuted, afflicted, perplexed, struck down, and all of this certainly shows weakness. We and our gospel appear in this way, however, in order to show that the real power belongs not to us, but to God. For that is what the turn of the ages means: life is manifested in death. Therefore we are each day given up to death for Jesus' sake, so that the life of Jesus may be shown in our daily dying.

4:16–5:5

The true apostle, therefore, does not lose heart. His daily death is his daily renewal, and it points to his ultimate life. We will not always stand at the juncture of the ages. The Spirit is the down-payment of God's promise that our dying will be wholly swallowed up by life.

5:6–10

The true apostle, therefore, is always of good courage. Whoever walks altogether within the old age walks by sight and will be discouraged. We walk, however, not by sight, but by faith, looking toward the *parousia* in hope.

5:11–15

The apostle stands at the juncture of the ages, on the one side facing human beings, but on the other side being really known only to God. Therefore, he must give his congregation grounds for answering those who boast of the appearance of their faces (*hoi en prosōpō kauchōmenoi*), thus assuming that the congregation's way of knowing is the same as their own. Whoever judges visible ecstasy to be a reliable sign of apostleship shows that his manner of perception is bound to the old age. It is not somatic ecstasy, but rather the love of Christ which controls us, inasmuch as we discern that one died for all. Therefore all died. He died on behalf of all for a definite purpose: that their lives might be lived no longer for themselves, but rather for him who for their sake died and was raised.

5:16–21

This great turn of the ages in Christ's death/resurrection is *the fact. From now on*, therefore, we regard no one according to the flesh. Even if we formerly regarded Christ according to the flesh, *no longer* do we do so.

Therefore if anyone is in the realm of Christ, there is a new creation. The old age has passed away. Open your eyes, the new has come! All of this is from God who causes the new to break in by reconciling the world to himself through Christ, and by entrusting his powerful word of reconciliation to the ambassador who stands at the turn of the ages.

6:1–10

For now is the long-awaited time. Now is the day of redemption. And since the old-age way of knowing is past, the old standards for identifying an apostle are shown to be invalid. The true apostle is not powerful, but rather weak. He looks like an impostor. When one gazes at him, one sees a man who is unknown and therefore not worthy of regard. One sees a person who is dying, being punished, in sorrow and in poverty. Yet, paradoxically, he is true, well known, thoroughly alive, a person of joy who makes many persons rich and himself possesses everything.

If this sketch presents the line of Paul's thought with essential accuracy, then the context alone answers our first three questions.

(1) The expressions *mēketi* ('no longer'), *apo tou nun* ('from now on'), and *nun ouketi* ('no longer'), are altogether harmonious with the clear indications given throughout 2 Cor 3–6 that Paul is centrally concerned with the turn of the ages in the death/resurrection of Jesus. The decisive point is not a private event, treasured by Paul as a radical change in his self-understanding.[16] As the second half of v. 17 shows, it is an event of cosmic, apocalyptic proportions, and Paul describes it in a manner worthy of an Enthusiast: 'New creation!' 'Everything old has passed away!' 'Look! Everything has become new!'[17]

(2) Verse 16, far from being a digression, is precisely the explicit statement of the epistemological concern which has been the twin to Paul's discussion of eschatology right from 2:14 onward.

---

[16] Bultmann saw this quite clearly, *Probleme*, 17; cf. Dahl, *Volk*, 250.

[17] Here and elsewhere, capitalizing the word Enthusiast, I speak in the first instance of persons in the early church who emphasized the present, already accomplished dimension of God's redemptive act in Christ. In his own way, Paul was himself an Enthusiast, a matter to which we will return below.

(3) That, in turn, tips the balance decisively in favor of reading the *kata sarka* phrases adverbially.[18] Paul is not speaking about a 'fleshly Christ.' He is certainly not saying that he was acquainted with Jesus prior to the crucifixion. Nor is he considering *in the first instance* 'how a person should be understood and regarded.'[19] He is saying that there are two ways of knowing, and that what separates the two is the turn of the ages, the apocalyptic event of Christ's death/resurrection. There is a way of knowing which is characteristic of the old age.[20] In the past Paul himself knew in that way.[21] And, since Paul now knows Christ (Phil 3:8), there must be a new way of knowing that is proper either to the new age or to that point at which the ages meet.

But now that we have answers to these three questions, we recall that, in reading the letters of Paul, the answer to a question proves more often than not to be yet another question. Indeed, at the present juncture there are two further issues of considerable import: Fourth, what precisely does Paul intend with the expression by which he refers to the old-age way of knowing; and how are the Corinthians – and later the pseudo-apostles who invaded the Corinthian church – likely to have understood that expression? Fifth, why is Paul satisfied merely to imply the new manner of knowing; and what Greek words would he have employed, had he elected to speak explicitly of this new epistemology?

The Old-Age Way of Knowing

To refer to the old way of knowing, Paul allows the phrase *kata sarka* to modify the verb 'to know,' using the word *sarx* ('flesh') to refer to the realm of the old age.[22] He thus coins an epistemological locution – to

[18] There are, of course, other arguments which support the adverbial reading. See the commentaries and Oepke, '*Irrwege.*' See also Schubert, 'New Testament Study,' 565.

[19] Bultmann, *Probleme*, 16: 'In the context, the question is how a person should be understood and regarded.' I should be satisfied had Bultmann written, '. . . how a person understands.'

[20] The *apocalyptic* frame of reference provided by the context tells us that, with the *kata sarka* phrases, Paul refers to the old-age way of knowing. These phrases are fundamentally domesticated, then, in the translation 'from a human point of view' (NRSV).

[21] The *ei kai* clause of v 16 tells us that at one time Paul himself regarded Christ in accordance with the old-age way of knowing. Lietzmann (125) was right in his initial comment: 'The sentence is not contrary to fact (*ei egnōmen*); it has the form of the real condition. On purely linguistic grounds, one can translate, "If, as is the case, . . ."'

[22] To some extent this locution is based on one Paul had earlier coined to refer to the evangelistic labors of the Teachers who invaded his Galatian congregations (chapter 1 above). There, speaking of the founding of Law-observant churches among the Gentiles, Paul had used the phrase *kata sarka* adverbially, attaching it to the verb *gennaō* ('to

know by the norm of the flesh – by which he refers to the passé, old-age manner of acquiring knowledge. Prior to the turn of the ages, Paul himself knew only in that way. A somewhat philosophically inclined citizen of Corinth would have had no great difficulty with Paul's expression. To such a person it would have meant to know on the basis of sense perception, for there is a time-honored connection between the term 'flesh' and speculation of an epistemological sort. Alexander Aphrodisiensis, for example, queried whether it is the flesh itself or something in it that has the power of perception.[23]

Many persons of the Hellenistic age would have answered Alexander's question in a fundamentally religious way. Agreeing that the flesh is somehow the seat of a certain kind of perception, and noting that Paul speaks *negatively* about knowing on the basis of the flesh, they would have agreed that the power of true perception stems neither from the flesh nor from something in it. On the contrary, sense perception is so misleading that the bodily senses must be curbed before one can truly know. Consider the opening paragraph of *Poimandres*:

> One day, when I had begun to reflect on the things that truly exist and my thoughts had soared aloft, while my bodily senses (*aisthēseis sōmatikai*) were bridled like those borne down by sleep through surfeit of food or fatigue of the body, it seemed to me that a being of vast, immeasurable size drew near

---

beget'). Referring to the Teachers' demand that their Gentile converts be circumcised, he said that Law-observant Gentile churches are *kata sarka gennētheis* ('begotten by the power of the flesh;' Gal 4:29). Opposite those churches, Paul saw others that were being begotten by the power of the Spirit (*kata pneuma gennētheis*; ibid.). In these adverbial constructions in Galatians, then, the word *kata* can be translated with the phrase 'by the power of' (see Martyn, *Galatians*, on Gal 4:23). Much the same is true of the phrase *kata sarka* in 2 Cor 5:16, except that here 'by the power of the flesh' denotes 'by the means of the flesh' or better 'by the norm of the flesh, the epistemological focus of the old age.' Unlike the Teachers in Galatia, the pseudo-apostles who invaded Paul's Corinthian church did not demand circumcision, but, as we will see in the closing section of this chapter, Paul considered them – and the Corinthian Enthusiasts as well – to be bound to the flesh, in the sense of taking it to be the norm/means of their knowledge.

[23] See Schweizer, '*sarx*,' 103. That Alexander was active about A.D. 200 is not important here. Earlier references are readily available, as one would surmise from Parmenides' reproach of those who trust daily experience as the basis for knowledge, from Protagoras' theory that knowledge is perception, and from Plato's concerted argument against Protagoras' theory. A Platonist reading Paul's expression would surely have thought of his master's careful distinction between *epistēmē*, 'knowledge' and *doxa*, 'opinion.' To know by the power of the flesh would strike such a person as 'to hold a mere opinion.'

and called me by name and said, 'What do you wish to hear and see and by thinking come to learn and know?'[24]

If *Poimandres* is to be dated later than Paul, the same is not true of Philo.[25] And numerous passages in Philo's writings reflect a dual conviction: The flesh is the seat of sense perception (e.g. *de Agric.* 97), and that fact as a liability to true knowledge.[26] The understanding which is endowed with true vision is unfortunately weighed down by the pleasures of the flesh (*de Migr. Abr.* 14). Indeed, 'there are no two things so utterly opposed to one another as knowledge (*epistēmē*) and pleasure of the flesh' (*Qoud Deus Imm.* 143).[27] Thus, the royal way which is Philo's passionate concern is 'a straight high road, and it is when the mind's course is guided along that road that it reaches the goal which is the recognition and knowledge of God. Every comrade of the flesh hates and rejects this path' (ibid.).

From such texts it is obvious that in Philo's view there are two kinds of human beings: the person who is a representative of the many and the person who is the true mystic.[28] One of the things that distinguish them is of considerable importance. The many do not have God's spirit abiding in them, whereas the mystic does. Here, then, we encounter an epistemological view with both negative and positive aspects: Whereas the flesh is a deterrent to true perception, the divine spirit which abides in the mystic makes knowledge possible.

> One sort of man only does it (*to theion pneuma*) aid with its presence, even those who have disrobed themselves of all created things and of the innermost veil and wrapping of mere opinion (*doxa*). With their minds unhampered and naked they will come to God (*de Gig.* 53).[29]

---

[24] I have given the translation of Nock's text by F. C. Grant in R. M. Grant (ed.), *Gnosticism*, 211.

[25] Geographically Philo of Alexandria was far removed from Corinth. Certain elements of his religious philosophy, however, were surely represented there. See Brandenburger, *Fleisch*; Borgen, 'Philo of Alexandria.'

[26] Just how Philo's thought is related to proto-gnostic speculation of the sort represented by Poimandres is a complex problem in itself. Cf. H. Köster, 'Paul and Hellenism' (Gnosticism is a presupposition of Philo's philosophy; 191) with Borgen, 'Philo' and 'Philo of Alexandria.'

[27] Here and subsequently I cite Philo according to *LCL* (occasionally with slight changes). On the subject of polar opposites, see chapter 7 below.

[28] Cf. Goodenough, *Light.*

[29] My attention was called to this passage by Wilckens, *Weisheit*, 140. One should also consider passages from the literature of Qumran, e.g. 1QS 4:20–22: 'God will then purify every deed of man with his truth; He will refine for himself the human frame by

Had Philo employed Paul's expression 'to know by the norm of the flesh' – and he could easily have done that – he would have meant that it is the mass of people who know in that way, whereas the initiate knows in a higher way by the aid of the divine spirit. Many other texts could be cited to show that for various religious circles in the first century Paul's words about knowing by the norm of the flesh would have been readily understandable. But can we be more specific? How will the Corinthians have construed Paul's negative reference?[30]

How was 2 Corinthians 5:16 Heard by the Enthusiasts Resident in the Corinthian Church?

Whatever we are to say about the situation in the Corinthian church when Paul wrote 2 Corinthians – see below – we can be confident first of all that the epistemological statement of 2 Cor 5:6 was heard and seriously pondered by the major group we see reflected in 1 Corinthians. One of several cliques, this was a group of Enthusiasts who understood themselves to be in possession of divine wisdom and true knowledge.[31] Certain that they were the perfected recipients of the Spirit, able to converse with angels in angelic tongues, these Enthusiasts were also sure that – as individuals – they were already filled with perfect knowledge, already in possession of complete freedom, and thus already liberated

---

rooting out all spirit of falsehood from the bounds of his flesh . . . And he shall be plunged into the spirit of purification that he may instruct the upright in the knowledge of the Most High and teach the wisdom of the sons of heaven to the perfect of way' (Vermes).

30 Regarding the value of asking about the understanding of the text by its original hearers, see chapter 13 below.

31 Numerous texts in 1 Corinthians reflect the presence of these gnosticizing, pneumatic Enthusiasts. See Schrage, *Korinther*, 38–62, especially 52; and cf. Thrall, *Corinthians*; Mitchell, *Rhetoric*. In view of the reading of 1 Cor 2:6–16 to be suggested below, two characteristics of Paul's polemic against the Corinthian Enthusiasts prove to be significant. First, his critique reveals the kind of ambivalence that arises when one is arguing with an opponent with whom one has extensive agreement, at least in a formal sense. Paul proclaimed the crucified Christ when he came to Corinth (1 Cor 2:2), but he preached Christ in a thoroughly enthusiastic, Spirit-filled way (1 Cor 2:4). Of the various cliques that developed in the Corinthian church after his departure, Paul stood closest, therefore, to the Enthusiasts when he wrote 1 Corinthians (note even in 2 Cor 6:2 Paul's enthusiastic exegesis of Isa 49: 8a). Second, his critique shows that a keen interest in knowledge is characteristic both of himself and of these Enthusiasts. In 1 Cor 8:1, for example, Paul can quote without direct polemic one of the Enthusiasts' slogans (did they adopt this slogan from Paul himself?): 'All of us possess knowledge.'

from the constraints imposed both by bodily existence and by responsibility for the neighbor (1 Cor 4:8; 10:23–30; 6:12–20; 13:1).[32]

Highly interesting, then, is 1 Cor 2:6–16, a paragraph in which, speaking mainly to these epistemologically sophisticated Enthusiasts, Paul distinguishes from one another two kinds of knowers – the *psychikos anthrōpos* ('the unspiritual person') and the *pneumatikos anthrōpos* ('the spiritual person'):[33]

(2:6) Yet among the mature (*teleioi*) we do speak wisdom, though it is not a wisdom of this age . . . (9) On the contrary, we speak, as it is written, 'What no eye has seen, nor ear heard, nor human heart conceived, namely what God has prepared for those who love him.' (10) For God has revealed these things to us through the Spirit. For the Spirit searches everything, even the depths of God. (11) For what human being has knowledge of human matters except the human spirit that is within? So also no one knows God's matters except the Spirit of God. (12) Now we have received not the spirit of the world, but the Spirit that is from God, so that we may know the gifts bestowed on us from God. (13) And the words we use to speak of these things are taught us not by human wisdom but rather by the Spirit, so that we discern (*sugkrinontes*) spiritual things by means of spiritual things. (14) The unspiritual person (*psychikos anthrōpos*) does not receive the matters that come from God's Spirit, for to such a person they are foolishness, and he cannot really know them, because they are spiritually discerned (*pneumatikōs anakrinetai*). (15) The spiritual person (*pneumatikos*), however, discerns (*anakrinei*) all things, but is himself subject to no one else's power of discernment (*anakrinetai*): (16) 'For who has known the mind of the Lord so as to instruct him?' But we have the mind of Christ. (1 Cor 2:6–16)[34]

[32] The Enthusiasts' view may have included an ontological dimension, achieved by a gnostic re-interpretation of apocalyptic motifs (cf. Sellin, as cited by Schrage, *Korinther*, 57 n. 160; and note Schrage himself, ibid. 61–62). To a significant extent, however, the temporal frame of reference, clearly reflected in Paul's use of the adverb 'already' (1 Cor 4:8), was a factor in the theologies of all of the actors in the Corinthian drama.

[33] The quotations from Philo given earlier suffice to show that Brandenburger is correct when he says that the opposition between the *psychikos anthrōpos* and the *pneumatikos* is absent in Philo only in the literal sense (Fleisch, 135; see especially Philo *Heres* 259–266).

[34] This astonishing paragraph played a key role in inspiring Reitzenstein to write *Mysterienreligionen*, the book in which he concluded that Paul was himself a gnostic, But see Wilckens, *Weisheit*, where Paul is credited with using the *language* of some of the Corinthians, while having his own anti-gnostic intentions. Cf. now Kovacs, 'Gnostic Opponents;' Schrage, *Korinther*; A. R. Brown, *Cross*.

The entirety of 1 Corinthians shows that Paul has his own polemical intentions vis-à-vis the Enthusiasts (see notably 1 Cor 4:8–13). It seems clear, however, that in composing 1 Cor 2:6–16, he draws on their vocabulary and – in formal terms – comes astonishingly close to their own epistemological views.[35] For, like the Enthusiasts, Paul affirms two ways of knowing. There is an *anakrinein psychikōs* (an 'unspiritual way of knowing') that is proper to the passé 'wisdom of [the old] age'; and there is an *anakrinein pneumatikōs* (a 'spiritual way of knowing'). How will the Enthusiasts have understood this distinction? Similar to Philo, they will have recognized in it a key way of differentiating themselves from their inferior brothers and sisters, the unspiritual members of the Corinthian church, the *psychikoi*.

With this observation, we can return to our major text, for the Enthusiasts' understanding of 1 Cor 2:6–16 is surely a key to their interpretation of 2 Cor 5:16. That is to say, when they heard this latter text, they understood Paul to speak of the way of knowing that – as foreign to them as it was to the Apostle himself – was characteristic of their inferior fellows in the Corinthian church:

> Our unspiritual brothers and sisters (the *psychikoi*) are precisely the ones who know by the norm of the flesh. For example, they demonstrate that they are filled with the anxiety of the old age rather than with the spiritual knowledge of the new age, when they are afraid to eat meat that may have been sacrificed to an idol. For they think that an idol has real existence! Indeed, being unable to discern the matters of the Spirit in the present time, they long for deliverance via a future resurrection of the body itself! Clearly they know in a way which takes the flesh as its norm (*anakrinein psychikōs* = *ginōskein kata sarka*).

By the same token, however, the Enthusiasts will surely have heard in the negative comment of Paul in 2 Cor 5:16 an impressive and thoroughly positive implication:

---

[35] Far from monolithically rejecting the Enthusiasts' vocabulary and motifs, Paul draws no less than they – formally speaking – on dualistic wisdom traditions evident in Philo (see again Brandenburger, *Fleisch*) and on gnosticizing motifs as well. In addition to the opposition between the *psychikos anthrōpos* and the *pneumatikos* (found literally only in gnostic texts), note that Paul speaks of the *pneumatikoi* as the *teleioi*, and that he is as certain as are the Enthusiasts that only the *teleioi* receive the Spirit's revelation of the depths of God. Our understanding of Paul's own epistemology will be deepened if, instead of trying to draw a complete contrast between the apostle and the Enthusiasts, we ask *how* he employs the Enthusiasts' own vocabulary and motifs. How, e.g. does he himself identify the *teleioi*? See Schrage, *Korinther*; and cf. the conclusion to the present chapter; Cousar, *Cross*; A. R. Brown, *Cross*.

With his denial that he now knows by the norm of the flesh, does not Paul mean to imply a positive counterpart? Those who are spiritual – Paul and we ourselves – know by the power of the Spirit!

In short, we can easily imagine that, having learned little from Paul's critique of their position in 1 Cor 4, 8, 10, 15, etc. the Enthusiasts, on first hearing Paul's words in 2 Cor 5:16, applauded them. The Enthusiasts will probably have understood the Apostle to be denigrating the inferior way of knowing characteristic of their unspiritual fellows, and, by implication, to be affirming their own superior and completely perfected epistemology, knowledge by means of the Spirit.

How was 2 Corinthians 5:16 Heard by the Pseudo-Apostles Who Invaded Paul's Corinthian Church?

When we turn our attention from the Enthusiasts resident in the Corinthian church to the 'pseudo-apostles' whose coming to Corinth spelled so much new trouble for Paul, we are conscious of moving into a conceptual orb which is more Jewish.[36] These persons identified themselves, in fact, as Hebrews, Israelites, descendants of Abraham (2 Cor 11:22). More important, they soon acquired considerable influence in the Corinthian church, probably in the main by readily meeting the Corinthian Enthusiasts' expectations of an apostle: a person of ecstatic

---

[36] Although numerous questions about Paul's opponents in 2 Corinthians remain unsettled, I think the fundamental thesis of Käsemann and Barrett ('Legitimität' and 'Opponents' respectively) enjoys a high degree of probability (*pace* Furnish, *II Corinthians*, 48–54): Those whom Paul calls 'pseudo-apostles' (2 Cor 11:13) are the invaders of his Corinthian church, while the 'super-apostles' (2 Cor 11:5; 12:11) are resident in the Jerusalem church. Far away from Corinth, the latter play, however, an indirect role in the Corinthian tensions by virtue of the fact that the itinerant pseudo-apostles claim to be sponsored by them (cf. now Belleville, 'Spirit,' 294 n. 44; 297 n. 63). Thus, the pseudo-apostles in Corinth are similar to the Teachers who came into Paul's Galatian churches, both groups being able to claim a significant degree of authorization by the church in Jerusalem (chapter 2 above). It seems clear that, at the time Paul wrote the letter now preserved in 2 Cor 10–13, the pseudo-apostles had acquired enormous influence in the Corinthian church, not least because of their claim to be authorized by the Jerusalem church (2 Cor 11:4; cf. Barrett, 'Opponents,' 251; Theissen, *Social Setting*, 41, 65; Kolenkow, 'Opponents'). It is equally likely, however, that, although less influential at the earlier date at which Paul wrote 2 Cor 1–9, they had already arrived and commenced their work in Paul's Corinthian church (no matter whether 2 Cor 1–9 constitutes one letter [so Furnish, *II Corinthians*, 41–44] or several [so H. D. Betz, *2 Corinthians 8 and 9*, 25–36, 141–144]). For Paul refers to these pseudo-apostles in 2 Cor 2:17; 3:1; 5:12. They were therefore among those who heard 2 Cor 5:16, and they must have arrived at their own interpretation of that verse.

visions, miracle-working powers, oratorical skill, and especially the possession of complete, spiritual knowledge (2 Cor 10:10; 11:6; 12:12).

Regarding their probable reading of 2 Cor 5:16, there are three major clues: (*a*) their quickly-won influence over the Corinthian Enthusiasts; (*b*) their sophisticated employment of the word 'face' (*prosōpon*); and (*c*) their own adverbial use of the phrase *kata sarka*.[37]

(a) The Pseudo-Apostles' Influence Over the Enthusiasts

The Enthusiasts whom we have met in 1 Corinthians believed, as noted above, that their initiation into Christ granted them *all* of the blessings of the new age, especially the gift of spiritual knowledge. Indeed, not only their knowledge, but also their way of knowing (*anakrinein pneumatikōs*) was complete. But persons who harbor such ideas are always in need of daily reinforcement, for they are constantly affirming the presence of ultimate eschatological blessings in the midst of a world that appears to be unchanged.[38] The pseudo-apostles' influence with the Enthusiasts suggests that they supplied the needed reinforcement. They were able, that is, to provide assurance by claiming to have received in their own private visions more than sufficient proof that they already possessed the wisdom and knowledge of the new age.[39]

(b) The Pseudo-Apostles' Faces

But where, specifically, will one look and how will one look in order to see the new age? There are indications that the pseudo-apostles answered the question – at least in part – not only by speaking of the Spirit, but also by referring to their visions of God, and by linking their visions with a sophisticated use of the term 'face.'

---

[37] Initially one might pause – but only briefly – over the further possibility that, being in possession of traditions about Jesus' deeds and teachings, the pseudo-apostles heard Paul's words *kata sarka* as an adjectival phrase, attaching it in 2 Cor 5:16 to *Christon* and thus hearing a reference to their knowledge of Jesus of Nazareth (cf. Käsemann, 'Legitimität,' 494–495). Their own adverbial use of the phrase *kata sarka* in 2 Cor 10:2 does not support this suggestion.

[38] For a modern comment, consider two sentences from a marvelously illuminating letter written by Martin Buber in 1926: 'Meinem Glauben nach ist der Messias nicht in einem bestimmten Augenblick der Geschichte erschienen, sondern sein Erscheinen kann nur das Ende der Geschichte sein. Meinem Glauben nach ist die Erlösung der Welt nicht vor 19 Jahrhunderten geschehen, sondern wir leben noch immer in der unerlösten Welt . . .' For a perceptive reference to Buber's letter, see Meyer, 'This-Worldliness.'

[39] Contrast Paul's own use of the terms *hikanotēs* and *hikanos* (2 Cor 2:16; 3:5), and see Georgi, *Gegner*, 220–225; *Opponents*, 231–234.

There is first the matter of seeing God's face. We have already considered the passage in 1 Corinthians in which Paul speaks of the two ways of knowing (2:6–16). There is another revealing passage in 1 Corinthians in which he again speaks of the two ways:

> Is there knowledge? It will vanish away; for our knowledge . . . [is] partial, and the partial vanishes when wholeness comes . . . Now we see only puzzling reflections in a mirror, but then we shall see face to face (1 Cor 13:8–12 NEB).

We may be sure that the pseudo-apostles did not impress their Corinthian hearers by claiming to have experienced visions in which they saw puzzling reflections in a mirror. For them that is surely the old-age way of seeing. On the contrary there are good reasons for thinking that in some sense they claimed to have seen God in their visions, perhaps even face to face.[40] Here again Philo may be our best guide.

> If . . . thou art worthily initiated and canst be consecrated to God . . . (then) instead of having closed eyes, thou wilt see the First (Cause) . . . For the beginning and end of happiness is to be able to see God (*Qaest. Exod.* ii. 51).[41]

But how precisely will the pseudo-apostles have substantiated their claim to have seen God? Pondering this question, we may recall 2 Cor 5:12, where – in the immediate context of 2 Cor 5:16 – Paul characterizes the pseudo-apostles as persons 'who boast on the basis of the face rather than on the basis of what is in the heart.' Here interpreters

---

[40] See Paul's counter-claims in 2 Cor 12:1, 7. The ancient Israelite traditions that refer to seeing God face to face clearly imply that the experience should bring death. But bold interpreters could have taken advantage of certain ambiguities (e.g. Exod 24:9–11), especially if they claimed their visions as an eschatological blessing. The author of the Fourth Gospel evidently had in mind persons who made a similar claim (for Moses? Cf. Exod 33:20 with Deut 34:10) when he said pointedly, 'No one has ever seen God' (John 1:18; see Meeks, *Prophet-King*, 299). Cf. also the opponents mentioned in Col 2:18.

[41] I should not want to present Philo as a clear witness for the pseudo-apostles' views. His comments about seeing God reflect a reserved ambivalence that may have been foreign to those haughty and overbearing braggarts. He was careful to say that mortals cannot see God in his being (*de Post. Caini* 168). He took seriously the famous passage in which God tells Moses that 'no one shall see me and live' (Exod 33: 20; e.g. *de Fuga* 165). To boast of seeing the invisible God is to yield to arrogance (*Quest, Exod.* ii. 37). On the other hand, to speak of seeing God is to refer to the goal of the entire Jewish mystery, and Philo was so attracted by the goal that on this subject, as on others, he had a somewhat divided mind. See Goodenough, *Light*, 212–213, and Wilckens, *Weisheit*, 140–141, where Pascher is quoted. What I am suggesting above is that the pseudo-apostles who came to Corinth were not so scrupulous as was Philo.

commonly take Paul to be speaking metaphorically, drawing a contrast between what is outward (the face) and what is inward (the heart). But Paul's other references to 'face' in 2 Corinthians – notably those in 2 Cor 3; see below – suggest that in 5:12 he is speaking of the pseudo-apostles' literal references to their faces.

That is to say, these interlopers seem emphatically to have reminded their hearers that the person who sees God (especially face to face) experiences a remarkable change in his (own) face. The classic example in the pseudo-apostles' store of tradition appears to have been Moses, whom God knew face to face (Deut 34:10).[42]

> For we read that by God's command he [Moses] ascended an inaccessible and pathless mountain . . . Then after . . . forty days . . . he descended with a face (*opsis*) far more beautiful than the one he had when he ascended, so that those who saw him were filled with awe and amazement; nor even could their eyes continue to stand the dazzling brightness that flashed from him like the rays of the sun (*de Vita Mos*. ii, 70).[43]

It is likely that the pseudo-apostles did in fact speak explicitly about Moses' face, affirming its remarkable radiance.[44] They seem even to have compared themselves with Moses.[45] And they may have done the same with Abraham, about whom Philo writes in a revealing way:

> Thus whenever he was possessed, everything in him changed to something better, eyes, complexion, stature, carriage, movements, voice. For the divine spirit which was breathed upon him from on high made its lodging in his soul, and invested his body with singular beauty, his voice with persuasiveness, and his hearers with understanding (*de Virt*. 217).[46]

It is probable, then, that the pseudo-apostles referred to such ancient worthies in order to say with emphasis that their own possession of the Spirit of true knowledge was attested by their ecstatically radiant faces.[47]

---

[42] LXX renders the well-known Hebrew expression with the Greek *prosōpon kata prosōpon*. Philo uses the preposition *pros* (*Heres* 262); cf. 1 Cor 13:12.

[43] My attention was called to this passage by Georgi, *Gegner*, 259; *Opponents*, 254.

[44] See Schulz, 'Decke;' Georgi, *Gegner*, 258–282; *Opponents*, 254–271.

[45] Cf. Furnish, *II Corinthians*, 244.

[46] Cf. Georgi's comments on this passage, *Gegner*, 80; *Opponents*, 58.

[47] Notice Paul's own statements in 2 Cor 3:18 and 4:6. He claims to behold the Lord's glory (Shekinah) with an *unveiled* face, being thereby changed into the Lord's likeness from one degree of glory to another. But he is careful not to say that his own face is what is changed. The face-heart polarity which is an overt part of Paul's polemic in 5:12 lies behind 4:6. God has shone in *our hearts* to give the light of the knowledge of the glory of God in the face of *Christ*.

(c) The Pseudo-Apostles' Adverbial Use of the Phrase kata sarka

From the foregoing we can see how important the term 'face' is for the epistemological question. 'In order to behold the apostolic signs of the Spirit, look at our faces,' say the pseudo-apostles. And should a loyal Corinthian convert of Paul call attention to the one who first brought the gospel to Corinth, the answer is simple: 'Look at his face. It is weak and inferior, not glorious like our faces and that of Moses. Lacking what you yourselves know to be the signs of a true apostle, he does not provide proof that Christ speaks in him. Indeed, when one considers his general demeanor, one sees that he lives his daily life by the totally unspiritual and woefully inadequate norm of the flesh' (*kata sarka peripatein*; 10:1; 12:11; 13:3; 10:2).[48]

These are thoroughly epistemological affirmations, and in the last of them the pseudo-apostles themselves use the prepositional phrase 'by the norm of the flesh' adverbially, referring to Paul's daily conduct by saying that he 'walks by the norm of the flesh' (10:2). All of these observations suggest that the pseudo-apostles will have grasped the negative dimensions of 2 Cor 5:16 quite as readily as the Enthusiasts. Like the latter, the pseudo-apostles will have been certain that knowing in a way which depends on the norm of the flesh is a thing of the past. Indeed, as just noted, they seem to have added that one needs only to observe Paul's fleshly (weak) life in order to see as much!

But the pseudo-apostles too must have thought of the positive statement implied by Paul's negative: 'Having left behind a knowing by the norm of the flesh, we now know in a spiritual manner.' And the meaning which that positive expression will have had for them is clear from what we have said about their use of the term 'face.' When they stood before the congregation, they boasted on the basis of a radiant face, that of an ecstatic (2 Cor 5:13), the face of one who was possessed by (and who possessed) the Spirit. In the state of ecstasy, the true charismatic knew God face to face, and his knowing in that way was reflected on his own face. The Corinthians, especially the Enthusiasts – so the pseudo-apostles assumed – had a considerable portion of the Spirit. Spirit is perceived by spirit (1 Cor 2:14). The pseudo-apostles will have been confident, then, that, gazing into their transformed faces,

---

[48] Taking 2 Cor 10–13 to be a letter later than 2 Cor 1–9, one can suggest that, being 'unscathed by the subtle polemic of 2 Cor 5:16,' the pseudo-apostles picked up Paul's adverbial use of the phrase *kata sarka*, turning it against him (Jewett, *Terms*, 127).

the Corinthians would perceive the work of the Spirit.[49] In their case too, then, we encounter the assumption that the true way of knowing is *kata pneuma* ('by the norm/means of the Spirit').

What Did Paul Intend With 2 Corinthians 5:16?

We have now seen reasons for thinking that in wording 2 Cor 5:16 Paul has uppermost in mind the Enthusiasts in the Corinthian congregation. Anticipating their certainty that they know by the norm/means of the Spirit, Paul thinks precisely of them when he speaks of knowing by the norm of the flesh! For, carried away by the radiant faces of the recently arrived members of an ecstatic acting company, the pseudo-apostles, the Enthusiasts are currently showing that, contrary to their own protestations, their discernment is still oriented to the flesh. That is to say, to be awe-struck by another's face – however ecstatic – is to discern by that old-age norm. Indeed, that way of discerning is the equivalent of knowing Christ himself as a religious ecstatic, rather than as the Kyrios who died for us all (2 Cor 5:14; cf. 3:17). The negative dimension of 2 Cor 5:16, then, is a sharp wake-up call, issued in the first instance to the Enthusiasts.

It is also, however, a rhetorically evangelistic invitation, by which, having waked them up, Paul puts his arm around the Corinthians, thus inviting them to see themselves as quite distinct from the pseudo-apostles. That is to say, when Paul says 'From now on, therefore, *we* do not know anyone by the norm of the flesh,' he invites the Corinthians – and especially the Enthusiasts – to join him in recognizing the *end* of that way of knowing. With regard to the matter of epistemology, he calls the whole of the Corinthian church back to the company of those who, in Christ, have been removed from the old-age way of knowing.[50]

---

[49] With regard to the Corinthians' ability to perceive the meaning of the pseudo-apostles' radiant faces, compare the final words of Philo *de Virt.* 217 quoted above.

[50] In the early chapters of 2 Corinthians, Paul often speaks of two parties, using the plural pronoun 'we' to refer to himself as an apostle, and addressing the Corinthians as 'you (plural).' In 2 Cor 3:2, however, he speaks of three parties, himself, the Corinthians, and the pseudo-apostles, and he does the same in 5:12. Then, in 5:16, he uses the emphasized 'we' in order to continue in a rhetorically effective way to refer to the same three parties. That is to say, with the 'we' of 5:16, he invites the Corinthians to recognize their own identity. Together with him, they are those who have left behind the old-age way of knowing, whereas, proud of their transfigured faces, the pseudo-apostles hold fast to the passé mode of discerning (cf. Jewett, *Terms*, 126 n. 3).

But that negative message can scarcely be in itself good news. Were not all of the original readers of 2 Cor 5:16 right in surmising that Paul implied a positive counterpart to his negation? There is, of course, the unbridled positive note of 2 Cor 5:17 – new creation in which all has become new. But, when, in 2 Cor 5:16, Paul denied a knowing by the norm of the flesh, did he not intend in that verse itself to imply a new way of knowing? And pressed for an explication, would he not have had to revert to the terms of 1 Cor 2:6–16, thus speaking again of a knowing by means of the Spirit (*ginōskein kata pneuma*)? Numerous interpreters have thought so. Indeed, in light of Paul's positive use of the expression *anakrinein pneumatikōs*, 'to discern in a spiritual way,' in 1 Cor 2:14, we can be sure that this reading is not totally incorrect. The norm of the old-age way of knowing, the *sarx*, has been replaced by the norm of the new-age way of knowing, the *pneuma* given by God. As we have noted earlier, Paul was quite uninhibited in his own type of enthusiasm.

We can be confident, however, that by the time Paul penned 2 Cor 5:16, he had learned how easy it was for the Corinthians to misread his words. Specifically, recalling the effects of his first plunge into the epistemological waters, 1 Cor 2:6–16, he doubtless knew that to repeat the motifs of that passage would be to invite large-scale misunderstanding. He had, therefore, every reason to choose his words carefully, and from the text he produced we can see that he consciously avoided certain expressions, allowing the positive side of the epistemological issue to be inferred from the context.

Specifically, given the fact that both the Enthusiasts and the pseudo-apostles were thoroughly attached to the motif of spiritual knowledge, Paul must have realized that he could not use again the expression 'to discern by the power of the Spirit.'[51] Had he done so, he would have been understood to imply that, with them, he himself was already living totally in the new age. He is careful, therefore, to imply that the opposite of the old-age way of knowing is not that of the new age – this point must be emphasized – but rather the way of knowing which is granted at the juncture of the ages. He speaks neither of seeing God's face (contrast Rev 22:4) nor of knowing by means of the Spirit. For, with the whole of the Corinthian church, he does not live entirely in the new

---

[51] The parallelism so often noted between 2 Cor 5:12 and 2 Cor 5:16 is surely one of Paul's clever means of argument. He wants to say that his opponents who claim to be freed from the bonds of sense perception in their states of facial ecstasy only demonstrate by that very claim that they themselves know *kata sarka*.

age, but rather at the painful and glorious juncture where some are being saved and some are perishing (2 Cor 2:15). Then what is the way of knowing which is granted at this juncture of the ages? The context provides the answer. In that context (see the section above titled Three Initial Questions) it is clear that the implied opposite of knowing by the norm of the flesh is not knowing by the norm of the Spirit, but rather knowing *kata stauron* ('by the cross').[52] Those who recognize their life to be God's gift at the juncture of the ages recognize also that until they are completely and exclusively in the new age, their knowing by the Spirit can occur only in the form of knowing by the power of the cross.[53] For until the parousia, the cross is and remains the epistemological crisis, and thus the norm by which one knows that the Spirit is none other than the Spirit of the crucified Christ.[54]

The essential failure of the Corinthians consists in their inflexible determination to live somewhere other than in the cross. So also the essential flaw in their epistemology lies in their failure to view the cross as the absolute epistemological watershed. On a real cross in this world hangs God's own Messiah, the Lord of glory (1 Cor 2:8)! How can that be anything other than an epistemological crisis? The apostle, the divinely authorized herald of the glorious new age comes to Corinth bringing this foolish word of a crucified Messiah, and he himself has a weak and inferior face (2 Cor 10:1, 10). That too is an epistemological crisis. For the riddle, How can the best of news be proclaimed in the midst of an unchanged world?, a riddle to which the pseudo-apostles had a ready but false answer, is precisely the riddle, How can the

[52] The word *stauros*, so important in 1 Corinthians, is absent from 2 Corinthians, but only in a literal sense. A more important problem is raised by my expression 'knowing *kata stauron*.' Can one speak of a *way* of knowing by allowing the preposition *kata* to govern a noun which refers to something *outside* the knower (as opposed to *sarx* and *pneuma* which are, so to speak, inside the knower)? A full answer to this question would be constructed, I think, on the following points: First of all, when Paul speaks of knowing *kata sarka*, he does not intend the term *sarx* to refer *exclusively* to the flesh of the knower. He intends it to point fundamentally to the realm of the old age, as noted earlier. So also *pneuma* points not only to an entity which is now in the believer, but also to the new age. Conversely, the *stauros* is not entirely outside the knower whose way of knowing is granted neither in the old age, nor in the new age, but rather at the painful and gracious juncture (Gal 2:19–20; Rom 6:3). Of course Paul's opponents know the *stauros* as an object of knowledge (although even this affirmation would be qualified by the apostle). They do not know *kata stauron*, inasmuch as to do so is to have one's own *stauros*.

[53] Regarding the expression 'by the *power* of the cross,' note that in 2 Cor 10:2–4, Paul places opposite *sarkika* the word *dynata* (Jewett, *Terms*, 127). See also note 22 above.

[54] Note the accent on Paul's christologizing of the Spirit in Vos, *Pneumatologie*.

resurrection be proclaimed in the midst of the cross? This is just the point. The cross is the epistemological crisis for the simple reason that while it is in one sense followed by the resurrection, it is not replaced by the resurrection.[55]

Thus, the new way of knowing is not in some ethereal sense a spiritual way of knowing. It is not effected in a mystic trance, as the pseudo-apostles claimed, but rather right in the midst of rough-and-tumble life (note that 2 Cor 6:1–2 is followed by 6:3–10). And that rough-and-tumble life is not the private experience of an individual ecstatic who partakes of the Lord's supper by himself (1 Cor 11:21). On the contrary, it is life in the midst of the new-creation community, in which to know by the power of the cross is precisely to know and to serve the neighbor who is in need.

To be sure, in this community the veil is taken away, the creation is new, the old has passed away, look!, the new has come (2 Cor 5:17; 6:2). Yet all of this can be seen only by the new eyes granted at the *juncture* of the ages. Thus, the one who knows by the Spirit cannot demonstrate that way of knowing by performing mighty works, congratulating himself on his individual prowess. Nor has seeing in a partial way been replaced by seeing face to face. On the contrary, it has been replaced by the faith that is active in love in the community (2 Cor 5:7).[56]

---

[55] Pondering the famous church and synagogue statues which stand on opposite sides of the Strasbourg cathedral's south portal, one can imagine Paul's ordering a radical change. 'Replace the veil, so that it is the proud figure with the crown, the noble bearing, and the mace-like cross who is blindfolded and the weak figure with the broken lance and the humiliated countenance (*kata prosōpon tapeinos*) who is able to see.'

[56] Drawing a partial contrast between the Pauline labors of J. C. Beker and myself, A. R. Brown is right to ask how Paul's apocalyptic epistemology is related to his view of daily life. And as the re-wording of the present sentence shows, I am myself instructed by her answer (see notably Brown, *Cross*, 149–169). The church is the locus in which the epistemology of the cross creates the new pattern of the *communal* life of mutual love. Brown and I seem to agree in avoiding a simplistic use of the term 'decision' (see chapter 10 below, and Brown, *Cross*, 167). And we might agree in conversation that the term 'ethics,' as it was employed by Paul's contemporaries – and especially as it is widely used today – defines a common way of domesticating Paul's apocalyptic theology (see chapters 14 and 15 below). In any case, Brown speaks convincingly, I think, of *living* the freedom one sees (169). That is a crucial point. But, by the same token, Paul does not refer to persons *abandoning* the old world (cf. Brown, 159). Nor does he think that he is *offering* an alternative world (160), or an alternative epistemology that provides the positive *impetus to re-locate* in the new world (163). On the contrary, he says that the old world was taken away from him, as he 'suffered the loss of all things' (Phil 3:8). Thus, he does not *call* for an end to the old world (Brown, 163). Having suffered its loss, he *announces* both its end and the dawn of the new creation precisely in 2 Cor 5:16–17.

For, as the second half of 2 Cor 5:16 and the first half of v. 17 show, the epistemology characteristic of this community is thoroughly and without remainder christological. That is to say, together with the community that is being formed in him, *Christ* defines the difference between the two ways of knowing, doing that precisely in his cross. The cross of Christ means that the marks of the new age are at present hidden *in* the old age (2 Cor 6:3–10). Thus, at the juncture of the ages the marks of the resurrection are hidden and revealed in the cross of the disciple's daily death, and *only* there.[57]

> For Christ's love controls us. That is to say, [looking at the cross], we have discerned (*krinantas*) that one died on behalf of all. Thus, all died! And he died for all, in order that those who live might live no longer for themselves, but rather for him who for their sake died and was raised (2 Cor 5:14–15).

For he harbors in his own way an enthusiastic strain, greatly underestimated by Beker, but essential to the distinction between cosmological and forensic apocalyptic (see de Boer, 'Apocalyptic Theology;' cf. chapter 9 below and Glossary). In short, Paul's gospel is the performative *announcement* that, against all anti-God powers, God is at work *making* the new creation in which 'true power is born not of control or force, but of solidarity in divine love' (Brown, 164).

[57] Several important limitations are set to the epistemological question by Paul himself; our concentration on the single verse, 2 Cor 5:16, must not be allowed to obscure that fact. (1) 2 Cor 5:17 makes it quite clear that God's deed of reconciliation in Christ is a cosmic event. It involves more than the granting of a new way of knowing. (2) In 1 Corinthians Paul was very careful to qualify the epistemological question by means of an insistence on God's election. The datives of 1 Cor 1:18 certainly point to different perceptions on the part of different groups, but by means of the surprising *imbalance* between *mōria* ('foolishness') and *dynamis theou* ('the power of God'), Paul says forcefully that the preached word is not served up as a first step, so that as a second step the Corinthians may apply to it their superior powers of discernment. Rather, in the preached word God is himself powerfully present and active. (3) 1 Cor 4:3 tells us that the Corinthian Enthusiasts had a propensity for judging others. That is not at all surprising. But notice that in this passage Paul, far from claiming for himself the capacity to judge (contrast 2:15!), insists that only the returning Lord is capable of judgment. These three passages should suffice. By citing them, we may return to our theme: until all stand before the *bēma tou Christou*, there is only one point at which the epistemological question can be legitimately posed: the death/resurrection of Christ and the daily death/life of the disciple.

7

Apocalyptic Antinomies

Galatian Embarrassment

At several junctures in the history of its interpretation, Paul's letter to the Galatians has been seen as the embarrassing member of the Pauline letter family, the one refusing to be brought into line with the others, and even, in some regards, the one threatening the unity and good-natured camaraderie of the family. Luther, to be sure, called on the familial image in an entirely positive sense, when he confessed himself to be happily betrothed to the letter. Others have considered that betrothal the prelude to an unfortunate marriage, in which Luther was led astray, or led further astray, by this intractable and regrettable letter.

In our own century the dominant cause of the letter's being regretted is the obvious fact that, when Paul wrote it, he was in a state of white-hot anger. More is involved here than merely the enlightened preference for equanimity, and thus for the Apostle's happy words in the final chapter of Philippians. There is notably the matter of Paul's stance toward the Law of Moses. Christian exegetes have been repeatedly embarrassed when their Jewish colleagues cite Paul's intemperate and quasi-gnostic comments about the Law in Galatians (e.g. 3:19–20).[1] In the state of embarrassment more than one Christian interpreter has turned to the seventh chapter of Romans, in order to remind the Jewish colleagues that when Paul was in his 'reasonable and balanced mind,' he characterized the Law as holy, just, and good. Similarly, made uneasy by Paul's polemical account of the Jerusalem meeting in Galatians 2, interpreters have frequently repaired, in one regard or another, to Luke's more even-handed account in Acts 15. And while all are pleased with the letter's characteristic celebration of freedom, some interpreters feel somewhat embarrassed that Paul should have written the letter in a

---

[1] See Martyn, *Galatians*, Comment 38, and chapter 5 above.

111

state of unrepentance for the inflexible and even hostile words he spoke to Peter in the presence of the entire church of Antioch (Gal 2:11–14). All of these factors, and others as well, have led a number of interpreters to a degree of regret that Paul should have written such an angry, unbalanced, and unrepentant letter.

Recent decades have seen the emergence of a new reason for regretting Galatians. To a growing number of interpreters the letter is the uncooperative maverick, not because of its belligerent tone, but because it does not support the thesis of a Pauline gospel consistently focused on what is being called an apocalyptic view of the future. In two seminal essays of 1960 and 1962 Ernst Käsemann set the cat among the pigeons by identifying apocalyptic as the mother of Christian theology, and by taking Paul as his crowning witness.[2] Now, a number of years later, one would have to admit that the pigeons are still circling, continuing their disturbance of the peace; and as regards Galatians the scene is particularly unsettled. Käsemann wrote his articles without explicit reference to the theology of Galatians (he took Gal 3:28 to be the slogan of the pre-Pauline Hellenistic community), and when his critics succeeded in eliciting from him a definition of apocalyptic, it proved to be 'the expectation of an imminent Parousia,'[3] a definition that threatened to exclude Galatians from the apocalyptic form of the Pauline canon by default.[4] As Pauline exegetes have taken sides for and against Käsemann's apocalyptic Paul, the letter has sometimes been allowed its voice, but precisely as the member of the family who does not fit in. If one was opposed to the picture of Paul as a thoroughgoing apocalyptic theologian, surely one could refute that picture by citing the letter that contains no reference to an imminent Parousia.[5] If one supported the picture of Paul as the consistent apocalyptic thinker, one had to admit that Galatians was an embarrassment, to which one would have to respond by questioning its right to be a bona fide member of the Pauline canon.

The chief witness to this new form of Galatian embarrassment lay before us in the first edition of J. C. Beker's *Paul the Apostle, the Triumph*

[2] Käsemann, 'Beginnings;' 'Apocalyptic.'

[3] Käsemann, 'Apocalyptic,' 109 n. 1.

[4] It is important to see, however, that Käsemann himself found 'the relics of apocalyptic theology . . . *everywhere* in the Pauline Epistles' ('Apocalyptic,' 131; emphasis added). For analysis and critique of Käsemann's views, see notably de Boer, *Defeat*; Way, *Lordship*.

[5] I have encountered this argument in oral discussions.

of God in Life and Thought (1980). This book is monumental on a number of counts, mainly because of its thoroughgoing exploration of the thesis that apocalyptic is the heart of Paul's gospel. What, then, could be said of Galatians? Lacking all traces of a passage corresponding to 1 Thess 4:13–18; 1 Cor 15; Rom 8:18–25, that letter does not support the thesis, but Beker demonstrated a certain patience with its uncooperative character, considering it to have been written in a situation that suppressed 'the apocalyptic theme of the gospel.'[6]

It may be well to return thanks for instruction received at the hands of Käsemann and Beker by suggesting another route. The thesis advanced and developed by these two colleagues may be essentially correct: Paul's theology is thoroughly apocalyptic, and is different from the theology of early Christian enthusiasm primarily in its insistence (*a*) that the world is not yet fully subject to God, even though (*b*) the eschatological subjection of the world has already begun, causing its end to be in sight. To cite Käsemann, 'No perspective could be more apocalyptic.'[7] One may ask, however, as Beker now sees – with characteristic openness – in the preface for his second edition (1984), whether that thesis is to be maintained at the expense of Galatians, indeed whether it can be maintained without the support of Galatians. And asking that question leads us to give the uncooperative letter another hearing. Could Galatians perhaps be allowed to play its own role in showing us precisely what the nature of Paul's apocalyptic was?[8]

Apocalyptic and Antinomies

That question can be honestly posed if we are willing to begin with a certain amount of ignorance as to the definition of apocalyptic, and of Paul's apocalyptic in particular. One may be reminded of the Socratic dictum of H. G. Gadamer: 'In order to pose a genuine question, one must wish to know. But that involves knowing that one does not know.'[9] In a state of some ignorance, then, we turn to the text of Galatians, taking our bearings initially from its closing paragraph.

---

[6] Beker, *Paul*, x. Note that indirectly Baumgarten confirms the assumption that Galatians lacks the apocalyptic perspective, concentrating his attention on 1 Thess 4–5, 1 Cor 15, and Romans 8 (*Apokalyptik*, 58).

[7] Käsemann, 'Apocalyptic,' 133.

[8] See the appendix to chapter 10 below.

[9] Gadamer, *Wahrheit und Methode*, 345.

In that paragraph Paul draws a final contrast between himself and the circumcising Teachers who are now active among his Galatian congregations.[10] He draws the contrast as though he intended to place before the Galatians a choice between two mystagogues, and thus a choice between two ways of life:

> For these circumcised people do not even keep the Law themselves! Their insistence on circumcising you springs, then, from their desire to boast in regard to your flesh. As for me, God forbid that I should boast in anything except the cross of our Lord Jesus Christ . . . (Gal 6:13–14a)

In the next breath, however, Paul does not speak of two alternatives, between which the Galatians might make a choice. He speaks, rather, of two different worlds:

> . . . except the cross of our Lord Jesus Christ, by which the cosmos has been crucified to me and I to the cosmos. For neither is circumcision anything nor is uncircumcision anything. What is something is the new creation. (Gal 6:14b–15)

Here Paul refers, as I have just said, to two different worlds. He speaks of an old world, from which he has been painfully separated, by Christ's death, by the death of that world, and by his own death. And he speaks of a new world, which he grasps under the arresting expression, new creation.[11]

These statements are of the kind to make the head swim. One might even wonder whether they do not constitute a flight from reality. To be sure, Paul seems to bring these cosmic announcements into relationship with some sort of realism, by placing between them a statement directed to what many interpreters consider to be the specific issue of the letter, circumcision as the sign par excellence of observance of the Law. To say that some sort of realism is involved only makes it possible, however, to define the major problem of Paul's closing paragraph. Exactly what sort of realism do we find? New creation, after all, is the kind of expression that easily trails off into the nebulous realm of pious rhetoric. We have, then, to ask Paul precisely how he understands his two cosmic

---

[10] On the Teachers see chapter 1 above.

[11] Taken by itself the expression 'new creation' scarcely decides the issue we are addressing, but it is pertinent to note that the expression is at home in apocalyptic. See Stuhlmacher, 'Erwägungen;' G. Schneider, 'Neuschöpfung.' On the triple death in Gal 6:14 see Minear, 'Enigma.'

announcements to be related to the specific negation of circumcision and uncircumcision.

We begin to deal with that question by attending to the form of the negation itself, for what is striking about the negation is exactly its form (cf. Gal 5:6 and 1 Cor 7:19). In the immediate context, as we have noted, Paul has just referred to the circumcising Teachers. One is prepared, therefore, to find him striking a final blow, directly and simply, against observance of the Law. Paul should say 'Neither circumcision, nor the food laws, nor the keeping of the sabbath is anything.' As is so often the case, however, Paul says the unexpected. He surprises his readers by negating not merely Law observance, but also its opposite, non-Law observance. In a word, that to which Paul denies real existence is, in the technical sense of the expression, a pair of opposites, what Aristotle might have called an instance of *t'anantia*,[12] and what I will refer to as an antinomy.[13]

---

[12] Aristotle spoke of *t'anantia* 'the contraries', as one of the modes of opposition, *Metaphysics* 1018a; cf. 1004b and 986a. He also spoke of pairs that admit an intermediate, such as black, grey, white. Gal 5:3 shows that Paul does not understand Law-observance and non-Law-observance to admit the intermediate phenomenon of partial Law-observance. Nor in 6:15 does Paul think of complementarity in the sense that circumcision and uncircumcision encompass the whole of humanity. As we will see below, Paul embraces as a major factor in his theology the pattern of mutually exclusive opposition. The concern of the present essay is to approach the question of 'Paul and apocalyptic' by taking one's bearings from pairs of opposites, a task as pertinent to the study of the other letters as it is to the study of Galatians. The path followed is distinct from the one that is pursued in studies of the antithesis as a rhetorical form, although there are points of contact. See particularly N. Schneider, *Antithese*, 30–31; Siegert, *Argumentation*.

[13] I use the term 'antinomy' in an idiosyncratic way, namely to render the numerous expressions by which the ancients referred (in many languages) to a pair of opposites so fundamental to the cosmos, being one of its elements, as to make the cosmos what it is (see both the following note and chapter 8 below). The most obvious of the ancient examples is the list of oppositional pairs that Aristotle attributed to the Pythagoreans: Limit and Unlimited; Odd and Even; Unity and Plurality; Right and Left; Male and Female; and so on (*Metaphysics* 986a). For examples from Persia, Egypt, and Palestine, not least Isa 45:7, see the texts and works cited in Lloyd, *Polarity*; Martyn, 'Apocalyptic Antinomies,' 422 n. 12. I must emphasize the difference between my idiosyncratic use of the term and that of rhetoricians such as Quintilian (cf. Vos, 'Antinomie'). For Paul, as for the Pythagoreans, an antinomy is more than an antithesis, for an antinomy lies at the foundation of the cosmos, whereas in common usage an antithesis is a form of rhetoric, a product of human thought. Moreover, in Paul's view, as we will see, the antinomies of God's *new creation* have their origin in the apocalypse of Christ and of his Spirit. For this reason, they are fundamentally different from Marcion's ontological anti-theses.

THEOLOGICAL ISSUES IN THE LETTERS OF PAUL

This observation may prove to be of considerable help in our efforts to hear the text as the Galatians themselves heard it. For when we note that Paul speaks about a pair of opposites – an antinomy – and that he does so between the making of two cosmic announcements, we may recall how widespread in the ancient world was the thought that the fundamental building blocks of the cosmos are pairs of opposites. In one form or another we find that thought in Greece, from Anaximander to the Pythagoreans to Aristotle; in Persia, from Zoroaster to the magi; in Egypt, from the Pythagorean traditions to Philo; and in Palestine itself, from the Second Isaiah to Qoheleth to Sirach to the Teacher of Righteousness to some of the rabbis.[14]

We might indeed pause to note the formula in Sirach, in which (as in Isa 45:7) cosmic duality is attributed to the creative hand of God:

[14] For *Greece* the first collection of pertinent texts was made by Kemmer, *Polare*. We have now the finely nuanced interpretation by Lloyd, *Polarity*. The traditions of primary importance are those of Heraclitus, the Pythagoreans, Parmenides, the Hippocratic corpus, Plato, and Aristotle, the last being our major source for the role of polar structure in Pythagorean philosophy. See also the orphic papyrus discussed by O. Schütz, *Archiv für Papyrusforschung und verwandte Gebiete* 13 (1939) 210–212, and for Stoic traditions on the *antikeimena* von Arnim, *Fragmenta*, 2, 70–83, and Pohlenz, *Die Stoa* (1948) 48. For *Persia* see notably Widengren, 'Apokalyptik.' For *Egypt* one notes certain recurrent antitheses in ancient Egyptian religion (Lloyd, *Polarity*, 29 n. 3), and above all Philo's use of the Pythagorean tradition of opposites (chapter 8 below). For *Palestine* see Isa 45:7, where God is the one who now creates light and darkness, salvation and woe; Qoh 3:1–9; and especially 7:14; Sir 11:14; 33:14–15; 42:24–25. Sirach provides the classic example of the use of the theory of cosmic polarity in service of the doctrine of the Two Ways; note also the motif of complementarity in Sir 42:24–25, reflecting Sirach's concern to avoid a split in God by affirming that God created a split world. In Qumran literature the major text is 1QS 3:13–4, 26, where one finds a connection between pairs of opposites and the expectation of the new creation: the struggle between the two Spirits is characteristic of the cosmos until God establishes the new creation by destroying the Spirit of Evil; the new creation is thus connected with the termination of cosmic polarity. The wisdom traditions show the thought of archaic polarity serving the doctrine of the Two Ways; Qumran can represent the tendency in apocalyptic traditions to use the thought of archaic polarity also in the service of the doctrine of the Holy War. The pertinent rabbinic data, fully collected and arranged, wherever possible, by date, would make a study in themselves; it will suffice to mention the continuation of the use of pairs of opposites to serve the doctrine of the Two Ways; *m. 'Abot* 2. 9; 5. 7; 5.19; and the sometimes philosophical discussions of the *zugoth* in which the accent generally lies on complementarity rather than on opposition, e.g. *Gen. Rab.* 11:8, where the Sabbath asks God for a partner (*zug*), and is given Israel as a partner; (cf. *Pesiq. R.* 23:6); Eccl 7:14 is taken up in several places, e.g. *b. Hag.* 15a where, however, under the name of Akiba, the motif of opposition is added to that of cosmic complementarity. It is well known that the so-called doctrine of the syzygies was a favorite of the gnostics and also plays an important role in Jewish-Christian traditions now found in the Pseudo-Clementine literature; see e.g. Strecker, *Judenchristentum.*

All the works of the Most High, are in pairs, one the opposite of the other (Sir 33:15).[15]

This text is one of numerous witnesses to the theory that from creation the *archai* (the foundational elements) of the cosmos have been pairs of opposites. We can say that in the world of Paul's day, the thought of archaic, cosmic polarity was very nearly ubiquitous. The Galatians, then, are almost certain to have known, in some form, the thought that the structure of the cosmos lies in pairs of opposites; and that is precisely the pattern of thought which Paul presupposes in Gal 6:15.

He is making use of that theory, however, in a very peculiar fashion. He is denying real existence to an antinomy, in order to show what it means to say that the old cosmos has suffered its death. We can bring the matter into sharp focus, if we can imagine, for a moment, that Paul is a Pythagorean, who has been compelled by some turn of events to say about the Table of Opposites (the *systoichiai tōn enantiotōn*):

> Neither limit nor unlimited is anything; straight is not the opposite of crooked; and odd and even do not really exist.[16]

For a Pythagorean to say such things would certainly be grounds for him to announce that the cosmos had suffered its death. *Mutatis mutandis* for Paul the Pharisee to say that neither circumcision nor un-circumcision is anything is for him to make a cosmic statement no less radical. In making that statement, Paul speaks in specific terms about the horrifying death of the cosmos. With that observation we have come far enough to advance an hypothesis:

> Perhaps in this final paragraph Paul is telling the Galatians that the whole of his epistle is not about the better of two mystagogues, or even about the better of two ways, and certainly not about the failure of Judaism. He is saying rather, that the letter is about the death of one world, and the advent of another. With regard to the former, the death of the cosmos, perhaps Paul is telling the Galatians that one knows the old world to have died,

---

[15] The formula is also cited in the *T. 12 Patr.* (*T. Ash.* 1:4; 5:1); cf. further *T. Jud.* 19:4; 20:1; *T. Levi* 19:1; *T. Naph.* 2:10; 3:5; *T. Jos.* 20:2; *T. Benj.* 5:3. In Sir 42:24–25 the formula is used to express complementarity rather than opposition, a tendency to some degree characteristic of the interpretation of duality in wisdom traditions and in rabbinic literature (see preceding note), not to mention the important role complementary duality plays in Greek philosophy (e.g. Heraclitus) and in the history of medicine from the Hippocratic corpus to the writings of C. G. Jung.

[16] See again Aristotle, *Metaphysics* 986a, where the ten principles of the Pythagoreans are listed in two columns of opposites (*systoichiai*).

because one knows that its fundamental structures are gone, that those fundamental structures of the cosmos were certain identifiable pairs of opposites, and that, given the situation among their congregations in Galatia, the pair of opposites whose departure calls for emphasis is that of circumcision and uncircumcision.

Obviously one tests this hypothesis by re-reading the entire letter, and, in the course of doing so, one sees that in Galatians Paul speaks of antinomies with astonishing frequency, referring both to the disappearance of old antinomies and to the emergence of new ones.

The Disappearance of the Old Antinomies

Moving back into the letter from Gal 6:15, we see that at several previous junctures Paul anticipates that climactic statement, doing so in such a way as to suggest that the disappearance of the old antinomies is an apocalyptic event. It is true, as noted above, that in Galatians Paul does not use images that are obviously apocalyptic – falling stars, a blood-red moon, an earthquake, the trumpet of God, etc. – but his language seems as thoroughly cosmic and as fully apocalyptic as it would have been, had he done so. Citing an early Christian baptismal tradition, for example, Paul emphatically says that the cosmos, founded as it was on religious pairs of opposites, does not any longer exist:

> For when all of you were baptized into Christ, you put on Christ as though he were your clothing.
> There *is* neither Jew nor Greek;
> there *is* neither slave nor free;
> there *is* no 'male and female;'
> for all of you are One in Christ Jesus (3:27–28).

By citing this tradition, Paul takes the Galatians back to the moment of their own baptism, in order to remind them of the true nature of that event. The baptismal scene was highly dramatic. As persons who were acquainted with some form of the tradition of elemental, oppositional pairs, the Galatians heard in the baptizer's words a list of the oppositional elements that had ceased to exist. In that declaration, they suffered *the loss of the cosmos*, as though a fissure had opened up under their feet, hurling them into an abyss.

Elsewhere in the letter, moreover, Paul repeatedly reinforces this matter of loss of cosmos. Using Jewish terms because of the nature of the Teachers' message, Paul nevertheless presents a universal picture.

That is to say, finding the Law to be an enslaving power precisely in its opposition to the Not-Law, Paul denies the existence of numerous pairs of opposites that, in one form or another, are identified by all people as the beacons from which one gains one's bearings:

to sin	to observe the Law (2:17–19)
to be wrong	to be set right by observing the Law (2:16, 21; 3:12)
to be dead	to be made alive by the Law (3:21).[17]

We return, then, to the climactic end of the letter:

> . . . the cross of our Lord Jesus Christ, by which the cosmos has been crucified to me and I to the cosmos. For neither is circumcision anything nor is uncircumcision anything. What is something is the new creation.

In baptism all of the Galatians were *crucified with Christ*. They all suffered the consequent loss of the world of religious differentiation, the world, that is, that had as one of its fundamental elements the antinomy of the Law / the Not-Law. For crucifixion with Christ means the death of the cosmos of religion, the cosmos in which all human beings live. Swept away are the basic guidelines which – in one form or another – all people had formerly considered permanently dependable.

The Emergence of the New Antinomies

With equal emphasis, however, Paul also says that in its death, the cosmos (cf. 'the present evil age;' 1:4) has been replaced by the new creation. Here two major pictures make their appearance, and both involve the apocalyptic relationship between cosmos and sets of antinomies.

New Unity

Interpreting the baptismal formula cited above (Gal 3:28), Paul says that *polarity* in the cosmos has been replaced by *unity* in Christ. The old

---

[17] The emphasis Paul places in Galatians on the termination of such elemental pairs of opposites reflects, of course, the polemical character of the letter. It is crucial, however, to note the nature of that polemic. Paul is concerned with the Teachers' failure to announce the termination of these oppositional pairs, because the result of that failure is the falsification of the gospel in the sense that it hides from the Galatians *the real world.* For the Teachers not only presuppose the antinomies Paul knows to be gone. They also explicate these antinomies and their unreal cosmos by developing a full-blown Table of Opposites – in Greek *t'anantia* – which they claim to find by reading the Law. See chapter 12 below.

cosmos had pairs of opposites. The new creation, marked by anthropological unity in Christ, does not have pairs of opposites, for with the eclipse of Jew/Gentile, slave/free, and male/female, 'all of you are One in Christ Jesus' (3:28b).

New Pairs of Opposites

Reading elsewhere in Galatians, however, we see that, important as this anthropological pattern may be, it presents only part of the picture. At numerous junctures, Paul says quite clearly that in the horrifying crucifixion of the cosmos, God is bringing to birth not only anthropological unity in Christ, but also a new set of antinomies. Two examples can be seen without difficulty.

There is, first, the Spirit and the Flesh. Paul speaks of these two powers as one would speak of a cosmic pair of opposites (5:17; chapter 15 below). The Spirit and the Flesh are an oppositional pair that cause the world to be what it *now* actually is.

Second, Paul speaks several times of a new-creation antinomy made up of the death of Christ versus the Law. Since God has elected to make things right via the death of his Christ, rather than via the Law (2:21), there is now – emphatically for the Galatian situation – a specific antinomy between the cross and circumcision, between the rectifying death of Christ and all religion (e.g. 5:11; 6:12–14; cf. 4:8–11). And since the Law (*scil.* religion) is in fact impotent to curb the Flesh, it is crucial to see that the true and potent opposite to that monster is the Spirit, rather than the Law (chapter 15 below).

Beyond unity in Christ, then, one notes in Galatians the antinomies of the new creation (see Paul's Table of Opposites in chapter 2 above and chapter 12 below). Like the old-age antinomies, those of the new creation are cosmic in scope. They are also thoroughly apocalyptic, in the sense that they are being born in the apocalypse of Christ (Gal 3:23–25). Six motifs play their roles in Paul's vision of the new creation, as it dawns with its new and dynamic pairs of opposites.

The Dawn of the New Creation

(1) The Spirit and its opposite, the Flesh, are not timeless first principles, called into being by God at the beginning (contrast not only Sir 33:15, but also 1QS 3:13–4:26).

(2) This pair of opposites owes its birth to God's *new*-creative act. It is born of the new event, God's sending both his Son and the Spirit of his Son into the present evil age (Gal 1:4; 4:4–6).

(3) The advent of the Son and of his Spirit is thus *the* cosmic, apocalyptic event. There was a 'before,' and there is now an 'after.' And it is at the point at which the 'after' invades the 'before' that the Spirit and the Flesh have become a dynamic pair of opposites. They form an apocalyptic antinomy characteristic of the dawn of God's new creation.

(4) This apocalyptic antinomy receives its dynamism both from the event that gave it its birth and from the warfare begun with that event (chapter 15 below).[18] The motif of warfare between pairs of opposites could remind one of the philosophy of Heraclitus; 'War [between the opposites] is the father of all things;' (*Frag.* 53) or, nearer to Paul, of the theology of Qumran, in which there is strife (*rib*) between the two Spirits. But in both of these views the struggle is thought to inhere in the cosmos. Indeed in the perspective of Qumran, the warring antinomy of the Spirit of Truth versus the Spirit of Falsehood, stemming as it does from the original creation, will find in the new creation not its birth, but rather its termination (1QS 4:16, 25). In Paul's apocalyptic, the picture is quite different. The Spirit and the Flesh constitute an apocalyptic antinomy, in the sense that they are two opposed orbs of power, actively at war with one another *since* the advent of the Spirit. The territory in which human beings now live is a newly invaded space, and that means that its structures cannot remain unchanged.

(5) It follows that when the Galatians follow the Teachers, beginning to live as though the effective opposite of the Flesh were the Law, they show that they have abandoned life in the creation that has now been made what it is by the advent of Christ and of his Spirit. It is they who are not living in the real world. For the true war of liberation has been initiated not at Sinai, but rather in the apocalypse of the crucified one and in the coming of his Spirit.

(6) All of the preceding motifs come together in the central question of the Galatian letter: What time is it? One hardly needs to point out that the matter of discerning the time lies at the heart of apocalyptic; and in none of his other letters does Paul address that issue in terms

---

[18] It is worth noting that Widengren identifies as the two main motifs of apocalyptic thought (1) cosmic changes and catastrophes and (2) the war-like final struggle in the cosmos ('*Apokalyptik*,' 150).

more clearly apocalyptic. What time is it? It is the time after the apocalypse of the faith of Christ (3:23–25), the time of things being set right by that faith, the time of the presence of the Spirit, and thus the time of the war of liberation commenced by the Spirit. In a word, it is the time of the dawn of the new creation with its new antinomies. The result is a holistic vision, in scope categorically cosmic and emphatically apocalyptic.

The Embodiment of the New Creation

Even in the face of this vision, one may ask whether the new creation has an embodiment. In the common sense of the expression, can Paul point to it? In effect, the apostle gives three mutually illuminating answers. The new creation is embodied in Christ, in the church, and thus in the Israel of God.

Christ

Paul connects the christological note of Gal 6:14a with the cosmic, new-creational note of 6:14b and 15. Just as it is in the cross of Christ that God has inaugurated the new creation, so there is a significant sense in which Christ *is* the new creation (note the word 'seed' in 3:16 and the term 'One' in 3:28, and cf. the expression 'the one man, Jesus Christ' in Rom 5:17; cf. further 1 Cor 15:22, 45). Sent by God, Christ is the descendant whom God promised long ago to Abraham (3:16), the one who is, as it were, the seed of the new creation (chapter 10 below).

The Church

At numerous junctures in Galatians, Paul speaks of the church's incorporation in this new-creation Christ. It is by being Christ's – by being baptized into him, by putting him on as though he were their clothes (3:27), by having his Spirit in their hearts (4:6), by having him determine the form of their communal life (4:19), by belonging utterly to him, the cosmocrator of the new creation (5:24) – that the Galatians (with all other members of God's church; 1:13) are Abraham's corporate seed and God's new creation in Christ (3:29).

The Israel of God

Finally, as Paul says at the close of Gal 6:16, the new creation is also the Israel of God, the people (the *qahal*) that God is now calling into existence in Christ, rather than in the Law.[19] However furious he may be with the Teachers, Paul will not allow their view of the nomistic people of God to separate him either from the God of Israel or from Israel itself. God's new creation is not a romantic haven in which the individual can hug himself to sleep (chapter 4 above). It is embodied in those who, recreated by Christ's love, serve one another in the new community of mutual service (5:13), God's Israel.

---

[19] See further chapter 10 below; and Martyn, *Galatians*, Comment 52.

8

Christ and the Elements of the Cosmos

The Data

In Gal 4:3 and 4:9 Paul mentions *ta stoicheia tou kosmou,* 'the elements of the cosmos.'[1] In both cases he speaks of two contrasting periods, distinguished from one another by a radical change in the relationship human beings have to these elements. The earlier of these periods is that prior to the advent of Christ; the second is the one since that event.

Four striking motifs are dominant in Gal 4:3–5: (*a*) The elements of the cosmos had the power to enslave, and they exercised that power. (*b*) God has terminated that enslavement by sending his Son. (*c*) In their enslaving activity, the elements had some kind of connection or relationship with the Law. At the minimum the elements and the Law were functionally parallel entities: both enslaved, and God's sending of Christ has effected liberation from both. (*d*) The elements enslaved 'us,' that is to say all human beings.[2]

In the second passage, Gal 4:8–11, three of the motifs mentioned above are repeated: (*a*) enslavement to the elements; (*b*) the termination of that enslavement by something God has done (he has known the Galatians); (*c*) the close connection drawn between enslavement to the elements and observance of the Law. Moreover, the third motif is clarified: Gentiles who have been known by God, and who now *turn* to the Law by following its holy calendar, are not thereby confirming the end of their veneration of the elements. On the contrary, they are *returning* to that veneration.[3] The elements and the Law are

---

[1] It is important to read Galatians in its own right before making comparisons. Thus, the references to cosmic elements in Colossians, Hebrews, and 2 Peter (cf. *Herm. Vis.* 3.13.3) will be mentioned only in passing.

[2] See Martyn, *Galatians,* Comment 36.

[3] That the holy times mentioned by Paul have to do with the Galatians' incipient acceptance of the Law is clear from the context. See also Lührmann, 'Tage.'

therefore more than functionally parallel entities, both having the power to enslave. If veneration of the Law is one form in which human beings venerate the cosmic elements, it is highly probable that in some fashion or other the Law *is* one of those elements. Thus, the universal 'we,' who were held under the power of the elements (4:3), are almost certainly the same persons as 'those' who were held under the power of the Law (4:5).[4]

There are also three new accents: (*d*) By addressing the Galatians directly, Paul now specifies their former enslavement as their worship of the elements. (*e*) He denies that the elements are deities, implying that in the Galatians' original religious life, they worshiped the elements as gods. (*f*) He insists that the elements are, on the contrary, weak and impotent.

These two references to the elements pose one of the more interesting and also one of the more important issues of Galatians, especially if one asks how these two references may be related to Paul's christology and to his view of the Law.[5] Why should Paul speak to the Galatians about the elements of the cosmos, and how does he intend them to construe his references? What, precisely, are these elements, how did they enslave, and how is it that their universally enslaving power has been broken by the advent of Christ? Was it not sufficient in Paul's mind to characterize the period prior to Christ as one of imprisonment under the Law (Gal 3:23, 25)? Why speak also of imprisonment under the elements, somehow identifying the Law as one of them?

These are exceedingly thorny questions, as one can see from the extraordinary number of studies given to them, and from the strik-

---

[4] Cf. B. Reicke, 'Law,' 259–260. Other interpreters have argued that the 'we' of 4:3 are Gentiles, whereas the 'those' of 4:5 are Jews, supporting their reading in part by referring to 1 Cor 9:20–21. It is indeed clear that in this passage Paul differentiates Gentiles from Jews, identifying the former as persons 'not under the Law' (*hoi anomoi*) and the latter as persons 'under the Law' (*hoi hypo nomon*). But those very expressions show that in 1 Cor 9:20–21 Paul is following the tradition according to which all persons are identified by their relation to the Law. Jews (and the circumcision party in the Jerusalem church) are indeed *those of the Law*. But in the same terms, Gentiles also derive their identity from the Law by being *those of the Not-Law*. Different from both, Paul declares himself to be 'in the Law of Christ' (*ennomos Christou*), an affirmation that sounds the note struck in Gal 6:2. That is to say, to be in the Law of Christ is to be altogether beyond the distinction between the Law and the Not-Law.

[5] The author of Colossians considers the relationships among the elements, the Law, and Christ to pose issues requiring explicit discussion. Regarding corresponding issues in Galatians, see the conclusion to the present chapter, and chapter 14 below.

ing absence of a consensus.[6] Regarding the identity of the elements, we may begin with the four major possibilities listed by W. Bauer (BAGD):[7]

(1) 'Elements (of learning), fundamental principles.' As this is almost certainly the meaning of *stoicheia* in Heb 5:12, numerous exegetes, noting the motif of immaturity in Gal 4:1–2, have proposed it for the references in Galatians as well: Human beings were formerly given to the elementary and immature forms of religion, Jewish and Gentile. These have now been surpassed by the maturity of the new revelation in Christ.[8] But such a reading is precluded by the fact that the motifs of immaturity and maturity play a genuine role neither in Paul's picture in Gal 4:1–2 nor in his interpretation of that picture in 4:3–5 (one does not outgrow slavery!).[9]

(2) 'Elemental substances, the basic elements from which everything in the natural world is made and of which it is composed,' presumably the traditional four: earth, water, air, fire. The lexicographical labors of Blinzler and Rusam have shown this to be the most common meaning of the term *stoicheia*, and the only meaning attested for the expression *stoicheia tou kosmou*. One should accept it for any text of Paul's time, unless there is good reason not to do so.[10]

(3) 'Elementary spirits which the syncretistic religious tendencies of later antiquity associated with the physical elements.' This is the meaning favored by Bauer, H. D. Betz and others, but the sources for it are mostly later than Paul.[11]

---

[6] The basic bibliography is given in the Galatians commentaries of H. D. Betz, Borse, and R. N. Longenecker. See especially Blinzler, 'Lexikalisches;' Hawkins, 'Opponents,' 181–250. Several studies of Schweizer are especially helpful for the role of the elements in the Colossian heresy, but one must take care not to allow the study of the elements in Colossians to set the agenda for the investigation of their role in Galatians. See most recently Schweizer, 'Elements;' and cf. the constructive critique by DeMaris, *Controversy*.

[7] For additional possibilities see Blinzler, 'Lexikalisches,' and Hawkins, 'Opponents.'

[8] Recently R. N. Longenecker finds Paul to be building on the view of *ta stoicheia* as being first principles or elemental teachings. Gal 4:3 is thus a reference to 'the Mosaic law . . . [as the] "basic principles" given by God in preparation for the coming of Christ,' while Gal 4:9 is a reference to the 'veneration of nature and cultic rituals that made up the Gentiles' "basic principles" of religion' (*Galatians*, 165–166).

[9] Cf. also Hawkins, 'Opponents,' 183–185, 210–212.

[10] Blinzler, 'Lexikalisches,' 439–441; Rusam, 'Belege.' Examples include Philo *Heres* 134; Wisd 7:17; 19:18; 4 Macc 12:13; and, among Christian texts, 2 Pet 3:10 and 12, where the author refers to the dissolution of the world's elements in a final cosmic conflagration, a Stoic motif.

[11] Cf. Moore-Crispin, 'Galatians 4:1–9,' 211.

(4) 'Heavenly bodies.' A number of interpreters link this meaning with the preceding one; H. D. Betz, for example, speaks of 'demonic entities of cosmic proportions and astral powers which are hostile towards man.'[12] It is a reading that honors Paul's insistence that the elements held humanity in a state of slavery, clearly viewing them as inimical powers of some sort. Again, however, the thought that the astral elements are demonic and hostile to human beings is difficult to show by drawing on early sources.[13]

We can already draw an initial and tentative conclusion: Lexicographical observations strongly favor the second meaning listed by Bauer, the four traditional cosmic elements, earth, water, air, fire. As we have already noted, one must have a strong reason to read *ta stoicheia tou kosmou* in some other way.[14]

Interpretive disarray remains widespread, however, and, in any case, lexicography cannot settle an issue of such exegetical complexity. Would progress be made, perhaps, by inquiring into the history of the Galatians' linguistic experience? Paul employs the expression 'the elements of the cosmos' without explanation; he may very well be using the expression in his own way, but he seems able to assume that it already has some meaning in the Galatians' vocabulary. What can we say, first of all, then, about the Galatians' experience with the expression prior to their hearing Paul's use of it in his letter?

The Galatians' Linguistic Experience with the Expression 'the elements of the world' Prior to Hearing Paul's Letter

1. Before the Coming of the Teachers

We can know relatively little about the religion of the Galatians before they were seized by the Pauline gospel. Living in the somewhat rustic Anatolian cities of Ancyra and Pessinus (perhaps also in the trading center of Tavium), some of the Galatians may have been adherents of an

---

[12] H. D. Betz, *Galatians*, 205.

[13] Cf. R. N. Longenecker, *Galatians*, 165. Astutely leaving aside the motif of demonic hostility, Hawkins opts at the end of his investigation for 'the heavenly bodies which determine the sequence of calendrical observances' ('Opponents,' 249). As we will see, that may very well be the major meaning the term had for the Teachers; it is not, however, central to Paul's view.

[14] It is worth mentioning that over a period of some years Schweizer has written several pieces to show that both in Colossians and in Galatians the reference is to the traditional four elements. That is surely the reading with which to begin one's work, but as we will see below, the study of Galatians cannot come to rest there.

old Celtic religion. Pessinus, however, was the site of a major sanctuary dedicated to Cybele, the Great Mother of Life and the lover of Attis.[15]

Equally important is the fact that Paul can formulate an argument in the letter that presupposes a certain amount of intellectual sophistication. He can assume the Galatians' acquaintance with certain rhetorical conventions and with some expressions and terms that had acquired a degree of technical denotation, such as the verb *systoicheō*, 'to stand in the same oppositional column with' (Gal 4:25; chapter 12 below). Thus, whatever the form of their native religion(s), they were probably in command of some of the common philosophical theories about the structure of the cosmos. Specifically, they had almost certainly heard of some form of the ubiquitous speculation about the elements that constitute the world's foundation. If, as noted above, one of Paul's Galatian churches was in Pessinus, it may be of some importance that Apuleius mentions the temple of Cybele there as the place in which the Phrygians reverence Isis under the name of 'the Pessinuntine Mother of the Gods.' For in the same passage Apuleius identifies Isis as *elementorum omnium domina*, 'mistress of all the elements' (*Metamorphoses* XI,5; cf. XI, 25).

These observations direct our attention to the second of Paul's references to the elements. There he confidently says that in their past life the Galatians worshiped the elements as though they were gods. To be sure, the Galatians will almost certainly have referred to their gods – at least the major ones – by proper names. A newcomer to their cities will not have found them worshiping earth, air, fire, and water.[16] Yet, looking back on that earlier period, they may have concluded (especially under the tutelage of the Teachers; see below) that in their cults they were somehow reverencing the elements, at least as subordinate deities. That would represent nothing more than the insight of Philo, for example, who, continuing a tradition evident in Homer and Empedocles, speaks of persons who revere the elements as gods. They

> call fire Hephaestus . . . air Hera . . . water Poseidon . . . and earth Demeter. (*de Vita Cont.* 3)[17]

---

[15] Cf. Vermaseren, *Cybele*, 13–31; H. Koester, *Hellenistic Age*, 191.

[16] In this sense Vielhauer is right to follow Delling ('*stoicheō*') in saying: 'There is not a trace of a stoicheia-cult in Galatia,' *Geschichte*, 117; cf. idem, 'Stoicheiadienst.'

[17] Homer *Iliad* 20.67 (from Delling, '*stoicheō*,' 675); Empedocles Fr. 6; DK 1.311; Freeman, *Ancilla*, 52. The Greek text of the fragment of Empedocles is given also in Kirk and Raven, *Presocratic*, 323.

In Paul's time it is the common *Jewish* view that, when Gentiles worship idols, they are in fact worshiping the elements. Thus, the Galatians may have held, for example, to some form of the common belief that changes in the elements, including the movements of the stars, cause the turning of the seasons, and so affect the growing of the food necessary for the sustenance of life.[18] If they were adherents of the cult of the Great Mother, they may have engaged in orgiastic rites designed to assure the fertility of the earth.[19] However this may be, the Galatians are almost certain to have known the expression 'the elements of the cosmos' long before they laid eyes on either Paul or the Teachers – very probably as earth, air, fire, water – and Paul is able to assume some retrospective comprehension on their part when he links these elements with gods they worshiped before his arrival.

2. The Teachers May Have Commented on 'the elements'

None of the letter's explicit references to the Teachers and to their message indicates that they spoke to the Galatians about the elements of the world. As we have seen in chapter 1 above, however, reconstructing the major motifs of the Teachers' message requires casting a net that reaches beyond the explicit references. Passages in which Paul makes no direct reference to the Teachers suggest strongly, for example, that they tied their instruction about the Law to affirmations they made about Abraham. Might they have spoken about the elements, even though Paul does not mention their having done so? Two factors suggest that they did.[20]

(1) We know that comments about the elements played a role not only in some Jewish portraits of Gentiles but also in corresponding forms of Jewish apologetic directed to Gentiles. One thinks, for example, of Wisdom 13, a text strangely overlooked in most of the attempts to understand Paul's references to the cosmic elements:

---

[18] Schweizer, 'Elements,' 457–458, cites and translates an interesting text from Alexander Polyhistor (DK 1.449). For the most part, I follow Schweizer's translation: 'among the sensible bodies are the four elements, fire, water, earth, air, which throughout undergo changes and are altered. And from them there came into being the animate, intellectual world . . . Light and darkness, warm and cold, dry and wet have equal shares in the world (*isomoira . . . en tō kosmō*); [but there are variations in their strength]. By a predominance of warm, summer comes, by a predominance of cold, winter . . .' On this text, see now the comments of DeMaris, *Controversy*.

[19] On the different forms of the Magna Mater/Cybele Cult and their developments see Gasparro, *Cybele*.

[20] See also Lührmann, *Galatians*.

For all men who were ignorant of God were foolish by nature; and they . . . did not recognize the craftsman, while paying heed to his works; but they supposed that either fire or wind or swift air, or the circle of the stars, or turbulent water, or the luminaries of heaven were the gods that rule the world. If through delight in the beauty of these things, men assumed them to be gods, let them know how much better than these is their Lord, for the author of beauty created them. And if men were amazed at their power and working, let them perceive from them how much more powerful is he who formed them. For from the greatness and beauty of created things comes a corresponding perception of their Creator. (Wisd 13:1–5; RSV)[21]

This text forms a helpful background for Paul's charge that in their native religious life the Galatians worshiped the elements as gods (Gal 4:8). Three further motifs are also important: (*a*) The author of Wisdom lists not only fire, wind, air, and water, but also the stars, perhaps reflecting the widespread linking of the activity of the elements with the turning of the seasons and thus with the demarcation of sacred times.[22] (*b*) As a Jew of the Diaspora, he is concerned to bring the Gentiles to the true knowledge of God (note the imperative verbs – 'let them know' and 'let them perceive').[23] And (*c*) he is convinced that the elements do indeed provide the route to God: Gentiles can ascend the ladder of perception *from* contemplation of the world's elements *to* the knowledge of God. There is ample evidence that this proselytizing reference to the world's elements was characteristic of numerous Diaspora Jews of Paul's time. And the following observation leads to the same conclusion regarding the Christian-Jewish missionaries who made their way into Paul's Galatian churches:

---

[21] See also Wisd 7:17; 19:18; 4 Macc 12:13; *1 Enoch* 80:7. Disdain of those who revere the elements as quasi-deities is not an exclusively Jewish motif. Delling mentions as an example Menander's mocking of those who divinize the elements ('*stoichieion*,' 677).

[22] The claim that no pre-Pauline text includes the stars among the elements can be literally maintained even in the face of Wisdom 13, for the term *stoicheia* does not occur there. It seems clear, however, that in this text the author expands his other references to the elements (7:17; 19:18) to include the stars and, more broadly speaking, the luminaries of heaven. That the heavenly bodies created on the fourth day mark the holy times is said, for example in *Jub.* 2:8–10 (cf. *1 Enoch* 82:9). One notes also that Philo speaks of the four physical elements as the material out of which God created both *kosmos* and *ouranos*, four also being the number of the seasons determined by the stars (*de Op. Mundi* 52). See also Sirach, who relates the distinguishing of holy times to the elemental polarity set in the cosmos by God (Sir 33:7–9, 14–15). On the great spring festival of Attis, March 15–27, see Vermaseren, *Cybele*, 113–123, and H. Koester, *Hellenistic Age*, 192–194.

[23] Cf. Georgi, 'Weisheit Salomonos.'

(2) Some Jewish apologists formulated this teleological argument by referring to Abraham's understanding of the elements. Two examples will suffice:

Philo, recalling that Abraham was reared in the religion of the Chaldeans, speaks of the patriarch's ladder-like journey to the perception of the true God, doing so in a way quite similar to that portrayed in Wisdom 13:

> The Chaldeans were especially active in the elaboration of astrology and ascribed everything to the movements of the stars . . . Thus they glorified visible existence, leaving out of consideration the intelligible and invisible . . . They concluded that the world itself was God, thus profanely likening the created to the Creator. In this creed Abraham had been reared, and for a long time remained a Chaldean. Then opening the soul's eye as though after profound sleep, and beginning to see the pure beam instead of the deep darkness, he followed the ray and discerned what he had not beheld before, a charioteer and pilot presiding over the world and directing in safety his own work . . . (*de Abr.* 69–70)[24]

And Josephus speaks in a similar way of Abraham's teleological journey from polytheism to monotheism:

> . . . he (Abraham) began to have more lofty conceptions of virtue than the rest of mankind, and determined to reform and change the ideas universally current concerning God. He was thus the first boldly to declare that God, the creator of the universe, is one, and that, if any other being contributed aught to man's welfare, each did so by His command and not by virtue of its own inherent power. This he inferred from the changes to which earth and sea are subject, from the course of sun and moon, and from all the celestial phenomena; for, he argued, were these bodies endowed with power, they would have provided for their own regularity, but since they lacked this last, it was manifest that even those services in which they cooperate for our greater benefit they render not in virtue of their own authority, but through the might of their commanding sovereign, to whom alone it is right to render our homage and thanksgiving. (*Ant.* 1.155–156)[25]

Bearing in mind the weighty role played by Abraham in the Teachers' Gentile mission, we may make several suggestions with some degree of plausibility:

[24] Cf. Goodenough, *Light*, 137 n. 87; W. L. Knox, 'Abraham.'
[25] Cf. Feldman, 'Abraham.'

The Teachers are almost certain to have shared the Jewish view of Gentiles as people who ignorantly worship the visible parts of creation, and they may have spoken in this connection of the Gentile tendency to confuse the elements with God (cf. Wisd 13 and Gal 4:8). It is not difficult to imagine their saying to the Galatians themselves:

> The presence of idols in the temples of your former religion shows that you Gentiles ignorantly reverenced the elements as though they were gods. More tragic still, Paul did nothing really to terminate your ill-informed relation to the elements. It is true that, like other peoples, you were always aware of the role of the astral elements in signaling the seasons you celebrated as holy. You did not know, however, the true calendar established by God, and Paul did not convey it to you. In truth the stars are nothing other than servants of the God of Israel who made them and who gave them a role in relation to his holy Law. As servants of this God, the elements shift the seasons in order to fix the correct times for the true feasts, those ordained by him.

The Teachers will not have spoken in this vein, however, simply in order to charge their Gentile hearers with ignorance. If they referred to the elements, they will probably have spoken of them in an evangelistic way:

> You are to ascend from the foolish and idolatrous worship of the elements themselves to the knowledge of the true God who created them, celebrating the holy times ordained by him in his Law, and doing so at the junctures fixed by the activity of his servants, the astral elements.

Will they have offered the Gentiles a paradigm of this crucial ascent? In chapter 1 above we have seen grounds for thinking that the Teachers made extensive use of traditions that present Abraham as the first Gentile to come to the true knowledge of God, being thus the paradigmatic proselyte. Here, then, we can add the possibility that, in presenting this picture of Abraham, they will not have overlooked the traditions in which the patriarch is said to have made the journey to the knowledge of God by an astrological contemplation of the elements, being the first to observe the holy feasts at the correct times (e.g. *Jubilees* 16).

Thus, it may have been as part of the Galatians' new understanding of the season-causing elements that they took up the calendrical observances laid out by the Teachers. That is one reading of the connection Paul draws between two of his charges: the Galatians, he says, are (re-)turning to the worship of the elements (4:9), and they are taking up from the Teachers the observance of holy times (4:10). One might hazard an imaginary encapsulation of one paragraph in the Teachers' message:

> In making the ascent from the pagan contemplation of the elements to the true knowledge of God, you follow in the steps of Abraham, for he did the same. You become, indeed, Abraham's true, Law-observant descendants, knowing for the first time why the constantly changing elements cause the turning of the seasons. As servants of God, they do that to enable us to observe at the correct time the holy feasts ordained by God. (Gal 4:10)[26]

The Galatians Listen to Paul's Letter

If the suggestions offered above are cogent, then in two regards Paul and the Teachers are in agreement: Both say – at least in effect – that in their former life the Galatians worshiped the elements as divinities. And both identify that worship as altogether foolish.

When, however, we take into account the whole of Paul's second reference to the elements, and when we combine it with the first, we see that Paul clearly parts ways with the Teachers. He does not for a moment entertain a form of ladder theology, encouraging Gentiles to acquire true knowledge of God by lifting their gaze from the elements to their maker.[27] More dramatically still, he refuses to speak of the elements from the Jewish point of view, finding in element worship a characteristic of *Gentiles*. On the contrary, he says that prior to Christ's advent all human beings revered the elements.[28] As we have noted earlier, Paul considers the elements of the cosmos somehow to include both the falsely deified idols of Gentile religion and the Law. Thus, the formerly Jewish members of the church (in Jerusalem, in Antioch, etc.) – no less than the formerly Gentile ones (in Galatia) – were once enslaved to those elements. It follows, as we have seen, that, if formerly Gentile members *turn* to the Law, they in fact *return* to the enslaving worship of the falsely deified elements (4:9–10). One hardly needs to say that vis-à-vis the theology of the

---

[26] The Galatians' attraction to the ladder theology basic to the journey from contemplation of the elements to knowledge of God may be reflected in the irony employed by Paul in Gal 4:9.

[27] Contrast Rom 1:19–20.

[28] This point has been sensed by many interpreters, although most admit that it is difficult to explain. It is one of the major aspects of the *stoicheia* puzzle; see below.

Teachers these statements of Paul constitute strong and explicitly polemical medicine.

It is clear, to be sure, that Paul cannot intend to refer to Jewish Christians (and by implication to Jews) as persons who in the past literally worshiped idols, images they held incorrectly to be gods (note again the change to 'you [Galatians]' in 4:8–9; cf. Rom 2:22). Nor can he mean that Gentile Christians, in their former life, literally observed and were enslaved by the Law (cf. Rom 2:14–16, 26–27).[29] That he speaks of universal enslavement is, however, unmistakable; and this point will have been in itself enough to incite outrage on the part of the Teachers and their followers in the Galatian churches. Joining one of the Galatian congregations again, we can imagine hearing the Teachers' retort:

> Paul is suggesting that prior to the advent of God's Messiah the world was a monolith of enslavement to the elements. He is saying that Jews no less than Gentiles were held in bondage to them, indeed that the holy and just and good Law of God *is* one of these enslaving elements! Such talk is outrageous. *We* have never considered the elements to be gods; we know that the Law of God is not one of them; and being Abraham's seed, we ourselves have never been enslaved to anyone (cf. John 8:33).

We can also imagine that Paul anticipated such outrage. Not at all easy to understand is his expectation that his inclusion of the Law among the enslaving elements of the cosmos would prove even momentarily worthy of consideration when his letter was read aloud to the Galatians. This expectation is, in fact, one of the persistent puzzles of the letter.[30] Can it be made less puzzling?

An answer may lie in our noting again that Paul does not speak merely of the elements, but specifically in Gal 4:3 of the elements *of the cosmos*. It is, to be sure, a traditional way of referring to the elements of nature.[31] This expression may provide, however, a clue to the character of Paul's startling universalism, provided we allow it to pose a simple

---

[29] Correctly recognizing this point, Blinzler unfortunately flees from Galatians to Romans, concluding that by the elements of the cosmos Paul meant flesh, sin, and death ('Lexikalisches,' 442–443).

[30] Vielhauer is more right than wrong to say that Paul includes the Law among the enslaving elements 'in order to place the non-Jew and the Jew on the same level' ('Stoicheiadienst,' 553). We are left, however, with the puzzle mentioned in the text.

[31] Aristotle, for example, can use as an equivalent the expression *stoicheia tēs physeōs* (*Metaphysics* 986b), and Philo follows suit (*de Vita Mos.* 2.251). Cf. Blinzler, 'Lexikalisches,' 440–441.

question: *Of what cosmos*, specifically, were these enslaving elements the fundamental parts?

1. The Cosmos of Which Paul Speaks

We note first that Paul employs the word 'cosmos' at only one other point in the letter:

> . . . the cross of our Lord Jesus Christ, by which the cosmos was crucified to me and I to the cosmos. For neither is circumcision anything nor is uncircumcision anything; what is something is the new creation (6:14–15).[32]

In chapter 7 above we have noted Paul's assertion that the *cosmos* from which Christ's cross has separated him consisted of *pairs of opposites*. What is gone with the crucifixion of the cosmos is not simply circumcision, but rather both circumcision and uncircumcision, and thus the distinction of Jew from Gentile. Or, to take the matter to its root, what has suffered eclipse is not simply the Law, but rather the cosmos that had at its foundation both the Law and the Not-Law.

Equally important for our present concern is the background of this affirmation: In form it is a traditional way of referring to the totality of the cosmos, evident, for example, in Sirach:

> . . . all the works of the Most High are in pairs, one the opposite of the other. (Sir 33:15)

In this tradition the word 'cosmos' or its equivalent is intimately linked with pairs of opposites. It is obvious that in Gal 6:14–15 Paul shapes this tradition to his own theological concern, speaking of a *religious* pair of opposites so fundamental to life as to be called 'cosmos.' Given the identity of this pair, it is not difficult to see that its erasure brought about loss of cosmos for Paul, the Pharisee. But one sees also that Paul considers the erased cosmos to have been the cosmos of all human beings (Gal 3:26–28).

Do we have here, then, a clue to the puzzle posed by Gal 4:3, 8–9? What cosmos was it whose elements enslaved human beings and whose hegemony has been terminated in Christ? Was it a cosmos composed of elements that were themselves pairs of opposites? Is there precedent for

---

[32] Comparison with Col 2:20 is revealing: 'If you died with Christ, parting from (*apo*) the elements of the world, why do you submit to rules as though you were living in (*en*) the world?' As DeMaris observes, this text connects the *stoicheia tou kosmou* with *cosmos*: '. . . both terms seem to denote a sphere of existence . . . that one can part *from* or live *in*' (*Controversy*, 59).

linking pairs of opposites not only to the word 'cosmos' (so Gal 6:14–15) but also to the term 'elements' (Gal 4:3, 8–9), and thus to 'the elements of the cosmos?' These prove to be significant questions, because they point to an area in which we do in fact have information.

2. The Elements of That Cosmos

Among the widely varied speculations about the elements of the cosmos, a significant number compare the traditional four elements with one another; and, being compared, the elements are then arranged in pairs of opposites (in Greek often called *t'anantia*). This is, in fact, an ancient way of speaking not only of the cosmos, but also explicitly of its elements, not least when one wishes to refer to the elements' effects on (and in) human beings.[33] In Paul's own time, Philo draws on Pythagorean tradition in order to develop the pattern at some length. Dealing with God's act of creation, he speaks of the division of the elements of the cosmos into equal parts, referring to the elements themselves as pairs of opposites.[34] Philo arranges the columns of element-opposites in various ways, each involving the traditional four elements:

the rare			*the dense*		
air	versus		earth		
fire	versus		water		

the light			*the heavy*		
cold	versus	hot	wet	versus	dry
air	versus	fire	water	versus	earth.[35]

---

[33] The notion of opposition among the elements (sometimes *stoicheia* sometimes *archai*) can be seen as early as Anaximander, Heraclitus, and Empedocles. A particularly clear exposition is given by Aristotle; see, e.g. *Metaphysics* 986b, where, having cited the Pythagorean tradition of the opposites, he continues his account by the summarizing remark: *t'anantia archai tōn ontōn* ('the opposites are the first principles of what exists'), an affirmation in which, as is often the case, *ta stoicheia* are represented by a synonym, *archai* (cf. also *merē*). Aristotle is a clear witness, therefore, for the continuation of the ancient tradition in which the elements are the opposites (*ta stoicheia* = *t'anantia*); cf. also 1005a, *panta gar ē enantia ē ex enantiōn* ('for all things are either opposites or are derived from opposites').

[34] *Heres* 134–135; 146. Cf. *Heres* 207: 'Having taught us the lesson of equal division, the Scripture leads us on to the knowledge of opposites (*tēn tōn enantiōn epistēmēn*), by telling us that "He placed the sections facing opposite each other" (Gen xv.10). For in truth we may take it that everything in the world is by nature opposite to something else' (cf. the citations from Aristotle given above). Cf. also Philo *de Deo* 107–149 (Siegert, *Philon*, 29–31).

[35] Philo speaks of three matters that are intimately interrelated and that are pertinent to our interpretation of Gal 4:3, 8–9: the elements, the pairs of opposites, and the seasons, and thus times of special celebration.

Thus from Philo – and from other authors as well – we see the tradition in which the elements *are* the pairs of opposites that constitute the foundation of the cosmos (*ta stoicheia* = *t'anantia*). A number of thinkers close to Paul's time, including both Sirach and the author of Wisdom, would have readily agreed with the traditional statement: The elements of the cosmos *are* pairs of opposites.

When, now, we bring together two points in Galatians at which Paul speaks of the old cosmos – 6:14–15 and 3:28 – we can see that, in his own way, he has in mind precisely this tradition. In writing Gal 6:14–15, Paul expects the Galatians to understand his testimony: the cross of Christ separated him from a *cosmos* that consisted of a pair of opposites, circumcision and uncircumcision. This declaration of the end of a cosmos leads us back to 3:28, where the same pair – Jew and Greek (Gentile) – introduces the baptismal tradition focused on pairs of opposites that have disappeared. For those who are incorporated into Christ, there is no Jew and Gentile. Moreover, the baptismal formula is broader than the affirmation of 6:14–15, including the social pair of slave and free, and the creational pair of male and female.[36] Thus, a Christian baptizand acquainted with a traditional list of oppositional pairs – in whatever form – would have recognized in the baptizer's words a list of the oppositional *elements* that have now found their terminus in Christ, and thus a declaration of the end of the cosmos that was constituted by those elements.

Moreover, the formula of Gal 3:28 – with its announcement of liberation from enslaving pairs of element-opposites – constitutes a key part of the context in which, in 4:3–5, Paul explicitly speaks of liberation from the enslaving elements of the cosmos. It is, then, a reasonable hypothesis that, when he speaks in 4:3, 9 of the elements of that cosmos, Paul himself has in mind not earth, air, fire, and water, but rather the elemental pairs of opposites listed in 3:28, emphatically the first pair, Jew and Gentile, and thus the Law and the Not-Law.

To be sure, I have suggested above that, prior to hearing Paul's letter, the Galatians will have connected the expression *ta stoicheia tou kosmou* with the traditional earth/air and fire/water, the stars being

---

[36] Both of these additional pairs figure in the tradition ascribed variously to Thales, Socrates, Plato, and the later Rabbi Judah. More important is the fact that male and female stand both in the text of Gen 1:27 and in the Pythagorean list of the elemental pairs of opposites. See Aristotle *Metaphysics* 986a, where the fifth pair in the Pythagorean list is *arren* [*arsen*] *thēly*.

added. Can Paul expect them suddenly to make this shift with him, sensing a reference to the elements of religious polarity? Here, as elsewhere in this extraordinarily dense letter, Paul apparently assumes that the Galatian congregations will listen to the whole of the epistle several times and with extreme care. He takes for granted, that is, not only great perspicacity, but also considerable patience. In regard to what he calls the elements of the old cosmos, he seems to think that the baptismal reference to the termination of pairs of opposites (3:28), coupled with his climactic reference to the death of the cosmos made up of the first of those pairs (6:14–15) will alert the Galatians to his intention in 4:3, 9. From those other passages, then, one finds a reasonable reading of Paul's line of thought in 4:3, 9:

Having accented the baptismal confession of 3:28, with its reference to the dissolution in Christ of certain pairs of opposites,

Jew / Gentile
slave / free
male / female,

Paul takes for granted the widespread tradition in which pairs of opposites are themselves identified as 'the elements of the cosmos.' Thus, in 4:3 he uses that expression itself to refer to the pairs of opposites that are passé, noting indeed that these oppositional elements had in fact enslaved all human beings prior to Christ.[37] And just as he has said that the opposition of the Law to the Not-Law affected the whole of humanity, thus being a true element of the cosmos (4:3), so he can finally say that for the Not-Law Galatians to turn to the Law – distinguishing holy times from profane ones by careful observation of what they identify as the astral elements – is for them to return to the old cosmos of the Law/the Not-Law (4:9–10).

Heard in this way, Gal 6:14–15; 3:28; and 4:3, 8–9 constitute a typical instance of Paul's transformation of language.[38] In a word, Paul employs the ancient equation of the world's elements with archaic pairs of opposites to interpret the *religious* impact of Christ's advent. Following the baptismal formula, he applies that tradition not to the sensible elements, but rather to the elements of religious distinction.

[37] By juxtaposing Gal 3:28 and 4:3 Paul instructs the Galatians as to the identity of the oppositional elements. Cf. Philo's concern that people be led to knowledge of the opposites: *tēn tōn enantiōn epistēmēn* (*Heres* 207; cf. Wisd 7:17).

[38] Note, e.g., Paul's eschatological interpretation of Stoic maxims in Gal 6:2–10.

These are the cosmic elements that have found their termination in Christ. Specifically, the cosmos that was crucified on the cross is the cosmos that was founded on the distinction between Jew and Gentile, between sacred and profane, between the Law and the Not-Law. When we contemplate the identity of this crucified cosmos, it is not difficult to see how its departure could lead a Pharisee to speak emphatically and climactically of his own death (Gal 6:14).[39]

---

[39] What the death of that cosmos means for the role of the Law in the daily life of the church is a matter addressed in chapters 14 and 15 below.

9

God's Way of Making Right What Is Wrong

Gal 2:16 is one of the most tightly concentrated theological statements in all of Paul's letters. It is also the earliest of his references to rectification (*dikaioō*; *dikaiosynē*), and thus the text in which we are privileged to see this crucial element of his theology taking shape.[1] We can begin with a somewhat paraphrastic translation, grounds for which will emerge as we proceed:

Galatians 2:16

As Jewish Christians, we ourselves know that a person[2] is not rectified by observance of the Law, but rather by the faith of Christ Jesus. Thus, even we have placed our trust in Christ Jesus, in order that the source of our rectification might be the faith of Christ and not observance of the Law; for not a single person will be rectified by observance of the Law.

As the initial clause indicates, Paul says that he is citing a tradition about rectification that he shares with all Jewish Christians, including the Teachers. We cannot say precisely where the tradition ends and Paul's situational interpretation begins. Indeed one suspects that the sentence is not the sort that recommends such a literary exercise.[3] Still, the

---

[1]   Reasons for translating the Greek terms with the expressions 'to rectify' and 'rectification' are given in Martyn, *Galatians*, note on 2:16.

[2]   Lit. 'a human being.' The identity of this *anthrōpos* is a matter of great import. In the underlying Jewish-Christian tradition, it is the Israelite. In Paul's interpretation, the term refers to all human beings. In neither view, then, is it the Gentile, distinguished from the Jew, *pace* Gager, *Origins*, 233, who follows the suggestions of Gaston, *Torah*, passim, and M. Barth, *Ephesians*, 246.

[3]   Dunn has argued, to be sure, that such a literary division can be made ('New Perspective,' 111–113). Taking *ean mē* in 2:16a to mean 'except,' he suggested that that part of the verse is Jewish-Christian tradition: '. . . one is not rectified by works of the Law except [unless] those works be accompanied by faith in Christ Jesus.' In 2:16b, Dunn continues, Paul 'pushes what began as a Jewish-Christian] qualification on covenantal nomism into an outright [Pauline] antithesis' (113). It is an interesting suggestion, but one that falters, I think, on three grounds. (1) We can be almost certain that *ean mē* is to be taken here with its adversative force, 'but rather' (see Räisänen, 'Galatians 2.16'; Eckstein, *Verheissung*, 21). (2) Exploring the huge realm of possibility,

interpreter does well to begin by taking Paul at his word. It is as though – building on an earlier remark directed to Peter – Paul had said to the Teachers:

> You and I share a Jewish-Christian tradition about rectification. I cite this shared tradition, precisely in order to show that you are currently misleading my Galatian churches, by straying from convictions to which you yourselves feign allegiance!

A Jewish-Christian Tradition About Rectification

Is Paul referring to a Jewish-Christian rectification tradition to which we have access, which we know Paul to have known, and which is sufficiently well-formed to enable us to compare it with Paul's reading of it? In fact his own letters present us with several snippets of such a tradition, and three of those snippets prove to be of considerable importance, Rom 3:25; 4:25; 1 Cor 6:11:[4]

Romans 3:25 (plus 26a)

... Christ Jesus, whom God put forward as a sacrifice of atonement by his blood. God did this to demonstrate the power of his rectitude; in his divine forbearance, that is to say, he has forgiven the sins previously committed ...

Romans 4:25

... Jesus our Lord ... who was handed over to death for our trespasses and was raised for our rectification.

---

one might indeed entertain the thought that, on occasion, some Jewish Christians told their Jewish neighbors they would not be justified by keeping the Law unless they added faith in Christ. In fact, however, Dunn cites no Jewish-Christian tradition to support such an hypothesis, and support from data external to Gal 2:16 itself is exactly what is needed. (3) Finally, the Jewish-Christian rectification tradition known to Paul never refers to a circumstance in which rectification does *not* occur (Matt 5:20 is another matter). See below the discussion of Rom 3:25; Rom 4:25; 1 Cor 6:11, none of which contains a negative. We conclude that Paul is responsible for all of the negatives in Gal 2:16 (drawing the third from Ps 142:2).

[4] On pre-Pauline, Christian rectification traditions see Stuhlmacher, *Gerechtigkeit*, 185–188; Kertelge, *Rechtfertigung*, 45–62; 242–245; several articles in J. Friedrich, et al. (eds), *Rechtfertigung*: Hahn, 'Taufe' (104–117); Lührmann, 'Christologie' (359); Strecker, 'Befreiung' (501–505). See also Reumann (with responses by Fitzmyer and Quinn), *Righteousness*, 27–40; Schnelle, *Gerechtigkeit*; Hays, 'Justification.' I leave aside formulas lying outside the letters of Paul. It is impossible to know the relative ages of the three formulas cited below. We can say only that they are of Jewish-Christian origin; the application of the formula in 1 Cor 6:11 to Gentiles (fornicators, idolaters, etc.) is a secondary move on Paul's part.

1 Corinthians 6:11

And this is what some of you used to be [fornicators, idolaters . . . thieves . . . drunkards . . . robbers; v. 9]. But you were washed, you were sanctified, you were rectified in the name of the Lord Jesus Christ and in the Spirit of our God.[5]

While these Jewish-Christian formulas show variations, a picture of considerable coherence does emerge from them.

1. Rectification is an act of God

Drawing heavily on traditions in the Old Testament and on strands of Jewish thinking about rectification, the Jewish Christians who worded these formulas speak about an act of God.[6] There are rich traditions, to be sure, having to do with human deeds of rectitude (e.g. Tobit 4:5–6; Wisd 2:12). The makers of these formulas do not draw on those traditions. They speak about God's action (cf. Judg 5:11; Isa 46:13).

2. In that act God sets right things that have gone wrong

In accordance with the causative force of the *hiphil* of the Hebrew verb *ṣadeq* (clearly reflected also in Jewish traditions expressed in Greek), the authors of the Jewish-Christian formulas speak of an action by which God changes the human scene, creating integrity where things had gone wrong.

3. What has made things wrong is transgressions against God's covenant committed among God's people

Here we have a point that requires emphasis. The human scene envisaged in these Jewish-Christian formulas is that of the Jewish nation, and in that scene the need of rectification has arisen from the fact that members of God's people have transgressed commandments explicitly issued to them by God, thus proving unfaithful to God's gracious covenant.[7]

---

[5] On the texts in Romans, see particularly the commentaries of Käsemann, Wilckens, Meyer, and Dunn. Dahl has argued that Rom 3:25 and 4:25, along with Rom 8:32 and Gal 3:13–14, reflect the use of Akedah traditions by Jewish-Christians ('Atonement'). This hypothesis may have some force in the case of Rom 8:32, but it is of dubious pertinence to the other passages.

[6] Did the formula cited by Paul in Rom 3:25 contain the phrase *dia pisteōs* (NRSV 'effective through faith')? If so, then like the rest of the formula it must have referred to God's rectifying act as *his* active faithfulness to the covenant. See note 14 below.

[7] The covenantal theology of the formula cited in Rom 3:25 is noted by numerous interpreters, the pathbreaking work being that of Pluta, *Bundestreue*. See also Käsemann, *Romans*, 100.

4. What makes transgressing members of God's people right is God's forgiveness

Given Israel's sins, the need is for divine acquittal, forgiveness, remission of sins, and cleansing, so that the covenant can be unburdened and a new life begun.[8] Rectification is now accomplished, however, not by a sacrifice executed by a human being (such as the high priest acting on the Day of Atonement), but rather by Christ's death. And in this Jewish-Christian tradition, that death is understood to have been God's sacrificial act taken at his initiative. It is the deed in which God has forgiven the sins formerly committed in Israel, wiping the slate clean (Rom 3:25).[9]

5. God's rectification is therefore God's mercy

This definition is one of the points at which the Jewish-Christian formulas are similar to passages in the Qumran scrolls.[10] The formula of 1 Cor 6:11, for example, can be profitably compared with several Qumran texts:

1 Corinthians 6:11

[There was guilt as the result of many sins] but you have been washed, you have been sanctified, you have been rectified in the name of the Lord Jesus Christ . . .

1QS 11:13–15

He will draw me near by his grace, and by his mercy will he bring my rectification. He will judge me in the rectitude of his truth, and in the greatness of his goodness he will pardon all my sins. Through his rectitude he will cleanse me of the uncleanness of man, and of the sins of the children of men, that I may confess to God his rectitude. (Vermes, altered)

---

[8] This is a juncture at which the thesis of Thielman may be taken into account (*From Plight to Solution*), for that thesis may have some pertinence to the Jewish-Christian authors of the rectification formulas. *They* may have worked to some degree from plight to solution, though the terms would be better put by speaking of sin and salvation. In any case, Thielman's thesis is unconvincing as regards *Paul*. It is a matter in connection with which one recalls that K. Barth was an exegete as well as a systematic theologian; for over a considerable period of time he correctly emphasized that Paul saw Adam in the light of Christ, sin in the light of grace, and so on. Note, for example, the comments, '. . . it is only by grace that the lack of grace can be recognized as such' (*Church Dogmatics*, II.2, 92); '. . . the doctrine of election . . . defines grace as the starting-point for all reflection and utterance . . .' (93). In recent decades, Barth's point has been emphasized in a certain way by E. P. Sanders, *Palestinian Judaism*, 442–447.

[9] Cf. Breytenbach, 'Versöhnung,' 78; Hamerton-Kelly, *Violence*, 142.

[10] See O. Betz, 'Qumran;' E. P. Sanders, *Palestinian Judaism*, 305–312.

1QH 4:34–37

When I thought of my guilty deeds . . . I said 'In my sins I am lost . . .'
But then, when I remembered the strength of your hand and the fullness
of your mercy, I rose again and stood upright . . . for you will pardon
iniquity and you will purify man of sin through your rectification (Vermes,
altered).[11]

1QS 11:12

As for me, if I stumble, the mercies of God shall be my eternal salvation. If
I stagger because of the sin of flesh, my rectification shall be by the rectitude
of God which endures forever. (Vermes, altered)

The last passage is of particular importance because it places in parallel
God's mercy and God's rectification. The Jewish-Christian formulas do
something similar, equating rectification with God's forgiving initiative
in cleansing one from sins. They thus stand in a long and impressive
line of tradition: God's deed of rectification is God's merciful forgiveness
of transgressions for which atonement has been made (cf., e.g. *Pss. Sol.*
3:3–12).

6. *The Law is not mentioned because its continuing validity is taken for granted*

The ways in which the Jewish-Christian formulas draw on Old
Testament traditions, and the fact that they were made by Christians
who were distinctly Jewish, tell us that the transgressions referred to
were identified as transgressions on the basis of the Law.[12] Moreover,
while it may seem obvious, we must reiterate that, for the Jewish-
Christian authors, the God who has now enacted his rectifying
forgiveness is the God of Israel, the God of the covenant, the author of
the Law. By enacting his rectifying forgiveness in the death and
resurrection of Christ, God has established his right over his people
Israel, thus restoring the integrity of the nomistic covenant.

---

[11] On the understanding of sin in Qumran see Becker, *Heil*, 144–148, and the critique of Becker's work in E. P. Sanders, *Palestinian Judaism*, 272–284.

[12] In 'Types,' R. E. Brown has made some suggestions that are helpful for the identification of churches outside of Palestine. The church of Jerusalem was, however, another matter; and the same is true of the churches in Judea that were children of 'the gospel to those who are circumcised' (Gal 1:22; 2:7, 9). In their own eyes, all of these churches were thoroughly observant, Jewish-Christian communities, and the formulas we are discussing seem clearly to have been authored in them.

There is, therefore, no thought that God's rectification removes one from the realm of God's Law.[13] The three rectification formulas do not mention the Law either positively or negatively, because taking the Law for granted, they express the *novum*: God's gracious and rectifying forgiveness of sins in Christ.

7. God has accomplished his rectifying forgiveness in Christ, specifically in Christ's death and resurrection

Just as the formulas' silence about the Law shows that the Law's continuance is taken for granted, so that silence also indicates that rectification is not attributed to the Law (a point that will prove crucial to Paul). God has provided his rectifying forgiveness by acting in the atoning blood sacrifice that is Christ's death (Rom 3:25), or in the event of Christ's resurrection (Rom 4:25). And that accomplishment of God is made real for those who are being baptized, when the name of the Lord Jesus is pronounced over them and the Spirit of Christ descends

---

[13] The thought of being removed from the realm of the Law would have horrified both the Qumran covenantors and the Jewish-Christian authors of the three rectification formulas. The God whom the Qumran psalmist praises because he will 'pardon iniquity and purify from sin by . . . [his] . . . rectification' (1QH 4:37) is the God who has engraved his Law on the psalmist's heart (1QH 4:10). Similarly, for Jewish-Christians the God who has graciously rectified Israelite sinners in the sacrificial death of his Son is the one who graciously gave the Law, engraving it forever on the hearts of his people. At this point one may pause in order to ask an important question about the assumption that God's rectification is an act taken by him in the context of the Law. Does this assumption mean that the authors of the Jewish-Christian formulas fail to present God's rectifying deed in Christ as an act of grace? By no means! Like the Qumran covenantors (and other Jewish sages who deal with the subject of rectification) these Jewish Christians celebrate a new instance of God's grace in the undisturbed context of God's gracious Law. Just as the covenantors could throw themselves on the merciful rectification of God, without dreaming of abandoning God's Law, so the authors of the traditions preserved in 1 Cor 6:11, Rom 3:25, and Rom 4:25, celebrate rectification in Christ without contemplating the possibility that that deed of God might stand in tension with God's giving of the Law, or with their observance of it. Modern Christian interpreters sometimes say of Qumran that strict adherence to the Law spoils the confession of hope solely directed to God's rectification, turning it into something other than true *sola gratia*. But that is a reading forgetful of the fact that Qumran exemplifies the way in which Israel traditionally put together the deepest belief in God's mercy and the strictest observance of God's Law (cf. E. P. Sanders, *Palestinian Judaism*, 292). In a word, the covenantors do not move *away from* the confession of God's gracious rectification *to* the demand for punctilious observance of the Law, thus allowing the latter to 'spoil' the former. On the contrary, they are representative Jews in holding the two together: observance of the Law and confession of God's mercy. *Mutatis mutandis* the Jewish-Christians from whom Paul inherited 1 Cor 6:11, Rom 3:25, and Rom 4:25 did essentially the same.

on them (1 Cor 6:11). Thus the Jewish-Christians responsible for these formulas see an indelible connection – even an identity – between God's deed of rectification and God's deed in Christ.

8. *In these formulas one finds, then, God's messianic grace in the context of God's Law*

For that reason, the authors of these formulas would have found a polemic against rectification by Law observance entirely beside the point. They were making no such claim. Indeed, the Jewish-Christian tradition about rectification is a stranger to polemics. It seems to have been formulated in Jewish-Christian churches largely free of internal strife.

9. *God's rectifying forgiveness in Christ is confessed without explicit reference to faith*

Just as the formulas make no reference to the Law, so they do not mention faith, either on the part of members of the Jewish-Christian communities or on the part of Jesus Christ.[14] There is, therefore, no hint of a polemical antinomy that would place opposite one another Christ's faithful deed in our behalf and our observance of the Law.

In these nine points we have, with a reasonable degree of probability, the major outlines of a Jewish-Christian rectification tradition that antedated both Paul and the Teachers, a tradition that was shared by both of them, indeed a tradition that both claimed to revere. Can we speak with some confidence about the ways in which the Teachers and Paul interpreted this shared tradition?

The Teachers' Interpretation of This Jewish-Christian Tradition

Here two points are of major importance. First, we can be confident that the Teachers find in the tradition what we have seen actually to be there: the affirmation of God's forgiveness of Israel's sins in the sacrificial death of his Messiah. For the Teachers, as for the Jewish-Christian

---

[14] The question whether the phrase *dia pisteōs* (NRSV: 'effective through faith') was included in the pre-Pauline formula of Rom 3:25 is an issue much discussed and unlikely ever to be settled to the satisfaction of all interpreters. In any case, if *dia pisteōs* is to be taken as part of the Jewish-Christian tradition, Pluta's argument in *Bundestreue* stands: That phrase referred, *as did the formula as a whole*, to God's trustworthy deed in Christ, his rectifying act of faithfulness to his covenantal people. In that tradition it meant neither Jesus' faith nor faith on the part of the human being.

authors of the tradition, Jesus' death is the totally adequate sacrifice made by God himself, the sacrifice in which God accomplished the forgiveness of sins for Israel, the people among whom observance of the Law was and is taken for granted.

Second, however, as missionaries to Gentiles, the Teachers hear the Jewish-Christian tradition in a new context in which observance of the Law is not – and cannot be – taken for granted. And because they carry out their mission by inviting Gentiles to *enter* the people of Israel, they necessarily posit an explicit relation between rectification and observance of the Law. Where the Jewish-Christian tradition affirmed God's deed in Christ for an Israel in which Law-observance was taken for granted, the Teachers understand God's act of forgiveness in Christ to be God's gracious deed for Israel, *including* all Gentiles who *transfer* from their pagan existence into God's Law-observant people. That rectifying transfer, then, clearly requires that Gentiles take up observance of the Law.

Paul's Reading of the Tradition in Light of Developments in Galatia

Paul's interpretation of this Jewish-Christian rectification tradition is more complex, involving seven crucial points.[15]

(1) The Teachers' use of the Jewish-Christian tradition does not cause Paul to give it up. Nor does he provide the slightest hint that he disagrees with the tradition itself. Precisely the contrary; he calls the Jewish-Christian rectification tradition down on the heads of the Teachers. The way in which he does that proves to be of considerable interest.

(2) As he writes to his Galatian churches, the setting in which Paul hears this Jewish-Christian tradition is both similar to and fundamentally different from the setting in which the Teachers hear it. On the one hand, since both Paul and the Teachers are active in missions to Gentiles, like the Teachers Paul necessarily hears the tradition in that new context.

On the other hand, however, even that context is quite different for Paul. In stark contrast to the Teachers, Paul perceives every day that in his Gentile mission-field God is creating churches – actively beginning

---

[15] See again the works on justification/rectification by Stuhlmacher, Kertelge, Reumann, and Hays cited in note 4 above.

to make things right in the whole of the world – *apart from* observance of the Law. It is easy to see, then, that Paul does not hear a rectification tradition that speaks about the Israelite, the Jew, the transgressor of God's covenantal Law who, because of his transgression, stands in need of forgiveness. Nor does Paul hear a tradition pertinent to Gentiles who can be rectified by becoming members of God's people via Law observance. As we have noted, Paul hears a tradition that speaks to and about *anthrōpos*, the human being, both Jew and Gentile, without any distinction between the two (cf. Gal 2:16a and 3:28). Exactly how can he hear the tradition in this way?

(3) He notes in the Jewish-Christian rectification tradition a striking instance of *silence*. As we have seen, the tradition, referring emphatically to God's deed of rectification, does not even mention the Law. Specifically, it does not attribute rectification to observance of the Law. In the light of God's work as Paul observes it in his own mission, he sees, then, that the tradition's silence about the Law is no mystery. Indeed, in this silence he senses not only that the tradition itself is speaking generically about the human being; he senses also that it is saying, 'the human being is not rectified by observance of the Law.'

(4) Silent with regard to the Law, this Jewish-Christian tradition is eloquent with regard to Christ; and Paul is as sensitive to the eloquence as he is to the silence. For, given his theological anger at the Teachers' work in his Galatian churches, Paul hears the tradition's nomistic silence and its christological eloquence in a new way. He now hears God's voice formulating a new antinomy that links the verb 'to be rectified' both to a negative statement and to a positive one: The human being

is not rectified by	but rather by
observance of the Law	*pistis Christou Iesou*

And, to formulate the positive member of this gospel antinomy Paul coins an eloquent expression of his own, *pistis Christou*.

(5) Recent decades have seen an extended and vigorous debate as to the force of this expression, some interpreters taking it to mean human faith in Christ (a construction they usually call an objective genitive), some finding a reference to the faith of Christ (usually termed subjective, but best identified, somewhat loosely, as an authorial

genitive).[16] Supplementing arguments of Hays and others, one can mention two observations that tilt the balance decisively in favor of rendering *pistis Christou* as 'the faith of Christ.'

(*a*) The Jewish-Christian rectification tradition on which Paul is drawing had spoken about an act that God carried out in Christ. If Paul is hearing that tradition anew, without violating it fundamentally, a simple conclusion is to be drawn: When he says that God has made things right by *pistis Christou Iesou*, he is referring to God's rectifying act *in Christ* (centrally in his death, which Paul always understands to be part of a holistic event including his resurrection). *Pistis Christou*, in short, arises in Paul's vocabulary as his way of reflecting the tradition's reference to *Christ's* role in God's deed of rectification.

(*b*) That interpretation is firmly supported by a comparison of Gal 2:16 with Gal 2:21. Gal 2:16 is the opening sentence in the first rectification passage in the letter, the final sentence of that passage being 2:21. Both are pithy references to God's deed of making things right, and both are antinomous in form:

2:16	2:21
. . . the human being is not rectified by observance of *the Law*, but rather by *pistis Christou Iesou* . . .	. . . if rectification were through *the Law*, then *Christ died* for no purpose at all.

---

[16] To trace this debate one will do well to begin with Kertelge, *Rechtfertigung*, 162–219, noting Haussleiter's move from subjective genitive to genitive of authorship (*Glaube*). From Kertelge, one can then make one's way to Howard's articles in HTR and *ExpTim*; to the items mentioned in the papers of Hays, 'What is at Stake?' and of Dunn, 'Once More;' to those papers themselves; to B. W. Longenecker, '*Pistis*;' and to D. A. Campbell, 'Romans 1:17.' As P. W. Meyer pointed out in remarks made at the meeting of the Society of Biblical Literature in 1991, the objective genitive, strictly defined, demands not only a verbal ruling noun, but also one whose cognate verb is transitive. The verb *pisteuō* is itself transitive only with the meaning 'to entrust' followed by two accusatives. In the case of *pistis Christou*, we may be well advised, then, to speak of a genitive of authorship or of origin. Everyone must agree that Paul sometimes speaks of the faith had by human beings; and in Gal 3:2 and 5 he identifies the generative source of that faith: the proclamation of Christ's death. From those references, then, and also from Gal 3:22–25, one could draw a conclusion not far from that of Haussleiter: 'Christ accomplishes faith, in that he communicates himself . . . And then he remains active behind our faith, so that the redeeming power of faith lies in the fact that the living Christ is both the one who originates it and the one who consistently carries it along' (cited from Kertelge, *Rechtfertigung*, 164 n. 18).

If beginning corresponds to end, then in 2:16, as in 2:21, Paul is referring to an opposition between rectification by Law observance and rectification by the deed of God in Christ. It follows that *pistis Christou* is an expression by which Paul speaks of Christ's atoning faithfulness, as, on the cross, he died faithfully for human beings while looking faithfully to God.

(6) The result of this interpretation of *pistis Christou* is crucial to an understanding not only of Galatians, but also of the whole of Paul's theology. God has set things right without laying down a prior condition of any sort. God's rectifying act, that is to say, is no more God's response to human faith in Christ than it is God's response to human observance of the Law. God's rectification is not God's response at all. It is the *first* move; it is God's initiative, carried out by him in Christ's faithful death.

The antinomy of Gal 2:16, then – observance of the Law versus the faith of Christ – is like all of the antinomies of the new creation: It does not set over against one another two human alternatives, to observe the Law or to have faith in Christ. The opposites are an act of God, Christ's faithful death, and an act of the human being, observance of the Law. The one has the power to rectify, to make things right; the other does not.

To be sure, as Paul will say in Gal 3:2, Christ's faithful death for us has the power to elicit faithful trust on our part. Thus in 2:16 itself he speaks *in the second instance* of our placing our trust in Christ:

> Thus even we have placed our trust in Christ Jesus, in order that the source of our rectification might be the faith of Christ and not observance of the Law.

The point is that the Christ in whom we faithfully place our trust is the Christ who has already faithfully died in our behalf (cf. Rom 5:8) and whose prevenient death for us is the powerful rectifying event that has elicited our faith.[17]

(7) Finally, there is the matter of indicating plainly what rectification is. Here one notes that Gal 2:16–21 is only the first of the rectification

---

[17] When we trust God, Paul would say, we signal that we ourselves have been invaded by God's presuppositionless grace, and we confess that the locus of God's invasion is *especially* our will! Far from presupposing freedom of the will (cf. Hos 5:4), Paul speaks of the freeing of the will for the glad service of God and neighbor. And that freeing of the will reflects one of Paul's major convictions: Our trust in God has been awakened, kindled by God's trust-worthy deed in Christ. See Schlier, *Galater*, who, in interpreting *akoē pisteōs* in Gal 3:2, speaks perceptively of 'revelation that kindles faith' (122).

passages in that letter. The second is Gal 3:6–4:7. Pondering the differences between the first rectification passage and the second (see further below), we see that, in the first, Paul provides his own arresting instance of silence. He uses the verb 'to be rectified' three times in 2:16, a fourth time in 2:17; and, as a fifth reference, he employs the noun 'rectification' in 2:21. Yet he speaks in this initial rectification passage only of the means or the source of rectification, giving not a hint as to what rectification itself might be. Why this silence?

It is surely intended for rhetorical effect. In his speech to the Teachers, Paul says nothing about the Jewish-Christian definition of rectification as forgiveness, in order to clear the deck for a new definition. And that new definition does in fact emerge in the second rectification passage, Gal 3:6–4:7.

To begin with, one notes the number of actors on the stage on which God's rectifying deed occurs. The Jewish-Christian tradition presents a drama in which there are three actors, sinful human beings, Christ, and the God of the covenant who has accomplished in the blood sacrifice of Christ the true forgiveness of human sins. Without expressing a polemic against this tradition, Paul does go well beyond it in Gal 3:6–4:7, presenting there a new definition of rectification that involves a crucial increase in the number of actors. That is to say, in 3:6–4:7 we find a drama in which there are four actors: human beings, Christ, God, *and anti-God powers*, the last of these actors being variously identified:

the Law that has the power to curse (3:10);

the Law as it pronounces its curse on the crucified Christ (3:13);

sin functioning as the prison warden over the whole of creation (3:22);

the elements of the cosmos that enslave both Jew and Gentile (4:3).[18]

With the appearance of these anti-God powers, the landscape is fundamentally changed, indicating what has really gone wrong and what is really involved in God's making it right in the whole of the cosmos.[19]

---

[18] Note that from Gal 3:10 to 4:5 Paul uses the expression *hypo tina einai*, 'to be under the power of someone or something,' no less than eight times, thus referring seriatim to anti-God powers that enslave all human beings. See Martyn, *Galatians*, Comment 39.

[19] In Galatians it is the movement from the first rectification passage to the second that confirms the major thesis of Käsemann: For Paul, God's rectification in Christ is 'the rightful *power* with which God makes his cause to *triumph* in the world that has fallen away from him . . .' ('Righteousness,' 180, emphasis added; cf. Zahl, *Rechtfertigungslehre*). The fact that the formulaic *dikaiosynē theou* does not appear in

The cosmic landscape now proves to be a *battlefield*, and in that setting the need of human beings is not so much forgiveness of their sins as deliverance from malignant powers that hold them in bondage.

The change to this battlefield is particularly impressive as regards the way in which Paul perceives the relation of Christ's death to the Law. To be sure, building on Jewish-Christian atonement tradition, Paul still says that Christ died 'for us' (Gal 3:13). But now Christ's death is seen to have happened in *collision* with the Law, and human beings are not said to need forgiveness, but rather deliverance from a genuine slavery that involves the Law. In this second rectification passage, the Law proves to be not so much a norm which we have transgressed – although transgressions are involved (Gal 3:19) – as a tyrant, insofar as it has placed us under the power of its curse. And by his death, Christ is not said to have accomplished our forgiveness, but rather our redemption from slavery. With the apocalyptic shift to a scene in which there are real powers arrayed against God, rectification acquires, then, a new synonym, *exagorazō*, 'to redeem by delivering from slavery' (Gal 3:13; 4:5).[20] And one of the powers from whose tyranny Christ has delivered us is the Law in its role as the pronouncer of a curse on the whole of humanity.

The shifts involved in moving from the first rectification passage (Gal 2:16–21) to the second (Gal 3:6–4:7) provide, then, a major clue not only to Paul's definition of rectification, but also to the genesis of his carefully formed thinking on this subject. For in Gal 3:6–4:7, no less than in the earlier passage, Paul is formulating a polemic against the Teachers' discourses on rectification. Specifically, he is circumscribing

Galatians is thus of no consequence. The view of God's rectification as God's deed of *power* is present in a multitude of texts, ranging from pre-apocalyptic traditions in ancient Israel to the Dead Sea Scrolls and beyond. Translators are correct, for example, to render *ṣidqot yahweh* in Judg 5:11 (the Song of Deborah) 'the triumphs of the Lord' (NRSV). In a word, the institution of the holy war is the deep soil in which cosmological apocalyptic took root in Israel.

20 Paul effects the same kind of shift at Gal 1:4b. Having quoted Jewish-Christian tradition in which Christ is said to have given his life 'for our sins' (1:4a), Paul changes the frame of reference to that of apocalyptic deliverance from the powerful grasp of the present evil age (*exeletai*). While he does not use in this shift the language of rectification, one can say that the theological integrity of Galatians warrants taking *exaireomai* ('to snatch from the grasp of') as yet another Pauline synonym for rectification. And when we are speaking of synonyms, we must at least mention two further ones: For Paul, God makes things right by bringing life where there was death (Gal 3:21: Rom 4:17) and by creating community where there was division (Gal 3:28; note *heis* ['one']).

'the forensic apocalyptic theology of the . . . Teachers with a cosmo-logical apocalyptic theology of his own.'[21] Rectification thus remains, for Paul, God's act in the death of Christ. But now, having taken silent leave of the Jewish-Christian concern with the forgiveness of nomistic transgressions, Paul sees in Christ's death God's liberating invasion of the territory of tyranny.

The Place of Rectification by the Faith of Christ in Paul's Theology

Paul's use of rectification language has been thought to constitute a doctrine, and about that doctrine numerous interpreters have made three claims: It was polemical in its very nature. It led to unnecessary divisions in the early church. And, being itself unnecessary, it proves on inspection to have been marginal to the core of Paul's gospel. Is any light shed on these claims by our consideration of Gal 2:16, and by our comparison of the first two rectification passages in Galatians (the third is 5:4–5)?

The polemical nature of Gal 2:16 is beyond dispute. When Paul says,

> . . . the human being is *not* rectified by observance of the Law, *but rather* by the faith of Christ Jesus,

he is clearly involved in a battle marked by considerable theological fury (cf. Gal 5:12). It is scarcely surprising, then, that the doctrine of rectification did indeed play a role in early Christian tensions (e.g. Jas 2:18–26).[22] Historians have had some reason for suggesting that those tensions – variously qualified and supplemented – played a role in the ultimate divorce between the largely Gentile church of the Mediterranean basin and the older, distinctly Jewish churches of Jerusalem, Judea, and parts of Syria. None of these developments indi-cates, however, that Paul was himself an enemy of Jewish Christianity. The truth lies with the precise opposite.

No one in the early church held more tenaciously to the vision of church unity than did Paul, and no one paid a higher price for that vision. At the Jerusalem conference (Gal 2:1–10), it was Paul who was consumed by the comprehensive vision of God's great work proceeding along two parallel paths, between which he envisioned only mutual

---

[21] De Boer, 'Apocalyptic Eschatology,' 185; see Glossary.
[22] See L. T. Johnson, *James*.

support and respect. In his early work he was at peace with the Jewish-Christian churches of Judea (Gal 1:22–24), and to the end of his life he was certain, first that the unified church of God was drawn both from Jews and from Gentiles (Rom 9:24), and second that that unity demanded concrete expression in the collection he gathered from his own churches for the church in Jerusalem (the delivery of which led eventually to his death; Rom 15:25–32; Martyn, *Galatians*, Comment 24).

Given the history of the interpretation of Paul's letters, then, one can scarcely over-emphasize that Gal 2:16 shows Paul formulating a polemic neither against Judaism nor against Jewish Christianity. At the genesis of Paul's doctrine of rectification, the apostle understands himself to be in accord with Jewish-Christian rectification tradition, *as* he hears that tradition anew in light of God's gospel-invasion of the whole of the world.

Comparing Gal 2:16–21 with Gal 3:6–4:7, and seeing that the two passages present a theological integrity, we have found in the progression from the first to the second an essential clue to the polemical character of Paul's doctrine of rectification. In the first rectification passage, Paul emphasizes the antinomy between Christ's faithful death and observance of the Law. In the second passage, he then brings that antinomy into the perspective of cosmic apocalyptic, in which God has set things right by acting in Christ against real enemies (Gal 3:13; cf. 4:3–5). But that means that *Paul's* rectification polemic against the Teachers in 2:16 is nothing other than a reflection of *God's* rectifying polemic against his enemies. Among these enemies, Paul understandably gives his primary attention to the curse of the Law. Having earlier said that God does not make things right *by means of* the Law, Paul now says that God has had to make things right by entering into combat *against* the Law, in so far as it enacts its curse (Gal 3:10). And Christ's death on the Law-cursed cross is the point at which God has done that (Gal 3:13).

It is thus *God's* polemical act in Christ that causes Paul's doctrine of rectification to be polemical, and that means that one cannot minimize the latter without doing the same to the former. We have no evidence, it is true, that before writing to the Galatians Paul ever spoke directly and explicitly on the subject of rectification. Once his combat with the Teachers in Galatia led him, however, to craft that way of preaching the gospel of God's triumph, he never gave it up.

For while Paul may well have been a person to whom compromise was foreign territory, his personal idiosyncrasies do not explain his theological tenacity. At root, he was sure that his call to be an apostolic soldier was a reflection of God's identity as *the* soldier, intent on making things right. It is God's declaration of war in Christ against all of the forces enslaving the human race that formed the foundation of Paul's militant doctrine of rectification.[23] In short, *God's* rectifying declaration of war in Christ is what gave Paul total confidence that in the end Christ will hand over the kingdom to God the Father, *after* he has destroyed every ruler and every authority and power (1 Cor 15:24).

---

[23] Cf. chapter 15 below.

Part III

Interpreting Scripture

Part III

Interpreting Scripture

Whereas Paul, Hebrew born of Hebrews, possessed extensive knowledge of 'the scriptures' – reading, recalling, and pondering them until his dying day – the Gentiles who entered his churches, largely ignorant of those writings, must have been seen by Paul as persons in need of instruction. The apostle certainly did not speak of God's Son as an isolated fact.[1] Indeed, sure that the God who had sent him to those Gentiles was identical with the God who had made an indelible promise to Abraham, Paul used in his preaching expressions drawn from early Christian interpretations of scripture, such as 'Christ.' How extensively, however, did he function as a teacher of the scriptures? Specifically, did he take it as one of his tasks regularly to offer lengthy and detailed exegetical discourses to his congregations? His letters suggest no such thing. On the contrary, most of the sustained exegetical sections in Paul's letters are fundamentally polemics against scriptural instruction he knew his congregations to have received after his departure and thus from someone other than himself.[2] Here again the close reader finds

---

[1] See below the comments of Wilckens and Vielhauer (chapter 13 n. 30); and cf. Hays, *Echoes.*

[2] Prominent examples are Gal 4:21–5:1 (chapter 12 below) and 2 Cor 3:7–18. To be sure, account must also be taken of such passages as 1 Cor 10:1–13, Rom 4, and Rom 9–11, where Paul's exegesis of scripture gives no clear indication of being crafted in order to counter interpretations of the same texts by others. In 1 Cor 10:1–13, however, Paul writes in a way that does presuppose knowledge of some of the passages he treats (note '*the* cloud', etc.), and the Corinthian church may very well have acquired much of its scriptural knowledge from someone other than Paul. We know that that congregation was fascinated by exegetical instruction it received from impressive Christian-Jewish exegetes such as Apollos, and that Paul was aware of such instruction. Similarly, Paul may have known that the Roman church, not founded by him, was the recipient of scriptural instruction from some of its Christian-Jewish members (cf. Rom 2:17–21a; 4:1; 14:1–23). Most important, as he devised the exegetical passages in Rom 4 and 9–11, Paul was preoccupied in part of his mind with the possibility that the Jerusalem church might refuse the collection he had assembled for it from his Gentile congregations (Rom 15:25–31). And that threatening prospect was related, as Paul knew, to an awesome development in the Jerusalem church itself: some of its members

traces of the Christian Jews who invaded some of Paul's churches in his absence, and whom Paul considered false teachers (Part I above). The result is that in reading Paul's extended exegeses we can truly hear his own interpretations of scripture only when we also take into account the interpretations against which he was arguing.

---

were holding him responsible for the mysteriously slim results of their mission to their fellow Jews (Rom 9:1–5). In composing Romans 4 and 9–11, then, Paul was in part preparing himself to speak exegetically about that mysterious turn of events when he journeyed to Jerusalem to address the church there, the early Christian community that was exceedingly well versed in Christian-Jewish exegesis (see chapter 3 above; cf. Jervell, 'The Letter to Jerusalem'). Neither 1 Corinthians nor Romans indicates that Paul regularly offered extended exegetical discourses to his Gentile churches.

10

The Abrahamic Covenant, Christ, and the Church

I
Covenant and Christianity

How are Christians to think of the covenant God made with Abraham? Specifically, how are they to understand the relationship between that covenant and the corporate people of God? We do well to begin our quest for an answer by considering the document in which the term 'covenant' first entered into Christian literature, Paul's letter to the Galatians.[1]

'Covenant' plays a significant role in two passages in Galatians, 3:6–4:7 and 4:21–5:1. These passages share several major characteristics: (1) Both are fundamentally exegetical in nature, being the only such units in the Galatian letter. (2) In both passages Paul focuses his exegesis on scriptural traditions about Abraham, doing so in part (3) by using the word *diathēkē* (a human being's last will; God's covenant), linking that word to those Abrahamic traditions (3:15, 17; 4:24). (4) In both he further develops his Abrahamic exegesis by emphatic references to Christ (3:16, 29; 5:1), and (5) in both he speaks of the identity of the Galatian churches themselves (3:26–29; 4:7; 4:28–5:1). Twice, then, in his letter to the Galatians Paul weaves into a colorful, exegetical tapestry Abraham, covenant, Christ, and church.[2] Why does he do this, and what are the results? These questions can be answered only by careful analysis of both passages. In chapter 12 below, we will attend to Gal 4:21–5:1. Here we focus our attention on 3:6–4:7.

---

[1] That Galatians antedates the Corinthian letters – and thus the covenant references in 1 Cor 11:28 and 2 Cor 3:6, 14 – is clear from a comparison of Gal 2:10 with 1 Cor 16:1–2. See Martyn, *Galatians*, Comment 24. From Galatians and the Corinthian letters, one turns to Romans 4 and 9–11. See the final sections of the present chapter, and chapter 3 above. Cf. further Hays, *Echoes*, 54–57; Grässer, *Bund.*

[2] On Abraham in Galatians, cf. Hansen, *Abraham.*

II

Galatians 3:6–4:7

Gal 3:6–4:7 is made up of several sub-units, all serving in some way the closely related themes of descent and inheritance, and leading to a climactic statement of the identity already given by God to the Galatian churches. (1) Paul first constructs a lengthy catena of scriptural texts accompanied by exegetical comments and addressing several matters, beginning with descent from Abraham and ending with an antinomy between God's covenantal promise to Abraham and the later-arriving Law (3:6–18).[3] (2) Asking, then, why the Law should have come into the picture at all, Paul writes a paragraph dealing with the genesis of the Law, with the linked advents of faith and of Christ, and with the resulting antinomy between the Law and the faith of Christ (3:19–25).[4] (3) He then pens a first climax by functioning as an exegete, not of scripture, but of early Christian baptismal formulas: the Galatians are heirs of Abraham (literally 'seed of Abraham') by virtue of their baptismal incorporation into Christ (3:26–29). (4) Introducing a new sub-section with an illustration drawn from everyday life, Paul again turns to traditional, early Christian formulas, in order to craft the section's true climax, a statement of liberation by Christ from slavery and an affirmation of adoption by the Spirit into the family of God. By Christ and by his Spirit the Galatians are heirs of God himself (4:1–7).

As the first in his series of scriptural texts, Paul chooses Gen 15:6, thus announcing to the Galatians that he will now speak of the patriarch of patriarchs, Abraham:

> Things were the same with Abraham: 'He trusted God, and as the final act in the drama by which God set Abraham fully right, God recognized Abraham's faithful trust'. (Gal 3:6; Gen 15:6)

He then provides his exegesis of this text:

> You know, therefore, that those whose identity is derived from faith, these are the children of Abraham. (Gal 3:7)

It is a strange exegesis, placing emphasis on an expression not found in the text – 'the children of Abraham' – and answering a question not posed by the text – 'Who is it who can be said truly to be Abraham's children?'

---

[3] Regarding the term 'antinomy,' see the glossary and chapter 7 above.

[4] On the expression *pistis Christou* ('the faith of Christ') see chapter 9 above.

To consider this strange exegesis in the context of Gal 3:6–29, and to take also into account Gal 4:21–5:1, is to see that, while it is Paul who has chosen to begin the exegetical catena with Gen 15:6, it is not he who has first broached the subject of Abraham and his progeny. That has been done by the Teachers who invaded his Galatian churches after his departure.[5] It is from the Teachers, in fact, that Paul takes the emphasized expression and the question. It is they who have caused the Gentile Galatians to long to become children of Abraham, and it is they who have laid out the requirements for true descent: Gentiles are to transfer from their partial and illegitimate line of Abrahamic descent (via Hagar) to the full and true line (via Sarah), doing so by following Abraham in circumcision as the act by which they commence their observance of the Law.

Again, by taking into account both Gal 3:6–29 and Gal 4:21–5:1, we can see the probability that, in developing the motif of Abrahamic descent, the Teachers spoke to the Galatians not only about *Abraam*, the *eulogia tou Abraam* (the blessing of Abraham, 3:14), and the *sperma Abraam* (the seed of Abraham, 3:29), but also about the *diathēkē* (the covenant) God made with Abraham. Our first conclusion, then, is that 'covenant' is one of the Teachers' themes, not a theme Paul has introduced on his own.[6] Pondering it, we can grasp, in fact, some of the major elements in the Teachers' theology.

Motifs in the Teachers' Theology

Covenantal Nomism

In our reading of Galatians, we may employ E. P. Sanders' neologism 'covenantal nomism,' but, as Sanders correctly sees, not in order fundamentally to characterize the theology of Paul.[7] It is the Teachers who hold to the traditional Jewish marriage of covenant and Law, tracing the covenant-Law complex back to Abraham, the first proselyte, the first observer of the Law, the first recipient of God's covenantal blessing, and thus the primal parent of the holy *sperma*. Part of their theology is well encapsulated in a passage in *Jubilees*:

> And all the seed of his [Abraham's] sons would become nations. And they would be counted with the nations [they would be, that is, Gentiles]. But

---

[5] On the nomenclature 'the Teachers' see chapter 1 above.
[6] See especially Grässer, *Bund*.
[7] E. P. Sanders, *Palestinian Judaism*, 511–515.

from the sons of Isaac one would become a holy seed, and he would not be counted among the nations, because he would become the portion of the Most High . . .[8]

Redemptive History

In the case of the Teachers we may employ not only the expression 'covenantal nomism,' but also – with care – the term 'redemptive history.' The expression *sperma Abraam* is important to the Teachers because it refers to the salvific *line*, the line that began with Abraham, that extended through the generations of the corporate people of Israel, that now has become explicitly messianic in the nomistic gospel of the Jerusalem church, and that is being climactically extended to the whole of the world through the Teachers' own mission to the Gentiles.[9]

Transference Into the People of God

It is thus a crucial aspect of the arrival of the Messiah that the Gentiles now have the opportunity of transferring from their present existence as ethnē/goyim into the redemptive-historical line of the Abrahamic, nomistic covenant. By following Abraham in the rite of circumcision, they can enter the already-existent people of God, the sperma Abraam, Israel.

III

Covenant and Seed of Abraham in Paul's Theology

Given these developments in his Galatian churches, Paul is willing to make contact with the Galatians by allowing significant roles to Abraham, to the expressions *sperma Abraam* and *eulogia Abraam*, to the word *diathēkē*, and to the motif of a corporate people of God (*huioi theou*, 'sons of God').[10] He shifts the ground of the discussion, however, quite fundamentally, as one can see from the way in which he speaks of the *diathēkē* and of the *sperma Abraam*, the corporate people of God.

---

[8]   *Jub.* 16:17 (cf. Gen 21:13). In *1 Macc* 12:21 the Spartans and the Jews are said to be brothers, both being of the family of Abraham; cf. Clementine *Recognitions* 1.33.3; 1.34.1.

[9]   Regarding the adjective 'nomistic,' see the glossary.

[10]   Some interpreters have questioned whether Paul really includes the people of God as one of his own topical concerns in Galatians. Gal 3:29 should suffice to settle the issue. It is a genuine surprise to see, however, that, in writing to the Galatian Gentiles, Paul nowhere refers to a people of God existing prior to the advent of Christ. In this regard there is a truly significant change when one turns from Galatians to Romans. See both the conclusion to this chapter and chapter 3 above.

Diathēkē

Paul's first use of the word *diathēkē* comes in Gal 3:15:

> Brothers and sisters, drawing an illustration from everyday life among human beings, let me say that once a person has ratified his will (his *diathēkē*), no one annuls it or adds a codicil to it.

As is frequently the case in our reading of Galatians, we can efficiently come to the nub of the matter by asking about the linguistic history of the term *diathēkē* in the Galatians' own vocabulary:

(1) In the Hellenistic period, as in the classic one, *diathēkē* refers consistently to a person's 'last will.' The Galatians will long have known the term with that meaning.

(2) We can be confident that in founding churches – no less in Galatia than elsewhere – Paul conveyed to his Gentile converts some form of the tradition of 'the Lord's supper' (1 Cor 11:20); and in giving the cup-word he may have consistently included the expression 'new covenant' (*kainē diathēkē*; so 1 Cor 11:25; cf. Luke 22:20). If he did that in Galatia, it will have been from him that the Galatians first sensed that the word *diathēkē* could carry a meaning quite different from the one with which they were already familiar: the riches of the thought of a covenant made by God, as distinguished from a last will drawn up by a human being.[11] Now, in attending to Gal 3:15 they will have noted – perhaps with some surprise – that, making no reference at all to a new covenant, Paul reverts to the everyday meaning of a last will.

(3) The source from which the Galatians will have learned that the term *diathēkē* can be significantly related to Abraham is the instruction of the Teachers. In their discourse to the Greek-speaking Galatians the Teachers doubtless employed the Septuagintal tradition in which *berit* is rendered by *diathēkē*, noting that (in Genesis 17) God defined his covenant explicitly as the rite of circumcision.[12] Expanding somewhat

---

[11] Distinguished also from the 'old covenant.' To suggest that, in communicating a form of the eucharistic tradition to the Galatians, Paul may have introduced them to the use of *diathēkē* as covenant, is quite a different thing, however, from suggesting that he regularly and extensively instructed his Gentile churches on the grand subject of covenant.

[12] That the LXX translators should have rendered God's *berit* as God's *diathēkē* requires explaining, inasmuch as the Hebrew term never has the meaning that is consistently attached to the Greek term, a person's last will. E. Kutsch may be correct to say that the LXX translators were able to use the word *diathēkē* (contrast *synthēkē* in Symmachus and Aquila) by focusing exclusively on one facet of a person's final will: its being an arrangement that he and he alone determines (reference to Kutsch in Grässer, *Bund*, 6).

on what we have earlier noted under the rubrics of covenantal nomism, redemptive history, and transference, we can imagine a paragraph from one of the Teachers' sermons:

> The covenant God made with the first proselyte Abraham is the same as the covenant he re-affirmed through Moses, thus establishing in all its generations the ancient and venerable people of Israel. God's covenant is the event by which Israel came into being, a people set apart from all the other peoples of the earth by being the people of the covenantal Law. What are you Gentiles to do, then? You are to follow in the steps of Abraham, the first proselyte. By undergoing circumcision you are to make your way into the covenant people, the seed of Abraham, the true Israel, the church of God that has Jerusalem as its mother.[13]

(4) It is especially against the background of the Teachers' covenantal instruction, then, that the Galatians will have sensed two significant changes that characterize Paul's argument in Gal 3:15–18. First, as noted above, in his initial use of the word *diathēkē* (3:15) Paul returns it to its distinctly secular meaning, dissociating it from its connection with the Law of Sinai, and thus – for the moment – pointedly detheologizing it.[14]

Second, the argument of 3:15–18 shows that, in declaring a divorce between God's covenant and the Law, Paul prepares the way for a re-theologizing move of his own. Paul attaches the *covenant* exclusively to the *promise* God made to Abraham. And he uses the illustration of 3:15 to show in what way God's covenantal promise is different from the Law. That is to say, the example of a person's last will precludes the thought that someone can alter it, but that picture also suggests that someone might make the attempt. And who might that be? In the illustration Paul has offered, it is clearly a person other than the testator, for the latter could easily change his will at any time prior to his death.

---

[13] That the Teachers understood themselves to have Jerusalem as their mother (cf. Gal 4:26) was suggested more than a century ago by Holtzmann, *Einleitung*, 243. See chapter 2 above.

[14] On the rhetorical *topos* of dissociation in Paul's letters see Vos, '*Legem statuimus*.' See also Perelman and Olbrechts-Tyteca: 'By processes of *dissociation*, we mean techniques of separation which have the purpose of dissociating, separating, disuniting elements which are regarded as forming a whole or at least a unified group within some system of thought: dissociation modifies such a system by modifying certain concepts which make up its essential parts. It is in this way that these processes of dissociation are characteristic of all original philosophical thought' (*Rhetoric*, 190). See further Siegert, *Argumentation*, 182–185.

The illustration of Gal 3:15 has to do, then, with the distinction between the God who spoke the covenantal promise to Abraham and the angels who instituted the later-arriving Law in God's absence (3:19–20). With the illustration of 3:15, in short, Paul means absolutely to preclude the thought that the *angels* who are responsible for the Law (as though it were an attempted codicil, 'added,' 3:19) can have changed the promissory covenant (the unalterable will) *God* made with Abraham. It is the certainty with which Paul speaks of the Law's impotence to alter the promise – and in Galatians 3–4 it is only this certainty – that makes possible Paul's denial of a nomistically potent conflict between the Law and God's promise (3:21).[15]

Sperma Abraam ('seed of Abraham')

In re-theologizing the term *diathēkē* – in divorcing it from the Law and equating it with the promise – Paul gives a crucial role to his own interpretation of the expression 'seed of Abraham.' His key sentence, Gal 3:16, has three parts:

(1) Now the [covenantal] promises were spoken to Abraham 'and to his seed.'

(2) The text does not say, 'and to the seeds,' as though it were speaking about many people, but rather, speaking about one, it reads, 'and to your seed,'

(3) and that seed is Christ.

Paul uses the negative – *ou legei* ('the text does not say') – to deny one reading of a text from scripture, so that, with the clause introduced by

[15] The interpretation of Gal 3:21 is a matter of great importance. From Paul's denial that the Law is 'against' (*kata*) God's promises, numerous interpreters have drawn three conclusions: (*a*) Both promise and Law have their origin in God. (*b*) There can be no insoluble contradiction between the Abrahamic promise and the Law. (*c*) Given the temporal notes in 3:17, 19, and 3:23–25, the promise and the Law constitute a divinely ordained *sequence* of a redemptive-historical sort, even though they are not to be put on exactly the same level. Carefully related to its context, 3:21 seems to me to say something quite different: (*a*) With the assertion of 3:19 and with the partial syllogism of 3:20, Paul attributes the genesis of the Law to angels acting in God's absence (Martyn, *Galatians*, Comment 38). (*b*) There is indeed a sequence: first the promise, then the Law. But the thrust of that sequence is determined by the illustration of 3:15 and by the denial of 3:17: it is a sequence marked by the inability of its second member to invalidate the first member. Thus the sequence is not at all marked by a redemptive-historical continuity. In a word, it is the Law's *impotence* vis-à-vis the promise that makes possible Paul's pointed denial in 3:21: 'Having pictured the promise and the Law as an antinomy, I must pose an important question: Is the Law, then, opposed to the promise *in the sense that it has overpowered it?* Absolutely Not!'

alla ('but rather'), he can provide the correct reading. The correct reading is what, given developments in Galatia, Paul actually hears in Gen 17:8. Able to foresee what God is now doing, scripture speaks directly to the present situation (Gal 3:8; 4:30; cf. Philo *Leg. Alleg.* 3.118).

Note, however, that Paul could have communicated the correct reading of the text in a non-polemical manner. Omitting the second part of the verse, he could have dictated simply

(1) Now the promises were spoken to Abraham 'and to his seed,'

(3) and the seed is Christ.

Why does he include the second, clearly polemical part? The context shows that he is concerned specifically to deny the Teachers' covenantal nomism, their redemptive-historical interpretation of the 'seed of Abraham,' their notion of Gentile transference into the already-existent, covenantal people of God, and hence their view of the relationship between covenant and church.

IV

Theological Motifs Wrongly Attributed to Paul

These observations remind us that at numerous junctures in the history of Pauline interpretation, Paul has been credited with perspectives proper to theologians against whom he waged, in fact, a life-and-death battle.[16] The history of the interpretation of Galatians offers a particularly clear case.

Covenantal Nomism

It has been suggested that in Galatians Paul himself argued for a modified form of covenantal nomism: faith in Christ accompanied by observance of the Law relieved of what are called its overly restrictive and nationalistic aspects.[17] But, while it is true that even the Paul of Galatians can clearly hear the Law when it testifies to and indeed expresses the gospel (4:21; cf. 5:14; 6:2), it is altogether beside the mark

---

[16] See also chapter 13 below.

[17] Two articles of Dunn are of direct pertinence: 'Works,' and 'Theology.' Consult now his commentary and his volume on the theology of Galatians. For four critiques, see (*a*) Räisänen, 'Galatians 2.16;' (*b*) Martyn, 'Events;' (*c*) Wright, 'Curse and Covenant: Galatians 3.10–14' in his *Covenant*; (*d*) Cranfield, 'Works.' In some regards, Wright and Dunn are in agreement. See now also, Dunn, *Partings*; Neusner, 'Really "Ethnic"?'; and – on observance of the Law in the church – chapter 14 below.

to attribute to him a modified form of covenantal nomism. As we have noted, he declares with polemical emphasis a divorce between the covenant and the Law.[18]

Redemptive History

A number of Pauline interpreters have recently revived the view of Paul as a redemptive-historical theologian.[19] But, considering again Gal 3:16, we can see that Paul's interpretation of the seed to whom God made the covenantal promise is as polemically *punctiliar* as it is polemically *singular*. As U. Luz has put it, the covenantal promise uttered by God to Abraham seems to have remained in a docetic state until the advent of the singular seed.[20] That covenantal promise did not create its own epoch, calling into existence a corporate *sperma Abraam* that would extend generation after generation – in a linear fashion – through the centuries. The distinction between linear and punctiliar is thus a distinction drawn by Paul himself. In Gal 3:16 he denies the Teachers' linear, redemptive-historical picture of a covenantal people, affirming instead the punctiliar portrait of the covenantal person, Christ.[21]

Transference Into the People of God

Here too, in some recent strains of interpretation, a theological motif is being given to Paul, whereas in fact it belongs to the Teachers. When one identifies as the subject of Galatians 'the condition on which Gentiles *enter* the people of God,' one presupposes that Paul is

18 Following a pattern of 'covenantal nomism' proposed by Hooker, Hansen suggests a reading of Galatians similar to Dunn's: Hooker's pattern of covenantal nomism 'not only represents the structure of the Old Testament covenants, it can also be seen in Paul's use of the Abrahamic promise in his letter to the Galatians' (Hansen, *Abraham*, 162).

19 To some extent, this revival is evident in the work of Beker, *Paul*, a matter discussed in the appendix to the present chapter. See the essays by Wright, Lull, and Scroggs in Bassler, *Pauline Theology, Volume 1*; and cf. Witherington, *Narrative*, a reading remarkably similar to that of Cullmann, *Christ and Time*. See also note 15 above; and Cousar, 'Romans 5–8.'

20 Luz, '. . . the promise . . . does not found an epoch . . . On the contrary, in Galatians 3, with an almost docetic shyness, Paul is careful not to make the promise available to an historical demonstration' ('Bund,' 322). One is compelled to say, then, that in the picture of Galatians 3 God's promise to Abraham is not an ethnic event any more than it is a religious event (chapter 5 above).

21 Is the result anti-Judaic, in the sense that in Gal 3:16 Paul denies the existence of corporate Israel as God's people? See the conclusion to the present chapter, and chapter 5 above.

concerned with the specific line of movement along which it is now possible for Gentiles to transfer from their sinful state to the blessedness of those who are descendants of Abraham.[22] This possible movement is their own,[23] and the goal of their movement is that of getting into the people of God. The question is how they can get in.[24]

To a large extent, as noted above, this formulation describes the theology of the Teachers, the theology against which Paul wrote the letter to the Galatians! In Paul's theology the fundamental and determining line of movement is God's, as we can see in part from a study of Paul's prepositions and verbs. In Gal 3:14, for example, Paul says that the blessing of Abraham has *come to* the Gentiles (*genētai eis*), not that the Gentiles have been granted the possibility of entering the blessed family of Abraham. Similarly Paul's frame of reference emerges in the verbs *erchomai* (to come, 3:23, 25), *exapostellō* (to send, 4:4, 6), and *exagorazō* (to redeem, 3:13; 4:5). He speaks, that is, not of the *possibility* of human movement into the family of Abraham, but rather of the *power* of God's already-executed movement into the cosmos, in the singular seed of Abraham, Christ. In a word, Galatians is a particularly clear witness to one of Paul's basic convictions: the gospel is about the divine invasion of the cosmos (theology), not about human movement into blessedness (religion). The difference between the two is the chief reason for Paul's writing the letter at all. Specifically, the demonstration

---

[22] E. P. Sanders, *Law*, 18 (emphasis added). Regarding the chart on page 7, where Sanders lays out the matter of transference, see chapter 9 above.

[23] The caveat offered by E. P. Sanders (*Law*, 14 n. 23) was written in response to my friendly critique of the typescript, and it is intended as a partial qualification of the diagram mentioned on page 7: '[The diagram] shows what happens, which Paul, of course, thought of as being "by grace," but which also involves human commitment.' It is true that Sanders (like Karl Barth before him) repeatedly emphasizes the priority of 'solution' over 'plight.' With consistency, however, Sanders considers God's grace to have opened up the *possibility* of human movement from condemnation to salvation. Thus, in a quasi-Bultmannian fashion he sees human possibility as a category fundamental to the analysis of Paul's theology (something that cannot be supported even by Col 1:13, where God is the subject of *metestēsen*). On this matter see further chapter 13 below (especially note 23). At its root, does Paul's good news belong to the category of human possibility or to that of the divine power that is invasive not only of the cosmos, but also of the human will? See Käsemann's comments on the translation of *dynamis* in Rom 1:16: *Questions*, 173 n. 4.

[24] 'Getting in,' 'entering,' and 'being included' are three of the expressions that run through the Pauline work of E. P. Sanders, Dunn, and Wright, to name only a few. What one might call 'entry language' is indeed characteristic of Qumran (e.g. 1QS 5:20). In the Galatian setting, it reflects the theology of the Teachers, not that of Paul.

of that difference is a major concern of Paul as he composes the exegetical section of Gal 3:6–4:7.

V

God's Non-Ethnic Election of Ancient Israel!

With these observations, two matters are now clear as regards Paul's view of the Abrahamic covenant and the corporate people of God. Addressing the Galatian churches about their own identity (3:29; 4:7), Paul attaches the term 'covenant' exclusively to God's promise to Abraham, divorcing that term from the Sinaitic Law. In this exegesis Paul also identifies 'the seed of Abraham' as Christ and those who have been incorporated into him, rather than as the lineal descendants of Abraham, generation after generation. These shocking aspects of Paul's exegesis bring us, in conclusion, to two vexing questions. In his exegetical battle with the Teachers over the matters of covenant and seed of Abraham, does Paul mean to deny God's elective creation of ancient Israel, linking the motif of election solely to the church? And if so, does he later rescind that denial in writing his letter to the Christians in Rome? First, in Galatians itself three further matters demand brief attention.

Galatians

Paul's use of the verb kaleō, 'to call into existence by election'

Every instance of this verb in Galatians refers to the genesis of the church (Gal 1:6, 15; 5:8, 13). Does Paul nevertheless understand that elective act to have its precedent in God's election of ancient Israel by the Abrahamic promise? Or, if Israel's election was not carried out in the promise, did it happen in the giving of the Law at Sinai?

The promise

We have already noted the thrust of Gal 3:16, 26–29. There Paul asserts that God is now creating the church by his elective word, incorporating human beings into the one seed of Abraham, Christ. We have also seen that that is an assertion the apostle makes only after painting a picture in which God's promise to Abraham remained in a docetic, unembodied state until the advent of the singular seed, Christ. And that picture is reinforced in 3:19. There, saying that the Law was added *until* the coming of the seed to whom – along with Abraham himself – God had spoken his promise, Paul implies that in the period of the Law there was no seed of Abraham.

The Law

That implication is shocking, for the resultant picture portrays God's election of ancient Israel neither in the Abrahamic promise nor in the giving of the Sinaitic Law.[25] For if God was absent at the genesis of the Law (3:19–20), a divine, nomistic election of Israel seems to be placed in question, if not excluded. Moreover, there is Paul's certainty that prior to the coming of Christ the human race was essentially an enslaved monolith, one of the enslavers being none other than the curse pronounced by the Law on both the observant and the non-observant (3:10; cf. chapter 8 above).

In Galatians, then, election is God's enactment of his promise in Christ, Abraham's singular seed. It is the act by which God is now creating his church (the new creation; 6:15), not a deed carried out by God either in the time of Abraham or in the time of Moses. If, then, we had only Paul's letter to the Galatians, we would have no reason to credit the apostle with a belief in the divine election of the ancient people of Israel. Indeed precisely the opposite.

Romans

Things are dramatically different in Romans, not to mention other letters of Paul.[26] Two passages in Romans are crucial, Romans 9–11 and Romans 4 (see also chapter 3 above).

Romans 9–11

In addition to using the verb 'to call into existence by election' (*kaleō*) in order to speak of God's acts in each patriarchal generation (Rom 9:7, 12), Paul several times refers to Israel as God's people, the people whom God foreknew (Rom 9:4–5; 11:2). Indeed, the whole of the argument in Romans 9–11 presupposes God's election of ancient Israel. To be sure, the view of Israel's election presented there is dialectically complex.

---

[25] Whether this picture is correctly characterized as anti-Judaic depends on one's assessment of the letter's primary polarity. See chapters 5 and 8 above.

[26] See, as examples, Phil 3:5; 1 Cor 10:1–5. The analysis offered here will show why I cannot fully agree with the unqualified statement of Sanders that Paul 'denies . . . the election of Israel' (*Law*, 208). See also Sänger, *Verkündigung*.

Shortly after listing God's special gifts to an apparently ethnic Israel, Paul relates God's elective grace to the distinction between

all Israelites	and	Israel
seed of Abraham	and	children [of Abraham]
children of the flesh	and	children of the promise (cf. Gal 4:23) = children of God (Rom 9:6–8).

And this distinction is related to another, that between God's hatred and God's love (Rom 9:13; quoting Mal 1:2–3)! These motifs in Paul's argument raise the question whether the distinction *within* Israel between children of the flesh and children of the promise may not play in Romans 9–11 a role similar to the one played in Galatians by the polemic of Gal 3:16. That is to say, even where Paul affirms the election of ancient Israel, as he does in Romans 9–11, that affirmation requires in Paul's mind a corresponding denial: God's election, being free of all presuppositions, cannot be traced through the generations of Israel on any basis other than the act of God himself, the one who issues the promise *newly* in each generation and *solely* on the basis of his own faithful perdurance, *so that* his purpose might *remain* without exception a matter of his election (Rom 9:11). An hypothesis follows: Perhaps both in Galatians and in Romans – although in different ways – Paul means emphatically to deny that God's elective grace was enacted in an ethnic, anthropological sense, either in the Abrahamic promise or in the giving of the Law (cf. Matt 3:9).

Romans 4

In the course of re-working Galatians 3 in order to form a new exegetical argument on the subject of Abraham, Paul refers in Romans 4 to Jewish Christians as the *plural* seed of Abraham who are inheritors of the promise *not only* on the basis of the Law *but also*, and fundamentally, on the basis of the faith of Abraham (Rom 4:16; cf. 4:12). It is true that the final clauses of Rom 4:16 are less than perfectly transparent.[27] Taking our guidance, however, from Rom 4:12 and 14, we can see Paul's concern to emphasize two points. First, the heirs of Abraham are not simply those who are defined as such by *the Law* (v. 14). Second, the competence to determine the identity of the heirs is indicated by *the promise* God spoke to Abraham before he was circumcised (v. 12). For

---

[27] See especially the Romans commentaries of Käsemann, Wilckens, Meyer, Dunn, and Fitzmyer.

'that is the only way in which the legacy can remain a matter of God's undeserved graciousness.'[28] Thus, even when Paul thinks of Jewish Christians – something he does not do in formulating the exegetical arguments of Galatians 3 and 4 – the elective point of departure proves to be the Abrahamic promise, not the Sinaitic Law. Yet, for these Jewish-Christians, the elective force of the Law is affirmed in a secondary way.

We are left, then, with a significant divergence between Galatians and Romans as regards the divine election of ancient Israel. In writing Romans, Paul certainly did rescind his earlier, implied denial of Israel's ancient election. Are we to say, then, that he changed his mind? At the minimum, we can be sure that Paul gave the subject further thought, especially if he was aware, when he wrote Romans, that parts of his Galatian letter had been communicated to the Jerusalem church by the Teachers (perhaps through the False Brothers), accompanied by their own sharply critical interpretation.

But that possibility simply emphasizes the fact that Galatians and Romans were written in quite different settings. To a considerable degree, therefore, the divergence is related to differences in those settings. When Paul wrote to the Romans, events required that he consider in depth both the anomaly presented by the Jewish people's massive rejection of the gospel of Christ, and the charge that he himself was largely indifferent to that development, if not in fact partially responsible for it (Rom 9:1–3). Moreover, in his consideration of that mysterious anomaly and in his answer to the charge of personal indifference, he found the existence of Jewish-Christians to be of great significance.[29]

In Galatians, by contrast, neither Israel's massive 'No' nor the existence of Jewish-Christians as such enters Paul's mind as an issue (the former had not yet occurred). The battle of this letter is fought altogether on the frontier of *the Gentile mission*. Active on that frontier, the Teachers are saying that God is now creating his church by adding Gentiles to Israel, the already-existent, ethnically and religiously distinct people of God. Given this development, Paul is driven to say that neither God's promise to Abraham nor the Sinaitic Law was a divine act of ethnic election. That is, then, a denial that Paul hurls specifically at

[28] Meyer, 'Romans,' 1142.
[29] See not only Rom 4:16, but also the 'remnant' in Rom 9:27–28 (Isa 10:22); and the 'elect' in Rom 11:7.

the Teachers who are working among the Gentiles in Galatia. It is addressed neither to the Jerusalem church, whose members are active in the mission to the Jews, nor to the Jewish nation.

The Non-ethnic Seed of the Non-ethnic Abraham: Christ and His Church

Crucial is the fact that the denial in Galatians is an element of Paul's christology. What negates the Teachers' portrait of the election of ancient Israel – and thus *their way* of relating the Abrahamic covenant to the corporate people of God – is the non-ethnic character of Christ, Abraham's singular seed. In *Christ* there is neither Jew nor Gentile (Gal 3:28). It is therefore Christ who reveals the non-ethnic character of God's covenantal promise to Abraham, both at its inception and in its fulfillment. In Paul's view, then, the Abrahamic covenant itself establishes the non-ethnic character of God's elective grace, not only in the present, but also in the past. Paradoxically the non-ethnic character of God's elective grace means two things. First, that the God who elected newly in each patriarchal generation is precisely the God who thereby *defined* enduring dependability (Rom 9:11). Second, that this same God is *now enacting* his covenant with Abraham, doing so in such a way as to *create* a corporate people in Christ, the singular seed of Abraham.[30]

---

[30] I emphasize 'now enacting' and 'create,' because of (*a*) the past dimension of Paul's linking the terms 'Israelites' and covenant in Rom 9:4–13 and (*b*) the future dimension of Paul's linking the expressions 'all Israel' and covenant in Rom 11:26–27 (the only two instances of *diathēkē* in Romans). On these passages, see notably Walter, 'Römer 9–11;' Grässer, *Bund*; Hofius, 'All Israel.' Regarding the use of the term 'race' in the interpretation of Paul's letters, see now Roetzel, 'Race.'

Appendix to Chapter 10

A Review of
Paul the Apostle:
The Triumph of God in Life and Thought
by J. Christiaan Beker
(Philadelphia: Fortress, 1980)[31]

J. Christiaan Beker has given us a full-dress study of Paul's thought, characterized by comprehensiveness, exegetical discipline, theological penetration, and a passion for a responsible contemporary hermeneutic. Beker first introduces his readers to what he considers to be the character of Paul's thought, namely its apocalyptic texture and the ubiquitous dialectic between its 'coherent core' and its 'contingent expression' (Part One). He then dives into Galatians and Romans – both are considered to be situational – in order to explore Paul's way of doing theology always in relation to a given setting (Part Two). Here attention is focused on the contingency of the gospel, and thus on the versatility of Paul the preacher. The bulk of the book follows as an exploration of the gospel's coherence, significantly introduced by a penetrating return to the matter of apocalyptic, which thus serves as a sort of bridge from the treatment of contingent expressions to the quest for coherent core. That core, distinguished from 'timeless doctrine,' Beker says, emerges as Paul's apocalyptic is explored under the rubrics of cross, sin and death, the Law, indicative and imperative, responsible life in Christ, the church, and the destiny of Israel (Part Three). A conclusion draws many of the threads together under the theme of the book, the final triumph of God. Among the attempts that have been made in recent times to issue a comprehensive, full-scale treatment of Paul's thought, this book is surely one of the strongest and most compelling. Indeed for three reasons one makes no contribution to our cinematic tendency to inflate adjectives by identifying the book as magnificent.

First, its scope reflects a remarkably disciplined determination to move toward an understanding of 'the whole Paul' (ix). The complexity of Paul's theology has driven many a scholar to issue a monograph on this aspect or that. Not Beker. Obviously the fruit of many years of

---

[31] The footnotes in this appendix have been added in the course of its slight editing for the present volume.

research and teaching, the book treats virtually every facet of Paul's thought.

Second, its comprehensiveness is of the truly brave sort, rather than being an encyclopedic matter. We already have the encyclopedic volume by Herman Ridderbos, and it is good to have it at hand, because it can often serve as a next step after one has consulted the concordance.[32] But its comprehensiveness is so thoroughly analytical that one is unlikely to meet in it the cantankerous and aggravating human being called Paul. Beker's book, on the other hand, is written by a nervy sort of fellow, who wants to take seriously in a holistic fashion the body of Paul's thought, as that of a living, breathing, moving human being, even though doing that is difficult and risky for the interpreter.

Third, Beker takes the risk of a holistic interpretation because of a clear and often contagious commitment to what is sometimes called Biblical Theology. There is a fairly large debt to some aspects of the broad movement that for years went under that name, revealed not least in the role granted to 'salvation history.' At the same time, Beker clearly knows how to go his own route as he attempts to avoid timeless interpretation by focusing his efforts on Paul's apocalyptic hermeneutic, Paul's peculiar way of relating coherence to contingency. That focus, Beker believes, will help to make Paul hermeneutically relevant to our own theological situation.

The major issue raised by the book is the one posed by every essay on what we blithely call 'Paul's Theology,' namely the way in which one moves from the mass of data before us in seven situational and highly variegated letters to the presentation of something that is recognizable as a coherent structure of thought. Most of us are not satisfied to speak indefinitely of the thoughts of Paul, but the rub comes when we ask exactly how we go about avoiding that.[33] From what I have said above it will already be clear that Beker's route is focused on apocalyptic. Drawing on the work of Ernst Käsemann, yet also following his own exegetical paths, Beker is able to argue that apocalyptic 'constitutes the heart of Paul's gospel' (173), that 'only a consistent apocalyptic interpretation of Paul's thought is able to demonstrate its fundamental coherence' (143), that 'the death and resurrection of Christ in their apocalyptic setting constitute the coherent core of Paul's thought' (207). I suppose it is in part our common debt to Käsemann that causes me to

[32] Ridderbos, *Paul.*
[33] See now Meyer, 'Proposal.'

find this interpretive route basically congenial.[34] Exploring Paul's particular and peculiar grasp of apocalyptic seems to me to offer the only hope of perceiving something that approaches coherence. Hence, as regards the basic issue of the book I am in complete agreement.

Massive agreement can lead to boredom. That never happened, however, in my reading of the book, and I believe the reason lies largely in Beker's considerable talent to make one think, a *sine qua non* for interpreters of Paul. Again and again I paused over a paragraph, being driven to re-read the texts under discussion, and to ponder at length that treacherous path that leads or appears to lead, from contingency to coherence. The result is an imagined conversation with Beker of a most instructive and stimulating sort, not least because of points of disagreement. I want to mention four of these as tokens of appreciation.

There is, first, the fundamental matter of reaching a working definition of Paul's apocalyptic. Preferring the lead of K. Koch to that of Vielhauer, Beker opts for a definition that plays down the disjunctive dualism of the two ages, accenting instead the linear matter of God's victorious faithfulness as it is directed toward the future consummation of his gracious plan.[35] Paul does not balance his references to the Old Age by mentioning explicitly the New Age, a fact that Beker takes to indicate a brand of apocalyptic primarily focused not on dualistic patterns of thought, but rather on the continuum of a history that God is directing toward his final triumph. It follows that in the course of exploring Paul's thought, Beker is able to discover a kind of marriage between apocalyptic (as core) and salvation history (as structure?). My own opinion is that the marriage, as presented in this book, is more arranged by Beker than discovered in Paul. Yet just here we have one of the gifts Beker proffers to us in the imagined conversation. For the critical reader will see that the book has the effect of posing an important question: If salvation history is to be a useful term at all in our efforts to interpret Paul, how are we to see its relation to apocalyptic?[36]

Second, that question is posed nowhere more clearly than in our attempts to hear Paul's letter to the Galatians, and to allow that hearing

---

[34] See notably Käsemann, 'Apocalyptic.'

[35] See K. Koch, *Apocalyptic*; Vielhauer, 'Introduction.'

[36] In his creative critique of Bultmann, Käsemann himself re-introduced the positive use of the expression 'salvation history,' but without a clear and forceful definition that would have precluded confusion. See Way, *Lordship*. On both apocalyptic and salvation history, see further chapter 10 above and chapter 13 below; and cf. Comments 3 and 38 in Martyn, *Galatians*.

a role in our quest for coherence in Paul's thought. For Beker, Galatians was written in a setting that made it necessary for Paul to 'suppress the apocalyptic theme of the gospel' (x). It is not surprising, then, that although he treats both Galatians and Romans when he is exploring the contingency of the gospel, his account of Paul's Apocalyptic Theology (the heart of the book) is written without reference to Galatians. But here again the critical reader who is willing to converse with Beker will find that yet another weighty question emerges: Is the apocalyptic theme of the gospel suppressed in that letter in which Paul says with unmistakable emphasis that the truth of the gospel is a matter of apocalypse (Gal 1:12, 16; 2:2, 5, 14)? One is driven to ask whether it is not Paul's voice in Galatians that is being suppressed, perhaps because that letter is felt to be offensive on two counts: It contains very few references to God's future triumph, that is, to what Beker views as the core of the coherent apocalyptic core, and it can be read as revealing a conscious avoidance of – if not an attack on – the continuum of salvation history.[37]

This second offense committed by Galatians may play a crucial role in Beker's assessment of the letter. For if one has arranged an indissoluble marriage of apocalyptic and salvation history, one may be tempted to say that the absence of one proves the absence of the other. But there may be another route! Could Galatians perhaps be allowed to play its own role in showing us precisely what the nature of Paul's apocalyptic was?[38] If one should answer that question in the affirmative, one would be driven back to the issue of the relationship between apocalyptic and salvation history.

Our wrestling with that question requires, in the third place, our examining and re-examining Paul's utterances about the Law and about Israel. And on both of these counts the major problems arise for us because we have both Galatians and Romans. The present review is scarcely the place to attempt yet another approach to these problems.[39] Romans seems to prove almost as victorious in Beker's comments on the Law as it does in his treatment of the destiny of Israel. But if Romans 9–11 can stand virtually alone because it has no proper counterpart in Galatians, the same cannot be said of Romans 7. The history of Pauline

---

[37] See again chapter 10 above.
[38] Note the admirable readiness to listen to others that Beker expresses in the preface to the Paperback Edition (1984); and see chapter 7 above.
[39] See chapter 3 above.

interpretation shows, I think, that Paul's words about the Law in Galatians 3:19–25 and his similar and dissimilar words about the Law in Romans 7 have usually combined to form a fish-bone in the throat of every interpreter who has attempted to formulate a coherence in Paul's understanding of the Law.[40]

That fact leads me to the fourth and final point of appreciative critique. The structure of Beker's book could cause one to think that he conceives the interpretive route to be a one-way street from contingency to coherence. At numerous junctures, however, he indicates that the two are dialectically interrelated. Perhaps Beker would agree that our work with Paul is always a movement around the circle of contingency and coherence, each being more sharply brought into focus as we return to it from the other. For example, we can move toward a coherent core of Paul's theology of the cross only after we have worked exegetically at his contingent proclamation of the cross in letter after letter. And that attempt at synthesis can lead, in turn, to a refined grasp of the contingent proclamation in, say, 1 Corinthians; and so on. It follows that when a scholar sends his manuscript to the publisher, he is in fact giving a report about the circular journey he has been able to make thus far.

The question is whether the scholar pauses to give his report as he is moving from contingency to coherence or as he is moving from that degree of coherence he is able to discover back to contingency. Given Beker's passion for Biblical Theology, it is not surprising that for the most part the structure of his report is dictated by its being given on the way to coherence. I have to admit a preference for the structure of the book by Leander Keck (*Paul and His Letters*). Equally aware of the interpretive circle, Keck chose to issue the final part of his report at the point at which one is moving from coherence to contingency. Two advantages result: (1) The interpreter reports while experiencing the same movement Paul experienced as he wrote his letters, thus increasing, perhaps, the chances of exegetical empathy. (2) The interpreter may find it easier to avoid the posture of a theological distiller by consistently taking risks of contingency parallel to those taken by Paul. In a word, it is not difficult to imagine Paul applauding Keck's emphases on matters the apostle considered worth fighting for, while being enormously grateful for Beker's determined focus on apocalyptic.

---

[40] Romans 7 is interpreted with uncommon perception in Meyer, 'Worm' (cf. chapter 16 below). On the Law in Galatians, see chapter 14 below.

Finally a prophecy. This book by J. Christiaan Beker will grace our Pauline shelves for a very long time, not least because readers will sense that the theological passions that raged in the heart and mind of Paul incite a contagious resonance in the heart and mind of the distinguished author.

11

The Textual Contradiction Between
Habakkuk 2:4 and Leviticus 18:5

In Gal 3:11 and 3:12, Paul quotes from Hab 2:4 and from Lev 18:5. He knows that these two texts do not at all say the same thing. Both speak of future life (*zēsetai*), but whereas Hab 2:4 says that faith leads to life, Lev 18:5 says that the route to life lies in observance of the Law. We will call the form displayed in Gal 3:11–12 a Textual Contradiction.

The Textual Contradiction

Ancient instances of the Textual Contradiction fall into two broad types. The first of these consists of traditions that display abstract rules developed in scholastic discussions lacking a genuine polemical cast. This type of Textual Contradiction is of limited help in illuminating the line of thought in Gal 3:11–12, for Paul does not compose those verses in order to put himself at ease, by showing how a mind-troubling contradiction between two scripture texts can be resolved.[1] On the contrary, these verses fit well into the section begun at Gal 3:6 by continuing the polemic in which Paul pits his own exegetical argument quite specifically against that of the Teachers.

Truly significant parallels are found, therefore, in a second type of Textual Contradiction, one that reflects actual conflict between two parties – often in the setting of a courtroom – the first of whom finds support for his position in one of the law's statements, whereas the second supports his position by citing a contradictory statement from the law. It is the strength of a recent study by J. S. Vos to have provided this truly comparable material, drawing it both from the rhetorical

---

[1] The materials collected in the classic essay of Dahl, 'Contradictions,' provide needed assistance, but they are largely of the abstract type, suggesting in effect that the contradiction between Hab 2:4 and Lev 18:5 may have kept a lonely Paul awake at night until he 'solved' it. See also Kennedy, *Interpretation*, 149. On the textual contradictions in Mark 9:11–13 and 12:35–37, see Marcus, *Way*, 94–110, 152.

recommendations made by Cicero, Quintilian, and other rhetoricians, and from Jewish sources.[2] Two factors are of particular importance, and they lead to a reasonably well-defined form.

First, although we will continue to call the form a Textual Contradiction, we also note that *the point of departure* from which it is constructed is not the contradiction between two laws or texts, but rather, as noted above, the substantive conflict between assertions made by two parties who are in actual disagreement with one another.[3] The parties' citation of contradictory texts is secondary to their voicing of contradictory assertions.

Second, because both parties take for granted that the law (or scripture) cannot ultimately be in conflict with itself (Quintilian, *Inst. Orat.* 7.7.2), one or the other of the parties must be able to find a resolution that affirms both texts.

The resulting form shows five steps:

1. An assertion (in Jewish traditions a *halakah*) is made by Party A.

2. Party A cites an authoritative text in support of that assertion.

3. A contradictory assertion (in Judaism a *halakah*) is made by Party B.

4. Party B cites an authoritative and contradictory text in support of that assertion.

5. One of the parties wins the debate by giving a new interpretation to his opponent's text, being thereby able not only to honor both texts as aspects of the indivisible law, but also to show that, correctly read, both texts support his own assertion.

Philo's treatise on the unchangeableness of God provides an excellent example, for as Vos points out, the pertinent discussion there reflects an actual conflict.[4] One can represent it in the form given above:

1. Philo asserts that God is not like a human being.

2. In support of that assertion he cites Num 23:19, 'God is not like a human being.'

3. Some persons known to Philo make a contradictory assertion: God is like a human being (note 'some persons,' *tines*, in *Quod Deus Imm.* 52).

[2] Vos, 'Antinomie.'
[3] Cicero *Top.* 26.96 (from Vos, 'Antinomie,' 260).
[4] *Quod Deus Imm.* 51–73. Together with related ones, this passage was cited and discussed by Dahl in 'Contradictions' (166–168), but without the insight into its polemical cast that is now added by Vos.

4. These persons support (or Philo knows that they can support) their assertion by citing Deut 8:5, 'Like a human being he [God] shall train his son.'

5. Philo then victoriously solves the textual contradiction by showing that, at the level of intention, both Num 23:19 and Deut 8:5 support his assertion. Deut 8:5 speaks not of God's own nature, but rather of God's concern to provide instruction, something definitely needed by those who think that God is like a human being!

Paul Anticipates The Teachers' Use of the Textual Contradiction

It is no long step from this example to Gal 3:11–12, provided we begin with a likely hypothesis: As Paul composes these two verses, he anticipates the Teachers' reaction to his assertion in 3:11a – 'Before God no one is being rectified by the Law' – and to his citing Hab 2:4 in support of it (3:11b). In a word, given the relatively fixed tradition of the Textual Contradiction, Paul can be confident that, upon hearing his letter, the *Teachers* will employ that tradition, in order to say something like this:[5]

1. As Paul's messenger read his letter aloud, we noted his lethally misleading assertion: Before God no one is being rectified by the Law.

2. To undergird that assertion he cites a text from the Law itself, specifically from the prophet Habakkuk: 'The one who is rectified by faith will live.'

3. We assert, on the contrary, that one is indeed rectified by observing the Law.

4. And we find clear support for our assertion in the same divinely given Law from which Paul draws his text, for in the book of Leviticus it says: 'The one who does the commandments will live by them.'

5. We can say in conclusion, then, that, being the word of the one God, the Law does not really contradict itself. At the level of intention, the text quoted by Paul and the text quoted by us actually say the same thing. Habakkuk's reference to life by faith is God's assurance of

---

[5] Can we assume both the Teachers and Paul to have known this form as a relatively fixed tradition? An affirmative answer is suggested by the breadth of the comparative material collected by Dahl, 'Contradictions,' and Vos, 'Antinomie,' and by the fact that in its five-step form the Textual Contradiction is both simple and reflective of common sense.

life to the one who faithfully observes God's commandments, as stated in Leviticus.[6]

Paul's Use of the Textual Contradiction

Paul's line of thought now emerges, when we see that, anticipating the Teachers' use of the tradition of the Textual Contradiction, he alters that form quite significantly:

1. On the basis of the truth of the gospel, I make a fundamental assertion: Before God no one is being rectified by the Law.

2. I then undergird that assertion with a quotation from scripture: 'The one who is rectified by faith will live.'

3. In light of the way in which the Teachers quote – and will continue to quote – from the Law, I must add a second assertion: the Law does not have its origin in faith.

4. Finally, given that second assertion, I cite a text from the Law that does not have its origin in faith – I think it is one of the Teachers' favorite texts – 'The one who does the commandments will live by them.'

Here three factors are revealing: Line 4 (Paul's citation of the text from Leviticus), Line 3 (Paul's second assertion), and the absence of Line 5.

Line 4

As suggested earlier, Paul's citation of Lev 18:5 is a pre-emptive strike. Confident that the Teachers will cite it if he does not do so first, he adheres to the form of the Textual Contradiction by allowing his opponents' text to make up Line 4.

Line 3

It is important to note that Paul could have followed the standard form in this line as well, reproducing the assertion he knows the Teachers to be making. In Line 3, that is, he could have said 'Those who are troubling your minds are saying, to be sure, that one is rectified by observing the Law' (note Line 3 in the example from Philo). And given

---

[6] Cf. the interpretation of Hab 2:4 in 1QpHab 8: 'Interpreted, this [text] concerns all those who *observe the Law* in the House of Judah, whom God will deliver from the House of Judgment because of their suffering and because of *their faith* in the Teacher of Righteousness' (Vermes, emphasis added).

the mental agility we know Paul to have possessed, we can be sure that, after stating the Teachers' assertion in Line 3, and after citing their text in Line 4, he could have completed the form of the Textual Contradiction with a fifth line in which he showed that Hab 2:4 and Lev 18:5 are to be harmonized in favor of his own assertion in the first line.[7]

That is not at all Paul's way of using the tradition of the Textual Contradiction. In Line 3, he formulates a second assertion of his own: The Law extolled and quoted by the Teachers does not have its origin in the faith about which Habakkuk speaks, the faith elicited in Abraham by God's promise, and the faith that has now arrived with the advent of Christ (Gal 3:6, 25).[8] Paul thus speaks of the origin of the Law to which the Teachers appeal, preparing the way for his assertion in Gal 3:19–20 that angels instituted that Law in God's absence (Martyn, *Galatians*, Comment 38). By taking over Line 3 for a second assertion of his own, Paul accomplishes several things.

(*a*) Addressing the issue of origin only for the Law represented in Lev 18:5 and not for the scriptural promise represented in Hab 2:4,

---

7 Neither Dahl nor Vos argues in precisely this way, but, assuming that Paul means to affirm both Hab 2:4 and Lev 18:5, these interpreters manage to find the essence of Line 5 in the later verses of Galatians 3. Dahl credits Paul with demonstrating the validity of Lev 18:5 by arguing in Gal 3:19–25 that 'the entire law of Moses itself [was] . . . a provisional, interim arrangement, valid only for pre-messianic times' ('Contradictions,' 172–173). But, as Hays points out, Paul gives no indication in 3:19–25 that he is explaining how Lev 18:5 can be affirmed (*Faith*, 221). Vos argues somewhat differently. Crediting the apostle, in effect, with Quintilian's dictum that the Law cannot finally stand in contradiction with itself, he assumes that Paul found both Hab 2:4 and Lev 18:5 in the substantively indivisible Law of God ('Antinomie,' 265). For Vos, therefore, the tension between Paul and the Teachers is a 'conflict between two parties each of whom calls on a different passage *in the same scripture*' (ibid., emphasis added). In short, in Vos's view, Paul argues as follows: True enough, the promise (Hab 2:4) and the Law (Lev 18:5) seem to contradict one another, the first supporting my gospel, the second supporting the gospel of the Teachers. In fact, however, when one considers both the letter of the Law and the intention of the Law-giver, God, one sees that there is no contradiction. For although Lev 18:5 says literally that the observer of the Law will live, one finds that God had something else in mind when he gave it: the Law should serve the cause of life in a quite indirect way. Placing the whole of humanity under the power of Sin (3:22), the Law paved the way for the fulfillment of the Abrahamic promise. Although gladly indebted to Vos for the comparative material mentioned earlier, I am compelled for reasons that will emerge in the following analysis to disagree with his conclusions.

8 In making this fundamental change, Paul employs, to be sure, a motif at home in the tradition of the Textual Contradiction. As Vos points out, the rhetoricians recommend that under certain conditions one should ask about the origin of a given law (Hermogenes, *Peri staseōn* [ed. H. Rabe; Leipzig: Teubner, 1913], 87).

Paul distinguishes the two from one another, but he also does more. He creates an imbalance in which it is only the Law that is placed in question, the divine origin of the promise being taken for granted. (*b*) Paul's assertion that the Law does not have its origin in the faith of which Habakkuk speaks does not suggest merely that Paul considers the Law of Lev 18:5 to be inferior. It shows that Paul does not adhere to a major presupposition of the Textual Contradiction, the assumption that the two texts, Hab 2:4 and Lev 18:5, have their origin in a monolith that is larger and more fundamental than either of them. (*c*) The foundational place of such a comprehensive monolith is given by Paul to the faith that is elicited by God's promise, as one sees it in Hab 2:4. Thus the benchmark from which all else must be judged is not a harmony that can be discerned between two texts drawn from the same source. That benchmark is quite simply the faith elicited by God's promise. (*d*) Far from thinking, then, that Hab 2:4 is itself drawn from the Law, Paul uses it to disqualify the Law before he quotes from the Law. The result: not having its origin in the benchmark of faith, the Law speaks a false promise when it says 'The one who does the commandments will live by them.'[9]

Line 5

The absence of this line cannot now come as a surprise. The fundamental premise of the Textual Contradiction, that the Law (or scripture) cannot ultimately be in conflict with itself, has for Paul no pertinence to the contradiction between his text from Habakkuk and the Teachers' text from Leviticus. From the time of Paul's own participation in the crucifixion of Christ (Gal 2:19), he has been unable to assume in a simple way the integrity of a Law that contains both the blessing uttered by God and the curse spoken by the Law (see chapter 14 below). Or, as noted above, although Paul continues to believe that there is a benchmark from which all else is to be judged, he can no longer identify that benchmark as a Law in which one can find both his text and the text of the Teachers. The benchmark is God's own blessing, the promising gospel spoken to Abraham ahead of time (Gal 3:8) and thus the faith elicited by that gospel.[10] In Hab

---

[9] Arguing on the basis of Gal 3:21b and Rom 8:3, Hays also concludes that Paul considered Lev 18:5 to be 'unconditionally false' (*Faith*, 221).

[10] This promise (Gal 3:8) was spoken to Abraham by scripture, that is to say by the *promissory, scriptural Law* functioning in God's behalf. There is here, then, a hint of

2:4 Paul hears nothing other than that blessing promise and that elicited faith. In Lev 18:5, however, he hears nothing other than the voice of the Law that, failing to have its origin in faith, can utter only a false promise, doubtless one means by which it enacts its universal curse.[11]

It follows that Paul is not at all concerned to 'solve' the contradiction between two texts he considers to have been drawn from the same Law, showing thereby that they can be harmonized in favor of his original assertion (Line 1). On the contrary, he is concerned to emphasize the contradiction between the two texts. He sees that God's promise in Hab 2:4 – rectifying faith will lead to life – is the truth of the gospel. And given the work of the Teachers in his Galatian churches, he also sees that the Law's promise in Lev 18:5 – observance of the Law will lead to life – is the falsification of the gospel.[12]

The contradiction between these two texts is altogether essential. For it is the result of the gulf between the voice of the cursing Law and the voice of the blessing God, and that gulf is not to be hidden. It is to be emphasized, until one sees that, in the cross, gulf became contradiction, and contradiction became collision, and collision became defeat for the Law's curse and victory for God's blessing (3:13).[13] Finally, then,

---

Paul's view that the Law has two distinguishable voices, indeed two modes of existence (chapter 14 below). Prior to 4:21; 5:3, 14; 6:2, however, one finds at most a hint of this view.

[11] In chapter 14 below we will consider in detail the three passages in Galatians in which Paul speaks of the Law in a decisively positive way, hearing in it God's own promise (Gal 4:21b; 5:14; 6:2). It is striking that in 5:14 Paul quotes from Lev 19:18, 'You shall love your neighbor as yourself.' The fact that Paul should find in Leviticus both a false promise (Lev 18:5) and the positive statement of the Law of Christ (Lev 19:18) is clear indication of his conviction that, with the coming of Christ, the two voices of the Law have been brought out into the open.

[12] Regarding Paul's citation of Lev 18:5 in Rom 10:5, see Martyn, *Galatians*, note on Gal 3:12.

[13] Paul's concern to portray a *conflict* that issues in defeat for the Law's curse and victory for God's blessing could remind one that Quintilian asks which of two conflicting laws is the stronger (*Inst. Orat.* 7.7.7). That is indeed a question fundamental to the argument Paul formulates in Gal 3:15, 17, and 21a, where, far from saying that the Law's impotence to grant life merely puts it 'at a disadvantage' (Vos, 'Antinomie,' 266), Paul says that the Law is doubly impotent: It cannot grant life, and it is unable effectively to oppose God's promise in the sense of being strong enough to annul that promise. It is, then, the contradiction between a true and potent promise and a false and impotent one that lends a striking note of discontinuity to Paul's exegetical argument, whereas we can be confident that the Teachers found a redemptive continuity in the integrity of the scriptural witness.

Paul's use of the tradition of the Textual Contradiction in Gal 3:11–12 reflects his concern to distinguish one spirit from another.[14] We might even credit Paul with an emended form of 1 John 4:1:

> Beloved [Galatians, in light of the Teachers' work in your midst], do not believe every spirit [or every text], but test the spirits [and the texts] to see whether they are from God.[15]

---

[14] Note the perceptive remark of Käsemann: 'The apostle is not afraid to apply *to scripture* . . . the distinguishing of spirits demanded of the prophets in 1 Cor 12:10' (*Romans*, 286, emphasis added). Cf. Beker, *Paul*, 54.

[15] Here we must remind ourselves that in Galatians 4, 5, and 6 Paul has other very important things to say of the Law, some of them seeming to involve more than a change in vocabulary (chapter 14 below). For example, in Gal 4:21 Paul no longer speaks of the blessing God and the cursing Law. On the contrary, in composing the letter's second exegetical section (4:21–5:1), he presupposes that *the Law itself* has two voices. One is the cursing voice of Lev 18:5, whereas the other is the promissory voice that – speaking in God's behalf – can be heard in Gen 12:3; Hab 2:4, Genesis 16–21, and Isa 54:1. Important as these changes prove to be, however, none of them negates what Paul says in Gal 3:11–12.

12

The Covenants of Hagar and Sarah:
Two Covenants and Two Gentile Missions

An Interpretive Context in the Twentieth Century

With the end of the Second World War and the full revelation of the
Nazi regime's mad attempt to exterminate European Jewry, a number
of church bodies began to draft statements, declarations, even confessions designed to heal some of the wounds, and thus to better the
relations between Jews and Christians. A declaration of guilt was issued
in Stuttgart within months of the end of the war in 1945, and it has
been followed by numerous others.[1]

All of these declarations and confessions draw on scripture in one
way or another, and, as is always the case, those who draft such
statements reveal their own inner-canonical canon. This is true of the
influential resolution issued in 1980 by the Synod of the Rheinische
Landeskirche, a few parts of which will occupy our attention in the
present chapter.[2] Because the Rheinland resolution is drafted in the form
of a confession, and because it is explicitly the result of a burning

---

[1] The books of Croner, *Stones* and *More* collect many of the pertinent documents, the
earliest being 'The Ten Points of Seelisberg' (1947). In the present essay the 1980
resolution of the Landessynode der Evangelischen Kirche im Rheinland will claim our
attention, not least because it has influenced subsequent statements, such as the one
issued in 1987 by the Presbyterian Church USA.

[2] Cf. Baumbach, 'Schriftbenutzung.' The extensive and sometimes heated discussion
elicited by the Rheinland resolution is a subject in itself. One can begin with the
bibliography in Brocke, *Augapfel*; see also the essays in that volume, notably the study
of Schrage, 'Skandalon.' I give here parts of the Rheinland resolution that will prove to
be pertinent to the present chapter:

> (1) Stricken, we confess the co-responsibility and guilt of German Christendom for
> the Holocaust . . .

> (3) We confess Jesus Christ the Jew, who as the Messiah of Israel is the Savior of the
> world and binds the peoples of the world to the people of God.

> (4) We believe in the permanent election of the Jewish people as the people of God,
> and we recognize that through Jesus Christ the church is taken into the covenant of
> God with his people . . .

concern for the renovation of relations between German Protestants and Jews, one is not greatly surprised to see several quotations from Paul's letters, and notably from Romans 9–11. Great weight is laid, for example, on a statement of Paul often taken to be a reminder to Gentile Christians of their indebtedness to Judaism, and doubtless for that reason placed with emphasis at the beginning of the resolution:

> . . . it is not you that support the root, but the root that supports you. (Rom 11:18b)[3]

In the same vein the Rheinland Synod declares as the fourth point of its confession:

> (4) We believe in the permanent election of the Jewish people as the people of God, and we recognize that through Jesus Christ the church is taken into the covenant of God with his people.

These two quotations would seem to reveal the heart of the Rheinland Synod's inner-canonical canon: New Testament passages – dominantly ones in Romans 9–11 – considered to be supportive of the view that the church has been *taken into* God's covenant with God's people Israel.

The limits of the Synod's inner-canonical canon are no less clear than its heart. Excluded by silence are Paul's comments about 'the Jews who killed both the Lord Jesus and the prophets' in 1 Thess 2:14–15, his nearly gnostic portrait of the Law's genesis in Gal 3:19–20, the sharp polarity involved in his positing of two covenants in Gal 4:21–5:1 and 2 Cor 3:6, 14, and so on.[4] The major reasons for such

---

(7) Therefore we declare: Through the centuries the word 'new' has been directed against the Jewish people in Christian biblical exegesis. The new covenant has been understood as the opposite of the old covenant, the new people of God has been seen as the replacement of the old people of God . . .

See the German text in the booklet *Zur Erneuerung* (graciously sent to me by E. Bethge).

[3] The identity of the root is an important exegetical issue. A strong case can be made that Paul intended to refer not to the Jewish people, but rather to *God's gracious election*, enacted newly in each patriarchal generation, and climactically in Christ. See especially the perceptive essay of Walter, 'Röm 9–11.'

[4] On 1 Thess 2:13–16 see Holtz, *Thessalonicher*, and bibliography there; also Pearson, 'Interpolation;' Baarda, 'toorn;' Donfried, '1 Thess 2:13–16;' Broer, '1 Thess 2,14–16;' Schlueter, *Measure*. For a contrasting and thoroughly odious canon within the canon, see the New Testament 'cleansed of Jewish relics' by the Institut zur Erforschung des jüdischen Einflusses: *Die Botschaft Gottes* (Weimar, 1941).

practical exclusion are not far to seek. The history of the interpretation of these latter passages includes some dark and altogether regrettable chapters. One thinks immediately, for example, of the famous statues that, flanking the south portal of the Strasbourg Cathedral, portray a proud and triumphant church, and a humbled and blindfolded synagogue. Consciously those statues were thought to present Paul's theology as it emerges in 2 Corinthians 3. Unconsciously they reflect the forms of anti-Semitism that were widespread among Christians in medieval Europe.[5]

Small wonder that a group of European Christians, living after the Holocaust and admirably intent on rectifying some of the most grievous wrongs done to Jews by Christians, should concentrate their attention on certain parts of the Pauline corpus, to the practical exclusion of others. All exegetes work with an operative canon within the canon, their own context and thus their own history inevitably playing a significant role in their interpretive labors.[6]

It is equally true, however, that the suppressed parts of the canon often have a way of reasserting themselves, to the surprise of those who have ignored them. I am quick to say that the present chapter is not designed with the presumptuous intention of instructing the framers of the Rheinland resolution as to the breadth of the Pauline canon.[7] Recognizing, however, that the term 'covenant' plays a truly significant role in the resolution and that the resolution draws at several points on Paul's letters, we may at least ask whether it is wise to pen a covenant-oriented, largely Pauline resolution without reference to the earliest covenant passages in the Pauline corpus, those in the letter to the Galatians. Thus the modest goal of the present chapter: to re-examine some of the issues that emerge in one of the excluded passages, Gal 4:21–5:1, as those issues might be pertinent to genuine conversation

---

[5] See the illustrations in Charlesworth, *Jews and Christians*, 126 and following. In an admirably honest way the Rheinland Synod arranged for sermonic Bible studies on some of the 'problematic' texts, including 2 Corinthians 3 (E. Bethge) and Matthew 23 (E. Schweizer), *Zur Erneuerung*, 56–71 and 72–78.

[6] Jansen points to the remarkable fact that there is not a word about Gal 4:21–31 in Karl Barth's comprehensive treatment of Galatians in *Die Kirchliche Dogmatik* (Zürich, 1932–1967) IV.1, 712–718; and the passing reference in II.2,237 does nothing to lessen the silence in IV.1: 'Allegorie,' 107 n. 20.

[7] Nor is it my intention to offer a comprehensive critique of the Synod's work, beyond saying that, in my opinion, a number of the resolution's aspects are well conceived and should prove helpful to Christians and Jews, as they seek faithful ways of relating to one another.

between Jews and Christians today (regarding Gal 3:6–4:7, see chapter 10 above).

Galatians 4:21–5:1 and Genesis 16–21

Gal 4:21–5:1, the letter's second exegetical argument, is framed by two questions: 'Tell me, you who wish to live under the power of the Law! Do you really hear what the Law says?' (4:21) and 'But what does the scripture say?' (4:30). The vocabulary with which Paul constructs this argument shows that he is interpreting the texts of Genesis 16 and 21, while taking side glances at Genesis 15 and 17, and developing the motif of promise from Genesis 15 and 18. To a considerable extent Paul stays close to the Genesis texts (adding in Gal 4:27 the quotation of Isa 54:1).[8]

In the stories of Genesis 16–21 there are, however, weighty matters to which Paul gives no attention at all. In Genesis 17, for example, God explicitly defines the covenant he is making with Abraham. It is the commandment of circumcision (Gen 17:10). In the Genesis stories that is a crucial matter, yet one to which, in constructing his exegesis, Paul makes no explicit reference (but see the discussion of 'flesh' under 'Two Begettings' below). Like all other exegetes, he is selective.[9]

He is also creative. As surely as the texts of Genesis 15–21 include motifs he chooses to suppress, so they also fail to supply him with some of the terms and expressions that are central to his interpretation. He does not hesitate to provide them himself, and in every verse:

Gal 4:22   two (sons)
                  the free woman

---

[8] See Verhoef, *Geschreven*, 89–104, 167–168, 200–211; D. A. Koch, *Schrift*, 204–211; Hays, *Echoes*, 111–121.

[9] Paul's silence regarding the definition of the Abrahamic covenant as circumcision is only one facet of his apparently arbitrary exegesis of Genesis 16–21. If one leaves aside Paul's interpretive point of departure, the two Gentile missions in his own time, one can see that Ben Chorin is justified in saying that in Gal 4:21–5:1 Paul turns the patriarchal stories completely upside down (*Paulus*, 132). Cf. Klein, 'A more brutal paganizing of what professes to be redemptive history can scarcely be imagined' (*Rekonstruktion*, 168). In order to see what Paul is talking about and what he is not talking about, one considers not only his silence regarding weighty factors in the Genesis texts, but also his silence regarding equally weighty factors in his own setting: He refers nowhere to the people he will later call, in Rom 9:3, 'my kinsmen by race.' He does not mention the gospel mission to this people (contrast Gal 2:7, 9). And he does not speak of those who pursue that mission, while gladly accepting as part of God's work the circumcision-free mission to Gentiles.

Gal 4:23	was begotten by the power of the flesh … (was begotten) by the power of the promise[10]
Gal 4:24	allegorical matters
	two covenants
	Sinai
	bearing children into the state of slavery
Gal 4:25–26	[entire; note particularly the following:]
	is located in the same oppositional column with the present Jerusalem;
	is in slavery
	children
	the Jerusalem above
	mother
Gal 4:27	Isa 54:1 with its two contrasts, a woman who is barren versus a woman who is fecund, and a woman who has a husband versus a woman who has none
Gal 4:28	children of the promise
Gal 4:29	the one begotten by the power of the flesh persecuted (cf. Jewish traditions based on Gen 21:10) the one (begotten) by the power of the Spirit
Gal 4:30	of the free woman
Gal 4:31	children of the free woman.

Why does Paul suppress certain motifs in his texts, while creating others? The best guidance lies, first, in several of Paul's added verbs: 'to stand in the same oppositional column with,' 'to beget a child,' and 'to bear a child.' Paul's unprecedented expression, 'two covenants,' and his two Jerusalems provide further clues (the last of these has received its own treatment in chapter 2 above).

The Verb 'to stand in the same oppositional column with'

Using the technical term *systoicheō*, Paul says in 4:25 that Hagar 'stands in the same oppositional column with' the present Jerusalem (regarding

---

[10] The noun 'promise' and the verb 'to promise' do not occur in the Abraham stories Paul is interpreting; indeed they are scarcely to be found in the Old Testament. But when, speaking of Isaac, Paul coins the expression 'begotten by the power of the promise,' he is certainly developing a key theological motif of these stories. The birth of Isaac happens only as a result of God's assuring word and, indeed, because of God's advent: 'I will surely return to you in the spring, and Sarah your wife will have a son' (Gen 18:10; cf. 18:14; 15:4–5).

columns of opposites, see chapter 7 above). In its context that sounds like a correction. Knowing that the Teachers are interpreting the Genesis stories by means of columnar pairs of opposites, Paul is concerned to put the columns in correct order. We might paraphrase 4:25, then, as follows (with one clause from 4:24):

> In their reading of the stories of Abraham, Sarah, Hagar, Isaac, and Ishmael, the Teachers carry out their interpretation by referring to columns of polar opposites. Well and good. They tell you, for example, that, standing opposite the free woman Sarah, Hagar is in the same column with slavery, and so she is. But they have not taught you to hear the Law fully and accurately. For they have hid from you the astonishing truth: Hagar, the slave girl, represents Mount Sinai, the locus of the genesis of the Law; *and* she stands in the same column with the present Jerusalem. One can see as much because the present Jerusalem is like the slave Hagar in that she is even now in slavery, together with the children to whom she is giving birth.

Noting this correction, and drawing on other motifs in the context, we can display, with a reasonable degree of probability, the columns of opposites the Teachers are finding in Genesis 16–21 (the Teachers neither cite nor interpret Isa 54:1)

Hagar	*Sarah*
slave	free
Ishmael	Isaac
the son who is not the true descendant of Abraham, having come through the slave girl, Hagar	the true Law-observant descendant of Abraham, as one can see from the fact that he was born on the day of the Feast of the First Fruits (*Jub.* 16:13)
Abraham's illicit descendants via Hagar, the Ishmaels	Abraham's true descendants via Sarah, the Isaacs
those who, uncircumcised in their flesh, are strangers to the covenant of Sinai and thus subject to the Impulsive Desire of the Flesh (see chapter 15 below)	those who constitute the people of God, circumcised in their flesh, observant of the covenant of Sinai, and thus free of the Impulsive Desire of the Flesh
Gentiles	Jews
the half-converted Gentile churches of the Pauline orb that are, properly	the true church of the circumcised – 'our mother Jerusalem' – and the

speaking, divorced from the mother church in Jerusalem, having been denied by Paul God's greatest gift, the Law confirmed to eternity by the Messiah, Jesus.

offspring to which she is giving birth in our Law-observant mission to Gentiles.

When we have analyzed the major clues to Paul's own interpretation, we will be able to see the columns of opposites as he senses them.[11]

The Verbs 'to beget a child' (Gal 4:23, 29), and 'to bear a child' (4:24)

Referring in Gal 4:23 to the births of Ishmael and Isaac, Paul avoids altogether the birthing verb used in Genesis 16–21, *tiktō*, putting in its place *gennaō*, used with its masculine meaning 'to beget' in vv. 23 and 29, and with its feminine meaning 'to bear' in v. 24. Is this properly speaking a substitution, and if it is, why should Paul make it?

Leaving aside Gal 4:21–5:1 (and the different case in Rom 9:11), we note that Paul employs the verb 'to beget,' linking it with the noun 'child/children,' only in speaking of the genesis of Christians and of Christian churches through the power of the gospel entrusted to him by God:

I appeal to you for my child Onesimus, whom *I begot* in my imprisonment. (Phlm 10)

I do not write this to make you ashamed, but to admonish you as my beloved children. For though you have countless guardians in Christ [Apollos, for

[11] No passage in Galatians has had a more interesting – and a more misleading – history of interpretation than 4:21–5:1. Although there have been some variations and a few reservations, one reading has dominated from the time of Marcion to the present, and it can be summarized in 6 points: (1) The pattern of two oppositional columns is accented. (2) The prepositional phrases by which this polar opposition is largely expressed – 'according to the flesh' versus 'according to the Spirit,' etc. – are taken to be adjectival identity markers, differentiating from one another two existent peoples. There *is* a people 'according to the flesh,' and there *is* a people 'according to the Spirit.' (3) These two existent peoples are understood to be respectively the Jews and the Christians; the polarity of the passage is thus focused specifically on Judaism and Christianity. (4) Judaism is consequently characterized as the religion of slavery and Christianity as the religion of freedom. (5) Verse 29 is taken to be a reference to the synagogue's mid-first-century persecution of the church. (6) Verse 30 is then read as an affirmation of the resulting supersession – according to God's will – of the synagogue by the church. Henceforth Christians are God's people; Jews are not. See note 16 below; and Martyn 'Hagar and Sarah.'

example], you do not have many fathers. For *I begot* you in Christ Jesus through the gospel (1 Cor 4:14–15).[12]

In light of these examples one notes the absence of the verb 'to beget' in Gal 4:19, 'My children, I am going through the pain of giving birth to you all over again, until Christ is formed in your congregations.' There Paul calls the Galatian churches his children, but the work of the Teachers makes it impossible for him to say simply that at a point in the past he begot them.

Passing, however, from Gal 4:19 to 4:21–5:1, we see that Paul suppresses his mission-oriented verb 'to beget' only for a moment. When he turns to the exegesis of the birth stories in Genesis 16 and 21, he brings that verb to the fore, as we have noted, even though it is not found in the texts he is interpreting. Why? Clouded as it is, the real begetting and birth – and consequent identity – of the Galatian churches remains his subject in 4:21–5:1, as a paraphrase of 4:28 demonstrates:

> Brothers and sisters, given the identity of your mother, the Sarah-like heavenly Jerusalem, your own identity is clear: you are children begotten by the power of God's promise, just as Isaac was (cf. 4:31).

Even in speaking so positively of the Galatians' birth identity, however, Paul does not leave behind the dark and foreboding tones of 4:19, as we can see from the fact that he speaks of two begettings and of two births.

Two Begettings

Not only does Paul employ his missioning verb 'to beget' in the interpretation of texts that lack it. He also modifies it with two prepositional phrases, thus producing a pair of opposites that he introduces into his own oppositional columns: '(Ishmael) begotten by the power of the flesh' and '(Isaac) begotten by the power of the promise/the Spirit' (4:23 and 29). On the contemporary level the Galatians are the Isaacs, begotten by God's powerful promise, the Spirit (cf. 4:29 with 4:6 and 3:3). Some other contemporaries are the Ishmaels, being begotten by the power of the flesh. Who are these other people?

---

[12] Birth was a metaphor employed very widely for conversion. See the passages about proselytizing in *b. Yebam.* 22a and *Cant. Rab.* 1,3,3; and note in the latter passage the use of the verb 'to form,' which may be compared with the use of the corresponding verb in Gal 4:19. See also Kuhn, '*prosêlytos*;' Nock, *Conversion*; Gaventa, *Darkness*; Malherbe, *The Thessalonians*.

Our first clue to the identity of this group is the term 'flesh.'[13] In the Genesis story, Ishmael is the son produced by the physical union between Abraham and Hagar, a human act rather than a divine one, and thus a deed of the flesh rather than of the Spirit (cf. Isa 31:3). All of this lies in the ancient narrative. When Paul coins the expression 'begotten by the power of the flesh,' however, he reflects a contemporary reality, namely the Teachers' demand that Gentiles enter the Sinai covenant by circumcising the flesh (Gal 3:3).

One may pause to note that 'to beget by circumcision' could be a way of referring to the proselytizing strain in some Jewish traditions. But the activities reflected in those traditions were probably unknown to the Galatians. Why should Paul speak to the Galatians about a matter regarding which they very probably know nothing? Moreover, Paul has referred in 4:19 to the missionary activity of the Teachers, not to that of Jewish proselytizers.

In coining the oppositional expressions having to do with the siring of a child, then, Paul employs the verb by which he elsewhere refers to missionary labors. He does not speak, therefore, of the begetting of individuals, but of the begetting of churches. In short, modifying the verb 'to beget' with the polarized phrases 'by the power of the flesh' and 'by the power of the promise/the Spirit,' Paul speaks of two different ways in which churches are being begotten among Gentiles at the present time, and thus of two different Gentile missions.[14] This interpretation is further supported when we note Paul's use of the feminine motif of a mother giving birth to a child.

Two Births

Begotten by the power of the promised Spirit (4:28–29), the Galatians are the contemporary Isaacs, born to the Sarah covenant, the Jerusalem that is above. True, however, to the patriarchal birth stories of Genesis 16–21 and to his reading of them in terms of polar opposites, Paul speaks also of another birth, and it too has a contemporary reference. In 4:24, thinking of the birth of Ishmael, the son begotten by the power of the flesh, Paul uses the image of giving birth in order to describe the Hagar/Sinai covenant. That covenant is bearing children into the state of slavery. A single observation suffices to indicate that on the con-

---

[13] See Jewett, *Terms*, 95–116.
[14] The double use of the verb 'to beget' in 4:29 is Paul's way of referring to the two Gentile missions.

temporary level Paul refers here to the work of the Teachers in their Law-observant mission to Gentiles.

It is the matter of the time reference of the clause in which Paul says that the Sinai covenant is 'bearing children into the state of slavery.' We have seen that in 4:22 Paul begins his exegetical section with the past tense, honoring the story-line from his text: Abraham had two sons, one begotten from the slave girl, one begotten from the free woman. With the exegetical notice, however, that these things are to be interpreted allegorically (4:24), Paul shifts, not surprisingly, to the present tense, maintaining that tense in every subsequent verse. We can be sure, however, that we are not dealing with the timeless present generally characteristic of allegory. In 4:29 Paul refers typologically and emphatically to the real present ('so also now').

The same thing is true of the participial clause 'bearing children into the state of slavery,' for with this clause Paul refers to births that are even now taking place in a mission distinct from, but also concurrent with, the mission in which the Galatians themselves were born.[15] The Hagar/Sinai covenant is not the *old* covenant, now superseded by the *new* covenant. On the contrary, the Hagar/Sinai covenant is presently active, giving birth to children begotten by the power of the flesh – that is by circumcision – bearing these children, as befits the *Hagar*/Sinai covenant, into the state of slavery.

The conclusion is as clear as it is important. Paul draws into his columns of polar opposites not only his missioning verb 'to beget a child,' but also the verb 'to bear a child.' Looking back to Gal 4:13–15, we are reminded of the fact that, when Paul thinks of his initial contact with the Galatians, he is filled with joy. Indeed, when he reads Genesis 16–21, he can recall those happy days, knowing that in Galatia, as elsewhere, the circumcision-free mission was God's instrument for producing Isaac-like churches, begetting them by the power of God's promised Spirit, and giving birth to them via Sarah, the free woman, the Jerusalem above. Thus, from his exegetical argument itself Paul draws a conclusion regarding the Galatians' identity: happily they are the liberated children of the free woman (4:28 and 31).

---

[15] To be sure, Erasmus – representing many interpreters from Marcion onwards – credited Paul with speaking in the past tense of Judaism: 'the first [testament] *gave birth* to a people subject to servitude of the law . . .' (Sider, *Erasmus*, 119; emphasis added). Had Paul wished to say this, however, he would surely have used the finite form of the simple past tense (aorist).

He comes to that matter, however, only by distinguishing the kind of begetting and birthing process that brought them into being from its polar opposite, an utterly different begetting and birthing process that is presently threatening to bring them into a different state of being, slavery.[16] Given that threat, Paul reminds the Galatians of their true birth identity, and he instructs them to maintain that identity by expelling from their churches the representatives of the Gentile mission associated with Sinai and the present Jerusalem (4:30).

Two Covenants

This conclusion is further reinforced when we consider the fact that Paul has even taken into his two columns of opposites the sacred words 'covenant' and 'Jerusalem,' moves of his own that have, we can be sure, no correspondents in the Teachers' columns of opposites. Immediately after indicating that the Genesis stories are to be read allegorically/typologically – that is to say by noting pairs of opposites in those stories that refer to specific pairs of opposites in the current scene – Paul identifies the two women as two covenants (4:24); and later he relates the two women to two Jerusalems (4:25–26). As noted earlier, the doubling of Jerusalem is a matter we have considered separately (chapter 2 above). Here we attend to the two covenants.

The reference in 4:24 is Paul's only use of the term 'covenant' in Gal 4:21–5:1. The first observation to be made about it is that it does not correspond to the use of the term in the Genesis stories Paul is interpreting. Three points are clear about the term 'covenant' in those stories:

[16] We have already noticed the present-tense force of the clause 'bearing children into slavery.' Now we can add another weighty point. The phrase 'into slavery' is clearly adverbial, modifying 'bearing children.' The resulting clause, therefore, does not present a static characteristic of Hagar that could as well be expressed by the sentence 'Hagar was a slave.' These two factors compel us to contest the standard interpretation sketched in note 11 above. From Lightfoot to H. D. Betz, there is a steady tendency to interpret all of the prepositional phrases laid out above on the basis of the last of them, the one in 4:29, and thus – in a way that is incorrect even for v. 29 – to take them as fundamentally adjectival, rather than as adverbial. Explicating the columns of opposites, H. D. Betz speaks of 'two kinds of people, those who are "according to [the] flesh" . . . and those who are "according to [the] Spirit"' (*Galatians*, 249). But in the text, Paul consistently has the contrasting prepositional phrases modify the verb *gennaō* (in finite and in participial form). Consequently he does not at all speak statically of persons who *are* according to the flesh and persons who *are* according to the Spirit. He uses the prepositional phrases to refer to two different birthing processes, two different modes of birth.

(*a*) There is only one covenant, and it includes both the promise of progeny and the commandment of circumcision:[17]

> On that day the Lord made a covenant with Abram, saying . . . I will establish my covenant between me and you, and your descendants after you throughout their generations, for an everlasting covenant, to be God to you and to your descendants after you. (Gen 15:18; 17:7)

> This is my covenant, which you shall keep, between me and you and your descendants after you: Every male among you shall be circumcised. You shall be circumcised in the flesh of your foreskins, and it shall be a sign of the covenant between me and you . . . So shall my covenant be in your flesh an everlasting covenant. (Gen 17:10–13)

(*b*) Abraham observed God's covenant without exception. He circumcised himself, his sons, and every male in his household (Gen 17:23–27; 21:4).

(*c*) Although, responding to God's command, Abraham circumcised Ishmael, just as he circumcised every other male in his house, God established his covenant with Isaac and emphatically not with Ishmael, as the exchange concerning the birth of Isaac shows.

> [God promises Abraham a son by Sarah; Abraham laughs in disbelief, and preferring the certainty of the son he already has via Hagar, he pleads with God:] 'Oh that Ishmael might live in your sight!' God said, 'No, but your wife Sarah shall bear you a son, and you shall name him Isaac. I will establish my covenant with him . . . As for Ishmael, I have heard you; I will bless him . . . But I will establish my covenant with Isaac'. (Gen 17:18–21)

At all three of these points Paul departs from the text of Genesis. He announces two covenants. Separating promise and nomistic commandment, he defines one covenant as that of promise (and of the Spirit, 4:29), the other as that of the Law of Sinai (and of the circumcision of the flesh). He then identifies the second of these covenants as the covenant of Hagar and her son, ignoring the pointed absence in Genesis of a covenant involving Hagar and Ishmael.

In one regard the way in which Paul uses the term 'covenant' in Gal 4:21–5:1 departs even from his own earlier usage. In Gal 3:15, 17, having divorced the promise from the Law, much as he does in the

---

[17] God makes his covenant with Abraham and with his multiple descendants, but there is no thought that its being passed from generation to generation causes it to be several covenants. Regarding the term 'covenants' in Rom 9:4, see Grässer, *Bund*, 18.

present passage, he spoke of only one covenant, tying it exclusively to the promise, and thus issuing a divorce between the terms 'covenant' and 'Law' (chapter 10 above). In Galatians 3 Paul nowhere refers to the Sinai *covenant*; nor does he even hint that there might be two covenants. What was it that drove Paul – surely against all of his Pharisaic training – to bring the term 'covenant' into the frame of reference set by the two columns of polar opposites, thus speaking of two covenants?

Paul sees that the Teachers are enticing the Galatians to long for inclusion in the venerable covenant of Sinai via circumcision as the commencement of Law observance.[18] He sees also that the Teachers' reading of Genesis 16–21 plays an important role in this seduction. In light of these developments, Paul is compelled to use the term 'covenant' himself, but he is forced to conclude that the Teachers' work has split the covenant into two. In the Teachers' labors among *Gentiles*, Paul sees the activity of the enslaving nomistic covenant of Hagar/Sinai. In his own work he sees the effects of the liberating, promissory covenant of Sarah/Jerusalem above. In short, Paul identifies the two women as two covenants, in order to speak of these two missions.[19] For that purpose the one-covenant picture of Galatians 3 will not suffice. Gal 4:21–5:1 is the passage in which Paul faces most openly and squarely and explicitly and analytically the existence of the Law-observant Gentile mission.[20]

[18] With respect to the way in which the Teachers' message addressed the female members of Paul's Galatian churches, see Meeks, *Urban*, 75–77; Cohen, 'Crossing,' 24; Lieu, 'Circumcision.'

[19] On Paul's later references to two covenants (2 Cor 3:6, 14), see notably Furnish, *II Corinthians*; Grässer, *Bund*, 77–95; Hafemann, *Moses*.

[20] It is important to see that Paul takes the unprecedented step of referring to two covenants only in order to establish the integrity of God's one church. When we recall Gal 2:7, 9, we remember Paul's passion regarding the unity of the church. By the mission to the Jews (presupposing their continued non-salvific observance of the Law), and by the circumcision-free mission to the Gentiles, God is calling into existence this one church. But the Teachers – and the supporters they have in the Jerusalem church – wish to produce this unity under the banner of the Sinai covenant, demanding that Gentile members of the church enter that covenant. Sure that this Law-observant mission to Gentiles is not God's work, Paul says that it produces nothing other than a new form of Gentile enslavement. If, then, Paul is sure that the Law-observant mission, the Hagar covenant, is *not* God's work, can he mean to imply that God is ultimately the author of both covenants? Does he think, e.g., that God used the Hagar covenant to imprison humanity until, climactically, he should provide the liberating covenant of Sarah? There is tradition for the view that God can change his own covenantal promise (e.g. Deut 28:62–68), but that view has no pertinence to the two *simultaneously active* covenants of Galatians 4. Since the Hagar covenant *is* the Law-observant mission to Gentiles, Paul does not in any way suggest that it has its origin in God (*pace* Grässer, *Bund* 95, among others). It stands under God's curse (Gal 1:8–9)! We are not surprised,

Conclusion

With the help of Isa 54:1, Paul finds that, when the columns of polar opposites are correctly arranged, the stories in Genesis tell a tale radically different from the one heard in those stories by the Teachers (for the Teachers' columns see earlier display):

Hagar	*Sarah*
slave	free
Ishmael	Isaac
the son begotten by the power of the flesh, that is by circumcision	the son begotten by the power of God's promise/the Spirit
begetting father: circumcision of the flesh	begetting father: the promissory Spirit
bearing mother: the covenant from Mount Sinai	bearing mother: the covenant of God's promise
the nomistic covenant, represented by Hagar and by Sinai, is bearing children – that is to say Gentile churches, small in number (v 27) – into the state of slavery via the Law-observant mission to the Gentiles	the promissory covenant, represented by Sarah, is mother to those who escape from slavery, being the churches, large in number (v 27), that are resulting from the circumcision-free mission to the Gentiles

Galatians 4:21–5:1 After the Holocaust

In footnote 11 above I have sketched the reading given most frequently to Gal 4:21–5:1, from the time of Marcion to our own day. We can now see that this reading is fundamentally flawed. To be sure, Gal 4:21–5:1 is one of those Pauline passages marked by polar opposites, and thus a text for which Marcion was, so to speak, waiting in the wings. The possibility of Marcion's reading is, however, something of which Paul had no premonition. Specifically, he did not have in mind a polar opposition between Judaism and Christianity, but rather the crucial

---

therefore, to note that, in speaking of the Hagar covenant, Paul employs no expressions corresponding to the *hina* clauses that function in Gal 3:22, 24 to indicate God's use of the Law to his own purpose. In the Hagar covenant, by contrast, the Law is being put to a use contrary to God's will, a fact showing clearly that the Hagar covenant is not the Law as such. At least in passing, we may also note in the Septuagintal form of Psalm 83 (LXX 82) the reference to a covenant that is dangerous to God's people (for Paul the church of God) and that is authored by God's enemies, specifically, among others, by the Ishmaelites and the Hagarites.

distinction between the two Gentile missions, one observant of the Law and one circumcision-free.[21] We may say that Judaism stands somewhere in the *background*, not least because other passages show Paul's firm conviction that the Law is *everywhere* impotent to curb the enslaving power of the Evil Impulse and Sin (e.g. Gal 5:16–18; Rom 3:9; see chapter 15 below). In this paragraph, however, Paul is far from launching a comprehensive attack against Judaism.

He knows of churches in Judea, for example, that retain traditional links with Judaism, in the sense that all of their members continue to observe the Law. For these communities he has only the warmest of fraternal feelings, so long as they do not attempt to impose the Law on Gentiles, as though it were salvific (Gal 1:22–24). Paul is altogether serious about the rule that 'every one should remain in the state in which he was called . . .' 'Was anyone at the time of his call already circumcised? Let him not seek to remove the marks of circumcision. . . .' (1 Cor 7:20, 18). Paul must himself have lived essentially in a Law-observant fashion during the meeting in the Jerusalem church (Gal 2:1–10; cf. 1 Cor 9:19–23). To be sure, he speaks in our passage of a causative connection between the Sinai covenant and enslavement. We have seen, however, that he does not here draw that connection by focusing on the Sinai covenant as such, but rather by speaking of that covenant as it is imposed on Gentiles in the Law-observant mission.[22] Hence in Gal 4:21–5:1 it is Paul's intention to listen attentively to the Law, as he hears it testifying against the Law-observant mission to Gentiles and for the circumcision-free mission; it is a grave mistake to speak here of a polemic against Judaism itself.[23]

---

[21] The history of the interpretation of Gal 4:21–5:1 would be basically different, had interpreters agreed to observe a hermeneutical rule attributed by oral tradition to Walter Bauer: Ask first how the text was understood by the initial readers, and only second how it was intended by its author. See chapter 13 below.

[22] An interesting study of Gaston, 'Enemies,' springs from an admirable motive, and includes some perceptive comments; but the argument is on the whole remarkably arbitrary, involving, for example, a tortured paraphrase of Gal 4:25 ('Enemies,' 410), and ending with a conclusion that owes far more to the Teachers than to Paul (the latter being credited with the view expressed in Eph 2:12, 17!). Gaston never deals in a truly exegetical way with 'two covenants' and with 'bearing children into slavery.' To some extent the arguments of Dunn in 'Works' are similar to those of Gaston (note again the use of Ephesians [2:13–16] to explicate Galatians!); to that extent Dunn's arguments are subject to similar critique.

[23] Were one to judge simply on the basis of Gal 4:21–5:1, one would say that, unlike Marcion and his descendants, Paul did not attack the synagogue in order to identify the Law-observant mission to Gentiles as a movement hostile to God's outreach into the

It follows that the framers of the Rheinland resolution – and the theologians who have admirably drafted similar documents in other contexts – had no need to avoid this text for fear that it provides a basis for anti-Judaism and a support for the doctrine of supersession. It does nothing of the sort. On the contrary, it develops a theology that could prove clarifying in conversations between Jews and Christians, precisely because it is a theology of missions *to Gentiles*.

Vis-à-vis our passage, however, the framers did have grounds for unease in light of the fourth point of their confession, quoted earlier:

> We believe in the permanent election of the Jewish people as the people of God, and we recognize that through Jesus Christ the church is taken into the covenant of God with his people.

The first clause of this sentence, clearly a polemic against the doctrine of supersession, can stand alongside Gal 4:21–5:1, in the sense that that passage says nothing about Christianity taking the place of Judaism. The theology expressed in the second clause, however, is another matter entirely, for it voices, within the context of what some are now calling a post-Holocaust theology, a view for which no support at all can be found in the author of Gal 4:21–5:1.[24] *It is the Teachers, not Paul,* who anticipated part of the Rheinland confession, by holding quite sincerely that through their ministry God was bringing Gentiles into the covenant of Sinai. And just as clearly, as we have seen, it is their active determination to bring Gentiles into the nomistic covenant of Sinai

---

world. That this passage has *implications* for Paul's perception of the synagogue has already been noted above. Galatians 4 presents Paul's Old Testament hermeneutic with unmistakable clarity: apart from the liberating gospel of Christ the scripture is read and heard without being understood (cf. 2 Corinthians 3; Grässer, *Bund* 91; Hafemann, *Moses*; chapter 13 below).

24 Regarding a Christian 'post-Holocaust theology,' see Klappert and Starck, *Umkehr;* Rendtorff and Stegemann (eds), *Auschwitz;* Jansen, *Auschwitz;* Grässer, *Bund,* 212–230; 259–270. One recalls that in 1934 K. Barth raised with G. Kittel the question – symptomatic that it should have been necessary – whether the church could see in the 'glorious' events of 1933 a second source of revelation alongside the Bible (Vos, 'Antijudaismus/Antisemitismus,' 99)! We hardly need to say that the Holocaust is another matter altogether: see Haacker, 'Holocaust.' For Christians the Holocaust does most surely provide new hermeneutical lenses, without eclipsing the radical hermeneutic of the rectification of the ungodly! Even with these lenses, however, one cannot truly find in Paul's letters – including the one to the Romans – support for the view that the church has been taken into the covenant of an already-existent people of God. See the discussion of Rom 11:27 in Grässer, *Bund,* 20–25, Walter, 'Röm 9–11,' the Nachwort of Grässer, *Bund,* 312–315, and Hofius, 'All Israel.'

that drove Paul – caught as he was in birth-pangs, and compelled by the theology of the Teachers to become for a moment a covenant theologian himself – to speak of the two incompatible covenants that were being carried out in the two incompatible Gentile missions.[25]

Genuinely theological conversation between Christians and Jews is comparatively rare. It is also essential to the faithful health and future of both. One is therefore grateful to those who took the step represented in the Rheinland resolution. One is also deeply thankful that, after centuries of persecution at Christian hands, Jews are yet willing to enter into dialogue.[26] In such thanksgiving, some Christian theologians might choose, in fact, to follow the Teachers who came into Paul's Galatian churches rather than Paul, affirming both a single covenant and God's inclusion of the church in it. They would need, however, to know whom they are following, and they would do well to make the identity of their theological forebears clear to their readers; explaining, presumably, that centuries of Christian guilt – unquestionably a grave matter with which Christian theologians must deal – make it necessary to derive crucial aspects of Christian theology not from Paul, but rather from his Galatian opponents.[27]

---

[25] Again 2 Corinthians 3 comes to mind, with its picture of two covenants, markedly similar to the picture in Galatians 4, but also different. Two points may be mentioned here. (*a*) In 2 Corinthians 3 the two covenants are clearly sequential, whereas in Galatians 4, as we have seen, they are simultaneous. (*b*) Whereas in Galatians 4 Paul speaks of his circumcision-free mission as the (Sarah) covenant itself, in 2 Corinthians 3 his mission is in the *service* of the (new) covenant, a locution that may help us to understand how in Galatians Paul can include himself among the children of the Sarah/circumcision-free mission (note '*our* mother'). On 2 Corinthians 3 see Käsemann, 'Spirit;' Furnish, *II Corinthians*; Grässer, *Bund*, 77–95; Hafemann, *Moses*.

[26] See especially Boyarin, *Politics.*

[27] In the case of the Rheinland Synod we can be confident that we are not dealing with theologians who consciously intend to substitute the theology of the Teachers for that of Paul. One might speculate that, when Paul's letter to the Romans is read through the lenses of remorse for what the Synod called 'the co-responsibility and guilt of German Christendom for the Holocaust,' it sounds in some regards similar to a letter the Teachers might have written. Thus far the result of such reading is in part, however, historically and theologically confusing, and one has to doubt that this confusing part has genuine power to eradicate anti-Semitism among Christians. It is crucial for Christian theologians to listen carefully to their Jewish counterparts (see, for example, the attempt made in chapter 4 above), but such listening does not relieve them of the responsibility to do their own theological work on the basis of their own sources, as R. J. Zvi Werblowsky pointedly reminded the Rheinland Synod in a remarkable address on 7 January, 1980: 'Trennendes und Gemeinsames.' Note his comment: 'It cannot be that Christians should get their theology from Jews. Indeed, God deliver us from such a development. They must themselves work out their Christian theology in their own

Do we not find a better route, however – and one that will both clarify and deepen genuinely theological conversation between Jews and Christians today – by recognizing that the Paul whom we see in Gal 4:21–5:1 is not asking how the church of God (Gal 1:13) is related to the Israel elected by God (Rom 11:1–2). As he writes this passage, Paul is concerned, in a tightly focused way, to combat the work of the Teachers by bearing witness to the power of God's promissory covenant. In the circumcision-free mission to Gentiles, *that* covenant is giving birth to multitudes of liberated children.[28] Far from planting seeds of anti-Judaism, this Paul proves to be the theologian who, when he reads scripture, hears the Law itself saying with emphasis: The God who is now reaching out for the whole of the world – in Christ and apart from observance of the Law – is the God who promised Abraham and Sarah that he would one day do that.

---

demanding disciplines – exegetically, systematically, historically' (35). Looking at the period since the Holocaust, one can identify two developments that are threatening to the faithful integrity of both Jews and Christians: the danger of underestimating the degree to which that event can and must affect Christian theology; the danger of concentrating one's attention so tightly on that event as to reduce Christian theology to anti-anti-Judaism. As one thinks of Christian responsibility for Christian theology, one notices with concern that the Rheinland resolution appears nowhere to speak of the rectification of the ungodly, and thus does not address the crucial issue of the relationship between that theological assertion and the affirmation of God's election of and complete redemption of Israel (Rom 5:12–21; 9:6–13; and 11:25–27, 32). See Käsemann, *Romans,* 319–321; Meyer, 'Romans;' Hofius, 'All Israel.'

[28] In light of some of the Pauline work of Gaston (e.g. note 22 above) and its influence on the labors of others (e.g. Gager, *Origins*; Van Buren, *Theology*), I must add a note regarding Paul's consistent conviction that God's salvific action *in the gospel of Christ* was directed to *the whole* of the enslaved world, 'to the Jew first and also to the Greek.' The thought never entered the apostle's head that the gospel mission to the Jews be abandoned, it being God's will that Jews should follow the path of the Law, while Gentiles should follow the path of the gospel. In writing Rom 9:6–11:24 Paul presupposes the faithful continuation of the (largely unsuccessful) mission to the Jews *until the parousia*; and the anxiety Paul experienced when he thought about the conversations he was shortly to have in the Jerusalem church (Rom 15:30–32) would have been quite differently focused had it been his view that that church should abandon 'the gospel to the circumcised' (cf. Gal 2:7, 9).

13

John and Paul on the Subject
of Gospel and Scripture

Reading as Listening

Let me begin[1] by inviting you to take a brief trip, chronologically back in time to 1957, and geographically to the delightfully low-key university town of Göttingen. For me it was a Fulbright year, and the main attraction of Göttingen was the presence there of two very different New Testament scholars, Joachim Jeremias and Ernst Käsemann. The year left indelible marks on me from both men. At the moment, however, thinking about the year 1957–58 takes me back to two other Neutestamentler, Walter Bauer and Ferdinand Christian Baur. And pondering aspects of the work of the two Bau(e)rs leads me, in turn, to two observations about the learning process that has claimed my allegiance over the third of a century since 1957, and that, more than anything else, has led to several changes of mind.

The first of these observations has to do with Walter Bauer. He had been in Göttingen when Jeremias arrived from Greifswald in 1935. In 1957 this grand old man, then 80 years of age, was still there, in retirement, and the multiple aspects of his legacy were much in evidence. The one that became most important to me is not to be found in any of his writings, so far as I know. It was a piece of circulating oral tradition, which had it that Bauer had propounded a hermeneutical rule to be used in interpreting early Christian documents: 'On the way toward ascertaining the intention of an early

---

[1] The basis of this chapter is a lecture that was given by invitation at the annual meeting of the Society of Biblical Literature in 1990, with critical responses by Professors Beverly R. Gaventa and Paul W. Meyer (lecture series 'How My Mind Has Changed'). For the present chapter – with additions drawn from yet another lecture ('Paul and His Jewish-Christian Interpreters,' *USQR* 42 [1988] 1–15) – there have been revisions, but for obvious reasons the lecture form has been retained.

Christian author, the interpreter is first to ask how the original readers of the author's document understood what he had said in it.'[2]

It is, at the minimum, an intriguing suggestion. In formulating it, Bauer presupposed, of course, that a thoughtful reader of a document in the New Testament will be concerned to learn everything possible about the author's intention, a clear indication that the famous essay of Wimsatt and Beardsley on the intentional fallacy had not yet made its way across the Atlantic.[3] For Walter Bauer, however, one begins one's reading not by inquiring after the author's intention, but rather by asking how the author's text was understood by those who first read/heard it.

I should admit that when I initially heard this rule, I was not uncontrollably enamored of it, having developed a certain allergy to discussions of hermeneutics. In retrospect I can see that it eventually got past my anti-hermeneutical bastion because of a striking experience while sitting in a seminar offered by Jeremias. Others will remember, as I do, one's amazement, the first time one saw Jeremias stride to the blackboard, open his New Testament to the Gospel of Mark, and, holding it in one hand, begin with the other hand to write the text in Aramaic. It was a case of instant translation, or, as he thought, instant retranslation.

To one who had struggled with Aramaic under the genial tutelage of Marvin Pope at Yale, it was an astonishing feat. Soon, however, I began to sense a head-on collision between Jeremias' act of instant translation and Bauer's rule; and I had no great difficulty in sorting the matter out. The exegetical stance of Jeremias clearly by-passed the first hearers of the Gospel of Mark, the hearers, namely, whom Mark had in mind when he wrote his tome in the Greek language. It seemed no accident, in fact, that the initial hearers of Mark's gospel and the evangelist himself disappeared simultaneously.[4]

---

[2] Note the *somewhat* similar comment of Kümmel about Matthäus Flacius Illyricus (*Clavis Scripturae Sacrae* [1567]); 'Flacius recognizes that to ascertain the literal meaning of a Biblical text, it is necessary first to understand the text in the way it was understood by its original readers. *From that point*, then, one proceeds to discern the goal that the Biblical author had in mind . . .' (Kümmel, *Testament*, 23, emphasis added). Cf. the helpful references to the hearers' perception of Galatians in Stanton, 'Law of Christ;' Downing, 'Preparation.'

[3] Wimsatt and Beardsley, 'The Intentional Fallacy.' This essay is itself widely misconstrued in our time, as Hays has recently remarked: *Echoes*, 201 n. 90.

[4] Let me add that I had and have great respect for Jeremias, both as an interpreter and as a person of integrity.

Thinking of Bauer and Jeremias, one could say, on the pedestrian level, that one Göttingen colleague was having a very brief affair with a Greek lexicon on which another colleague had spent a large portion of his lifetime. At a deeper level much more was involved, namely the question whether both initially and fundamentally the New Testament interpreter necessarily has a responsibility that somehow involves the original hearers, in order to be able to discharge his responsibility to the author who had those hearers in mind as he wrote. An affirmative answer seems to me to be demanded. Bauer's rule is one of the chief things I have learned and tried to practice over the years; it has more than once led to a change of mind.

The second observation from 1957 is focused on the labors of an earlier Baur, the one without the 'e,' Ferdinand Christian. I had already read fairly widely in Ferdinand Christian Baur's writings, but the year in Göttingen drove me back to his work in a decisive and unexpected way. That happened primarily as a result of truly formative and very enjoyable debates with Ernst Käsemann about the Gospel of John. We found ourselves in considerable disagreement, but the disagreement was focussed on a question we agreed to be crucial: Where does the document we are reading belong in the strains and stresses characteristic of early Christian history?[5] With regard to every early Christian document, that was one of the chief questions for Ferdinand Christian Baur. During the Göttingen year it became a truly burning question for me.

What needs to be added is the fact that the period in Göttingen also led – with the passing of time – to a conscious confluence of the hermeneutical rule of Walter Bauer with the historically dynamic, interpretive framework of Ferdinand Christian Baur. The confluence is not hard to explain. First, one thinks again, for a moment, of the rule of Walter Bauer.

On its face Bauer's rule may seem quite simple, even simplistic. Pursued both rigorously and poetically, however, the rule proves to be immensely complex and immensely rich. For it involves all of the imagination and all of the disciplines necessary for a modern interpreter to take a seat in an early Christian congregation, intent on borrowing the ears of the early Christian neighbors, in order to hear the text as they heard it.[6] To mention only a few of these disciplines, the exercise of Bauer's rule involves:

[5] See now Käsemann, *Testament*; Martyn, 'Jewish Mission.'
[6] See now the attempt in Martyn, *Galatians.*

1. Resurrecting the hearers' vocabulary, as it is similar to, and as it is different from, the vocabulary of the author.

2. Straining to hear the links between the hearer's vocabulary and their social and cultural world, as those links are strengthened and assailed by the author's words.

3. Ferreting out the way in which certain literary and rhetorical forms are likely to have worked on the first listeners' sensibilities.

4. Trying to match the first listeners' ability to hear a fine interplay between figure and narrative, and on and on.

But how, then, does Walter Bauer's rule lead one back to the labors of Ferdinand Christian Baur? If the interpreter's initial step is the attempt to hear an early Christian document with the ears of its first hearers, it follows necessarily that, in addition to the partial list just given, one will have to hear the text as it sounded in the midst of the strains and stresses in early Christian theology that were of major concern to those first hearers, and to the document's author as well.

That is to say, one listens to an early Christian writing, as far as possible, with the ears of the original hearers. And, listening with those ears, one hears not only the voice of the theologian who authored the document in question – and not only the voices of, say, various itinerant teachers in rural Palestine, and of various street preachers and artisan-philosophers in this or that essentially Greek city – but also one hears the voices of other Christian theologians who prove, more often than not, to be saying rather different things, and in some instances to be saying those different things quite effectively. If one does not hear the chorus of these other voices, one does not really hear the voice of the author as his first hearers heard him.

I mention Göttingen, the year 1957, Walter Bauer, and Ferdinand Christian Baur in order to confess that the interpretive confluence I have just sketched goes a long way toward defining the location and the passion of my own exegetical labors through the years. And, as I have already said, it is that interpretive confluence that has more than once changed my mind, that is to say has taught me something.

I do know that there are other ways of reading early Christian texts, and some of those ways are, I think, helpful. I have learned, even in my old age, from scholars whose exegetical stance is different from my own. At the moment, however, I am concerned simply to point out that lying in wait for every interpreter is the omnipresent and dangerously un-conscious tendency to domesticate the text, to cage the wild tiger. Every serious interpreter, therefore, is looking for an antidote to that domesticating tendency. In my judgment a truly powerful antidote has been given to us in the heritage that has come our way from Walter Bauer and from Ferdinand Christian Baur.

Listening to John and Paul

Let me briefly offer two examples that may illustrate the way in which the interpretive confluence I have just sketched has taught me some things. The general issue to be addressed is that of scripture and gospel, and the two examples arise when we interview John and Paul with that issue in mind. How do John and Paul see the relationship between scripture and gospel? I hardly need to say that the area to which this question points is massive and highly complex. Having been approached in the main by asking how Paul and John interpret scripture, it is also an area much studied.[7]

Something a bit different might emerge, however, when we ask not how these first-century theologians interpret scripture, but rather how they see the relationship between scripture and gospel, a distinguishable even if closely related question. Moreover we will interview them by imaginatively taking up residence in their circles, in order first of all to try to listen to their writings with the ears of their first hearers. And finally we will mount a galloping horse, in order to see whether attending to both John and Paul in a single lecture may enable us to sense an aspect of early Christian theology we may have missed on more pedestrian sorties.

Gospel and Scripture in John

When we take up temporary residence in the Johannine community, what do we hear? The first thing we note is that without exception John's references to scripture are references to the law, the prophets, the writings. When, therefore, he relates scripture to gospel, he is relating the law, the prophets, the writings to the gospel of Jesus Christ.

The second thing we sense, as we listen, is that a number of John's references to these ancient scriptures are couched in a distinctly

---

[7] See, as examples, Vielhauer, 'Paulus und das Alte Testament;' D. A. Koch, *Schrift*; Juel, *Exegesis*; Hays, *Echoes*; Stanley, *Scripture*; Beutler, 'Use;' Liebers, *Studien*; Aageson, *Written*.

polemical tone of voice. To take just one example, Jesus says to the crowd of people who have seen him raise the paralytic:

> You search the scriptures, because you think that in them you have eternal life; and it is they that bear witness to me; yet you refuse to come to me that you may have life. (John 5:39–40)

When John is speaking about or quoting scripture, his voice often has an edge to it. In part, that edginess is doubtless a rhetorical stratagem, but with Ferdinand Christian Baur at one's elbow, one may also think that this stratagem is designed to play a role in a rather tense setting in the history of early Christian thought and life.[8]

Further listening may convince one, then, that there have been – and probably still are at the time of John's writing his gospel – theologians both in and around John's community whose understanding of the relationship between gospel and scripture is not only different from that of John, but is also an understanding of gospel and scripture that sets his teeth on edge. In order to hear the Gospel of John with the ears of its original listeners, we must make every effort to hear in the background of John's text the voices of these other theologians. For the sake of convenient reference, I will refer to these other persons as 'the simple exegetical theologians in John's setting'; and let me repeat that they seem to be located both in and around John's community.[9] How do they view scripture and gospel?

In a word 'simply.' Both the exegetical theologians who accept Jesus as God's Son, and those who do not, share one fundamental conviction: They believe that whenever God acts newly, he does so in a way that is demonstrably in accordance with scripture. Thus all of these exegetical theologians prefigure C. H. Dodd's book, *According to the Scriptures*, by agreeing that the scriptures form the sub-structure of true theology.

We can be still more specific. These exegetical theologians presuppose a clear trajectory from the scriptural expectations connected with various 'messianic' figures to the figure of the Messiah. They believe, in turn, that all theological issues – including ones having specifically to do with christology – are *subject to exegetical discussion*.

---

[8] See Ashton, *Understanding*, 107–198; Smith, *Theology*, xi; de Boer, *Perspectives*, 31–33; Martyn, 'Jewish Mission.'

[9] Some of these theologians have elected to remain in the synagogue; others are in the Johannine community. With regard to the relationship between scripture and gospel, they are essentially of one mind.

Now, tuning our ears for John's own voice brings surprises. For when we do that, while hearing the voices of the simple exegetical theologians ringing in the background, we notice that John's theology is radically different from theirs. To be sure, there is some common ground, and that common ground is important. Like the simple exegetical theologians, John gives considerable attention to the interpretation of scripture; and he several times speaks explicitly about the exegetical process itself, making clear that exegesis of scripture is part of the totality of preaching the gospel.[10]

For John, however, the relationship between scripture and gospel is anything but simple and innocent. He is sure, in fact, that exegesis of scripture can blind the blind and deafen the deaf. There is, accordingly, a striking subtlety and even, as we will see, a radicality to John's understanding of gospel and scripture. Three major points stand out.

First, John finds that the story of Jesus contains numerous geological faults (Verwerfungen), radical disjunctures that cause the gospel story to be a landscape over which it is impossible for human beings to walk.[11] Again and again, the hearer of this gospel senses John's concern to demonstrate the impossibility of human movement. Again and again, the evangelist hears Jesus say, in effect, 'You cannot get here from there' (see, for example, John 6:44; 6:65). One does not walk into the community of the redeemed across the terrain that reaches from the past into the present, for there seem to be no bridges that reach over the geological fault created by the advent of Christ, the Stranger from Heaven.[12]

Second, in the evangelist's opinion, the impassable geological faults are nowhere more evident than in the relationship of scripture to Jesus Christ, for that relationship is as riddly and elusive as are Jesus' words themselves. Contrary to the opinion of the simple exegetical theologians, exegetical discussion does not offer a route beyond the geological faults.[13] It is thus a fundamental error to think that, if one will only persevere with one's interpretation of scripture, one can leap over the geological faults from this side.[14]

---

[10] See now Beutler, 'Use.'

[11] For a suggestive use of the term 'Verwerfung' in the sense of a geological fault see Bornkamm, 'Towards,' 91.

[12] See Meeks 'Man from Heaven;' de Jonge, *Stranger*; Ashton, *Understanding*, 205–237; Smith, *Theology*, 91–101.

[13] Martyn, *History and Theology*, 126–128.

[14] For John, Jesus' own lack of scribal education, for example, is a clear warning that his identity cannot be perceived on the basis of exegetical exertion (John 7:15).

Does John believe, then, that scripture has lost its voice altogether? Hardly! The evangelist several times speaks of memory in order explicitly to address the issue of the relation between the proclamation of the gospel and the exegesis of scripture. When we pause in order to listen with Johannine ears to John's use of the verb *mimnēskomai* ('to remember'), we sense one of John's basic convictions. And it is a conviction all members of John's community will have recognized as polemical with respect to the views of the simple exegetical theologians: Only after Jesus' resurrection/glorification were his disciples given the power of a memory that could believe both scripture and Jesus' words (see notably John 2:22 and 5:46–47).[15]

The connecting link, then, between scripture and gospel is a matter of great importance, but for John that link is given by the gospel story itself, a fact that tells us two things: The gospel story has to do with the same God who granted to Isaiah a vision of Jesus' glory (John 12:41) and who allowed Abraham to see Jesus' day (John 8:56). But, the fundamental arrow in the link joining scripture and gospel points from the gospel story to scripture and not from scripture to the gospel story. In a word, with Jesus' glorification, belief in scripture *comes into being* by acquiring an indelible link to belief in Jesus' words and deeds.[16]

Third, while I can do little more here than mention it, John's acknowledgement of the geological faults also produces a radicality in the matter of origins, and thus a view of history that must have been as strange to the simple exegetical theologians as was his view of the relation of scripture to gospel. Here the question is not whether John can speak positively of the Jews and of Israel. Clearly he can, and he does. The question is whether for him scripture points to a linear entity that in a linear fashion prepares the way for, and leads up to, the incarnation of the Logos. In this regard, we have simply to note in the Gospel of John the absence of a linear sacred history that flows out of scripture into the gospel story.[17]

---

[15] Those who do not believe Jesus show thereby that they do not believe Moses. On 'believing in Moses,' cf. Meeks, *Prophet-King*, 295.

[16] In Luke 24:6, 8, a similar motif involves the use of the verb *mimnēskomai*. What is absent in Luke is a sense for the gospel-created geological faults, and thus a theological allergy to the naive promise-fulfillment hermeneutic. See Schubert, 'Luke 24.'

[17] In the scenes presented in John 1:35–51, disciples of the Baptist confess Jesus to be the Messiah, the one of whom Moses wrote, Son of God, and King of Israel, thus seeming to make their way from scriptural expectations to Jesus. I take this material

Indeed the redemptive-historical perspective is more than absent; it is a perspective against which John is waging a battle. In his gospel, the origin, the beginning, the point of departure for the doing of theology is not to be found in the linear development of a linear history. In the very beginning with God, there was the Logos, the Word. He has no precedent in any history, for nothing and no one anteceded him. The Logos alone has been with God. Two consequences follow: He alone is the exegete of the Father (John 1:18). Other than the Father whom *he* makes known, therefore, nothing and no one can provide the criterion against which he is to be measured, not even scripture.

Gospel and Scripture in Paul

When we turn to Paul's letters, asking about gospel and scripture, 1 Thessalonians brings an immediate surprise. That letter contains not one exegetical paragraph. It is both true and important, as Hays has recently argued, that the voice of scripture is more weighty to Paul himself than one would think on the basis of his explicit exegeses.[18] Still, the absence of even one of these in 1 Thessalonians is impressive. If we had only this earliest of Paul's letters, we would have no reason to think that the apostle ever caused his Gentile converts to trouble their minds over the relationship between the gospel and scripture.

1 Corinthians

Pondering the surprise of 1 Thessalonians, we turn to a passage in which, insisting that he preaches only the gospel of Christ, Paul nevertheless explicates that proclamation by quoting from scripture:

Christ did not send me to baptize but to proclaim the gospel,
and not with eloquent wisdom, lest the cross of Christ be
emptied of its power.
For to those who are perishing the word of the cross is
foolishness,

---

to be tradition which John accepts only because he can enclose it in a gospel that proves over-all to be opposed to redemptive history. See Fortna, *The Fourth Gospel,* 15–47; Martyn, *John,* 104–107. See also, however, the response below by Professor Gaventa.

[18] Hays, *Echoes.*

to those of us, however, who are being saved, it is
God powerfully stepping on the scene.[19]
For it stands written (in scripture)
> I will destroy the wisdom of the wise,
> and the discernment (*synesis*) of the discerning I will
> thwart (Isa 29:14).

Where is the one who is wise? Where is the scribe? Where is the debater of this age? Has not God made foolish the wisdom of the world? For since, in the wisdom of God, the world did not know God through wisdom, it pleased God through the foolishness of our proclamation to save those who believe. For Jews demand signs, and Greeks seek wisdom, but we preach Christ crucified, a stumbling block to Jews and foolishness to Gentiles, but to those who are called, both Jews and Greeks, Christ the power of God and the wisdom of God.
(1 Cor 1:17–24)[20]

What does this remarkable passage tell us about Paul's view of the relationship between the gospel and scripture?

Attempting to listen with the ears of the Corinthians, we hear an utterly outrageous affirmation. Paul is not playing the language game according to the rules. Knowing – as everyone knows! – that the opposite of foolishness is wisdom, Paul should speak in a rational way, saying in 1 Cor 1:18,

> To those who are perishing the word of the cross is
> considered to be *foolishness*;
> to those of us, however, who are being saved it is
> considered to be *wisdom.*

Expressing himself in this manner, Paul would reflect what one takes to be a simple fact. The proclamation of the gospel must be like the proclamation of any other message. It involves a two-step dance, does it not? First, through the apostle God serves up the gospel. As a second and separable step, the human being assesses that message – responds to it, as we say – discerning it to be, in his judgment, either foolish or wise. And on the basis of that discernment, the human being decides, in this second step, either to believe or not to believe.

---

[19] The last line reads literally '. . . it is the power (*dynamis*) of God.' To study Paul's use of this expression is to see that in the apostle's mouth it is consistently verbal in character, referring not to a thing, but rather to an event: God newly exerting his own very strange kind of power in the world of human beings.

[20] On this text see especially Schrage, *Korinther.*

Returning to the text, we see that this two-step dance is the picture that Paul seems to portray in the first line, whereas, in the second line, he clearly says, in effect, that that picture is foreign to the event of the gospel.[21]

> To those who are perishing the word of the cross is
>   considered to be *foolishness*;
> but to those of us who are being saved it is
>   *God powerfully stepping on the scene!*

Those who are perishing think that the gospel is an it. Once it is delivered as the first step, then, as the second step, they think that they can assess it on the basis of perceptive criteria they already possess. And, in fact, on the basis of those criteria, they do pronounce the word, 'Foolishness!,' thinking that in that pronouncement they are making their own sovereign decision.

Looking at those who are being redeemed, Paul sees that the scenario is different, not least in that the two-step dance is excluded for all concerned. The gospel is not an it that God serves up as the first step, afterwards withdrawing to see what the human being will make of it. On the contrary, the gospel is God's advent! And for that reason, those who are being redeemed discover that in the event of the gospel God invades their wills, rearranging the very *fundamenta* of their existence.[22] As event, the gospel is inseparable from God because God himself comes on the scene in that proclamation in the fullness of his power (*dynamis theou*).[23]

---

[21] In fact Paul presupposes the two-step dance neither in the second nor in the first line. Those who are perishing are not exercising freedom of will. They are suffering God's active judgment *in* the gospel!

[22] See chapter 6 above.

[23] We have here a major issue facing the New Testament guild, and one of fundamental theological import. There are two camps. (1) On the one side are scholars who understand Paul to have viewed the gospel as the event that defines the category of God's power, being itself God's powerful invasion of the cosmos for the purpose of bringing about new creation. The seminal essay here is that of Käsemann, 'Righteousness;' see especially the footnote on his page 173. (2) The other camp credits Paul with the view that the gospel, rather than being itself God's powerful invasion, is a message that establishes a human possibility. The Gospel, in short, is a new edition, in effect, of the ancient doctrine of the Two Ways. In this second camp there are two subgroups. (*a*) Numerous Christian theologians have said, in essence, that what is novel about the gospel is that it offers faith in Christ as a new way to God, a way that is the preferable alternative to the way of works. The gospel, announcing a new possibility, teaches one that it is better to believe than to work. In addition to making a caricature of Judaism, as though it were a religion of works-righteousness (helpfully corrected by

This is the point the Corinthians will have seen in Paul's certainty that the gospel creates its own language game, producing new pairs of opposites.[24] They will have noted, that is, that whereas in the context of 1 Cor 1:18 Paul speaks repeatedly of foolishness and wisdom as a pair of opposites, he does not do so in referring to the event of the word of the cross. The surprising linguistic imbalance of 1 Cor 1:18 is one of the major keys to the text.[25] By means of that imbalance, Paul not only speaks of the gospel as God's performative word. He also denies that this performative word – the gospel of the crucified Christ – is subject to human evaluation, whether that of the Gentiles or that of the Jews (1 Cor 1:22–24). And in this denial Paul obliterates in one stroke the thought that the gospel is subject to criteria of perception that have been developed apart from the gospel!

It is precisely with respect to scripture, then, that the offensive nature of the gospel reaches its climax. For to say that the gospel – as the word of the cross – is not subject to perceptive criteria that have been developed apart from it is to say that the gospel is not subject to criteria developed prior to it. And that, in turn, is to place an italicized question

---

E. P. Sanders, *Palestinian Judaism*), this line of interpretation surrenders the good news of God's powerful invasion to the impotence of a merely human decision to have faith. To cite one example, E. P. Sanders' fascination with two questions – What does the human being do in order to get in? and What does he do in order to stay in? – leads this very accomplished scholar to an overuse and an oversimplification of the category of decision, not altogether unlike the pattern one finds in the writings of Bultmann, a scholar Sanders has no intention of following (see chapter 10 above)! Strange as it may seem to us, Paul speaks fundamentally of what God has done, is doing, and will do; and in this way the apostle holds as his central concern God's power, not some fancied human decision. (b) In addition to those who concentrate their attention on decision, there is in this second camp another sub-group who, with equal effectiveness, reduce the gospel to the category of possibility. Concerned that ethics has often disappeared into a cloud of triumphalism, these interpreters understandably accentuate Paul's demand for obedience. Here the problem arises from the fact that, unless one is both precise and explicit about it, obedience is inevitably viewed as the human alternative to disobedience. To cite, again, a single example, the learned article of Donfried, 'Justification,' was not written, I think, with the conscious intention of suggesting that the gospel merely presents human beings with a new chance to be obedient. To a considerable extent, however, that is the effect of the study. Perhaps in exegetical discussion we would agree that for Paul the antidote that actually conquers human disobedience is not the human decision to be obedient, but rather the active power of God's mercy (Rom 11:30–32), mercy so powerful as to overcome disobedience by eliciting the active obedience of faith (Gal 3:2).

[24] See chapter 7 above.
[25] Cf. Wilckens, *Weisheit*, 24.

mark alongside the patriarchal traditions. Here one has the impression that Paul requires his reader (now, no less than in his own time) to lean out over a horrifying abyss.

What calls for emphasis is Paul's own stance in relation to this abyss. One thinks of Paul's words about himself in the first chapter of Galatians. Looking back from the event of the gospel, Paul says that his own zeal for the patriarchal traditions led him to persecute severely the group he now knows to be the church of God. With equal clarity – and this is the point of greatest importance for us – he implies that the patriarchal traditions did not provide him with the criteria of perception that enabled him to recognize God's good news when it came along. What brought Paul to the gospel was not his decision about God, based on criteria learned in his scribal study of scripture, but rather what one might call God's apocalyptic decision about him: 'But when [God] was pleased to apocalypse his Son to me . . .' (Gal 1:15–16).

For Paul, then, there are no through-trains from the scriptural, patriarchal traditions and their perceptive criteria to the gospel of God's Son. Taking a final glance at 1 Cor 1:17–24, we can be certain, that Paul did not make his way *from* Isaiah's words about God's destroying the discernment of the discerning *to* the foolish word of the crucified Messiah. His hermeneutic worked exactly the other way around, from the previously unknown and foolish gospel of the cross to the previously known and previously misunderstood scripture (cf. Gal 1:13–16).[26]

Galatians

We might explicate this finding by turning finally to the letter to the Galatians, for the exegetical sections in that letter are indeed produced by the radical hermeneutic we see in the first chapter of 1 Corinthians. Consider, for example, Gal 4:21–5:1, Paul's exegesis of the stories in Genesis 15–21 about Abraham, Sarah, Hagar, Ishmael, and Isaac.[27] When we listen to Paul's exegesis of the Genesis text with the ears of the Galatians, we notice several things.

(1) We are immediately thrown back into the company of the two Bau(e)rs, for the form of Paul's exegesis in Gal 4:21–5:1 shows us that, if we take our seat in the Galatian churches, we hear not only

---

[26] Cf. Vielhauer, 'Paulus und das Alte Testament.'
[27] See the more detailed interpretation of this passage in chapter 12 above; and note the analysis of Gal 3:6–4:7, the first exegetical section of the letter, in chapter 10.

Paul's words, but also the words of the Teachers who invaded those churches. It was in the Teachers' sermons, in fact, that the Galatian Gentiles first heard about Abraham, Sarah, Hagar, Ishmael, and Isaac. And in the interpretation given by those exegetical theologians they doubtless noted three major accents, all having to do with the term 'covenant':

(*a*) God's covenant with Abraham commenced a covenantal line that extended through Isaac to God's people, Israel.

(*b*) God provided a specific definition of his covenant: that covenant is the commandment of circumcision, observed repeatedly in generation after generation (Genesis 17).

(*c*) At the present time, via the good news streaming out from the Jerusalem church, the covenantal line is being extended to the Gentiles; for, through the Messiah Jesus, Gentiles are now invited to enter the line of the Abrahamic covenant by observing the commandment of circumcision.

(2) Now we turn with our other ear, so to speak, to listen to Paul's exegesis of Genesis 15–21, and doing that, we find a radically different picture:

(*a*) In his exegesis of Genesis 15–21, Paul gives to the term 'covenant' an emphasis at least equal to that given to this term by the Teachers.

(*b*) But departing radically from the plain sense of Genesis 15–21, Paul affirms two covenants, diametrically opposed to one another, something not at all to be found in the text itself.

(*c*) Paul is totally silent about the fact that in the Genesis stories God specifically defines his one covenant as his commandment of circumcision. Paul is equally silent about there being in his scripture no covenant attached to Hagar and her son Ishmael.

Of two things we can be confident. We can say that, when Paul's messenger had finished reading aloud this exegetical section of Galatians, both the Teachers and their Galatian followers must have risen to their feet, vociferously condemning it as one of the most arbitrary and unfaithful interpretations one can imagine.[28] We can be equally sure, however, that, when Paul had finished dictating this

---

[28] Jewish scholars of our time have understandably characterized it in similar terms. See, e.g. Ben Chorin: Paul turns the patriarchal stories of Genesis 15–21 'completely upside down' (*Paulus*, 132).

paragraph, he was certain that, by providing this exegesis of scripture, he had preached the gospel once again, and specifically the gospel that had been preached ahead of time to Abraham by scripture itself (Gal 3:8).

Pause, now, for a moment, and allow yourself the fantasy of being able to discuss with Paul the fact that ancient texts are often subjected to eisegetical domestication. And since you are indulging in a fantasy, you might as well imagine yourself suggesting to Paul that Gal 4:21–5:1 is a prime instance of such eisegetical domestication. If your powers of fantasy allow you to do that, then you also have enough imagination to hear Paul's response:

> Whether, in interpreting the stories in Genesis 15–21, I have used the gospel to domesticate the voice of scripture is a question that can be answered only on the basis of the gospel-event.[29]

One hardly needs to add that with that response Paul takes us back to the radical hermeneutic of the first chapter of 1 Corinthians, and we are thus faced with some of the specific dimensions of Paul's understanding of the relationship between gospel and scripture.

If the gospel is significantly related to scripture – and for Paul it is – and if the gospel of the crucified Christ nevertheless brings its own criteria of perception/discernment, then in the case of Paul, as in the case of John, it is misleading to speak of an even-handed, dialectical relationship between scripture and gospel.[30] That much should be clear from the fact that for Paul the text of scripture no longer reads as it did before the advent of the gospel. When one needs to do so – and most of

---

[29] If this Pauline response sounds hopelessly arbitrary, it is imperative to note at least that Paul believes scripture actually says exactly what he hears it saying. He is not constructing what some rabbis of the middle ages called *pilpul*, an exegesis one knows not to correspond to the original meaning. In fact, Paul does not think of one meaning back then and a second and debatable meaning now. For him the scriptural stories in Genesis 15–21 do in fact speak about the two Gentile missions, one Law-observant and one circumcision-free, thus uttering the gospel ahead of time (cf. 1 Cor 10:11).

[30] Cf. Vielhauer's statement: 'It is true [as Mr. Wilckens has said] that "the event of Christ cannot be recognized and understood – in its universal-eschatological meaning of salvation – as an isolated fact." [We cannot follow Mr. Wilckens, however, when he says that] "the event of Christ needs the witness of history, being history's fulfillment." For, while it is true that Abraham is for Paul of great theological significance, and whereas the promise does in fact take precedence over the Law, it is also true that the texts of Romans 4 and Galatians 3 do not portray the consequence of a history of election . . . The history of Israel as a sequence of events does not interest Paul in the slightest' (*Oikodomē*, 217–218).

Paul's formal exegetical exercises are polemical[31] – one can find in scripture a voice that testifies to the gospel. But one finds this testifying voice – the voice of God in scripture – only because one already hears God's voice in the gospel, that is to say in the story of the cross, the story that brings its own criteria of perception, the story, therefore, that brings its own criteria of exegesis.

Some Provisional Conclusions

To listen to John and Paul with ears borrowed from members of their own circles is – at least in my experience – to learn several things:

(1) To a considerable extent, the earliest history of Christian thought and life can be profitably analyzed as the history of various struggles over a single issue: Is the gospel of the crucifixion and resurrection of Jesus Christ subject to criteria of perception that have been developed apart from it?[32] And with regard to this issue, Paul and John share a number of convictions, not least the belief that prior to the event of the gospel, the human being does not possess adequate powers of discernment any more than he or she possesses freedom of will. One hardly needs to add that the issue of perceptive criteria became truly thorny when early Christians were asking whether the gospel was subject to criteria of perception one had inherited from scripture. For, to take one's bearings again from Paul and John, one would say that the human being cannot find these adequate powers of perception even in the scriptures themselves. 'You search the scriptures, because you think that in them you have eternal life; and it is they that bear witness to me; yet you refuse to come to me that you may have life' (John 5:39–40).

(2) When we analyze early Christian history in the light of this issue, listening to the multitude of voices that were directed to it, we see that, more often than we should like to admit, we have attributed a

---

[31] Regarding the thesis that Paul's exegetical efforts are mostly polemical, see Harnack, 'Das Alte Testament.' From the work of Grässer, *Bund*, it seems clear that all of the crucial covenant passages in Paul's letters – Gal 3:15–18; Gal 4:21–5:1; 2 Corinthians 3 – are exegeses formulated by Paul in an explicitly polemical form because of opponents who are providing his churches in Galatia and in Corinth with weighty exegetical discourses on the subject of covenant. Paul is an exegetically active 'covenantal theologian' only when compelled to be, *pace* Wright, *Covenant.*

[32] Cf. Bultmann, *Theology*, 2.119–127.

motif to John or Paul, when in actuality that motif is characteristic of theologians against whom these authors were waging a significant battle.[33]

(3) Why have we often done that? In part, I think, because we have been unconsciously afraid that, if Paul and John should prove to be anti-redemptive-historical theologians, they would also prove to have applied to scripture an anti-Judaic hermeneutic. That fear is unfounded.[34] Theologically it is important to note that neither Paul nor John was an absolute innovator. In scripture itself there is ancient tradition for theology oriented to the geological fault. Consider Second Isaiah.[35] The prophet, you will recall, several times calls on his fellow exiles to remember the things of old, to remember the exodus, in the sure hope of the new exodus. One time, however, he reflects on the ways in which tradition can blind eyes and stop ears. Thus he hears God say with emphasis:

> Do not remember the former things, nor remember the things of old. Behold I am doing a new thing; now it springs forth; do you not perceive it? (Isa 43:18–19).

(4) Even the similar note in Second Isaiah cannot forestall, however, a final question. Did Paul and John unwittingly prepare the way for Marcion? In the present context this question has to be posed for two reasons.

First, the battle that raged around Marcion was focused to no small degree on the issue to which we have been directing our attention, that of the relationship between scripture and gospel.[36] Second, when the emerging great church identified Marcion's theology as heretical, it did so, in part, by adopting a view of the relationship between scripture and gospel that, in general terms, looks rather similar to the view of the simple exegetical theologians against whom Paul and John struggled in the first century (see Justin Martyr; Rhodo; Irenaeus). If the orthodox theologians of the great church had had an accurate sense for the radical disjunctures in the theologies of Paul and John, would they not have been compelled to draw some degree of analogy between those two

---

[33] See chapter 10 above.
[34] Cf. chapter 5 above.
[35] See also Psalm 78.
[36] The study of Harnack remains a classic: *Marcion*. See also Hoffmann, *Marcion*; and Clabeaux, *Edition*; idem, 'Marcion.'

theologians and Marcion, thus raising some doubts as to the complete orthodoxy precisely of Paul and John themselves?[37]

The raising of the question can lead us to a closing point. If one of the most virulent heresies of the second century emerged in connection with the matter of gospel and scripture, may it not be that the same is true of the first century, except that, as one passes from one century to the other, the identities of orthodoxy and heresy undergo a remarkable reversal?

If we listen to Paul and John, and if, at least tentatively, we take our view of heresy from them (note the term *anathema* in Gal 1:8–9), then we could be led to ponder the possibility that the earliest heretical view of gospel and scripture was the embryonic *redemptive history* characteristic of the simple exegetical theologians known both to Paul and to John. It is the author of the letter to the Galatians, at any rate, who is the theologian of the cross, whereas the Teachers are theologians of an incipient and simple-minded redemptive history.

And it is against their view that Paul waged battle precisely in order to bear witness to the true identity of the God of Abraham by speaking of him as the Father of Jesus Christ. With his deed in the crucified Christ, that is to say, this God is announcing who he is, and thus showing that, however wrongly he may have been perceived in the past, he always was the one who rectifies the ungodly. It follows that this God is sovereign even over traditions celebrating his own earlier deeds. The struggle of Paul and John is one Second Isaiah would have understood.

Critical Responses to the Lecture

Professor Beverly R. Gaventa

In her critique Gaventa expressed a measure of agreement as regards Paul and some serious reservations with respect to John. In her remarks, I heard two major points: (*a*) The location of inadequacy to assess the gospel. Does it lie with scripture or with human beings? (*b*) The role of scripture in making the gospel intelligible. What is signified by the line that runs from gospel to scripture?

> *Regarding John*: The target [of John's polemic in 5:39–47] is not the adequacy of scripture to reveal Jesus Christ. The target . . . is the

---

[37] As the Gospel of John won its place in the canon only with difficulty, that development has rightly been said to have occurred 'through man's error and God's providence' (Käsemann, *Testament*, 75).

adequacy of human beings, who read scripture which does testify on behalf of Jesus, without seeing what it says. [Thus, while John practices an interpretation that reads scripture by means of the gospel and not the other way around, he nevertheless perceives a line . . . [that] begins with God and the Logos, . . . contains the history of Israel and, with it, scripture, and then culminates in the gospel. The Logos thus precedes scripture, but scripture in turn points toward the advent of Jesus [note particularly John 1:35–51].

Regarding Paul: [The apostle holds as a major conviction] the inadequacy of human beings to assess the gospel, [but] this conviction comes to expression in terms drawn from scripture (e.g. 1 Cor 1:19–31). [Paul does not reason from scripture to the cross, but – even in 1 Thessalonians – the words and echoes of scripture] provide the language with which Paul articulates the meaning of the gospel. [That is so because] the gospel . . . remains unintelligible apart from the language of scripture and the story of Israel. [In short, for Paul] scripture is not only a convenient mode for interpretation but a vital requirement.

This is, I think, a constructive critique. Both John and Paul focus the polemic I have discussed against other interpreters of scripture, while being able themselves, beginning with the gospel, to hear God's voice in scripture itself. But, as one ponders Gaventa's claim that scripture makes the gospel intelligible, what is one to make of Paul's words about the foolishness of the gospel in 1 Cor 1:17–24 (see above)? Moreover, how is one to understand Gaventa's use of the expression 'the story of Israel'? If, in Galatians, Paul reads scripture in such a way as to find in Abraham a point rather than the beginning of a line (Gal 3:16; cf. chapter 10 above), and if our word 'story' indicates a narrative always possessing some sort of linearity, then can we say that Paul articulates the gospel by drawing not only on the language of scripture, but also on the story of Israel?[38] One can cite, for instance, Paul's reference to Israel's wilderness generation in 1 Cor 10:1–22, but we should have then to ask whether this example – and others as well – is linear rather than punctiliar.[39] It is a service of Gaventa to express herself in a way that calls for further discussion.

[38] Cf. Hofmann, *Weissagung*. Bultmann accurately summarizes: '[Hofmann's] thesis is this: It is not the *words* of the Old Testament that are really prophecy, but the *history* of Israel, to which the Old Testament testifies' (Bultmann, *Essays*, 188).

[39] Note, on the one hand, the apparently punctiliar terms *typoi* and *typikōs* in 1 Cor 10:6, 11 and, on the other hand, the plural reference to 'our fathers' (1 Cor 10:1) and the linear reading proposed by Hays, 'Scripture,' 39–41.

Professor Paul W. Meyer

In contrast to Gaventa, and perhaps as much to her surprise as to mine, Meyer professed basic agreement with my remarks about John, while expressing a significant degree of skepticism about my reading of Paul.

> *Regarding John*: This gospel avoids making Jesus as Messiah dependent upon the Hebrew scriptures or any tradition of their interpretation. In John's theology, the Son is so carefully aligned with the Father who sent him, so completely transparent to the presence and reality of the God who confronts the world in him, that there is no possibility of any independent access to God to establish the credentials of the Son.[40]
>
> *Regarding Paul*: [For Paul scripture is far too important to be left in the hands of] those who are intent on domesticating the gospel to their own criteria of perception. It provides access not just to the continuities of Israel but to the God of Israel, who is the 'antecedent' of the gospel as well as its *ex post facto* authorizer, indeed who cannot be the latter without being the former, without whom the gospel too would have no validity. The appeal to Abraham does provide to Paul, in his own hands of course, a confirmation to his preaching of the gospel . . . that parallels the confirmation that God himself provided when he . . . 'raised Jesus our Lord from the dead.' Without this authentication from scripture, i.e. from God's side, Paul's argument would no more be believed and trusted than could the dead Jesus of Nazareth apart from his authentication from God's side.[41] It is not just criteria of perception that are at stake in the relationship of gospel and scripture. It is also a matter of categories of interpretation . . . and above all, within the historically concrete process of a life-and-death argument about God, a way of reaching beyond the tools of argument to a truth and reality that argument alone cannot establish or adjudicate. It requires a scripture that is more than a product of Paul's hermeneutic, one in which God speaks before human beings interpret. [The issue is] fundamentally the relationship between the Father of Jesus Christ and the God of Abraham, Isaac, and Jacob.

Like Gaventa, Meyer has provided a critique that is constructive, in that it raises in one's mind further questions. Let me mention three:

(*a*) Granted that Paul was in every instance concerned with a gospel-word that reaches beyond the tools of argument, can we say that his

---

[40] See now Meyer, 'The Father.'

[41] Regarding the issue at stake here, see again the disagreement between U. Wilckens and P. Vielhauer mentioned in note 30 above.

gospel meets that test? And if it does, can we identify the result? Is it scripture or the apocalypse of Jesus Christ that reaches beyond the tools of argument? Do we not need further conversation about the relationship between scripture and the apocalyptic character of God's deed in Christ? I myself want to learn how Meyer reads Gal 1:10–16.[42]

(b) Granted also that the God who sent his Son is the God who uttered his promise to Abraham. Both of these deeds are deeds of the same God; thus what one might call 'God's steadfast identity' is altogether crucial, especially in light of the continuing influence of a Marcionite type of thought in the modern church. Is it not in this regard that Gaventa speaks of 'the story of Israel' and Meyer of 'the continuities of Israel'? My lecture suffices to show, however, that I am somewhat uneasy with the linearity of Gaventa's expression and with the plural character of Meyer's. But again, that means only that we have an exegetical issue calling for further discussion among us. Specifically, how are we to relate 'the story of Israel' and 'the continuities of Israel' to Gal 3:16, 1 Cor 10:1–12, 18, and Rom 9:6–13?[43] I do not doubt that further conversation with Gaventa and Meyer will be instructive for me.

(c) Finally, the matter of God's identity could take us to yet another exegetical discussion of Romans 9–11, and in that conversation we might find ourselves pondering our own use of the terms 'identity,' 'identical,' and 'identify.' The issue is indeed, as Meyer says, the relationship between the Father of Jesus Christ and the God of Abraham, Isaac, and Jacob. And in this regard, Gaventa, Meyer, and I should surely agree that Romans 9–11 shows us a theologian who is thoroughly convinced that the God who sent his Son is *iden*tical with the God who elected Abraham. Is not this theologian also concerned to say, however, that, in sending his Son, this one God is newly *iden*tifying himself as the one who rectifies – and, paradoxically, has always rectified – the ungodly? And if so, is this dual use of the root *idem* something that was missed not once, but rather twice in the second century? Once

---

[42] Aspects of my own thinking in this regard are laid out in Martyn, *Galatians*, Comments 8, 9, and 10. Pending further instruction, I should not refer with Meyer to a scripture – or even to a gospel formulation – 'in which God speaks before human beings interpret,' for, in uttering his word, God invades the human will, thus immediately affecting the interpretive capacity. See again the comments on 1 Cor 1:17–24 above.

[43] On 'Israel according to the flesh' in 1 Cor 10:18 see Schrage, 'Israel.'

by Marcion, who failed to see God's identity, by denying that the Father of Jesus Christ is identical with the God of Abraham. And a second time by many of those who read Marcion out of the church, while failing to sense the motif of God's newly identifying himself in Jesus Christ. With hearty thanks to Professors Gaventa and Meyer, let me say that the discussion is to be continued.

Part IV

The Church's Everyday Life

Part IV
The Church's Everyday Life

In an earlier day Paul's letters were often thought to consist of a theological section followed by an ethical application. In fact, as 1 Corinthians amply demonstrates, Paul shows no tendency to draw a discernible distinction between theology and ethics. Indeed, if we define ethics as an investigation of the norms of human conduct that are focused on human decisions, duty, and virtue – what a member of the human race should will to do and what that human being should will not to do – we would have to admit that Paul's letters are notable in containing no decision-oriented ethics at all.[1]

The letters do indeed include hortatory sections, doubtless considered by Paul to be essential. When the apostle turns to exhortation, however, he is in fact *doing* theology, by speaking of God's continuing apocalyptic rectification in the daily life of the church. There is here a distinct linearity. Paul knows that in Christ God has created the new community (Gal 3:28, 6:15). He also knows, however, that God is

---

[1] 'The church's everyday life,' then – as I use the expression in Part IV – corresponds neither to what is often termed 'ethics,' nor to what is generally meant by the word 'morals.' Both of those terms, and the concerns and literary forms connected with them, were alive and well in Paul's time (see especially Furnish, *Ethics*; idem, *Moral Teaching*; Schrage, *Ethics*; Malherbe, *Moral Exhortation*; Meeks, *Origins*; Sampley, *Walking*; Hays, *Community*). It is easy to accept Meeks's carefully crafted definitions: Morality 'names a dimension of life, a pervasive and, often, only partly conscious set of value-laden dispositions, inclinations, attitudes, and habits.' Ethics is 'a reflective, second-order activity: it is morality rendered self-conscious; it asks about the logic of moral discourse and action, about the grounds for judgment, about the anatomy of duty or the roots and structure of virtue' (*Origins*, 4). It is also easy to see, however, that the pictures Paul presents in Gal 5:13–24, Rom 12:1–15:13, etc. are (*a*) thoroughly permeated by apocalyptic motifs and (*b*) tightly focused on God's *new* creation, the Christian community in which the criteria of discernment have been fundamentally changed (chapter 6 above). Thus, these pictures are at their root descriptive of daily life in the real world, *made what it is by the advents of Christ and his Spirit.* They are, then, grievously domesticated when they are pressed into the categories usually associated with morals and ethics, as these categories pertain to timeless concerns among human beings in general. See further notes 25 and 26 in chapter 15 below..

continuing to form that community in the image of Christ (Gal 4:19; 2 Cor 3:18) and to supply that community with the Spirit of Christ (Gal 4:6; 3:5; Rom 8:1–27). In his exhortations Paul speaks, therefore, to the community that is *newly addressable* because it bears Christ's form and is led by Christ's Spirit. That is to say, every one of Paul's hortatory sentences presupposes the presence of Christ and the constant activity of Christ's Spirit, as it causes the church to be able to hear. Thus, far from being decision-oriented ethics directed to the individual human will as such, Paul's exhortations are fundamentally descriptive of the corporate patterns of life that constitute God's continuing apocalyptic rectification. It is to those patterns of life that the church is called, but the church is called to them because it is fully equipped for them by virtue of its being the community in which Christ's Spirit is bearing its fruit.

14

The Crucial Event in the History of the Law

I

Pauline interpreters are unanimously of the opinion that, in Gal 5:13–6:10, Paul addresses issues pertinent to the church's daily life. It is no surprise to see, then, that when these interpreters ask how that daily life is related to the Law, they turn first of all to Gal 5:13–14, which in the NRSV reads as follows:

> For you were called to freedom, brothers and sisters; only do not use your freedom as an opportunity for self-indulgence, but through love become slaves to one another. For the whole law is summed up in a single commandment, 'You shall love your neighbor as yourself.'

Surprise sets in, however, with the discovery that in Gal 5:14 the NRSV committee offers 'For the whole law *is summed up* in a single commandment' as the translation of the Greek *ho gar pas nomos en heni logō peplērōtai*. The student of Greek knows that elsewhere in early Christian literature the verb *pleroō* is almost always translated 'to fulfill' (the RSV rendered Gal 5:14 'For the whole law *is fulfilled* in one word'). And the surprise deepens with the discovery that the NRSV was anticipated by the New English Bible – 'can be summed up' – and by the Jerusalem Bible – 'is summarised' (Revised English Bible: 'is summed up'). Why have the scholars responsible for these recent translations elected this new rendering?

Illumination arrives in Victor Furnish's perceptive work *The Love Command in the New Testament*. For, asserting the equivalence of Gal 5:14 and Rom 13:9, Furnish renders the crucial verb of Gal 5:14 'has been epitomized,' thus applauding the NEB and the JB (the NRSV had not yet appeared):

> The passive verb which I have translated 'has been epitomized' (literally 'has been fulfilled,' cf. *RSV*) is equivalent to the verb 'summed up' which Paul uses in Rom 13:9 (this is quite properly recognized in both *NEB* and *JB*).

The law is 'the law of faith' when its *essence* is recognized in the love commandment. . . . [For Paul] 'God's commands' [1 Cor 7:19] are *summarized* in the one commandment of Lev 19:18. When one is a new creature in Christ, he lives by a faith which becomes active in love, and that is *what really matters*.[1]

From several translations, then, and indeed from numerous studies parallel to that of Furnish, we know how Gal 5:14 reads if it is interpreted in the light of Rom 13:9.[2] That is to say, assuming Rom 13:9 to be a guide, one arrives at what is taken to be Paul's intention in Gal 5:14: When the Law is *summarized*, its *essence* – that about it which really matters – emerges, and that essence is the love commandment of Lev 19:18. But how is Gal 5:14 to be read, if one interprets it – as the Galatians did – in the context of the letter in which it stands?

II

By the time he reaches Gal 5:13–14, Paul can take for granted three major elements that form the background for his words there.

A. Galatians 5:3

Speaking to the former Gentiles who make up his Galatian churches, and who are being tempted to accept circumcision, Paul says in 5:3 that the one who in this manner starts out on the route of the Law must go all the way, observing the whole of the Law (*holon ton nomon poiein*).[3] And in the next verse (5:4), he insists that to seek rectification in this observance of the whole Law is to be separated from Christ. One sees, then, that, whereas in 5:14 Paul draws a positive link between 'the whole of the Law' and the life of the church, in 5:3 he says that observing 'the whole of the Law' can have nothing to do with the church's daily life.[4]

---

[1] Furnish, *Command*, 97 (emphasis added).

[2] In addition to Furnish, see, e.g., Schrage, *Ethics*, 206–207; Lührmann, *Galater*, 87: 'Zusammenfassung des Gesetzes.' Reading Rom 13:9 into Gal 5:14 is a venerable practice, doubtless much older than its attestation (*anakephalaioutai*) in the manuscript of 365 (twelfth or thirteenth century). The interpretation of Galatians in light of Romans remains very widespread in our own time, for the old assumption that Romans provides us with the quintessence of 'Paul's theology' endures in the unconscious, even where it is consciously questioned.

[3] The *linguistic* difference between *holos ho nomos* (5:3) and *ho pas nomos* (5:14) is without significance, *pace* Hübner, *Gesetz*, 37–40.

[4] The tension between Gal 5:3 and 5:14 has frequently been 'solved' by repeating the venerable tradition according to which Paul rejected the Law as the way of rectification (5:3), while affirming it as the criterion for ethics (5:14). See, e.g. Schrage: 'God "justifies without works of the law," and the law has ceased to be a way of salvation . . .

B. Galatians 4:21

This tension between the negative role of the Law in Gal 5:3 and its positive role in 5:14 leads us back to 4:21, where Paul speaks of a similar tension *internal* to the Law.

> Tell me, you who wish to live under the power of the Law! Do you really hear what the Law says [when it speaks of children begotten by the power of the promise]?

Here the Law as enslaving overlord stands in contrast with the Law as promise. Indeed, an essential part of Paul's point in Gal 4:21–5:1 is that the Law has two voices. The Galatians can come *under* the Law, thereby being enslaved by the power of its subjugating and *cursing voice* (4:21a; cf. 3:10), or they can *hear* the *promising voice* with which the Law speaks of the birth of circumcision-free churches among the Gentiles, thereby sensing their own true identity as children of God's promise (4:21b, 22, 27, 31).[5]

C. Galatians 3:6–4:7

From Gal 5:14, 5:3 and 4:21, then, we move further back into the letter, retracing certain aspects of Paul's exegetical argument in 3:6–4:7. For in constructing that argument, Paul again draws a sharp contrast between two voices. First, he portrays the contrast between the blessing/promising voice of God and the cursing/enslaving voice of the Law. Second and equally important, Paul finds precisely the same two contrasting voices *in* the Law. On the one hand, there is the Law of Sinai, the Law that forms one of the enslaving elements of the old

---

but this does not mean that Christians are dispensed from obeying the commandments (1 Cor 7:19). Therefore the Old Testament and its law are presupposed and enforced as the criterion of Christian conduct' (*Ethics*, 205). Furnish draws the same differentiation: 'Paul rejects the law as a way of salvation, but he does not reject it as a norm for the conduct of one's life' (*Command*, 95). And note more recently E. P. Sanders' distinction between 'getting in' – one enters the church by faith rather than by the Law – and 'staying in' – one remains in the church by keeping the Law (e.g. *Palestinian Judaism*, 513). Against this cherished tradition, one considers Paul's certainty that the church's daily life *is* the scene of God's rectification (so Gal 5:2–6:10). That is to say, God's act of making things right is for Paul 'God's sovereignty over the world revealing itself eschatologically in Jesus . . . the rightful power with which God makes his cause to triumph in the world . . .' (Käsemann, *Questions*, 180; cf. 188–195). See chapter 9 above.

5   Cf. chapter 12 above.

cosmos by being paired with the Not-Law (4:3; 6:15; 3:28).[6] In Galatians 3 and 4, this Sinaitic Law *is* the enslaving and cursing voice of the Law (3:10, 19–20; 4:4–5).

On the other hand, however, prior to the Sinaitic genesis of the Law/ the Not-Law as one of the paired and enslaving cosmic elements, there was the promissory voice of the Law.[7] This was the voice with which, speaking in God's behalf, the Law (as *hē graphē*) preached the gospel ahead of time to Abraham (and to Abraham's singular seed; 3:16–17) in the form, not of commandments, but rather of the covenantal promise: 'In you all the Gentiles *will be blessed*' (Gal 3:8; Gen 12:3).[8]

Being nothing other than promissory, this original voice also pronounced the promise that is a statement of God's rectifying good news: 'the one who is rectified by faith *will live*' (Gal 3:11; Hab 2:4).[9] We see, then, that Paul draws a clear distinction between that singular, true promise of the Law's original voice and the false promise of the Law in its plural and paired existence (Gal 3:12; Lev 18:5).[10] Thus,

---

[6]   See chapters 8 and 10 above.

[7]   It may seem illogical to speak of a period prior to the existence of a cosmic element. For Paul, however, it is the cosmos of religion that has as one of its elements the Law/the Not-Law. And Paul clearly considers the cosmos of religion to be younger than the cosmos created (in prospect) by God when he spoke his promise to Abraham (not to mention the cosmos God created in the time of Adam). For in Galatians, Paul's portrait of Abraham is that of a pre-religious and thus non-religious figure (chapter 5 above).

[8]   Note especially Paul's use of the rhetorical stratagem of dissociation. In Gal 3:15–18, he links the word 'covenant' to the Abrahamic promise, while divorcing that word from the Sinaitic Law. See chapter 10 above. One could be tempted for the sake of clarity to summarize the argument of Gal 3:6–29 by means of a chronological narrative, beginning with creation (assumed); then God's promise to Abraham; then, 430 years later, the curse of the Sinaitic Law; and finally the advent of Christ. One could then suggest that this narrative presents a redemptive-historical sequence: Both the promise and the Law have their origin in God, even though they are not to be put on exactly the same level (so Barclay, *Obeying*, 99–100). In fact, however, Paul's distinction between the cursing voice *of the Law* and the blessing voice *of God* makes this reading impossible (Gal 3:15–18; cf. 2:19). There is indeed a sequence: first God's covenantal promise to Abraham; then the advent of the cursing Law; then Christ. What Paul finds in this sequence, however, is sure proof of the impotence of the later-arriving Law to alter the earlier and potent promise (3:15, 21a). The sequence, then, is that of promissory potency and nomistic impotence, not that of a redemptive continuity.

[9]   Caring nothing about what we would call the historical place of Habakkuk, Paul hears in Hab 2:4 (as in Isa 54:1; Gal 4:27) an element in the original utterance of the Law (Gal 3:8). In the distinguishing of the two voices of the Law, chronology plays a role (3:17), but one that is secondary to the role played by Christ. See note 14 below.

[10]   See chapter 11 above.

both from Gal 3:11–12 and from the two halves of 4:21, the reader of Galatians learns – before coming to 5:3 and 5:14 – that, after hearing the promissory voice of the Law testify successfully *against* the Law's cursing voice, Paul cannot consider the Law to be a monolith.[11]

Does the distinction between the Law's two voices in Galatians 3 and 4 illuminate Paul's negative and positive pictures of the Law in 5:3 and 5:14?

Two additional steps will prove helpful in our attempt to answer this question. First, we will ask whether the distinction between the Law's two voices in Galatians 3 and 4 is related to the advent of Christ (III). Second, returning to the matter of the translation of Gal 5:14, we will ask whether Paul's statement about the Law in that verse is itself made in relation to Christ's advent (IV).

---

[11] In the second and third centuries, the drawing of distinctions within the Law became an important motif among Christian Jews, gnostics, and orthodox Christians. See especially the theory of false pericopes in the *Kerygmata Petrou* (HS 2.118–121 [Strecker]); the *Letter of Ptolemy to Flora* (Foerster, *Gnosis*, 154–161); Irenaeus, *Heresies* 4.24–29; and the *Didascalia Apostolorum* (Connolly, *Didascalia*). In the five books of Moses, Ptolemy found (*a*) the Law of God (itself composed of three sub-parts), (*b*) the additions of Moses, and (*c*) the traditions of the elders. Perhaps influenced both by Galatians itself and by Ptolemy, the author of the *Didascalia* spoke repeatedly of a clean distinction between the eternally valid first Law, which 'consists of the Ten Words and the Judgments,' and the *deuterosis*, the punitive Second Legislation with its cursing bonds of circumcision, etc. Similarities and differences between these writings and those of Paul warrant more investigation than they have received.
   Similarities: Three motifs in the *Letter of Ptolemy to Flora* and the *Didascalia* can be compared with motifs in Galatians: (1) The distinction(s) internal to the Law have been *revealed by Christ*: 'The words of the Saviour teach us that it [the Law] is divided into three parts' (Ptolemy 4:1); 'He teaches what is the Law and what is the Second Legislation' (*Didascalia*, p. 218; cf. 'If one accepts his [the true prophet's] doctrine, then will he learn which portions of the Scriptures answer to the truth and which are false,' *Kerygmata Petrou* [HS 2.119]). (2) Christ came in order to destroy the second law, with its injustice, thus *setting us loose from its curse* (Ptolemy 5:7; *Didascalia*, p. 224). (3) In his act of making distinctions in the Law and of liberating us from the second Law, Christ fulfilled, *restored*, and *perfected* the Law of God (Ptolemy 5:3, 9; *Didascalia*, p. 224).
   Two *differences* are also noteworthy: (*a*) Over against the second Law, Ptolemy and the author of the *Didascalia* place not the singular Abrahamic promise, but rather the plural Decalogue, as its commandments were perfected by Christ. (*b*) For the catholic author of the *Didascalia*, God is expressly identified as the author both of the first Law and of the Second Legislation, whereas Ptolemy attributes only part of the Law to God, considering the laws of divorce and corban to have come from Moses and the elders. In writing Galatians, does Paul come closer to preparing the way for Ptolemy? The apostle is, in any case, very far from linking God to the genesis of the Sinaitic Law (Gal 2:19; 3:19–20; 4:24–25). For that reason, he 'is not afraid to apply *to scripture. . .* the distinguishing of spirits demanded of the prophets in 1 Cor 12:10' (Käsemann, *Romans*, 286).

III

In Galatians, the Law's relationship to Christ is a subject best approached by noting, first, that the Law has done something to Christ, and, second, that Christ has done something to the Law.

A. *What the Law did to Christ*

In its Old-Age, paired existence with the Not-Law, the plural Sinaitic Law formed the inimical orb into which Christ came. Thus, like every other human being, Christ himself was born into a cosmos enslaved under the power of that Law (Gal 4:4; cf. Phil 2:7). Together, that is, with all others, Christ was subject to the curse of the Law in its plural mode of existence (Gal 3:10; 4:3). But in his case there was also a head-on and climactic collision with that curse. As Christ hung on the cross, dying for the whole of humanity (1:4), the Law pronounced a specific curse on him (Gal 3:13; Deut 21:23), doing that with the malignant power it possessed as one of the enslaving, paired elements of the old cosmos.

B. *What Christ did to the Law*

Nothing in Galatians suggests that – unlike the other elements of the cosmos itself – the Law has escaped the influence of Christ. Quite the reverse. When, then, we turn the question around, asking what Christ did to the Law, we see two motifs that are both distinct from and closely related to one another.

1. *Christ has defeated the cursing voice of the Law*

In the collision between Christ and the cursing voice of the Sinaitic Law, Christ was distinctly the victor (Gal 3:13; 4:5; 5:1). In his crucifixion, Christ bore the Law's curse for humanity, thus vanquishing the cursing voice of the Law, confining it – properly speaking – to the era before his arrival (3:17).[12] Christ's victory over the Law's cursing voice is, to a large extent, the good news that permeates the whole of the letter (cf. Col 2:14–15).

---

[12] To be precise, in Galatians the era of the Law in its paired existence began 430 years after Abraham and ended with the arrival of Abraham's singular Seed (3:17, 19). It is a paradox that to some extent the Law's cursing voice survived its collision with Christ at the cross. Thus, even though greatly weaker than the promissory voice (3:17, 21), the cursing voice still poses a threat even to the baptized Galatians. For they can lose sight of what time it really is, thus becoming again slaves under the curse of the Law (4:10; 5:3).

2. Christ has enacted – and is enacting – the promise of the Law's original voice, being the seed to whom, along with Abraham, the promise was spoken

(a) The promise of the Law's original voice in the time of Abraham. According to Galatians, the message that the Law (as *hē graphē*) preached ahead of time to Abraham did not consist of numerous commandments, or even of one commandment, such as covenantal circumcision.[13] In the time of Abraham, the Law consisted solely of God's promise, and, for that reason, it preached nothing other than the singular gospel of Christ himself (Gal 3:8). For Christ is the singular seed of Abraham, and there is no gospel other than his (3:16; 1:6). From its Abrahamic inception, then, the original voice of the Law was positively and closely related to Christ; and, from its inception, this voice was the singular, evangelical promise, not a plural series of commandments. By the same token, the true promise pronounced in Hab 2:4 was and is the promise of the gospel of the Christ who is now making things right by his faith and by the faith that his faith elicits (Gal 3:11).[14]

---

[13] In Galatians – contrast Rom 4:9–12 – Paul totally and systematically ignores every aspect of God's dealing with Abraham, except the promise. He thus suppresses the Abrahamic covenant of circumcision (Gen 17:10–14), and he eclipses Jewish traditions in which God is said to have given the Law itself to Abraham, thus enabling the patriarch to be observant prior to Sinai (*Jub* 16:12–28; Sir 44:19–20). In this letter the figure of Abraham is emphatically pre-Sinaitic, pre-religious, and thus non-religious.

[14] In his own mind, does Paul locate Habakkuk chronologically between Abraham and Christ, even putting him after the genesis of the Sinaitic Law? That is the sort of question to which Paul gives no attention. As we have noted above, a major concern in Gal 3:6–18 is the clean distinction between two voices, that of the cursing Law and that of the Abrahamic promise. In developing this distinction, Paul hears the voice of God in the scripture of Hab 2:4 (Gal 3:11), without naming or thinking of the individual through whom God spoke the rectifying gospel-word, and without thinking of that individual's date. In sharp contrast, Paul hears in Lev 18:5 (Gal 3:12) the false promise of the cursing and plural Law ('The one who does the commandmen*ts* will live by *them*'). He then returns in Gal 5:14 to the voice of God, hearing in another passage of Leviticus (19:18) an utterance of the singular Law in its guiding function ('You shall love your neighbor as yourself'). Does Paul not know that the whole of Leviticus falls after Sinai, being in fact the major collection of the priestly laws? And if so, how can he hear in any part of Leviticus the voice of God, almost as though Lev 19:18 were included in God's utterance to Abraham? Those are questions to which we can respond only by noting that Paul's consistent point of departure for reading the Law is the advent of Christ. It is *Christ* who has distinguished from one another the promising and cursing voices of the Law. For that reason, Paul can find those voices in various parts of the scripture/Law, paying no attention to what we might call the fine points of chronology.

(*b*) *The promise of the Law's original voice in the present.* These affirmations themselves speak of the present connection between the promissory voice of the Law and Christ. One is not surprised to see, then, that the circumcision-free mission, promised in the original, covenantal Law of Genesis 16–21 and Isa 54:1, is the mission in which the gospel of Christ is presently marching into the Gentile world, giving birth to churches among the Gentiles, and freeing them from the cursing voice of the Law/the Not-Law (Gal 4:21–5:1). In that mission, the gospel of Christ has unleashed the promissory voice of the Law (4:21b), affirming and enacting its distinction from the Law's cursing voice (4:21a), and thus restoring it to the singularity it had in the time of Abraham.

IV

We can now return to Gal 5:14. In light of indications earlier in the letter that Christ has done something to the Law – defeating its cursing voice and enacting its promissory voice – we may ask whether Paul words 5:14 as he does, because he is still thinking of Christ's effect on the Law. That question brings us back to Paul's use of the expression *ho gar pas nomos en heni logō peplērōtai* (RSV: 'For the whole law *is fulfilled* in one word;' NRSV: 'For the whole law *is summed up* in one commandment'). Reading this expression in the context of the Galatian letter, how is one to translate the verb *peplērōtai*?

A. The verb plēroō

In its literal use, the verb frequently refers to the filling of a container that was previously altogether or partially empty, the result being that the container is full (BAGD). Used as a trope, the verb has various shades of meaning, four of which could be suggested for Gal 5:14, where Paul employs the verb with reference to the Law.

1. 'is fulfilled.' The New American Bible joins the RSV in the venerable tradition in which the verb *plēroō* in Gal 5:14 is rendered 'fulfill.' Thus: the whole of the Law '*is fulfilled*' in the single commandment of neighbor love, in the sense that the one who loves the neighbor is considered to have *completely observed* the *essence* of the Law, thus fulfilling the Law's *real* requirement. If there were reason to think that, in using the verb *plēroō*, Paul was actually thinking of the verb *qum* (pi. 'to fulfill'), it could be pertinent to note that the rabbis sometimes used this verb to speak of the Law's being *completely*

observed.[15] But the broad context given by Paul's references to the Law in Gal 2:16–5:4 precludes this interpretation, not least because, as H. D. Betz has emphatically noted, in wording Gal 5:14, Paul uses the verb *plēroō* rather than repeating from 5:3 the verb *poieō* ('observe'). About this verbal change, Betz remarks,

> [In 5:14] the 'whole Law' is not to be 'done' (*poiein*), as individual laws have to be done (cf. 3:10, 12; 5:3), but is rather 'fulfilled' . . . According to him [Paul], the Jew is obliged to *do* the Torah (cf. 3:10, 12; 5:3; also 6:13), while the Christian *fulfills* the Torah through the act of love, to which he has been freed by Christ (5:1, 13).[16]

The comment of Betz is helpful. Fully to honor the verb *peplērōtai*, however, is to sense three grounds for avoiding the translation 'is fulfilled.' First, completely foreign to the text of Galatians 5 is Betz's reference to the Jew's obligation to observe the Torah, whereas the Christian fulfills it. Paul does not shift from the verb *poieō* to the verb *plēroō* in order to speak of Jews and Christians (chapter 5 above)! Second, in English parlance, the verb 'fulfill' very often takes as its direct object the noun 'requirements,' the result being indistinguishable from 'fully perform all required stipulations.'[17] As noted above, it is precisely Paul's shift to the verb *plēroō* that precludes in 5:14 the thought of Law observance in that sense.[18] Third, to anticipate one of the major

---

[15] E.g. *Yoma* 28b: 'Abraham fulfilled the whole Law.' There are rabbinic traditions in which the whole Law is said to be fulfilled in one commandment, but what is meant is either that that commandment is the 'great principle' of the Law or that that commandment is the point at which a non-Jew can enter into the Law, its being presupposed in *both* cases that the rest of the Law is also to be observed with undiminished rigor. These traditions have nothing to do, then, with what a post-Enlightenment thinker might identify as an 'essence' that can serve as a stand-in for the rest of the Law. If the expression 'to fulfill the whole of the Law' was current in Paul's time, it meant to keep the Law completely, observing the commandments without exception. The expression would be precisely represented in a Jewish-Christian reference to keeping the whole of the Law now found in James: 'For whoever keeps the whole Law (*holon ton nomon tērēsē*) but fails in one point has become guilty of breaking all of it' (Jas 2:10). Cf. Gal 5:3.

[16] H. D. Betz, *Galatians*, 274–275. See also Moule, 'Fulfillment Words.'

[17] It is not difficult to find instances in which, in the interpretation of Gal 5:14 and Rom 13:8–10, the verbs *peplērōtai* and *anakephalaioutai* are equated – finally – with the English verb 'to do,' in the sense that by loving the neighbor, one *does* all of the requirements of the Law.

[18] One of the most important motifs of Gal 5:14 is the singularity of its Law, in contrast to the plural nature of the Law of 5:3. Thus, one cannot link Gal 5:14 *in any way* to the fulfilling of discrete requirements and stipulations, not even via 1 Cor 7:19 and Rom

results to be reached below, by putting the verb in the *perfect passive*, Paul does not refer to something the Galatians are to do – as if, rather than observing the Law, they are to fulfill it. The translation 'is fulfilled' is therefore unacceptable.

2. 'is summarized.' As noted above, this translation is imported from Rom 13:9, rather than being an interpretation of Gal 5:14 in the setting provided by the remainder of the letter. We can now add that nothing in the letter suggests the rendering 'is summarized.'

3. 'is brought to completion.' The verb *plēroō* can also be used in connection with a promise or a prophecy. A promise, for example, can be thought of as partially empty, until it is fulfilled by being *brought to completion* (Matt 1:22; John 13:18; cf. Rom 15:19; BAGD, '*plēroō*' 3.; LSJ, III.3.).[19]

4. 'is made perfect.' finally, in a similar manner, *plēroō* can have the connotation of bringing to perfection. Something can be thought imperfect, until it is *made perfect* by being 'filled out,' thus becoming what it was intended to be (so, for example, 'your joy' in John 15:11; cf. Phil 2:2). Something could also be made perfect by being *restored* to its original identity, after having suffered some kind of deterioration or contamination.[20]

There are no purely lexicographical grounds for preferring one – or both – of the last two meanings. As we proceed, however, we will see that there are exegetical reasons for electing them.

13:8–10. The latter two texts are to be read in the light of Gal 5:14 and 6:2, rather than vice versa. See Martyn, *Galatians*, Comment 48, Appendix B. See also the extraordinarily perceptive essay of Lindemann, 'Toragebote.' Finding in Romans 14 a key to the interpretation of Rom 13:8–10, Lindemann remarks correctly, 'Love does not make it possible to observe the Torah commandments; on the contrary, love takes the place of these commandments' (262). Note also Lindemann's reference to an important comment of O. Hofius, 'Paul knows nothing of a "third use of the Law," that is to say of "a new, ethical use of the Mosaic Torah for the Christian church"' (262 n. 105). For a rather different analysis see Hays, 'Scripture.'

[19] See also *b. Mak* 24b, where *qum* is used to refer to the bringing of a prophecy to completion.

[20] Note the passages in Thucydides and Aristotle from which LSJ arrive at a rendering of the passive of *anaplēroō*: 'to be restored to its former state or state.' Note also *anaplērōsis* as 'restoration,' and cf. Gal 6:2, where Paul employs *anaplēroō* essentially as a synonym for *plēroō*. See, finally, the references in the *Letter of Ptolemy to Flora* (5:3 and 5:9) to Christ's restorative perfecting of the Law of God.

B. *The perfect tense of the verb peplērōtai*

Interpreters are unanimous in taking the verb *peplērōtai* as an instance of the gnomic use of the perfect tense.[21] Gal 5:14 is taken, that is, to be a timeless aphorism. In the tradition of the RSV ('the whole Law is fulfilled in one word'), Paul is understood to speak both in 5:13 and in 5:14 of the Galatians' action. First, he exhorts the Galatians to serve one another in love. Second, he provides an aphoristic explication of *their act* of loving service: 'You are to serve one another in love (v. 13), for it is always true – and thus true in your case as well – that when one loves the neighbor, one fulfills (the essence of) the Law (v. 14).'[22]

Could it be, however, that Paul selected the perfect tense in order to refer to the present state of affairs that is the result of a past action, the simple and most frequent sense of the Greek perfect?[23] On this reading, Paul intends in Gal 5:14 to speak of the present state of affairs with the Law itself, as that state of affairs is the result of something that has happened to the Law. In a word he speaks of a watershed event in the history of the Law. To take the third and fourth meanings above, one would then find Paul saying, 'The Law is now completed, as the result of its having been brought to completion, thus being restored to its original identity.'[24]

---

[21] Thus following, in effect, the texts in which the verb has been changed into the present tense (DFG, et al.).

[22] The translation 'is summarized' is no less gnomic, for the summary is timeless. Interpreting the perfect tense as gnomic, a number of exegetes credit Paul, in effect, with being a child of the eighteenth-century Enlightenment, who refers both in Gal 5:14 and in Rom 13:8–10, to the Law's *essential intention* (something done by no rabbi and by no early Christian; cf. note 15 above). See, e.g., the references to Schrage and Holtz in Lindemann, 'Toragebote,' 243 n. 5.

[23] BDF, §340, §342. Citing Acts 5:28, 'You have filled Jerusalem with your teaching,' BDF remarks, 'a perfect like *peplērōkate* . . . may be resolved into *eplērōsate kai nun plērēs estin* ("you filled it and it is now full").' See also R. Kühner and B. Gerth, *Ausführliche Grammatik der griechischen Sprache. Satzlehre I* (Leverkusen: Gottschalkscke Verlag, 1955) 147.

[24] Note well that I have not said 'thus being restored to its original intention.' See note 22 above. Since the translation I am suggesting is the most obvious way of taking into account the perfect tense in 5:14, its absence in the commentaries – even as a possibility – is astonishing. Mussner may take a step in the direction of this reading: 'Also in ethics Paul thinks in "salvation-historical" terms: the love which was manifested exemplarily in Christ's sacrificial death is the eschatological fulfillment and completion of the Law' (*Galaterbrief,* 370). In a footnote, however, he abandons even that modest step, taking Paul to be speaking of something the Galatians should do: 'To be sure, the perfect tense verb *peplērōtai* is gnomic, in the sense that the Law is always fulfilled when the love commandment is fulfilled.'

C. *The passive voice of the verb peplērōtai*

Had Paul put the verb in the active voice – 'Someone has brought the Law to completion' – how would he have identified the subject of that verb? He would scarcely have referred to an act performed by the Galatians, for his exhortation that they serve one another (5:13) is certainly not a plea that he bases on something they have already done to the Law. In light of Paul's references to what Christ has done to the Law (III above), an hypothesis virtually suggests itself: When Paul speaks in 5:14 of the effect of an event in the history of the Law – it has now been brought to completion – he thinks of a state of affairs that is the result of a deed of Christ. Christ has brought the Law to completion.

We recall that the freedom to which Paul refers at the outset of Gal 5:13 is the freedom Christ has won for the Galatians (and all others); and this freedom is precisely liberation from the tyranny of the Law's cursing voice: Christ has done something that has affected the Law (Gal 5:1). Moreover, there is a clear link between 5:14, with its reference to the Law's having been 'brought to completion' (*peplērōtai*), and 6:2, with its reference to the future event in which the Galatians 'will bring to completion' the Law *of Christ* (*anaplērōsete ton nomon tou Christou*).[25] Detailed exegesis of Gal 6:2 – in light of Rom 8:2 – would show that 'The Law of Christ' is the Law that has found its genesis in Christ's act vis-à-vis the Law. In a word, it is the Law in the hands of Christ (Martyn, *Galatians*, Comment 50).

That reading of Gal 6:2 takes us back to 5:14, with its positive announcement about the Law. To honor that announcement in the context of the whole of Galatians is to find in it two crucial motifs. First, Paul presupposes Christ's deed in distinguishing from one another the two voices of the Law (one could as well say distinguishing from one another the two Laws, the original Law of God and the later-arriving Law of Sinai). Second, given that distinction, Paul refers in

---

[25] In Gal 6:2, Paul clearly speaks of something the Galatians themselves will do. In bearing one another's burdens, *they* will bring to completion 'the Law of Christ.' How is their future deed related to the past deed of Christ? (*a*) Christ's having brought the Law to completion (5:14) is the deed in which he took possession of the Law, making it his own Law, the Law of Christ. (*b*) In bearing one another's burdens, the Galatians will themselves repeat Christ's deed, the major difference being that – as they follow in Christ's train – they will bring to completion the Law that is now the Law *of Christ.* 'Bear one another's burdens, and in this way you yourselves will repeat Christ's deed, bringing to completion in your communities the Law that Christ has already brought to completion in the sentence about loving the neighbor.'

5:14 to Christ's having brought the original Law of God – the pre-Sinaitic Law – to its completion. For in this announcement, Paul adds a crucial dimension to the portrait of that Law he has painted in earlier passages. We have already seen that, restored by Christ to its pristine state, the original Law proves to be the sure Abrahamic *promise* of God that is now *giving birth* to circumcision-free churches among the Gentiles (Gal 3:8; 4:21b–5:1). Now, in Gal 5:14, we see in addition that, thus restored, the original Law is also the *one imperative* of God, a dependable *guide* for the daily life of those churches, precisely in the form of the love of neighbor.[26]

The nature of this imperative, however, is a matter of great import. *In the first instance*, that is, Paul does not speak in Gal 5:14 about the imperative that really matters, but rather about the imperative that really exists, having been caused to exist by God's act in Christ (cf. the motif of existence in Gal 3:28). What really exists for the church's guidance in everyday life is not the Sinaitic Law, but rather the original Law of God, as that original Law has been brought to perfected completion by Christ.

Reading Gal 5:14 in its own letter, then, we are reminded in two regards of Paul's ubiquitous concern to differentiate anthropological possibility from christological power.[27] First, we sense that for Paul the difference between anthropological possibility and christological power is nowhere more evident than in the daily life of the church (cf. Gal 5:22–24). Second, we see that, in the church's life, that difference emerges precisely in relation to the question of the pertinence of the Law. In Gal 5:14, that is to say, the guiding imperative of the Law (Lev 19:18) is not the result of an insightful deed of *Paul*, his act of *reducing* the Law to its essence (his achievement of the *reductio in unum*).[28] On

---

[26] It is significant that Paul calls this imperative a sentence, not a commandment. Even in Rom 13:8–10, Lev 19:18 proves to be the *one* imperative of God. See again Lindemann, 'Toragebote,' 262–263.

[27] On possibility and power, see notably Käsemann, *Questions*, 173 n. 4 (the issue of the translation of *dynamis* in Rom 1:16); and cf. note 23 in chapter 13 above.

[28] One can ask whether, in linking Lev 19:18 to 'the whole of the Law,' Paul was influenced either by the sort of Jewish tradition we find in *Gen. Rab.* 24:7 (Akiba on Lev 19:18) or by Jewish-Christian tradition in which Jesus is credited with approving the link between Deut 6:4–5 and Lev 19:18 (cf. Furnish, *Command*, 94). The form of this latter tradition in Luke 10:25–28 suggests that the Jewish-Christians who preserved it may have known the combination of Deut 6:4–5 and Lev 19:18 to be a Jewish formulation antedating Jesus. See Fitzmyer, *Luke*, 879. In any case, both the Jewish tradition and the Jewish-Christian one are worlds removed from Paul's *announcement*

the contrary, that guiding imperative is the result of the powerful deed of *Christ*, his act of *loosing* God's Law from the Law of Sinai, thereby addressing God's Law to the church.[29] The Law taken in hand by Christ (Gal 6:2) is the Law that Christ has restored to its original identity and power (Gal 5:14).

Paul can relate the Law, therefore, both to the birth of the church (Gal 4:21–5:1), and to its daily life, because of Christ's powerful effect on the Law. Stated as a guide for the church's daily life, then, Gal 5:14 refers climactically to *the christological event in the history of the Law*:

---

in Gal 5:14 of an *event* in the history of the Law. Moreover, for all of those traditioners the issue was that of the comparative importance *among* the many commandments. There was no thought of deleting or negating some of them (N.B. the strict Jewish-Christian tradition *behind* Matt 22:40: 'On these two commandments hang *all* the law and the prophets;' cf. Matt 23:23). Cf. the later interpretation of the role of this Jewish-Christian tradition in Matthew's *mixed* church by Donaldson, 'The Law That Hangs.' In the setting of this mixed church, Matthew sees that significant aspects of the written Torah have been abrogated. In 22:40, then, Matthew uses 'a rabbinic formulation in the service of an unrabbinic interpretation of the Torah' (696).

[29] My use of the verb 'to loose' is intended to reflect the polemical cast of Gal 5:3 and 5:14, against the background of the same polemic in Gal 3:10–18. The Teachers who invaded Paul's Galatian churches presupposed the integrity of the Abrahamic blessing/ promise and the Sinaitic Law. Paul sees that Christ has liberated the former from the latter. Note a partially similar reading in Lührmann's perceptive comment on Gal 6:2 (*Galater*, 96–97): 'The new teachers in Galatia may have used the expression "the Law of Christ" to indicate that the Law of Sinai is still valid in the Christian church . . . [Paul, however, sees a] splitting of the Law into the Law of Sinai and the Law of Christ, a view that is later completed in the opposition between "the Law of the Spirit of life" and "the Law of Sin and death" in Rom 8:2. The "Law of Christ" is possible only through liberation from the Law that was given on Sinai' (author's translation).

The present chapter is tightly focused on Gal 5:14 and other texts in that letter, not least Gal 4:24–25; 5:3, where Paul draws a connection between the plural, *Sinaitic* Law and enslavement. Were we to take account of 1 Cor 7:19 and Rom 13:8–10, we would see that, in settings different from the one that developed in Galatia, Paul could speak affirmatively of *some of the commandments in the Decalogue*, understanding them to be commandments *of God*. Noting, however, the reminiscence of Gal 5:14 and 6:2 in Rom 13:8–10 – thus recalling Paul's certainty that Christ has distinguished the promising and guiding Law from the cursing and enslaving Law – we can arrive at a new paraphrastic translation of the *latter* text: 'Owe no one anything at all, except to love one another. For the one who loves another has brought the Law to completion (*nomon peplērōken*). What do we say, then, of the commandments, "You shall not commit adultery; You shall not murder; You shall not steal; You shall not covet"? Like the whole of the Law, these and all other commandments are brought to their completing sum-total (*anakephalaioutai*) in this sentence: "You shall love your neighbor as yourself." Love does no wrong to a neighbor, such as the wrongs mentioned in the commandments. For that reason, taking the place of the commandments, love is the completion of the Law (*plērōma nomou*).'

For you were called to freedom, brothers and sisters . . . through love, be genuine servants of one another. For the whole of the Law has been brought to completion [by Christ] in one sentence: 'You shall love your neighbor as yourself.'

15

The Daily Life of the Church in the War Between the Spirit and the Flesh

The Problem of Providing Specific Guidance
For the Church's Daily Life

In chapter 14 we have seen that, according to Gal 5:14, the whole of the Law *post Christum* is the Law that Christ has loosed from its paired and plural mode of existence, restoring it to the original singularity in which it spoke God's own word. It is the singular Law of love, and nothing other than that. We have also seen that this is the Law that is positively related to daily life in the church, because it does nothing other than reflect the pre-eminence of Christ's love. For that reason, it is the Law apart from which the church does not live. Turning from Gal 5:14 to 5:15–24, we note, however, that when Paul takes up the matter of specific and detailed guidance for the church's everyday life, he repairs neither to the plural Law of Sinai nor to the singular Law of love. He could easily have done the one or the other.

He could have reverted to the Sinaitic Law, drawing on the Jewish traditions in which the Law is said to be the antidote to vice and the producer of virtue.[1] Thus, he could have said in effect that, although the plural, Sinaitic Law has nothing to do with the rectifying event that occurs at the point of one's entry into the church (so Gal 2:16; 3:21; 4:24–25; 5:3–4), that Law nevertheless remains – with its commandments – the guide to the daily sustenance of Christian behavior, when circumcision, food laws, and regulations for holy times have been removed from it.[2] This seems to be the reading of Paul's ethics proposed by a number of interpreters.[3]

---

[1] On the Law as the antidote to vice, see comments below under 'The Guidance Provided by the Teachers.' The Law as the producer of virtue is a common Jewish motif: e.g., Josephus *Ap.* 2.170–171 (*eusebeia* and *aretē*), 291–296.

[2] This reading presupposes the venerable and untenable view that Paul drew a significant distinction between rectification and sanctification. See the following two notes.

[3] See note 4 in chapter 14 above.

For two reasons, it is also a reading that cannot be supported from Galatians. First, according to this letter, the daily life of the church *is* the scene of God's rectification, not an addition to it (the negative reference to nomistic rectification in 5:4 points forward to the pastoral section of 5:13–6:10).[4] Second, Galatians 5 and 6 show that Paul is worlds away from finding the guide to Christian behavior in the Sinaitic Law. Immediately before giving the first of two lists by which he speaks of daily life, he emphatically repeats his assurance that the Galatians are not under the authority of the Law (5:18). Consequently, in composing the pastoral section of his letter, Paul does not seek to guide the daily life of the Galatian churches by drawing on the commandments that are found in the Sinaitic Law.[5]

Nor does Paul develop a detailed picture of Christian life by drawing on various commandments in the singular Law of love (5:14), not least because, as we have seen in chapter 14, that Law does not consist of commandments. Even so, however, Paul could have turned to it for specific guidance. Drawing, that is, on the Jewish tradition in which the Law is said to be the producer of virtues, being itself the epitome of virtue, Paul could have considered one after another the various aspects of love – patience, kindness, endurance, and so on. Developing each aspect, he could have arrived at a comprehensive and detailed picture of behavior in a community that is informed in the whole of its life by the Law of love. That is the route Paul will later elect in writing 1 Corinthians 13, and it is not altogether unlike the way by which he proceeds to compose the second of his behavioral lists in Galatians itself (5:22–23a: love, joy, peace, and so on). The first of those lists, however – the effects of the Flesh – is not drawn from the Law of love (even negatively) any more than it is composed on the basis of various commandments in the Sinaitic Law.

Where will Paul turn, then, in order to provide the Galatians with specific guidance for the daily life of their communities? In reading Gal

---

[4] Cf. Käsemann, 'Neither can support be found . . . as has sometimes been thought, for distinguishing between the righteousness of the beginning and the righteousness of the end, between righteousness of faith and righteousness of life' (*Questions*, 171); cf. Way, *Lordship*, 259.

[5] The corresponding observation is made about Romans 14 by Lindemann, 'Toragebote,' 262; cf. Scroggs, *Text*, 167–183. Note, for comparison, the role of the Law in James; and cf. the statement of L. T.Johnson: 'For James the term *nomos* . . . finds its focus in the love of neighbor, but that love is explicated by specific attitudes and actions prescribed by Torah' (*James*, 32).

5:16–24, one sees that Paul takes four major steps. First, he issues a promise explicitly focused on the Spirit, rather than on the Law (5:16). Second, referring to one of the presuppositions of that promise, he speaks of the Spirit and the Flesh as two combatants, engaged in a war with one another (5:17). Third, certain that that war is the determinative context for the Galatians' daily life – that war being the scene of the Spirit's victory and thus of the Galatians' real life (5:25) – Paul gives the Galatians a description of the war. He provides specific guidance, that is, by transforming the traditional lists of vices and virtues into community characteristics in the midst of the war. On the one hand, there are marks of a community under the influence of the Flesh and, on the other hand, there are marks of a community in which the Spirit is fruitfully active (5:19–24). Fourth, centrally concerned with the Spirit's apocalyptic war against the Flesh, Paul employs the language of exhortation in the promise itself (5:16), thus giving to hortatory expressions a very peculiar stamp.

The Promise in Galatians 5:16, Foundational Guidance

We can begin fully to sense the impact of Paul's promise in 5:16 only by seeing first that, in wording it, he is keenly aware of current developments in the Galatian churches. He knows, that is, that the Galatians will hear his promise as a rewording of a promise they are already hearing from the Teachers. It is, then, in the differences between the two promises – and not least in the differences between their presuppositions – that we can see yet further into the issue of daily life as Paul perceives it.

The Guidance Provided by the Teachers

Identifying the Law as the God-given antidote to 'the Impulsive Desire of the Flesh' (see definition below), the Teachers are providing the Galatians with what they consider to be comforting assurance:

> If you Galatians will *become* observant of the Law, we can promise you that you will not fall prey to the Impulsive Desire of the Flesh.

It is a conditional promise, holding good *if* the Galatians do what the Teachers exhort them to do, *viz.* become observant of the Law. It is also a promise founded on a view of the Impulsive Flesh and the Law that is familiar to us from both Jewish and Jewish-Christian traditions.

1. The Flesh[6]

Drawing on these traditions about the Impulsive Desire of the Flesh, we can suggest six motifs that the Teachers probably included in their own instruction:[7]

(*a*) Internal to the individual, the Impulsive Flesh has the individual as its major locus of operations.[8]

(*b*) The Impulsive Flesh is to some extent an entity with a life of its own, but it remains within the individual.[9]

(*c*) It is dangerous to the individual.[10]

(*d*) But the individual can master the Impulsive Flesh by choosing to observe the Law.[11]

---

[6] The Teachers almost certainly speak of the *epithymia sarkos*, lit. 'the desire of the flesh,' that being their Greek rendering of the Hebrew *yeser basar*. Whether, like Paul, they also use the abbreviation 'the Flesh' (Gal 5:13, 17 (twice), 19, 24) we cannot say. In any case, in speaking both of the Teachers and of Paul, I employ interchangeably the expressions 'Impulsive Desire of the Flesh,' 'Impulsive Flesh,' 'Impulse,' 'Inclination,' and 'Flesh.'

[7] In each case I give in footnotes one or two illustrative citations. For the whole of these texts, for others like them, and for further interpretation, see Marcus, 'James;' idem, 'Paul.'

[8] 'For there are two ways of good and evil, and with these are the two inclinations *in our breasts*, distinguishing the one [way] from the other' (*T. Asher* 1:5). '[No member of the community] shall walk in the stubbornness of his heart, so that he strays after his heart, after his eyes, and after the thought of *his* Impulse (*mahasebet yisro*). On the contrary, they shall circumcise in the community the foreskin of the Impulse (*'orlat yeser*)' (1QS 5:5). Similarly, referring to an unfortunate state of affairs (and using the word 'spirit' to refer to the Inclination), the Jewish-Christian author of James speaks of 'the spirit that he [God] has made to dwell *in us*' (Jas 4:5; cf. Sir 15:14–17).

[9] 'Hear now, my sons, and I will uncover your eyes so that you may see and understand the works of God . . . so that you may walk perfectly in all his ways and not be drawn by *the thoughts of the guilty impulse* (*bemahsebot yeser 'asma*) and by lustful eyes' (CD 2:14–16). See also 1QS 5:5 cited in preceding footnote. At Qumran the Old Testament expression 'the inclination of the thoughts' has become 'the thoughts of the inclination,' suggesting that, in some sense, the Inclination has its own existence (Marcus, 'James,' 612). Essentially, however, it remains internal to the individual.

[10] 'If a man does not set bounds to his impulses and bridle them like horses which defy the reins, he is the victim of a well-nigh fatal passion, and that defiance will cause him to be carried away before he knows it' (Philo *de Spec. Leg.* 4.79). 'One is tempted by one's own desire (*epithymia*), being lured and enticed by it; then, when that desire has conceived, it gives birth to sin, and that sin, when it is fully grown, gives birth to death' (Jas 1:14–15). In Qumran the Inclination of an individual, if not resisted by strict observance of the Law, also presents a danger to the community (1QS 5:3–7).

[11] 'For God created man from the beginning . . . and gave him into the hand of his inclination (*yeser*). If you choose, you may keep the commandments . . . Death and life are before a man; that which he shall choose shall be given him' (Sir 15:14–17). In the metaphorical language of Qumran, the Inclination is a danger until it is circumcised (1QS 5:3–7).

(*e*) Viewed in the framework of the doctrine of the Two Ways, the Impulsive Flesh presents the individual with the necessity of making a choice; the individual is competent to make that choice, and is responsible for the effects of that choice.[12]

(*f*) To choose to observe the Law is not only to master the Impulsive Flesh; it is also to achieve perfection of virtue.[13]

2. The Antidote: Observance of the Law

Holding such views of the Flesh and of the Law, and concentrating their attention on human acts, the Teachers are exhorting the Galatians to make the right decision. By choosing to observe the Law, these Galatian Gentiles are to transfer from the path of the Flesh (an entity essentially internal to each of them as an individual) to the path of the Law, thus mastering the Flesh and achieving perfection of virtue (3:3).[14] For the human act of circumcising the flesh – as the commencement of Law observance – is the antidote to the human act of following the dictates of the Flesh.[15]

[12] 'And each one chose the stubbornness of his heart' (CD 19:20). Note also that the individual's freedom of choice is accented in the passage from Sirach cited in the preceding note. That freedom to choose is a gift of God. For, although God caused the Inclination to dwell in the human being, 'he gives all the more grace' (Jas 4:5–6). Thus the human being can yield to the Inclination, the result being sin and death. Or, by following God's commandments, he can choose to resist the Inclination, the result being life (Jas 1:2–4, 12–15). This point holds good in the framework of forensic apocalyptic as well as in that of the wisdom tradition of the Two Ways. See de Boer, 'Apocalyptic Eschatology', and 'forensic apocalyptic eschatology' in the Glossary.

[13] Note the motif of perfection in CD 2:14–16, and the reference to Abraham in CD 3:2–3: 'Abraham did not walk in it [the Inclination] . . . he kept the commandments of God and did not choose the will of his own spirit' (cf. Murphy-O'Connor, 'Missionary'). Regarding Abraham, see also *Gen. Rab.* 46:1, 4, where circumcision is said to have removed Abraham's only blemish; thereafter he was perfect (cf. *m. Ned.* 3:11). In Jewish-Christian tradition, Abraham's faith was brought to perfection by his observance of the Law (Jas 2:22).

[14] In chapter 10 above we have seen that this transfer has the corporate dimension of joining the people of Israel (truly represented in the church of Jerusalem); but, speaking to Gentiles, the Teachers focus their exhortation on the individual.

[15] In their own 'home' setting, that of Christian Judaism, the Teachers will doubtless have viewed Law-observance as a path made possible by God's grace in establishing his covenant with Israel (cf. the references to Qumran texts in chapter 9 above). Similarly, they will have seen their mission as the gracious, Messianic extension of that covenant to the Gentiles. As far as we can see from Galatians, however – not least from the Teachers' threat (4:17) – the Galatian Gentiles will have heard in the Teachers' instruction the demand that they themselves *do* something, namely commence observance of the Law, however clearly the Teachers may have thought that one can do this only with the help of God.

The Guidance Provided in Paul's Promise

1. The Flesh

In Gal 5:13–24, Paul speaks for the first time in this letter of the Flesh as a distinctly assertive actor (hence the capital 'F'), in all probability following the Teachers in doing so. Indeed, to some degree, he shows that he is in agreement with them. He believes, for example, that the Impulsive Desire of the Flesh exists, and that it is itself the major reason for the Galatians' need of guidance in daily life. Certain, however, that the opposite of the Flesh is not the Law, but rather the Spirit, Paul presents a picture of the Flesh that is different from that of the Teachers in regard to all six of the motifs mentioned above:

(*a*) As the Spirit is invading the present evil age by creating the new community in which it bears its fruit of love, joy, and peace, so the Flesh has its major locus of action in the community, not in the individual.

(*b*) As the Spirit is the Spirit of Christ, a power distinct from the Galatians, so the Flesh is an entity that has, to an important extent, a life of its own. It is not a mere part of the human being, less noble than other parts, 'our lower nature' (so NEB in Gal 5:13, 16, 17, 19). Both the Flesh and the Spirit are apocalyptic powers that do things not only in, but also to the Galatians (5:13, 17, 19–21a; 22–23a).[16]

(*c*) As noted above, the Flesh is a danger to the Galatian communities, being intent on maintaining in communal form its own orb of power, the present evil age (1:4; 5:13).

(*d*) Nothing is more foreign to Paul than the thought that the Flesh can be defeated by a course of human action.[17]

---

[16] In the early Christian church it was Paul who brought the Impulsive Flesh fully into the apocalyptic worldview, by viewing it as the opposite of the Spirit of Christ. See again Marcus, 'Paul.' To be sure, the Qumran community speaks of warfare between the spirits of truth and falsehood, attributing real power to them and noting ways in which their warfare affects the community (1QS 3:22–24). The Covenantors also focus considerable attention, however, on the general picture of humanity, and thus on the individual within whom the spirits act. 'The nature of *all the children of men* is ruled by these (two spirits), and during their life all the hosts of men have a portion in their divisions and walk in (both) their ways. And the whole reward for their deeds shall be . . . according to whether *each man's* portion in their two divisions is great or small' (1QS 4:15–16; Vermes). In Gal 5:18–24 Paul does not speak of humanity, but rather, consistently and exclusively, of the community of those who belong to Christ, those who have received the Spirit of Christ.

[17] See Marcus, 'Paul,' 15–16; de Boer, 'Apocalyptic Eschatology,' passim.

(*e*) As we will see in greater detail below, for Paul the Spirit and the Flesh are not related to one another in such a way as to call upon the Galatians to decide for the one or the other.

(*f*) In Paul's view, there is no thought that human beings can achieve perfection.[18]

2. *The Antidote: the Spirit*

Returning to Gal 5:16, one sees that Paul considers the Teachers' promise to be lethally false, not least because it presupposes fundamental misunderstandings of the Flesh, the Law, and the Spirit. Because the Spirit is the Spirit of Christ (4:6), because this Spirit – rather than the Law – is the opposite of the Flesh, and because the Flesh is known on the basis of its opposite, it follows that the true character of the Flesh, and of the drama in which it is an actor, has only recently been revealed. In 5:16, then, Paul issues a comprehensive correction, thus providing in his own promise the foundation for the specific guidance he believes the Galatians to need:

> Even after the advent of Christ and his Spirit, the Flesh does in fact continue to exist, and, unrestrained, it will destroy your communities. It is clear, however, that the restraining antidote to the Flesh does not lie in something you can do, *viz.* commence Law observance. The God-given antidote to the Flesh is the Spirit of Christ. And, since the antidote to the Flesh is the Spirit rather than the Law, the solution to the problem of the Flesh lies in something God has already done. For God has already sent the Spirit into your hearts, calling you into existence as his church. Continue to lead your communal life guided by the Spirit, then, and I can promise you that you will not end up carrying out the Impulsive Desire of the Flesh (paraphrase of Gal 5:16).

The Spirit and the Flesh as Warriors[19]

With the promise of 5:16, Paul provides the foundation for daily guidance, but he does not yet give details. From that promise, therefore, he moves first to one of its major presuppositions: the Spirit and the Flesh are engaged in a dramatic conflict (5:17). Then he turns to the

---

[18] On Phil 3:12–14, see Gnilka, *Philipperbrief.*

[19] The picture of a cosmic, dualistic struggle between good and evil is ancient and widespread. As we will see below in discussing the so-called catalogues of virtues and vices, Iranian traditions included mythological lists in which personified spirits of good and evil oppose each other. See Kamlah, *Paränese*; Fitzgerald, 'Lists;' idem, 'Catalogue.'

task of portraying the nature of that conflict, the basic character of its major actors, and the place of the Galatians in it (5:18–24). Remarkable is the fact that in referring to this conflict, and in analyzing its actors, Paul speaks in a thoroughly descriptive fashion: all of the verbs in 5:17–24 are in the indicative mood. Paul does not initially move from his foundational promise to specific details by means of exhortation. On the contrary, he seems to think that he can develop the promise of 5:16 into the particulars of daily guidance by first of all *describing* for the Galatians the world in which they actually live *post Christum*.

The War (5:17)[20]

Paul is quick to state the obvious presupposition of the promise of 5:16: The Spirit and the Flesh are at war with one another:

> For the Flesh is actively inclined against the Spirit, and the Spirit against the Flesh. Indeed these two powers constitute a pair of opposites at war with one another . . . (5:17a)

One recalls the weighty role Paul has given in prior sections of Galatians to the motif of divine invasion (chapter 10 above). That motif is also central to 5:13–24. As we have noted, the Spirit to which Paul refers here is not an inherent component of the human being, comparable, let us say, to an individual's heart.[21] It is the Spirit of God's Son, the Spirit that God has sent invasively into the human orb (4:6).

In a significant sense, peace is a result of that invasion, for the Spirit bears its fruit of love, joy, and peace in the community of God's church (Gal 5:22; contrast 5:15). In another sense, however, the divine invasion has certainly not happened peacefully. Indeed it has been necessitated by the fact that the human orb has been subject to an alien, occupying power, the Flesh. With the sending of the Spirit, then, God has invaded the territory of the Flesh (cf. Gal 1:4), inaugurating a war against that monster.

---

[20] On the relation between God's act of rectification and the motif of cosmic war, see chapter 9 above. The institution of the holy war is the deep soil in which cosmological apocalyptic took root in Israel, and it stands ultimately behind Paul's battle imagery. Cf. de Boer, 'Apocalyptic Eschatology.'

[21] Thus the antinomy between the Spirit and the Flesh is neither an anthropological dualism (H. D. Betz, *Galatians*, 278–280), focused on the inner psychic economy of the individual human being, nor an ethical dualism focused on alleged decisions made by the individual.

It follows that the opposition between the Spirit and the Flesh cannot be grasped either in the image of an infection and a medicinal antidote or in the picture of the Two Ways that are set before the human being, in order to call for a decision.[22] On the contrary, that opposition is a genuine conflict, an apocalyptic war. It is also of recent vintage. For the Spirit's war against the Flesh is neither an inherent part of creation (as in Qumran), nor a conflict that was inaugurated with the genesis of the Sinaitic Law, nor the result of a human decision to attack the Flesh. This war was declared by God when he sent his Son and the Spirit of this Son into the territory of the Flesh. This war is, then, the new-creational struggle, the apocalyptic war of the end-time, the war in which God's forces are the ones on the march (regarding the line of movement see chapter 10 above). The Spirit's weapons, however, are strange indeed. For example, the Spirit bears the fruit of communal *peace*, in order to overcome the *violence* engendered by the Flesh (vv. 15, 22; cf. Eph 6:10–20).[23]

The Galatians' Place in this War

1. Distant observers?

If Paul identifies the major actors in this war as the active belligerents, the Spirit and the Flesh, does he then portray a drama in which the Galatians themselves are essentially inactive characters, persons who view the battlefield from afar? One might think so for a moment, for, as we have seen, the two warriors are distinct from human beings.

A further moment of reflection shows that, although distinguished from the Galatians, the Spirit and the Flesh are at war in such a way as vitally to affect the Galatian communities. Just as the Spirit is distinct from the Galatians, being the Spirit of God's Son, so the Spirit is also *in* the Galatians as communities, having been sent by God *into* their hearts (4:6). And, as noted above, the Flesh is actively seeking a military base of operations *in* the Galatian communities (5:13). Those communities are not at all distant observers of the apocalyptic war of the end-time.

---

[22] Recognizing that Stowers is right to note the close relation between letters of exhortation and letters of advice (Stowers, *Letter Writing*, 91–152), Schrage nevertheless comments perceptively, 'In [ancient] letters focused on the giving of advice, the fundamental presupposition is the freedom to make decisions (Stowers 109). One can scarcely say that in the hortatory section of Galatians Paul only gives good advice' ('Probleme,' 12).

[23] Cf. Hamerton-Kelly, *Violence*.

Somehow permeable both to the Flesh and to the Spirit, the Galatian churches are very much in the thick of the battle.

2. Passive puppets?

Are the Galatians caught up in this war, however, essentially as puppets, incapable of decisive action? One could think so in the course of reading the whole of 5:17:

> For the Flesh is actively inclined against the Spirit, and the Spirit against the Flesh. Indeed these two powers constitute a pair of opposites at war with one another, *the result being that you do not actually do the very things you wish to do.*

What is one to make of the final, surprising clause? Why should the war between the Spirit and the Flesh lead to a failure to do what one wishes to do?

In chapter 16 below we will find that, using a plural verb – 'you (plural) do not actually do the very things you (plural) wish to do' – Paul speaks here to the Galatians who are trying to direct their allegiance both to Christ and to the Sinaitic Law. The result is that, although these converts of the Teachers earlier received the Spirit (3:2), they are now actually being led by the Flesh (cf. 3:3), thus being swept into a failure to avoid behavior they wish to avoid. In short, the note of tragic failure in 5:17 is one that Paul directs only to the Galatians who are attempting the impossible, that is, to follow both Christ and the Sinaitic Law. Elsewhere, notably in 5:13, he issues an exhortation that presupposes active engagement on the part of the Galatians. They are not puppets.

3. Soldiers

Indeed in 5:13, identifying the Flesh as a power seeking to establish a base of military operations in the Galatian communities, Paul exhorts the Galatians to resist. They have, then, an active role in the war. It was given them at their baptism. Just as they are the new communities begotten by the power of the Spirit (4:29), so, given the Spirit's war against the Flesh, they find themselves to be serving in the Spirit's army, fully equipped and nourished for that service by the Spirit itself. Is there not the need, however, for yet greater specificity as regards their daily life?[24] In Galatians 5, that is a question Paul answers largely by the lists of 5:19–21a and 5:22–23a and by the statements of vv. 21b and 24.

---

[24] Schrage is certainly correct to say that Paul is concerned with concrete specificity (*Einzelgebote*, 59–70; 'Probleme,' 23 n. 116).

Paul's Transformation of the Traditional Lists

At least a number of the Galatians will have sensed that Paul draws the lists of vv. 19–21a and vv. 22–23a from the widespread philosophic and religious tradition of compiling catalogues of vices and virtues. Momentarily, then, they may have thought that, having identified them as soldiers, Paul now lists in vv. 19–23 the *vices* soldiers *should avoid* and the *virtues* they *should cultivate*. In fact, however, taking as his basic frame of reference the apocalyptic war between the Spirit and the Flesh, Paul paints a picture far removed from that given in the traditional catalogues. He does not introduce the list in vv. 19–21a by identifying 'fornication . . . the worship of idols . . . outbursts of rage, etc.' as vices with which individuals can be charged, and from which, alternatively, they can abstain. On the contrary, for him this first list presents '*the effects of* the Flesh,' deeds accomplished in a significant sense *by* the Flesh as an apocalyptic power. Similarly, for Paul, the list of vv. 22–23a, 'love, joy, peace, etc.' is not a catalogue of virtues, but rather '*the fruit borne by* the Spirit,' communal evidence of the Spirit's own activity. Thus, none of the things in either list is an autonomous act of a human being that could be correctly called that individual's vice or virtue.[25] On the contrary, Paul lists actions that are without exception effected by the two warring powers, the Flesh and the Spirit. And all of the actions are communal in nature.

The effects of the Flesh are developments that destroy community – outbursts of rage, etc. – and the fruit of the Spirit consists of characteristics that build and support community – love, joy, peace, etc. Thus, in the apocalyptic war of the end-time, vices and virtues attributable to individuals have lost both their individualistic nature and their character as vices and virtues. They have become marks of community character, so that if one speaks of 'character formation,' one adds that it is the community's character that is being formed by the Spirit (cf. Gal 4:19). In the framework of the apocalyptic war, a community that has succumbed to the Flesh bears the marks of the Flesh. A community that is led by the Spirit shows in its common life the fruit

---

[25] Cf. Käsemann, 'the concept of virtue as used in our morality is fundamentally inapplicable to him [Paul]' (*Questions*, 194). But, just as the lists had originally to do with vices and virtues, so after Paul they lost the apostle's apocalyptic and corporate frame of reference, becoming again simply vices and virtues. Enjoying wide circulation and embroidering, they became in time 'The Seven Virtues' and 'The Seven Deadly Sins.' See Meeks, *Origins*, 66–71; Fitzgerald, 'Lists.'

borne by the Spirit. The profound radicality of Paul's apocalyptic picture is seriously domesticated when one credits him with speaking of vices and virtues.[26] We return, then, to our earlier question: in what sense are the Galatian soldiers persons who have an active role in the drama?

The Apocalyptic War, the Transformed Lists, and the Galatians' Acts

After listing communal developments that reflect the powerful effects of the Flesh, Paul does in fact warn the Galatians about *their* acts:

> Those who *practice* things of this sort will not inherit the Kingdom of God. (5:21b)

And after listing the communal fruit of the Spirit, he adds,

> Those who belong to Christ Jesus *have crucified* the Flesh, together with its passions and desires. (5:24)

As *combatants*, in whom and through whom the Flesh and the Spirit carry on their war, the Galatians are led into certain *acts* by the one

---

[26] Given the structure of the learned book of Meeks, *Origins*, there is an inevitable tendency to read Paul's letters through the lenses of second and third century sources, the latter being very well interpreted. But, to turn to such passages as Gal 5:19–23a, after quoting from the moral lists of Aristides and Pliny the Younger (both second century) – not to mention certain parts of the *Didache*, the *Epistle of Barnabas*, and the *Doctrina XII Apostolorum* – is to run the risk of missing the major surprise of Gal 5:19–23a: the degree to which Paul's apocalyptic view has transformed the language of the catalogue tradition (*Origins*, 8–9, 15, 66–71). As we have seen, it is the Teachers, not Paul, who view the problem of the Impulsive Flesh in light of the doctrine of the Two Ways, and who therefore accept the ancient pattern in which vices and virtues exemplify precisely that doctrine. True enough, Meeks himself speaks of the Christian development in which 'humility,' for example, is transformed by being juxtaposed with 'the metaphoric pattern' of Christ's crucifixion and resurrection (15; cf. 66; 84–90). But, on the whole, Meeks's willingness to analyze early Christian moral sensibilities as developments reflecting 'socialization' and 'resocialization' leaves largely out of account the degree to which apocalyptic frames of reference – notably the motif of cosmic warfare – led Paul to a radically new view of the cosmos itself, and thus to an apocalyptic transformation of the language of vices and virtues. Thus, if one were able to imagine a conversation in which one could teach Paul the modern usage of such inelegant terms as 'resocialization,' one would also be able to imagine him coining the still more inelegant term 're-cosmos-ization,' in order to refer to the deed by which God is bringing about the death of the old and enslaving cosmos, in order to create a community so novel as to be called the new creation, a community in which language itself is transformed. After Paul, the kernel of his apocalyptic vision was mostly lost, and socializing attempts were indeed made to foster patterns of morality, without reference to the radical foundation of God's re-cosmos-ization. But these attempts cannot serve as the key to Paul's own views. A better commentary on Paul is Flannery O'Connor's reference to the burning away of virtue (see chapter 17 below).

belligerent power or by the other. The Galatians themselves do things as communities. In a significant sense, then, they are responsible actors. And because they are responsible actors, Paul does more than give them a description of the apocalyptic war between the Spirit and the Flesh. He speaks to them in the imperative mood. Even in what we might call Paul's apocalyptic ethics there is a place for exhortation.

The Nature of the Imperative in 5:16

The nature of Paul's imperative is, however, a crucial matter. We return briefly to the imperative verb with which he begins the promise in 5:16:

> In contradistinction to the Teachers, I, Paul, say to you: *Lead your daily life guided by the Spirit*, and, in this way you will not end up carrying out the Impulsive Desire of the Flesh.

Granting that Paul disagrees with the Teachers as to the identity of the Flesh's opposite – it is the Spirit rather than the Law – a number of commentators think that Paul nevertheless agrees with the Teachers on a truly significant point: Paul is said to see in the opposition between the Spirit and the Flesh a new edition of the doctrine of the Two Ways. Does not the promise of 5:16 show, after all, that Paul thinks of the Flesh and the Spirit as two alternatives placed before a human being who is competent to decide for the one or for the other? In fact, this interpretation reflects a failure to see the centrality of the metaphor of warfare, analyzed above, and for that reason it presents a false reading of Paul's imperative in Gal 5:16 (and a consequent misreading of the hortatory dimensions of 5:25–6:10).

That is to say, it is easy to misunderstand the thrust of the promissory sentence of 5:16, as though Paul intended it to be the equivalent of a simple condition, focused on the *inception* of a relationship with the Spirit: '*If* you will *commence* a life with the Spirit, then I can promise you that you will not carry out the Impulsive Desire of the Flesh.' It is true that the promise of the second clause is predicated on the imperative given in the first. That imperative itself, however, is predicated on three major factors that *precede* it, reflecting Paul's awareness that, in formulating his promise, he is not speaking to humanity in general. On the contrary, he is addressing the Galatian churches that have been created as addressable communities by the invasive Spirit. In a word, the promise presupposes the history of the Galatians' relationship with the Spirit.

(1) Some time ago Paul preached the gospel of Christ to the Galatians. The power of that gospel elicited their faith, and the result of this faith-kindling gospel was that they received the Spirit (Gal 3:1–2). In short, the beginning of the Galatians' life as members of the church was not the result of a human act of deciding for the Spirit rather than for the Flesh. At that beginning lay God's act of sending the Spirit into their hearts, begetting them by the power of the Spirit (4:29), and freeing their enslaved wills for obedience to him in the Spirit (4:6). In their baptism, the Galatians crucified the Flesh (5:24), but they did that under the direction of the Spirit, just as their cry to God as Father was in fact the deed of the Spirit.

(2) Because God continues to supply the Spirit to the Galatians (3:5), the Spirit itself remains active in their corporate life, continuing to cry out to God through their own mouths, and continuing to bear the fruit of love in the corporate life of their communities (5:22).

(3) Through the invasive Spirit, then, God has created and continues to create the Galatian churches as *addressable communities*, communities that are able to hear God's imperatives *because of* the indwelling Spirit.[27]

In light of this history, two readings of the imperative of 5:16a are excluded.

First, it is a mistake, as noted above, to treat that imperative as the equivalent of an inceptive conditional clause, as though Paul had said, '*If* you will *commence* a relationship with the Spirit, I can make you a promise.' Knowing the history of the Spirit in the Galatian churches, Paul does not lay the Spirit before the Galatians as a new possibility, a mere alternative to the Flesh. He does not exhort them, therefore, to make a sovereign choice between the two, as though the Spirit and the Flesh were two paths, both of which lay equally open before them. On the contrary, with his imperative, Paul calls on the Galatians steadily to be what they already are.[28] Metaphorically speaking, the Spirit is the

---

27 Cf. Schrage, 'Probleme,' 13–14.

28 In this Bultmannian formulation, one sees a crucial dimension of Paul's understanding of the will. Were the Galatians to fail to continue the life they are being given in the Spirit (5:22–23a), they would not be exercising freedom of will. On the contrary, they would find that they are again slaves of the Flesh, and thus in the state properly called bondage of the will. For there is only one form of free will, and that is obedience to the leading of the Spirit.

general who has already affected the Galatians' will itself, inciting them to service in its war against the Flesh.

It is also a mistake to read the promise of 5:16 as though Paul were informing the Galatians of the availability of the Spirit, the Spirit being a *resource* on which they can call for help in *their* struggle against the Flesh. As we have seen, the war against the Flesh is in the first instance the Spirit's war (5:17), the war declared by the Spirit upon its advent, and carried out by the Spirit as it bears its fruit in the daily life of the church. Thus, the Spirit is and remains the primary actor in the military engagement. The Galatians are soldiers already enrolled in *the Spirit's* army, not contestants in a struggle that is theirs, and in which they are merely free to call on the Spirit for aid. Their deeds are first of all the acts of the Spirit (5:22; cf. 4:6), and secondly the acts of themselves as persons into whose hearts the Spirit has made its entrance (5:24).[29] The imperative element in 5:16 is conceptually equivalent, then, to the hortatory element in 5:25:

> If then we live in the Spirit – and it is certain that we already do – let us carry out our daily lives under the guidance of the Spirit. (5:25)

Similarly, the promise of 5:16 can be fully rendered

> Stay consistently in line with the Spirit. For, as you are led by the Spirit – the victorious power already sent into your hearts by God – you will not fall victim to the Spirit's enemy, the Impulsive Desires of the Flesh.

Conclusion

In writing to the Galatians, Paul is far from reducing daily life to a matter of morals vis-à-vis an ethical code, however conceived. At its root, behavior in the church of God is a subject Paul takes up in the first instance, not by giving a hortatory prescription of 'what ought to be,' but rather by providing a description of 'what is,' now that, by sending the Son and the Spirit of the Son, God has commenced his invasive – and ultimately victorious – war against the Flesh. 'What is' proves therefore to be the war in which God is calling into existence his new creation, the church, with a view toward ultimately delivering the whole of humanity – indeed the whole of the cosmos (Gal 3:22; Rom 8:21) – from the grip of the powers of the present evil age, the curse of the Law, Sin, the elements of the old cosmos, and not least the Flesh.

[29] See Duff, *Humanization*, 61.

In this war, the church is God's cosmic vanguard, the soldiers who receive their behavioral bearings in the midst of and from the contours of this war. It is therefore by describing the Spirit's victorious war against the Flesh, and by portraying the Galatians' place in this war, that Paul speaks with specificity in 5:13–24 of the behavior for which the church is fully inspired, to which it is summoned, and for which it is responsible.

It is both true and important that, pursuing the motif of responsibility, Paul turns from the essentially descriptive paragraph of 5:13–24 to a series of imperative and hortatory verbs in the next paragraph, 5:25–6:10. He is free to do that, however, only because in 5:13–24 he has descriptively portrayed the activity by which God has graciously created an addressable community, a church that, led by the Spirit, is able to hear the imperative and to be thankful to God for it.

16

A Formula for Communal Discord!

Galatians 5:17

In Gal 5:17 Paul speaks of the dynamic relationship between the Impulsive Desire of the Flesh and the Spirit of Christ, identifying that relationship as an apocalyptic war that has been raging since the advent of the Spirit:[1]

> For the Flesh is actively inclined against the Spirit, and the Spirit against the Flesh. Indeed these two powers constitute a pair of opposites at war with one another . . .

In the context set by Gal 5:13-24 (see also 3:2, 5; 4:6, 29) this statement is both clear and understandable. In formulating the promise of Gal 5:16, for example, Paul has just portrayed the Spirit and the Flesh as powers that are actively opposed to one another in the corporate life of the Galatian churches. Far from transparent, however, is the final clause of 5:17, in which Paul describes the result of the war between the Spirit and the Flesh:

> . . . the result being that you do not actually do the very things you wish to do.[2]

---

[1] With consistency Paul uses the term *pneuma* in Galatians to refer to the Spirit of Christ, and the Galatians are very likely to have noted this consistency, for from their baptism onwards, the identity of the Spirit will have been essentially clear to them. It is not a natural part of themselves, a spirit with which they were born, corresponding to the body they were given at birth. Nor is it one of the amorphous spirits abroad in the world. It is the Spirit of the Son, drawing its characteristics from him, and being sent by God into their hearts (Gal 4:6). In Gal 5:13–24 Paul consistently employs the word *sarx* (5:13, 17 [twice], 19, 24) as an abbreviation for *epithymia sarkos* (5:16), the Impulsive Desire of the Flesh, the *yeser* as an apocalyptic power arrayed against the Spirit of Christ. See Marcus, 'Paul.'

[2] Grammatically the *hina* clause can be taken to state either result – on *hina* as a substitute for the infinitive of result, see BDF §391.5, and add to the Pauline passages listed there 2 Cor 7:9 – or purpose, the latter reflecting the goal had in mind by one or the other of the two combatants (or by God? cf. Barclay, *Obeying*, 115 n. 23). The strongest

What are we to make of this surprising clause? If Paul intends the Galatians to rest assured in the promise of 5:16 – a community that leads its daily life guided by the Spirit can know that it will not end up carrying out the Impulsive Desire of the Flesh – how can he follow that promise – indeed how can he ground it (note the word 'for' [*gar*] at the outset of v. 17) – with the apparently discouraging assertion that the war between the Spirit and the Flesh leads to a failure to do what one wishes to do? After the promise, we could expect Paul to speak with a confidence that is contagiously enthusiastic:

> In contradistinction to the Teachers, I, Paul, make you a solemn promise: Lead your daily life guided by the Spirit, and, in this way you will not end up carrying out the Impulsive Desire of the Flesh. For the Flesh is actively inclined against the Spirit, and the Spirit against the Flesh. These two powers constitute a pair of opposites at war with one another, and the result of this war is precisely the positive basis of my promise: The Spirit is in the victorious process of liberating you from the destructive power of the Flesh!

Why does Paul portray instead an apparently negative result to the war between the Flesh and the Spirit? Faced with this question, interpreters have elected in general one of three readings:[3]

First, Paul has been thought to refer mainly to the Spirit's role in the war, thus striking precisely the positive note mentioned above. Far from intending finally to portray a stalemate between the Flesh and the Spirit, Paul announces in Gal 5:17 itself the encouraging news that the Spirit successfully frustrates the desires of the Flesh. Jewett, for example, finds in this verse a decided imbalance. The human being is paralyzed only if

---

argument for the purposive reading is the thesis that in 5:17 Paul intends to warn the Galatians against libertinism. Taking the clause to speak of the purpose of *the Spirit* in its war against the Flesh, and translating the relative pronoun *ha* with the word 'whatever,' Barclay, e.g., finds just such a warning: In its war, the Spirit's purpose is to see to it that 'the Galatians are not in the dangerous position of being *free* to "do *whatever* you want"...' (*Obeying*, 115; emphasis added). But does not this reading import the motif of dangerous freedom into 5:17? Together with virtually the whole of 5:13–24, the clause *hina mē poiēte* is almost certainly descriptive rather than purposive. Paul *describes* the result of the warfare: Given the war between the Flesh and the Spirit, the Galatians *are not doing* what they wish to do.

3   Cf. Barclay, *Obeying*, 113–114. In addition to Barclay's own interpretation (note 2 above), see the reading proposed by O'Neill: Gal 5:17 – where 'spirit' and 'flesh' refer to the two complementary parts of every human being – is one of the Jewish moral aphorisms included in 5:13–6:10, a section inserted into Paul's letter by a later hand ('Spirit'). Cf. Smit, 'Speech,' 25.

'he identifies his own will with that of the flesh.' If he walks by the Spirit, the Flesh has no success in its attempt to lure him away.[4] One can indeed find the essence of this thought in 5:16, and in 5:18 as well. But to read the promise of 5:16 into 5:17 is to beg the question, thus giving no genuine explanation for the fact that Paul *ends* the latter verse on the note of an emphasized failure. And 5:18 is introduced by a contrastive instance of the expression *ei de* ('if, however'), indicating that in speaking there of the successful leading of the Spirit, Paul pictures a state of affairs different from that portrayed in 5:17.[5] This first reading is unconvincing.[6]

Second, Paul has been taken to speak equally of the Flesh and the Spirit, thus formulating an anthropological theory true of every human being: The self experiences a wrenching inner dualism that produces impotence of will because of an essential parity between the Flesh and the Spirit. In the battle each of these powers has as its successful intention the frustration of the other one. Paraphrasing Burton, R. N. Longenecker comments, for example:

> The flesh opposes the Spirit with the desire that people not do what they want to do when guided by the Spirit, and the Spirit opposes the flesh with the desire that people not do what they want to do when guided by the flesh.[7]

Third, Paul has been thought to refer mainly to the role of the Flesh in the life of the Christian. The intention of the Flesh in its war against the Spirit is revealed in the fact that it always stands ready to mislead the

---

[4] Jewett, *Terms*, 106–107. It is significant, of course, that Jewett holds Paul to have turned his attention in Gal 5:13 from nomists to libertinists (*Terms*, 101).

[5] The adversative reading of *ei de* in 5:18 is strongly suggested by 5:24, where Paul refers to the victory over the Flesh that is characteristic of a community belonging *exclusively* to Christ.

[6] Note the form of this reading proposed in Chrysostom's commentary on Galatians. Knowing some who find that Paul has divided the human being into two parts (*dieilen eis duo ton anthrōpon ho Apostolos*) – meaning body and soul in conflict with one another – Chrysostom is concerned to offer a refutation: When Paul speaks here of 'flesh' and 'spirit,' he does not refer to body and soul, but rather to two reasoning powers that are opposed to one another, virtue and vice (*peri duo phēsi logismōn . . . hē aretē kai hē kakia*). Then, having found in this text a reference to virtue and vice, and concluding from other texts that it is the soul that willfully lusts (and taking *hina* to indicate purpose), Chrysostom can offer a happy interpretation of the final clause of 5:17: The flesh and the spirit are opposed to one another, 'in order that you *not allow* the soul to proceed in her evil desires' (*hina mē sygchōrēsēs tē psychē poreuesthai en tais epithymiais autēs tais ponērais*; PG 61.672).

[7] R. N. Longenecker, *Galatians*, 246; Burton, *Galatians*, 302.

Christian, often frustrating his wish to be guided solely by the Spirit. On the one hand, while the tense conflict between willing and doing is the fate of all human beings, in the case of the Christian the Spirit can neutralize that conflict (Gal 5:16). On the other hand, however, still living *in* the Flesh, even the Christian can fall back into the conflict at any moment, thus experiencing impotence of will. Whereas he wishes to do the good, he actually does the evil (cf. Rom 7:19).[8]

Galatians 5:17 and the Standard Reading of Romans 7

Calling for analysis is the fact that most interpreters who propose the second and third readings do so by drawing explicitly or implicitly on a common interpretation of Romans 7. R. N. Longenecker represents numerous commentators when he says – following the statement quoted above – 'In effect, Gal 5:17 sets out in rudimentary fashion what is later spoken of more fully in Rom 7:14-25 . . .'[9] And the interpretation offered by H. D. Betz – for the most part a form of the second reading – is a particularly interesting case in point. To be sure, Betz mentions some of the differences between Gal 5:17 and Romans 7. In the final analysis, however, his interpretation of the verse in Galatians is heavily indebted to his reading of Rom 7:15, as one can see from his use of the pronoun 'I,' a word that plays a prominent role in Romans 7, while being absent from Gal 5:17. Having identified the Flesh and the Spirit in Gal 5:17 as 'impersonal forces acting within man and waging war against each other,' Betz finds in that verse an anthropological theory focused finally on the impotence of the individual's will.

> Man is the battlefield of these forces within him preventing him from carrying out his will. The human 'I' wills, but it is prevented from carrying out its will (*tauta poiēte*) because it is paralyzed through these dualistic forces within. As a result, the human 'I' is no longer the subject in control of the body . . . the human will is disabled from carrying out its intentions.[10]

---

[8] The last two sentences are virtual quotations from Borse, *Galater*, 196.
[9] R. N. Longenecker, *Galatians*, 246; cf. Borse, *Galater*, 195–196.
[10] H. D. Betz, *Galatians*, 279–281. In offering this reading of Gal 5:17, Betz proposes that its anthropological theory of human paralysis is basically pre-Pauline (280). The fullness of Paul's own view emerges in Gal 5:18, where he tells the Galatians that, for Christians, the battle between the Flesh and the Spirit does not issue in a stalemate. On the contrary, 'the Spirit takes the lead, overwhelms, and thus defeats evil' (281).

When we place Gal 5:17 and Rom 7:22-23, 15 (cf. 7:19) in parallel with one another, we can easily see how this reading of the former text has arisen:

Galatians 5:17	*Romans 7:22-23; 15 (19)*
17a. For the Flesh is actively inclined against the Spirit, and the Spirit against the Flesh. 17b. Indeed these two powers constitute a pair of opposites at war with one another,	22. I delight in the Law of God in my inmost self, 23. but what I see is a different Law, operative in my members. This different Law is in conflict with the Law of God to which I adhere in my intentions, and in this conflict the different Law keeps me imprisoned to itself, thus being the Law that controls me, the Law that has fallen into the hands of Sin.
17c. the result being that you do not actually do the very things you wish to do.	15. I do not recognize my own actions. For what I wish – the good – is not what I do; on the contrary, what I hate – the evil that I do not want – is what I actually do.[11]

The standard reading of Romans 7 credits Paul with centering his attention on two motifs, a split internal to the individual self and the resulting impotence of the self actually to carry out its own will. Regarding the first of these motifs, Michel, for example, identified what is distinctive about Rom 7:7-25 as 'its description of the cleavage of the human self;' and H. D. Betz now echoes Michel with his assertion that in Romans 7 'the "I" is split up into two.'[12] For many interpreters, the second motif, the impotence of the human will, seems so obvious in Romans 7 as to need no demonstration. Often, however, certain 'parallels' are offered, such as Ovid's 'I see the better and approve; the lower I follow' (*Metamorphoses* 7.21) and the reference of Epictetus to the man who 'is not doing what he wishes, and is doing what he does not wish' (*Diss.* 2.26.4; cf. 2.26.1).

---

[11] Basically this interpretive translation of Rom 7:22–23, 15 (19) is drawn from Meyer, 'Worm.'

[12] Michel, *Römer*, 225 n. 7; H. D. Betz, *Galatians*, 280.

From this reading of Romans 7 it would seem a short step back to the earlier passage in Gal 5:17. To be sure, as H. D. Betz points out, Paul does not speak in Galatians of a split in the self. Does he not refer, however, as Betz says, to the human body as a battlefield between two contesting forces? And does he not identify the result of this state of affairs as the disabling of the human will to carry out its intentions?

Pondering this apparently Romanesque reading of Gal 5:17, we are faced with three questions. (*a*) In Rom 7:15 (19) Paul says that the self *does not* do what it wishes to do – and does what it does not wish. He could have spoken explicitly of an impotence of the will, saying that the self is *unable* to do what it wishes (*ou gar ho thelō touto dynamai poiēsai*)[13] – and is unable to avoid doing what it does not wish. Is it really Paul's intention in Romans 7 to refer to an impotence of the will? (*b*) Given the absence of an explicit reference to that motif, is the standard interpretation of Romans 7 in need of significant correction? (*c*) If so, would that corrected interpretation of Romans 7 play a role in leading us to a different reading of Gal 5:17?

A New Interpretation of Romans 7

A phenomenal advance in the interpretation of Romans 7 was made in 1990 by Paul W. Meyer.[14] Agreeing with the dominant view that in Romans 7 Paul describes the human situation apart from Christ, Meyer nevertheless offers an analysis in which both of the motifs that characterize the standard interpretation are laid aside, the supposed split internal to the individual self and the resulting impotence of the self actually to carry out its own will.

First, in Romans 7 'both "inmost self" (v. 22) and "members" (v. 23) are but two aspects of the same self that is "sold under sin"' (Meyer, 'Worm,' 76). The tragic element in Romans 7 does not arise, then, from a divided self, but rather from the self's enslavement to the power of Sin, precisely as Sin has wrested the Law out of the hands of God. That is to say, rather than speaking of two parts to the self, Paul refers to *two Laws* (7:22–23, 25; 8:2), which prove to be the Mosaic Law functioning as the Law of God and the Mosaic Law as it has fallen into

---

[13] Both with the negative and without it, the locution *dynamai poiēsai* – and its equivalents – is, of course, very common. In early Christian usage see, e.g. Matt 9:28, and in Paul's letters cf. 1 Cor 15:50.

[14] 'Worm.'

the hands of Sin.[15] The terrifying *fundamentum* to the whole of Paul's argument is the fact that the Mosaic Law is not only God's Law, but also Sin's Law, a tool of Sin. One can see, then, that Romans 7 culminates in a cleavage, but that cleavage 'is in the *Law* and not in the self' (Meyer, 'Worm,' 78).

Second (continuing with Meyer), the result of this terrifying cleavage in the Law – the result of the fact that God's Law has fallen into the hands of Sin – is far more serious than a mere impotence of the human will. In Rom 7:15 (19) Paul's major accent lies not on inaction, but rather on action and result. Indeed, in the first clause of 7:15 Paul speaks explicitly of the result of his actions, saying that that result is a mystery to him; he himself does not recognize it. Clearly something much more sinister is involved than an impotence of the will. A menacing actor other than the self is on stage, and that actor uses for its deadly purposes precisely God's holy and just and good Law. In short, Paul speaks of Sin's power to deceive him via the Law, the result being that he *accomplishes* the *opposite* of what he intended.

The subject of the discourse in Romans 7, then, 'is not simple frustration of good intent, but good intention carried out and then surprised and dumbfounded by the evil it has produced' (Meyer, 'Worm,' 76). Moreover, the form in which this good intention is carried out is precisely that of observance of the Law. Thinking of the Law as God's Law, and of his own clearly willed, altogether admirable and blameless observance of it (Rom 7:12; Phil 3:6), Paul takes as his subject the power of Sin to corrupt the highest good. For in Christ he now looks back on the demonic power of Sin 'to use the Mosaic Law to effect just the opposite of what its devoted adherents expect, even and especially when it is obeyed . . .' (Meyer, 'Worm,' 80). In short, Paul's argument attaches impotence not to the human will, but rather to the

---

[15] In this reading Meyer takes *tēs hamartias* to be a genitive of possession, an interpretation supported by Rom 7:8–11 (seizing *the* Law, Sin used it to kill me). For an alternative reading see Winger, *Law*. There *tēs hamartias* and its equivalents are taken as genitives of source, 'identifying the power whose control is in turn identified by the term *nomos*' (195). This interpretation is related to Winger's finding in Rom 7:21 – with numerous other interpreters – a metaphorical use of *nomos* (force, rule, controlling power) that then sets the precedent for a metaphorical use of *nomos* in 7:22–23 (186 and 186 n. 138). Meyer, on the other hand, taking *ton nomon* in 7:21 to be an adverbial accusative of respect, arrives at a paraphrase in which Paul refers in that verse itself to the Mosaic Law: 'So then, as far as the (Mosaic) law is concerned, the outcome (of the above experience) is that for me, the very one who wishes to do the good, evil is what I find at hand' (79).

Law. The Law itself is the actor who proves to be disabled vis-à-vis the sinister power of Sin. Indeed it is for that reason that God sent his own Son in behalf of all, 'to deal with Sin as the Law could not (Rom 8:3–4)' (ibid.).

The New Interpretation of Romans 7 and a New Reading of Galatians 5:17

Does Gal 5:17 read differently when taken in light of Meyer's interpretation of Romans 7?[16] That is a question we can consider by noting both similarities and differences between these two texts.

The Bifurcated Law

The picture of a bifurcated Law in Romans 7 has its earlier form in Galatians, where Paul considers the Law to have two distinct voices, one could almost say two modes of existence (chapter 14 above). There is *the subjugating and cursing voice* of the plural, Sinaitic Law, ordained by angels in God's absence (4:21a; cf. 3:10), and there is *the promising and guiding voice* of the singular and original Abrahamic Law that, uttered by God himself, speaks of the birth and daily life of circumcision-free churches among the Gentiles (3:8; 4:21b; 5:14).

The Human Will

As we have noted above, in Rom 7:15 Paul does not say that he is *unable* to do what he wishes to do, but rather that he *does not* do what he wishes to do. Similarly, in Gal 5:17 Paul does not say that the Galatians *cannot* do the very things they wish to do (*hina mē ha ean thelēte touta dynēthēte poiēsai*), but rather that they *do not* do those things. Rom 7:15 and Gal 5:17 are similar, in that neither contains an explicit reference to an impotence of the will.

The 'I' of Romans 7 and the 'You (Plural)' of Galatians 5:17

The form of the texts, however, shows them to be in one regard significantly different. Romans 7 is marked by Paul's repeatedly speaking

---

[16] As I have noted previously, reading the earlier letter, Galatians, in light of the later – a common if usually unconscious procedure – can lead to serious misinterpretation. With caution, however, we can make comparisons, honoring the specifics of the Galatian setting (see below) and noting significant differences between the two letters.

of an '*I*,' whereas in Gal 5:17 he speaks *to* a '*you (plural)*,' the Galatians. In his Galatian letter, then, Paul does not speak anthropologically *of* a general failure to act on one's intentions. He speaks specifically and pastorally *to* the Galatian Christians about their failing to do something they corporately wish to do. This simple observation suggests the possibility that Paul intends the Galatians to hear a reference to a development that is to some degree peculiar to *their* corporate life. We can profitably ask, then, how Gal 5:17 will have been heard by the Galatians when Paul's messenger read it aloud.

The Law and Christ

Posing that question, we note first that in the context of Gal 5:17 Paul has emphatically referred to the Law – specifically in its bifurcated state – and to the relationship between this bifurcated Law and Christ. In 5:14 he has spoken of the original voice of the Law of God, the blessing and guiding Law that is altogether pertinent to the daily life of the church, being the Law of neighbor love that has been brought to completion by Christ (Lev 19:18; chapter 14 above). In 5:3, however, he has referred to the voice of the cursing Sinaitic Law, warning the Galatians who are commencing its observance that that Law has no pertinence to the daily life of their churches, being the Law that can be in no way combined with Christ (Gal 5:3-4). He also makes an indirect but clear reference to the Sinaitic Law in the verse immediately preceding 5:17, the promise of 5:16. For there he warns the Galatians that the Teachers are deceiving them with the claim that – as the God-given, fully potent antidote to the Impulsive Desire of the Flesh – the Sinaitic Law is the guide for their daily life.[17] And finally, Paul speaks explicitly of the Sinaitic Law in the verse following 5:17, telling the Galatians that, when lead by the Spirit, they are not under the authority of that Law (5:18). In a word, The Galatians will have heard the statements of 5:17 in a context heavy with Paul's insistence that the Sinaitic Law cannot be added to Christ.

From this observation we return to the form of Gal 5:17, and thus to the simple fact that in Paul's 'you (plural)' the Galatians will have heard a corporate reference to themselves, and thus neither to the individual human being in general – as though Paul were describing a pre-

---

[17] Chapter 15 above.

Christian anthropology – nor to all Christians everywhere – as though Paul were speaking in general of 'the Christian situation'.[18] Just as the Galatians will have sensed in 5:16 a promise Paul believes to be pertinent to their own corporate life, so they will have heard in 5:17 Paul's statement that *they* are corporately not doing what they wish to do.

The Galatians' understanding of 5:17 will have been affected, then, by their having just listened to 5:15 ('But if you snap at one another, each threatening to devour the other, take care that you are not eaten up by one another!'). That is to say, hearing that earlier verse, they will have been reminded of the almost animalistic dissensions currently raging in their churches. That pattern of communal life was something the Galatians surely wished to cease. As things presently stand, however, they are continuing it. Indeed, intending to live in harmony, they are accomplishing the opposite, intensifying their communal conflicts. From the context, then, one can surmise that in the last clause of 5:17 the Galatians will have heard Paul referring to their failure to cease their internal strife, and we can suppose that Paul intended them to hear that reference.[19]

But what does Paul mean when he says that this failure is the result of the war between the Flesh and the Spirit? That is a question best approached by recalling Paul's practice of speaking to the Galatian churches as a whole, when in fact he is thinking of the numerous members who are in the process of accepting the Law-observant theology of the Teachers (see, for example, Gal 1:6; 3:1). In 5:17, that is to say, Paul is thinking of the fact that many of the Galatians are commencing observance of the Sinaitic Law, confident that, by adding that observance to their allegiance to Christ, they will find the guidance in daily life they sorely need (5:3–4). But how, exactly, does Paul think that their failure to cease their dissensions is characteristic of the Galatians who are commencing observance of the Law? And how can he say that that failure is the result, for them, of the war between the Spirit and the Flesh? Two observations may prove helpful.

[18] As we will see below, Käsemann's statement that Gal 5:16–17 describes 'the Christian situation' does not take the Galatian setting sufficiently into account (*Romans*, 208). Note also Meyer's reservation, 'Worm,' 69.
[19] Note that in 5:26 Paul draws the word *phthonos*, 'grudging envy of the neighbor's success,' from the list of the effects of the Flesh (5:21), thus suggesting that it has specific pertinence to the situation in the Galatian churches.

On the one hand, throughout Gal 5:13–26 Paul presupposes a war that has been commenced only with the coming of the Spirit. Addressing the Galatians who have experienced the Spirit's advent in baptism, he portrays quite specifically the situation of the Galatian churches as communities that have been called to the battlefield by the Spirit (chapter 15 above).

On the other hand, the failure to avoid undesired acts, as it is portrayed in 5:17, can be characteristic neither of the Christian freedom Paul has so compellingly pictured in 5:1 and 5:13, nor of the loving communal life that is the fruit of the Spirit (5:22–23a). We return, then, to the hypothesis that in 5:17 Paul is speaking to the Galatians about the stance being taken on the battlefield by those among them who are trying to direct their allegiance both to Christ and to the Sinaitic Law. In this attempt at a dual allegiance, they have, in Paul's view, nothing more to do with Christ, having fallen out of the realm of grace (5:4). Baptized persons summoned to the war by the victorious general, the Spirit, they are looking elsewhere for their guidance!

Read in the light of this hypothesis, the puzzling final clause of Gal 5:17 proves to be an instance of Pauline abbreviation. Here Paul is able to use a kind of shorthand because, addressing the Galatians in their own setting, he can presuppose (1) their having been called by the Spirit to their place in its war against the Flesh, (2) their incipient observance of the Law, (3) the continuance of communal strife in their churches, and (4) the cause of that continued strife, not the paralyzed impotence of their will, but rather the impotence of the Sinaitic Law to curb the power of the community-destroying Flesh.[20] What the Sinaitic Law promises it cannot produce.[21] With the result clause of Gal 5:17c, then, Paul describes the effect of the Spirit–Flesh warfare on those who, in its midst, look to the Sinaitic Law for their guidance. When they desire

---

[20] Two supplementary comments: (*a*) A fifth presupposition hovers in the background. The impotence of the Sinaitic Law to curb the Flesh is related to the yet more distressing fact that the Law and the Flesh are, in effect, secret allies! Via the nomistic circumcision of the flesh, the Flesh has the capacity to draw the Law to its side in its battle against the Spirit. See Gal 3:3; 4:23, 29. (*b*) The major accent in Paul's list of the effects of the Flesh (Gal 5:19–21a) lies on the ways in which the Flesh destroys the *communal* life that is created by the Spirit.

[21] In Galatians Paul does not hesitate to say that the promise spoken by the Sinaitic Law is false. Gal 3:12 can be paraphrased as follows: 'Not having its origin in the benchmark of faith, the (Sinaitic) Law speaks a false promise when it says "The one who does the commandments will live by them"' (Lev 18:5). See chapter 11 above.

277

and expect the good – harmonious communal life – they find its opposite, without being aware of the reason.[22]

With this reading, we can sense the line of thought that runs through the whole of Gal 5:16-18. Speaking to the Law-observant Galatians – and to others tempted to follow them into the same cul-de-sac – Paul first issues the corrective promise of 5:16. Shortly thereafter, he explicates that promise *positively* in the confident statement of 5:18. Before doing that, however, he grounds the promise *negatively* in 5:17, speaking in such a way as to imply that Christ plus the Sinaitic Law is a formula for communal discord:[23]

> (5:16) *But*, in contradistinction to the Teachers, I, Paul, say to you: Lead your daily life guided by the Spirit rather than by the Sinaitic Law; and, in this way, you will not end up carrying out the Impulsive Desire of the Flesh. (5:17) *For*, to find a negative proof of this promise, consider carefully the war between the Flesh and the Spirit. In your case the outcome of that war is nothing other than your failure to do what you wish to do. When you wish, that is, to end the dissensions that plague your communities, you succeed only in intensifying them. Why? Because, even though you have received the perfectly potent Spirit (4:6; 5:16), you are now turning to the Law for your guidance. But, unlike the Spirit, the Law is impotent to provide the guidance that actually curbs the Flesh, and that impotence leads to the continued discord in your churches. (5:18) *If, however*, in the daily life of your communities you are consistently led by the Spirit, then you are not under the authority of the Law, the weakling that cannot deliver you from the power of the Flesh.

---

[22] Yet another difference between Gal 5:17 and Romans 7 demands at least brief comment. In Galatians the split in the Law lacks the complex profundity characteristic of that motif in Romans 7. In Galatians, that is, the Sinaitic Law – far from being holy, just, and good (Rom 7:12) – is the product of angels who, in ordaining it, acted in God's absence, thereby establishing that Law as one of the enslaving elements of the cosmos (Gal 3:19–20; 4:3; chapter 8 above). Paul does not describe the deception experienced by the Law-observant Galatians, then, by speaking of their admirable and blameless devotion to what Paul himself knows to be the highest good. (Contrast Meyer's comment about Romans 7: '[In the hands of Sin] God's own good Law takes on a quality and character opposite to that which a person knows to be true . . . ;' 'Worm,' 80). In Galatians Paul views Law-observant deception in simpler terms. Rather than the result of Sin's beguiling use of God's Law (Rom 7:11), the Galatians' deception is the work of the Teachers (Gal 3:1); and it consists of the Galatians turning to what the Teachers *falsely* define as the highest good.

[23] It should now be clear that this interpretation does not truly fall under any of the three readings catalogued near the beginning of this chapter.

17

From Paul to Flannery O'Connor
with the Power of Grace

The Unredeemed World and Handel's Hallelujah Chorus[1]

In 1926 Martin Buber, the truly majestic German Jewish philosopher, wrote a letter to the editor of a German newspaper in which he addressed the Christian confession with characteristic clarity, precision, and candor:

> In the perspective of my faith, the word spoken to Jesus by Peter at Caesarea Philippi – 'You are the Messiah' – was sincere but nevertheless untrue; and its repetition over the centuries has not brought it any closer to the truth. According to my faith, the Messiah has not appeared in a definite moment of history, but rather his appearance can only mark the end of history. In the perspective of my faith, the redemption of the world did not happen nineteen centuries ago. On the contrary, we still live in an unredeemed world . . .[2]

Is this letter an attack on the Church by a friend and teacher? Hardly! It is a serious challenge, no less pertinent in the time of bloody and intractable tensions in Northern Ireland, Rwanda, and Israel than in the shaky years of foreboding that preceded the rise of Nazism in Europe. Indeed Buber's comment cannot be far from the lips of every one of us. We do live in an unredeemed world, and the consequences of that fact have to be weighed no less seriously by Christians than by Jews (chapter 4 above).

For most of us who have been seized by Jesus Christ, however, abandoning the confession of him is not a genuine option. And the consequence is to realize that the Church has to live, as it has always lived, having on its hands, so to speak, both the magnificent triumphalism of

---

[1] The original form of this chapter was a lecture given in September 1980 to a group of lay women faithfully supportive of Union Theological Seminary in New York City.

[2] See H. J. Schoeps, Review of F. Hammerstein, *Das Messias Problem bei Martin Buber*, *TLZ* 84 (1959), 348–349, and note 38 in chapter 6 above. Note also Stegemann, 'Introduction [to Martin Buber].'

Handel's Hallelujah Chorus and a world staggering under the loads of poverty, genocide, war, and myriad other forms of dehumanization. That brings us to the necessary question: What does it mean to have inherited both the triumphant Hallelujah Chorus and the suffering world?

Christian theology is born with that question. Indeed the history of genuinely Christian thought and life is the history of attempts to come to terms with that question.

Over the stretch of twenty centuries two simplistic answers have dominated, and each of them has been formulated – in part – by drawing quotations from the Bible, and especially from Paul. The first is the answer of other-worldliness. One can confess Jesus as the Messiah in the midst of the unredeemed world if one holds that it was never God's intention to redeem this world. In this vein one can quote Col 3:1–2:

> So if you have been raised with Christ, seek the things that are above, where Christ is . . . Set your minds on things that are above, not on things that are on earth.

The second of the simplistic answers is that of this-worldliness. To confess Jesus as the Messiah in the midst of the unredeemed world is to hold oneself responsible for bringing the Kingdom of God to earth. Here one can cite Phil 2:12:

> . . . work out your own salvation with fear and trembling . . .[3]

Since both answers are made by invoking passages from Paul's letters, doubts remain that either option taken by itself is Paul's. And those doubts send us back to the apostle's letters.

Paul and the Bi-focal Vision of Apocalyptic

We come in on Paul as he is preaching in Corinth. Taking one of the ancient scrolls, that of the prophet Isaiah, and being a well-educated interpreter, he carefully quotes:

> [God says] At an acceptable time I have listened to you, and on a day of salvation I have helped you. (Isa 49:8)

Then, laying the scroll aside, Paul gives his interpretation in an arresting voice:

---

[3] For a decisively different and highly illuminating use of the expression 'this-worldliness,' see Meyer, 'This-Worldliness.'

Look! Now is the acceptable time! Look! Now is the day of salvation. (2 Cor 6:2)

These are impressive words. Bearing in mind Buber's challenge, however, we begin our conversation with Paul by lodging a serious protest. 'Paul, you have used the word Look! Well, looking the real world straight in the eye, from Calcutta to Harlem, to Seoul, Hebron, Buenos Aires, Belfast, Teheran, Baghdad, Oberammergau, if anything is obvious, it is that now is not the day of salvation.' In a word, we begin by charging Paul with poor reality testing. Buber at our elbow, we give Paul a failing grade for the way in which he carries out his exegesis of Isaiah.

The Apostle, however, is disconcertingly unimpressed, and certainly not silenced. We may imagine that he responds initially by uttering an arresting expression: 'Apocalypse Now!' Then he fills out at some length his apocalyptic perspective. It follows that if we are going to converse with Paul, rather than cite him in support of our own insights, we are going to have to come to terms with the strange world of Pauline apocalyptic.

'Apocalypse' is a Greek word which our English-speaking forebears and we ourselves have traditionally rendered by the term 'revelation.' It is one of the results of the Vietnam War that the Greek word has been introduced into the popular levels of the American language from the bestseller lists to the theater marquees. And that is an interesting development, for one of the major points to be made about apocalyptic, not least in Paul's letters, is that it draws quite essentially on images of war.[4]

In Paul's apocalyptic, as in war, there are two opposing sides, the Old Age and the new creation.

Old Age	*New Creation*
orb of evil and sin	orb of grace
sphere under the power of Satan, the rulers of this age	sphere under the power of God, the Spirit of Christ
slavery	freedom
death	life
the oppressive status quo	the genuinely new.

Here the imagery of apocalyptic war presupposes a provisional eschatological dualism. As in war, so in apocalypse, two sides are dynamically

---

4   See chapters 7 and 15 above.

interrelated. It would be a serious mistake to link them simply with heaven and earth as though the New Creation were statically existent *up there*, and the Old Age statically existent *down here*. Apocalyptic is not a matter of metaphysical transcendentalism, or of static polarization. On the apocalyptic landscape there is always movement, and for that reason the English word 'revelation' is an inadequate translation of the Greek term 'apocalypse.'

When we speak of revelation, we think of the drawing back of a curtain, resulting in the exposure of something previously hidden behind the curtain. There are elements of Paul's apocalyptic that can be related to that picture (e.g. 1 Cor 2:6–16). On the whole, however, the image of an uncovering or unveiling is woefully inadequate as an attempt to interpret Paul's apocalyptic. Paul's view is focused instead on the image of a dynamic invasion. This invasion inaugurates the *movement* on the apocalyptic landscape.

The resulting issue proves to be critical in our reading of Paul's letters. What has been made visible is not some *thing* previously enclosed behind a curtain, now revealed by pulling the curtain aside. Rather, the *One* who has been on the other side rips the curtain apart, steps through to our side, altering irrevocably our time and space.

It may help to recall Jesus' parable about the binding of the strong man:

> No one can enter a strong man's house and plunder his property, unless he first binds the strong man; then indeed he may plunder his house. (Mark 3:27)

Here Jesus interprets the powers of demon exorcism active in him, and he does so by drawing on the war-like imagery of apocalyptic (note particularly the verb *deō* 'to bind,' and cf. Rev. 20:2). Jesus' strength to exorcize demons from terrorized human beings is a sign of the powers of God's New Creation. They are invading the house of the Old Age, binding the Satanic Strong Man who is the major power of that Age, and freeing human beings from his grasp.

The same image of invasion informs Paul's apocalyptic, as one can see in the ease with which he uses interchangeably the verbs 'to be revealed,' 'to come,' and 'to be sent' (Gal 3:19–4:7). Paul sees that the coming of Christ is the invasion of Christ. And as invasion, that event has unleashed a cosmic conflict, indeed *the* cosmic conflict.

Here we pause. Given this eschatological dualism and the motif of war-like invasion, we ask, what is coming next in Paul's apocalyptic?

One thinks, for example, that after speaking of the Old Age and the new creation, Paul might call on his hearers to make a decision. He might think of the Old Age and the new creation as one thinks of two options, thus formulating a variant form of the ancient doctrine of the Two Ways. He might then address his hearers with an exhortation: 'As you are living in the orb of evil and sin, I beg you to repent, thus choosing grace and life.'

Paul does not speak in this way. The language of repentance, for example, is almost totally absent in his letters. Nor do his references to Christ's coming lead Paul to speak of new possibilities or potentials for human beings. In the apocalyptic war as Paul sees it, the focus is not on novel options. Rather, as in all wars, the focus is on power, and in the first instance the power question is posed because, as we have seen, the coming of Christ, the apocalypse of Christ, is the powerful invasion of Christ.

It follows that the basic characteristic of the present time is given in the fact that it is the juncture of the Old Age and the new creation.[5] To use a spatial image, it is the arena made what it is by the fact that God's new creation is invading the Old Age in a kind of jungle warfare. The 'now' about which Paul speaks as the now of salvation is the redemptive now because it is the now of God's apocalyptic war of liberation, not the now of a retreat from the real world.[6] The real cosmos, then, is not a harmony, but the scene of struggle. The area in which we now find ourselves is hotly contested territory. Individual battles are sometimes won, and sometimes lost. Whoever forgets this invites repeated experiences of disillusionment.

Finally, however, the results of individual battles do not constitute the ultimate issue. For, truly perceived, this apocalyptic war is a war whose outcome is not in question. In Paul's letters there is never a hint that God will ultimately lose. But, given the rampaging forces of evil, how can Paul be entirely confident in God's final victory?

Here we encounter the ancient linking of apocalyptic with the matter of vision.[7] We can notice this link by studying the ways in which Paul uses verbs of perception: 'to see,' 'to know,' 'to discern.' In this linking two issues are at stake: (1) whether one sees this peculiar apocalyptic war at all; (2) whether one sees its ultimate outcome. The first of these

[5] Cf. chapter 6 above.
[6] Cf. Meyer, 'This-Worldliness.'
[7] See the closing section of chapter 4 above.

is an issue because battles between the Old Age and the new creation are never simple public events in the usual meaning of that expression. The battles that concern Paul are not portrayed in their true perspective in the Evening News. For the true contours of these battles are not fully visible to the naked eye.

Why not? Because God's liberating invasion is not demonstrable in categories of the Old Age or with the means of perception native to the Old Age. The inbreaking is itself revelation, apocalypse. That event brings about an epistemological crisis, a crisis in the way one sees and perceives.[8]

If we are to converse with Paul, then, we are required to speak of bi-focal vision, an expression not found, of course, in Paul's letters, but one which may help us to understand those letters. The dictionary defines bi-focal, as regards eyeglasses, as a lens having two portions, one for near vision, one for far vision. In order to find a metaphor helpful to our interpretation of Paul, we will have to imagine looking *simultaneously* through both of these lenses. Looking in that manner would cause us to see everything in a new perspective.

To see bi-focally in Paul's terms is to see *both* the enslaving Old Age and God's invading and liberating new creation. It is an understatement to say that a crucial difference lies before us here: the difference between uni-focal vision, in which one sees on a single level, and bi-focal vision, in which one is given the grace, the power, to see simultaneously, two levels.

The Civil Rights Struggle in the Southern States

Transport yourself for a moment to the Sixteenth Street Baptist Church in Birmingham, Alabama, on an evening in the month of May, 1963.[9] Black people are in the middle of a struggle for one aspect of liberation in Birmingham. They come each evening to the church. On the evening in question, God has been invoked, prayers offered, hymns sung, with the contagious emotions found in the midst of struggle. Now it is time to hear from the visitors who have flown in during the afternoon. One of these is a greatly and justly loved figure from the sports world. He begins his speech by remarking, 'You people are doing a great thing here in Birmingham.' At this, one hears a few feet shuffling back and

---

[8] Chapter 6 above.
[9] See King, *Letter*.

forth. After three or four sentences he says again, 'It is a great thing you people are doing here.' Shuffling of the feet, to which is added a few clearings of the throat. Several sentences later he returns to what is now his theme. 'The whole world has its eyes fixed on you, because you are doing a great thing here in Birmingham.' Now, shuffling of the feet and clearing of the throat will no longer suffice. One of the old deacons interrupts the speaker, politely but firmly, calling out, 'We're not doing this! God is doing this!'

What does one make of such a remark? Is the deacon uttering a pious, other-worldly platitude? Hardly! He has been on his feet in the struggle all day. We have here one of those moments in which uni-focal vision is met by and corrected by bi-focal vision. The deacon is simply saying that the real struggle in Birmingham is a struggle in God's apocalyptic war. He is saying that the full contours of this struggle can be seen only in the bi-focal vision concentrated on what God is doing in the world.

Similarly, Paul's perspective links apocalyptic to vision, not in order to gaze into heaven in a mystic trance, but to bear witness that God has begun the apocalyptic war by striking the decisive blow in Jesus Christ, thus making certain that the ultimate future of the world is the future of Christ, the corporate One of the New Age.[10]

We must now pause to find our bearings. Paul's vision of God's apocalyptic warfare is impressive. But does it reach all the way as an answer to Martin Buber's challenge? I think not. The issue of the unredeemed world is not yet fully addressed. For, whoever will preach apocalyptic Good News in an unredeemed world by using the word 'Look!' will have to do so with his index finger firmly extended (cf. Grunewald's John the Baptist). As Paul preaches the Gospel of Jesus Christ, where does he point?

When one follows the line of Paul's index finger, one sees that the whole of the apocalyptic theater takes its bearings from the cross. For Paul the cross is no timeless symbol. On the contrary, the crucifixion of Jesus Christ is itself the apocalypse, after which nothing can be the same. There are two dimensions to the crucifixion of God's Messiah seen as invading revelation, as apocalypse.

(1) First, the crucifixion speaks to the question of the nature of the world's unredemption. Against the background of apocalyptic war, Paul

---

[10] Cf. Moltmann, *Hope*; Morse, *Logic.*

sees that Jesus' death is death *on the battlefield*, and that means that it is from Jesus' death that one begins to perceive the contours of the real battlefield. Consider for a moment the old question, Who crucified Christ? New Testament scholars have given various answers, involving the Roman soldiers, the Temple police, Pilate, and perhaps the Sanhedrin. The answers are various, but they are all this-worldly, all uni-focal. Paul passes through the midst of such answers when he says apocalyptically, 'The rulers of this age crucified the Lord of glory' (1 Cor 2:8). From Paul's thoroughly apocalyptic answer we see that in the crucifixion God meets on the battlefield not the Jews, not the Sanhedrin, not even the Gentile Romans, but rather Satan and his hosts, who act in and through and on human beings, but who are scarcely reducible to some discrete human group or individual. When the crucifixion of God's Messiah is seen as the event of God's apocalypse, the forces of oppression and dehumanization which cause our world to remain unredeemed are not to be explained by identifying them with any discrete group of human beings.

Here we can be reminded of the Swiss theologian Emil Brunner, lecturing at Wellesley College not long after the Second World War, not long, that is, after the horrors of the Holocaust. In the course of his lecture, Brunner referred several times to the Devil. One was not surprised, then, that in the question period a student asked him why he, a modern human being, should have mentioned the Devil. It was a polite question, behind which lay the recognition that we live in the scientific age. Brunner's response: 'I have referred to the Devil for two reasons. First, I find that he plays a very important role in scripture. And second, I have seen him.'

That response brings us back to the matter of bi-focal vision. When the offensive and horrifying crucifixion of God's Messiah is seen as the center of God's invading revelation, the battlefield is defined in ways that probe the mystery of cosmic evil, rather than in the reductionistic perspective that is focused on the ill will, the misconduct, the immorality, of this or that individual or group. The startling crucifixion of God's Messiah seen as invading apocalypse tells us that the world's unredemption is a matter of universal enslavement by cosmic forces of evil![11]

---

[11] We can also say that God's deed of raising Jesus from the dead is what gives assurance that the world's unredemption will give way to ultimate rectification, but in Paul's theology Jesus' resurrection is God's validation of Jesus' redemptive death, not the replacement of that death. Cf. Cousar, *Cross*; A. R. Brown, *Cross*.

(2) Second, the cross, God's invading apocalypse, speaks to the question of power. It is a truism that there is no issue in our time more crucial than the question of power. For Christians facing the unredeemed world, the question of power becomes again and again *the* question. Wherein does the power lie for the overcoming of the cosmic forces of evil that are revealed in the crucifixion?

For the most part we tend to answer the question of power with one or another form of law. We talk endlessly about legal justice and injustice, about procedures, programs, and cross-avoiding policies in which – however 'well intentioned' – the rich manage not to share the world's goods with the poor. We assume, for example, that the unredemption of the world lies fundamentally in what we call immorality, sexual violence, and lack of family values. The antidote we consider powerful, therefore, is effectiveness in numerous forms of law-enforcement. But in this way we are trapped by a new and thoroughly impotent legalism.[12]

The crucifixion of God's Christ – the horrifying nailing of Jesus to splintery pieces of wood – seen as God's invading apocalypse speaks in an utterly different way to the question of power. We say to Paul, 'Look! From Harlem to the ancient valleys of the Tigris and Euphrates, the oppressed are crying out for change, for liberation, for transformation, and we must find the power by which genuine change, liberation, and transformation can be brought about!' Paul responds: 'The people are indeed crying out. I myself cry out. Who is weak, and I am not weak? Who is made to fall, and I am not indignant?' (2 Cor 11:29) 'But look,' Paul continues, 'God is neither indifferent nor powerless. There is a word, one Word, which has the new power genuinely to change, liberate, transform, and that is the word of the cross.'

A strange Word with a stranger power that looks like weakness. It is not a word addressed to the will of the individual, exhorting that individual to do this or that. Neither is it a contingent word, laying down conditions that humans must meet if there is to be a movement toward human betterment. The word that is God's power is the indicative word of the cross as the apocalypse of God's genuine love and powerful grace.

---

[12] The references above and below to developments in the civil rights struggle reflect genuine political action on the part of people who were ready to strike an alliance with civil law on their own terms. Those terms inevitably involved them, however, in the politics of God, and thus in a kind of political action that includes, but cannot be reduced to, legal dimensions. See Duff, *Humanization*.

> But God proves his love for us in that *while we were still sinners* Christ died for us. (Rom 5:8)
>
> ... *while we were enemies*, we were reconciled to God through the death of his Son. (Rom 5:10)

At this point we are confronted with the mystery of God's strange way of making right what is wrong.[13] For the crucifixion of Christ proves to be the centerpiece in God's war in our behalf, the event of his powerful invading grace, in no way contingent on the fulfilling of a single presupposition from our side. On the apocalyptic battlefield Christ's death is the deed enacted in behalf of those who are enslaved under the power of Sin, and that means in behalf of all of us. Paul can even say, therefore, that in Christ's death God is the one who rectifies *the ungodly* (Rom 4:5). Here is the power of God's grace: that Christ did not die for the righteous, for the morally acceptable, for the noble of heart who are never anxious. Indeed Paul even sees in the crucifixion that Christ did not die for those who believe. Neither Christian faith nor faith of any sort is a presupposition to God's invading apocalypse of love in the crucifixion of the Messiah. On the contrary, the crucifixion is God's revelation of that gift of grace that, not assuming or presupposing faith, calls faith into existence.

But is this event of unconditional grace the power in the face of which the forces of evil are in fact deeply vulnerable? God's gift of grace in Jesus Christ often seems passive and weak.[14]

Recall again the civil rights struggle in the southern states. Turn in your imagination to Montgomery, Alabama in the winter of 1955–56. You remember the general scene: Mrs Rosa Parks has said 'No!' She has been arrested, and the bus boycott has begun.[15] You may remember the sequence in the Montgomery City Hall and in the Chamber of the City Commissioners. On one side of the table sit leaders of the black community; on the other side leaders of the white community.

Make no mistake about it. The game being played in this room *is* the power game. But what makes the scene fascinating is that across the table from one another, looking one another full in the face, are two kinds of power. The power of the city fathers is revealed to be the power of the Old Age, the power that is built solidly on the old principle of

---

[13] See chapter 9 above.
[14] See chapter 4 above.
[15] See King, *Stride*.

quid pro quo, this for that. The game played by this Old-Age power is a game set up for those who think they have the quid and who play at the expense of those who do not. Moreover, a major stratagem of the city fathers, the representatives of Old-Age power, is that of attempting to convince everyone that this is the only kind of power. In effect, they are saying to the leaders of the black community, 'If you wish to win, you will have to beat us at our own game, using Old-Age power yourself; and we all know that you have very little of that power.'

The scene is fascinating because the power on the other side of the table does not accept this agenda. Gathering evening by evening in its churches, the black community knows that there is power of a different order. What makes this power truly different and what makes it in the long run invincible is not visible to Old-Age eyes. What makes this a different power is its root and vitality in the graceful, uncontingent love of God revealed in the crucifixion of his Son.

In this scene the weapon of God's grace comes clear. It is the unconditional grace in the cross of Christ, the grace that is powerful enough to keep the black community walking on sore feet every day, instead of riding the segregated buses. It is the grace known by Rosa Parks and her sisters and brothers, as they sing into the face of the unredeemed world,

> Amazing grace, how sweet the sound that saved a wretch like me; I once was lost, but now am found, was blind, but now I *see*!

See that in the literal crucifixion of Jesus of Nazareth God invades without a single if. Not *if* you repent. Not *if* you learn. Not even if you believe. The absence of the little word if, the uncontingent, prevenient, invading nature of God's grace shows God to be the powerful and victorious Advocate who is intent on the liberation of the entire race of human beings. This is the victorious power that one saw in Birmingham and in Montgomery. It is also the power that Paul saw in the cross, the event in which the name Immanuel was enacted: 'God with us.'

Flannery O'Connor as Apocalyptic Novelist

Numerous scenes in Flannery O'Connor's story 'Revelation' remind us forcefully that this southern author was gifted with a sense of humor far superior to that of Paul! Her admirers enjoy reading her stories an indefinite number of times, finding, they say, new insights with each reading. Yet, for many readers, O'Connor's novels and short stores are highly problematic, even grossly offensive.

They are so, I suppose, on three major counts. O'Connor's stories and novels are overpopulated, to say the least, with grotesque characters. We encounter, for example, a Bible salesman prowling about, looking for girls with wooden legs. These grotesque characters are responsible for highly bizarre plot developments. And O'Connor's stories often seem to have no point beyond the grotesque and bizarre. In short, the images seem to be the message; the images are often unpleasant, one suspects that the message is unpleasant. Would one not do better, then, to repair to the novels of Anthony Trollope?

If you have read the collection of O'Connor's letters, *The Habit of Being*, you will recall that after the appearance of her early stories, some of her kinsfolk wrote to her mother suggesting that she use the motherly office, as it were, to inform Flannery that the real world contains some nice people. Why couldn't she write stories about them? Flannery's response to such instructive letters was a moment of amusement, after which she returned to her work, consistently posing for herself two questions: What is the real world? And how is that real world to be represented in fiction? Her own answers to these questions explain her use of the grotesque.

She speaks of the writer whose concern for *realism* causes him to lean away from typical social patterns toward the grotesque as it may convey mystery and the unexpected. She notes that what this writer sees on the surface will be of interest to him only as he can go through it into an experience of mystery itself. Thus far, we might conclude that we are in touch with nothing more than a talented writer who has a healthy respect for the power of metaphor.

Another of O'Connor's remarks hints, however, that she may intend to point to something more than metaphor. She continues,

> The writer of grotesque fiction is looking for one image that will connect or combine or embody two points; one is a point in the concrete, and the other is a point not visible to the naked eye, but believed in by this writer firmly, just as real to him, really, as the one that everybody sees.[16]

Bearing in mind the way in which she worked out these images in her stories, you will look a long time before you will find a novelist speaking more clearly of the germ of the apocalyptic perspective. When you read

[16] O'Connor, *Mystery*, 42.

or reread the whole of her essay on 'Some Aspects of the Grotesque in Southern Fiction,' try substituting the word apocalyptic for the term grotesque, and note the ways in which the grotesque proves to be cruciform.

The major point is that Flannery O'Connor was no less aware than Paul of the link between apocalyptic and bi-focal vision. Grotesque characters, she observes, seem to carry an invisible burden. Or changing the image slightly, she notes that the prophetic vision – a vision that is for her conveyed in the actions of grotesque characters – is a matter of seeing near things with their extensions of meanings, and thus of seeing far things close up. The *real* world emerges, she believed, in this kind of exaggerated, distorted, but also and fundamentally bi-focal vision.

Indeed, there is more to support the thesis that what we have here goes beyond metaphor. Not only do we find the bi-focal vision of apocalyptic, but also apocalyptic's dynamism. There is in O'Connor's stories no static polarization between 'near things' and 'far things.' On the contrary, there is always movement on the grotesque, apocalyptic landscape. And most important of all, that movement is fundamentally portrayed in the dynamic motif of invasion. 'I have found,' she says, 'from reading my own writing that the subject of my fiction is the action of grace in territory held largely by the devil.'[17] In a word, O'Connor saw very clearly the territory held largely by the devil; she saw very clearly the invading power of grace; and she saw that God's grace was more powerful than evil. Here again, one can scarcely avoid being reminded of Paul (cf. Rom 5:15; 11:32).

'Revelation'

Consider the story 'Revelation.' In this narrative O'Connor introduces Mrs Ruby Turpin, a white, middle-class woman of the South, a bit plump (but in a pleasing way), blessed with good skin, and grateful to Jesus that she is, in her own words, 'neither nigger nor white trash.' At night she lies awake pondering her place in the social and moral hierarchy. She and her husband Claude own their house and the land on which they farm hogs. That situates them above most blacks and all white trash, but below (and this troubles and confuses Mrs Turpin) the black dentist in town who owns two Lincoln Continentals. As she drifts

---

[17] O'Connor, *Mystery*, 118.

into sleep, confusion overcomes the neat categories in which she situates herself by day, and she dreams that 'all the classes of people are crammed in together in a box car, being ridden off to be put in a gas oven.' Mrs Turpin's apocalyptic revelation, her encounter with God's truth, begins in this disturbing dream.

It continues in the waiting room of a doctor's office where Mrs Turpin encounters, among others, Mary Grace, an over-weight college student with bad acne who accurately (almost supernaturally) perceives the older woman as THE enemy. As the group waits together, Mrs Turpin strives in her patronizing way to assert her superiority over the others present, including Mary Grace, whom she pities for having such an ugly face. Presently, we notice that battle lines are being drawn. The girl gazes on Mrs Turpin, O'Connor writes, 'as if she'd known and despised her all her life. All Mrs Turpin's life too, not just the girl's.' This gaze makes Mrs Turpin uneasy. What had she done to the girl to deserve this? She continues her smug self-justifying way of relating to the others, but becomes more and more aware of the girl's hostile gaze, until suddenly Mary Grace, by now in a seething rage, hurls her biology textbook, *Human Development*, across the room. The book hits Mrs Turpin above the eye and knocks her to the floor.

In the confusion that ensues, the girl is restrained and tranquilized, while Mrs Turpin enters into the depths of an apocalypse. She feels as though she were in an earthquake. First she sees everything as if through the wrong end of a telescope, and then in reverse, everything large instead of small. She feels 'entirely hollow except for her heart which swings from side to side as if it were agitated in a great empty drum of flesh.' And when her vision returns to normal, she finds herself looking directly into the fierce, brilliant eyes of Mary Grace. Like Jacob wrestling with the angel, Mrs Turpin demands a word from the girl who knew her in some intense and personal way beyond time and place and condition.

'What you got to say to me?' Mrs Turpin says, waiting '*as for a revelation.*' The girl replies in a whisper, 'Go back to hell where you came from you old wart hog.' At this pronouncement, Mary Grace's eyes burned, writes O'Connor, as if she saw with pleasure that her message had struck its target.

At this moment in the story, we are fully drawn into O'Connor's subject, the action of grace in territory held largely by the devil. We notice, for example, her use of the grotesque to shock us out of complacency, her focus first on false perception and then on an irruption that radically alters our vision, the earthquake, the penetrating words of judgment, the use of the expression 'as if,' so typical of visionary literature, and finally the pervasive imagery of battle. The ear trained by Biblical texts will hear the striking overtones of other apocalypses: the earthquake on Golgotha, the blinding light on the road to Damascus, the dream of a sheet coming down from heaven filled with creatures clean and unclean (Acts 10:9–16).[18]

The last image, the descent of the clean and unclean creatures, becomes more directly relevant as O'Connor brings Mrs Turpin deeper into her crisis and then turns her toward resolution. It is late afternoon of the same day, and Mrs Turpin, unable to rest since the trauma suffered in the doctor's office, starts down the road to the hog pen which she calls, delicately, 'the pig parlor.' Still stunned by the sharp and penetrating words of the girl, wounded and seeking justice if not revenge, she moves, 'single-handed, weaponless,' we are told, 'into battle.' As she hoses down her hogs, she complains to God, Job-like.

> What did you send me a message like that for? . . . There was plenty of trash there, it didn't have to be me. . . How am I a hog and me both? How am I saved and from hell too? . . . How am I a hog, exactly how am I like them?

As she continues defiant in the face of God, she sees Claude's truck, tiny in the distance, and imagines another truck hitting Claude's and killing him, leaving her alone. Now her loss and her lostness are magnified. Bracing herself for a final assault, as O'Connor put it, she cries out to God,

> Go on, call me a hog. Call me a hog again. From hell. Call me a wart hog from hell. Put that bottom rail on top. There'll still be a top and a bottom!

And then, shaken by a final surge of fury, she demands of God: 'Who do you think you are?'

For a moment there is silence, and 'the color of everything burns,' we are told, 'with transparent intensity,' as Mrs Turpin's question rolls across the meadow to the highway, and returns to her 'clearly, like an answer from beyond the wood.' Then she gazes, 'as if through the very heart of mystery' into the pen of hogs. In the setting sun they appear to 'pant with secret life.' From this sight her eyes are drawn upward, where in the purple-streaked sky she sees 'the whole vast horde of souls rumbling

---

[18] Cf. Minear, *The Golgotha Earthquake.*

toward heaven.' It is the band of saints and sinners, ascending, white trash, colored people, freaks, and lunatics, going on ahead 'shouting and clapping and leaping like frogs.' And then bringing up the end of the procession, she sees dignified people like herself and Claude, the only ones singing in tune, but now their 'shocked and altered faces' show 'that even their virtues are being burned away.' Seized into recognition, Mrs Turpin raises her hands in a gesture hieratic and profound. O'Connor ends the story with an apocalyptic audition that seals the message of Mrs Turpin's vision in ordinary experience:

> At length she . . . made her slow way on the darkening path to the house. In the woods around her the invisible cricket choruses had struck up, but what she heard were the voices of the souls climbing upward into the starry field and shouting hallelujah.[19]

It is no large step from Paul's apocalyptic vision to that of O'Connor. Indeed, by comparing them with one another, we may gain a better understanding of both. We begin by noting the word of revelation, 'Go back to hell where you came from, you old wart hog.' It is not simply a disclosure, an unveiling. On the contrary, this word is an event of powerful invasion. To use another image, Mary Grace's word of revelation is a cruciform fish-hook that makes its way into Mrs Turpin's soul, so that she cannot shake it off. It is a disclosure because it is an invasion that has power, the power to transform Mrs Turpin's world. Where does this power lie?

It lies in the grotesque image, the image of Mrs Turpin as a wart hog. This image functions on several levels. On one, it points to our unredeemed world, exhibiting it for what it is, a pig pen. The world is a world of hogs. On another level this grotesque image of Mrs Turpin as a hog – indeed, a wart hog – causes Mary Grace's word of revelation to be Mrs Turpin's crucifixion. That word is the *violent* action of grace invading territory held largely by the devil.

Return now to the final scene at the Turpins' 'pig parlor.' There are 'seven long-snouted bristly shoats . . . and an old sow a few weeks off from farrowing . . . lying on her side grunting . . . the shoats . . . running about shaking themselves like idiot children, their little slit pig eyes searching the floor for anything left.' Who is Mrs Turpin now? She is, of course, the grotesque figure in a bizarre scene, no less grotesque than

---

[19] With her permission I have taken this account of O'Connor's story from an uncommonly perceptive essay of Alexandra Brown, 'Word,' making slight alterations.

she was in the doctor's waiting room, and in surroundings no less bizarre. *But now*, Mrs Turpin's space, her world, her very self, have been invaded by the terrible, crucifying, fish-hook-shaped word of revelation (cf. Paul's 'But now . . .' in Rom 3:21). That word, God's weapon of grace, inaugurates the conflict in cosmic terms, portrayed by the ending of O'Connor's story. The Old Age does not give up without a struggle. Forces in Mrs Turpin now fight against the invading word of revelation. As this grotesque figure screams at God, struggling against God's uncontingent grace, Mrs Turpin poses the question of the *bi*-focal vision of apocalyptic. Shouting at God, she demands to know, 'How an I a hog *and* me both? How am I saved *and* from hell too?'

The end of the story confirms both O'Connor's bi-focal vision and the question it poses. There is first the near vision of the hogs:

> Mrs Turpin stood there . . . all her muscles rigid . . . Then like a monumental statue coming to life, she bent her head slowly and gazed, as if through the very heart of mystery, down into the pig parlor at the hogs. They had settled all in one corner around the old sow who was grunting softly. A red glow suffused them. They appeared to pant with a secret life.[20]

Secret life in hogs? What is that secret life? O'Connor portrays it not only in the near vision of the hogs but also in the far vision of the vast horde of beings, and the far vision consummates the cosmic conflict, as we have seen above. It brings about the crucifixion of Mrs Turpin's world:

> Until the sun slipped finally behind the tree line, Mrs Turpin remained there with her gaze bent to them [the hogs] as if she were absorbing some abysmal life-giving knowledge. At last she lifted her head. There was only a purple streak in the sky, cutting through a field of crimson and leading, like an extension of the highway, into the descending dusk. She raised her hands from the side of the pen in a gesture hieratic and profound. A visionary light settled in her eyes. She saw the streak as a vast swinging bridge extending upward from the earth through a field of living fire. Upon it a vast horde of souls were rumblings toward heaven. There were whole companies of white-trash, clean for the first time in their lives, and bands of black niggers in white robes, and battalions of freaks and lunatics shouting and clapping and leaping like frogs. And bringing up the end of the procession was a tribe of people whom she recognized at once . . . She leaned forward to observe them closer. They were marching behind the others with great dignity, accountable as they had always been for good order and common sense and respectable

---

[20] O'Connor, 'Revelation,' 217.

behavior . . . Yet she could see by their shocked and altered faces that even their virtues were being burned away. She lowered her hands and gripped the rail of the hog pen, her eyes small but fixed unblinkingly on what lay ahead. In a moment the vision faded but she remained where she was, immobile. At length she got down and turned off the faucet and made her slow way on the darkening path to the house. In the woods around her the invisible cricket choruses had struck up, but what she heard were the voices of the souls climbing upward into the starry field and shouting hallelujah.[21]

That final vision involves the cruciform death that is loss of cosmos, for in that vision – a vision of the burning away of virtues and thus a vision of tax collectors and prostitutes preceding you into the Kingdom of the God who rectifies the *un*godly (Matt 21:31; Rom 4:5) – Mrs Turpin's carefully ordered, 'comfortably moral' world is attacked by God's uncontingent grace, destroyed by God's grace, and re-created by God's grace.[22] But notice that the bi-focal vision, made up of the near vision and of the far vision, does not cause a hog to be not a hog. The concrete point is still there. The invading grace of the bi-focal vision causes a hog to be from hell and saved too (at the same time a sinner and rectified)! And the graceful vision has the destructive and creative power to do that. The out-working of the crucifixion in that terrible word of revelation uttered to Mrs Turpin is the uncontingent invasion of God's grace on God's own terms. Here the action of God's grace in territory held largely by the devil takes place in the crucifying word of revelation. Pondering the relation between that offensive word of Mary Grace and the offensive word of the cross, Paul would have said

> God forbid that I should boast in anything except the cross of our Lord Jesus Christ, by which the cosmos has been crucified to me and I to the cosmos. (Gal 6:14)

For Flannery O'Connor, no less than for Paul, the crucifixion is the invading apocalypse of God's unconditional grace that brings us to life in the midst of death.[23]

---

[21] 'Revelation,' 217–218

[22] Theologically the erasure of moral distinctions in Mrs Turpin's vision is closely related to the apocalyptic texture of the pastoral section of Galatians, and specifically to Paul's transformation of the language of vice and virtue there. See chapter 15 above.

[23] The *offensive* character of the gospel's inbreaking is a major motif in O'Connor's stories and novels. Similarly, although for Paul the cross and the resurrection constitute an indivisible whole, the pattern of the church's daily life is set far more by the cross than by the resurrection (e.g. Gal 2:19–20; 5:24; 1 Cor 2:2; 2 Cor 4:10). See Cousar, *Cross*; A. R. Brown, *Cross*.

Buber, Paul, and O'Connor

So the challenge of Martin Buber, the apocalyptic witness of Paul, and the apocalyptic fiction of Flannery O'Connor flow together to leave us with a question: Where are *we* in the truly real world, that is to say in this apocalyptic, cosmic conflict? The form of the question is not where should we be, but where are we *in fact*? And the answer is as clear as the question: Look! God has placed us in his struggle for redemption, the ultimate outcome of which is not in question. By the awful invading power of God's unconditional grace, without a single if, God has placed us in the front trenches of his apocalyptic war of redemption, so that in the power of his unconditional grace we may fight the only good fight in the world, the fight of the God who is the Passionate Advocate of every one of us.

Glossary

Amidah

The major prayer at synagogue services, consisting of eighteen or nineteen benedictions.

anacoluthon

A sentence that lacks the syntactical completion required by its beginning.

antinomy/antithesis

An antinomy is a pair of opposites discovered by human beings to be so fundamental to the cosmos as to constitute one of its elements. An antithesis consists of two contradictory statements or propositions formulated by a human being. See chapter 7.

cosmological
apocalyptic
eschatology

A specific understanding of what is wrong, and a view of the future: Anti-God powers have managed to commence their own rule over the world, leading human beings into idolatry and thus into slavery, producing a wrong situation that was not intended by God and that will not be long tolerated by him. For in his own time, God will inaugurate a victorious and liberating apocalyptic war against these evil powers, delivering his elect from their grasp and thus making right that which has gone wrong because of the powers' malignant machinations. This kind of apocalyptic eschatology is fundamental to Paul's letters. See de Boer, 'Apocalyptic Eschatology.'

covenantal nomism

An expression coined by E. P. Sanders to refer to the symbiosis that consists of God's covenant and God's Law. See chapter 10.

Diaspora	The Jewish communities scattered throughout many parts of the world outside Palestine, but not evident in ethnic Galatia.
enthusiastic	Emphasizing the present, already accomplished dimension of God's redemptive act in Christ (German: *schwärmerisch*).
Enthusiasts	Persons in the early church (notably in Corinth) who emphasized the present, already accomplished dimension of God's redemptive act in Christ.
forensic apocalyptic eschatology	A specific understanding of what is wrong, and a view of the future: Things have gone wrong because human beings have willfully rejected God, thereby bringing about death and the corruption and perversion of the world. Given this self-caused plight, God has graciously provided the cursing and blessing Law as the remedy, thus placing before human beings the Two Ways, the way of death and the way of life. Human beings are individually accountable before the bar of the Judge. But, by one's own decision, one can accept God's Law, repent of one's sins, receive nomistic forgiveness, and be assured of eternal life. For at the last judgment, the deserved sentence of death will be reversed for those who choose the path of Law observance, whereas that sentence will be permanently confirmed for those who do not. This kind of apocalyptic eschatology – focused on the religious doctrine of the Two Ways – is fundamental to the message of the Teachers who invaded Paul's Galatian churches. See de Boer, 'Apocalyptic Eschatology.'
Impulsive Desire of the Flesh	For the Teachers, as for other Christian Jews, the Flesh is the tendency of the human being to rebel against God. For Paul, it is one of the cosmic powers arrayed against God. See chapter 15.

Jewish-Christian and Christian-Jewish	Adjectives referring to churches that remained to a significant degree happily linked to Jewish legal traditions. In the hyphenated expression (whether adjectival or nominal), the second term is the dominant one. Churches, for example, that were essentially Jewish sects would be groups of Christian Jews, rather than groups of Jewish Christians. See chapter 1.
midrash	An interpretation of scripture.
nomistic	Legal in the sense of being derived from the Law of Sinai.
parenesis	'Admonition,' traditional exhortation designed to cultivate religious and moral life. Common in writings characterized by forensic apocalyptic eschatology.
religion	The various communal, cultic means – always involving the distinction of sacred from profane – by which human beings seek to know and to be happily related to the gods or God. Religion is thus a human enterprise that Paul sharply distinguishes from God's apocalyptic act in Christ.
Shema	Deut 6:4–9, the paragraph accenting the oneness of God, and beginning 'Hear, O Israel: The Lord our God, the Lord is one.'
the Teachers	The Christian-Jewish evangelists who came into Paul's Galatian churches after his departure. See chapter 1.
Two Ways	Various strands of Jewish and Jewish-Christian thought in the first century preserved and interpreted the ancient portrait of God's placing before Israel 'the way of life and the way of death.' To obey God's commandments is to live; to disobey them is to die (Jer 21:8; cf. Deut 27:12–13; Sir 2:12; 15:16; Matt 7:13–14; *m. 'Abot* 2:1; Jas 2:8–13). Within this frame of reference, the Teachers used the terms 'blessing' and 'curse' to

name the two actions of God they considered to be dependent on the path chosen by the Gentiles to whom they brought their message. Cf. 'forensic apocalyptic theology' above.

Bibliography

Aageson, J. W., *Written Also for Our Sake: Paul and the Art of Biblical Interpretation* (Louisville: Westminster/John Knox, 1993).

Abrams, M. H., *The Mirror and the Lamp* (Oxford: Oxford University Press, 1953).

Achtemeier, P. J., *The Quest for Unity in the New Testament Church* (Philadelphia: Fortress, 1987).

Amir, Y., 'Die messianische Idee im hellenistischen Judentum,' *Freiburger Rundbrief* 25 (1973) 195–203.

Ashton, J., *The Interpretation of John* (Philadelphia: Fortress, 1986).

——, *Understanding the Fourth Gospel* (Oxford: Clarendon, 1991).

Baarda, T., '"Maar de toorn is over hen gekomen . . .",' 15–74 in T. Baarda, H. Jansen, S. J. Noorda, J. S. Vos, *Paulus en de andere joden* (Delft: Meinema, 1984).

Baeck, L., *Aus Drei Jahrtausenden* (Tübingen: Mohr, 1938; 1958).

——, 'The Faith of Paul,' Kaufmann, *Judaism,* 139–169.

——, 'The Gospel as a Document of the History of the Jewish Faith,' Kaufmann, *Judaism,* 41–136.

——, 'Harnacks Vorlesungen über das Wesen des Christemtums,' *MGWJ* 5 (1901) 97–120.

——, 'Judaism in the Church,' cited by page numbers in Rothschild, *Perspectives.*

——, 'Mystery and Commandment,' cited by page numbers in Rothschild, *Perspectives*; cf. Kaufmann, *Judaism,* 171–187.

——, 'Romantic Religion,' Kaufmann, *Judaism,* 189–292.

——, 'Some Questions to the Christian Church from the Jewish Point of View,' *The Church and The Jewish People* (ed. G. Hedenquist; London: London International Missionary Council, 1954) 102–116.

——, *Wege im Judentum* (Berlin: Schocken, 1933).

——, *Das Wesen des Judentums* (Berlin: Nathansen & Lamm, 1905); *The Essence of Judaism* (rev ed.; New York: Schoken, 1948).

Baird, W. '"One Against the Other"', *The Conversation Continues: Studies in Paul and John in Honor of J. Louis Martyn* (eds R. T. Fortna and B. R. Gaventa; Nashville: Abingdon, 1990) 116–136.

Barclay, J. M. G., '"Do we undermine the Law?" A Study of Romans 14.1–15.6,' *Paul and the Mosaic Law* (ed. J. D. G. Dunn; Tübingen: Mohr/Siebeck, 1996) 287–308.

——, *Jews in the Mediterranean Diaspora from Alexander to Trajan: 323 BCE – 117 CE* (Edinburgh: T&T Clark, 1996).

——, 'The Jews of the Diaspora,' *Early Christian Thought in Its Jewish Context* (eds J. M. G. Barclay and J. Sweet; Cambridge: Cambridge Univ. Press, 1996) 27–40.

——, 'Mirror-Reading a Polemical Letter: Galatians as a Test Case,' *JSNT* 31 (1987) 73–93.

——, *Obeying the Truth: A Study of Paul's Ethics in Galatians* (Edinburgh: T&T Clark, 1988).

——, 'Paul Among Diaspora Jews,' *JSNT* 60 (1995) 89–120.

Barrett, C. K., 'The Allegory of Abraham, Sarah, and Hagar in the Argument of Galatians,' *Rechtfertigung: Festschrift für Ernst Käsemann zum 70. Geburtstag* (eds J. Friedrich et al.; Tübingen: Mohr/Siebeck, 1976) 1–16.

——, 'Paul's Opponents in 2 Corinthians,' *NTS* 17 (1971) 233–254.

Barth, K., *Church Dogmatics* (14 vols; Edinburgh: T&T Clark, 1936–1970).

Barth, M., *Ephesians* (AB; 2 vols; Garden City: Doubleday, 1974).

Bassler, J. M., *Divine Impartiality* (Atlanta: Scholars, 1982).

—— (ed.), *Pauline Theology, Volume I* (Minneapolis: Fortress, 1991).

Baumbach, G., 'Schriftbenutzung und Schriftauswahl im Rheinischen Synodalbeschluss,' *EvT* 48 (1988) 419–431.

Baumgarten, J., *Paulus und die Apokalyptik* (Neukirchen: Neukirchener, 1975).

Becker, J., *Das Heil Gottes* (Göttingen: Vandenhoeck & Ruprecht, 1964).

Beker, J. C., *Paul the Apostle* (Philadelphia: Fortress, 1980; Paperback ed. with new preface, 1984).

Belleville, L. L., 'Paul's Polemic and Theology of the Spirit in Second Corinthians,' *CBQ* 58 (1996) 281–304.

Ben Chorin, S., *Paulus, der Völker Apostel in jüdischer Sicht* (Munich: Taschenbuch Verlag, 1980).

Betz, H. D., 'Corinthians, Second Epistle to the,' *ABD*.

Betz, H. D., *Galatians* (Philadelphia: Fortress, 1979).

——, *2 Corinthians 8 and 9* (Philadelphia: Fortress, 1985).

Betz, O., 'Rechtfertigung in Qumran,' *Rechtfertigung: Festschrift für Ernst Käsemann* (eds J. Friedrich et al.; Tübingen: Mohr/Siebeck, 1976) 17–36.

Beutler, J., 'The Use of "Scripture" in the Gospel of John,' *Exploring the Gospel of John: In Honor of D. Moody Smith* (eds R. A. Culpepper and C. C. Black; Louisville: Westminster/John Knox, 1996) 147–162.

Billerbeck, P. and H. L. Strack, *Kommentar zum Neuen Testament aus Talmud und Midrasch* (4 vols; Munich: Beck, 1926–1928).

Blinzler, J., 'Lexikalisches zu dem Terminus *ta stoicheia tou kosmou* bei Paulus,' *Studiorum Paulinorum Congressus Internationalis Catholicus 1961* (Rome: Pontifical Biblical Institute, 1963) 2.429–443.

Bonhoeffer, D., *Letters and Papers from Prison* (New York: Macmillan, 1953).

——, *No Rusty Swords: Letters, Lectures and Notes 1928–1936* (ed. E. H. Robertson; New York: Harper & Row, 1965).

Boomershine, T. E., 'Epistemology at the Turn of the Ages in Paul, Jesus, and Mark,' *Apocalyptic and the New Testament: Essays in Honor of J. Louis Martyn* (eds J. Marcus and M. L. Soards; Sheffield: JSOT Press, 1989) 147–167.

Borgen, P., 'Judaism (Egypt),' *ABD*.

——, 'Philo,' *ABD*.

——, 'Philo of Alexandria,' *ANRW* 2.21.1; 97–154.

Bornkamm, G., 'Towards the Interpretation of John's Gospel: A Discussion of *The Testament of Jesus* by Ernst Käsemann,' *The Interpretation of John* (ed. J. Ashton; Philadelphia: Fortress, 1986) 79–96.

Borse, U., *Der Brief an die Galater* (Regensburg: Pustet, 1984).

Boyarin, D., *A Radical Jew: Paul and the Politics of Identity* (Berkeley: University of California Press, 1994).

Brandenburger, E., *Fleisch und Geist. Paulus und die dualistische Weisheit* (Neukirchen: Neukirchener, 1968).

Breytenbach, C., 'Versöhnung, Stellvertretung und Sühne,' *NTS* 39 (1993) 59–79.

Brinsmead, B. H., *Galatians – Dialogical Response to Opponents* (Chico: Scholars, 1982).

Brocke, E. and J. Seim (eds), *Gottes Augapfel* (Neukirchen: Neukirchener, 1988).

Broer, I., '"Antisemitismus" und "Judenpolemik im Neuen Testament."' Ein Beitrag zum besseren Verständnis von 1 Thess 2,14–16,' *Religion und Verantwortung als Elemente gesellschaftlicher Ordnung* (Beiheft zu den Siegener Studien, ohne Jahr) 734–772.

Brown, A. R., *The Cross and Human Transformation* (Minneapolis: Fortress, 1995).

——, 'The Word of the Cross, Pattern for Moral Discernment: From Paul to Flannery O'Connor,' *Doctrine and Life* 47 (1997).

Brown, R. E., 'Not Jewish Christianity and Gentile Christianity but Types of Jewish/Gentile Christianity,' *CBQ* 45 (1983) 74–79.

——, et al., *Peter in the New Testament* (Minneapolis: Augsburg, 1973).

Bultmann, R., 'Die Bedeutung des geschichtlichen Jesus für die Theologie des Paulus,' *Glauben und Verstehen*, 1 (Tübingen, 1954), 188–213.

——, *Essays Philosophical and Theological* (London: SCM, 1955).

——, *Exegetische Probleme des zweiten Korintherbriefes* (Darmstadt: Wissenschaftliche Buchgesellschaft, 1963).

——, *Theology of the New Testament* (2 vols; New York: Scribner's, 1951, 1955).

Burchard, C., 'The Importance of Joseph and Asenath for the Study of the New Testament,' *NTS* 33 (1987) 102–134.

Burton, E. D., *The Epistle to the Galatians* (Edinburgh: T&T Clark, 1921).

Bussmann, C., *Themen der paulinischen Missionspredigt auf dem Hintergrund der spätjüdisch-hellenistischen Missionsliteratur* (Bern: Lang, 1975).

Campbell, D. A., 'Romans 1:17 – A *Crux Interpretum* for the *Pistis Christou* Debate,' *JBL* 113 (1994) 265–285.

Charlesworth, J. H. (ed.), *Jews and Christians: Exploring the Past, Present, and Future* (New York: Crossroad, 1990).

Chesnutt, R. D., 'Joseph and Asenath,' *ABD*.

Clabeaux, J. J., *A Lost Edition of the Letters of Paul* (Washington, D.C.: Catholic Biblical Association, 1989).

——, 'Marcion,' *ABD*.

Cohen, S. J. D., 'Crossing the Boundary and Becoming a Jew,' *HTR* 82 (1989) 13–33.

Collins, J. J., 'Sybilline Oracles,' *OTP* 1.317–472.

Collins, J. J., 'Jesus and the Messiahs of Israel,' *Geschichte – Tradition – Reflexion: Festschrift für Martin Hengel* (3 vols.; eds H. Cancik et al.; Tübingen: Mohr/Siebeck, 1996) 3.287–302.

Connolly, R. H., *Didascalia Apostolorum* (Oxford: Clarendon, 1929).

Cousar, C. B., 'Continuity and Discontinuity: Reflections on Romans 5–8 (In Conversation with Frank Thielman),' *Pauline Theology, Volume III: Romans* (eds D. M. Hay and E. E. Johnson; Minneapolis: Fortress, 1995) 196–210.

——, *A Theology of the Cross: The Death of Jesus in the Pauline Letters* (Minneapolis: Fortress, 1990).

Cranfield, C. E. B., '"The Works of the Law" in the Epistle to the Romans,' *JSNT* 43 (1991) 89–101.

Croner, H. (ed.), *More Stepping Stones to Jewish-Christian Relations* (New York: Paulist, 1985).

—— (ed.), *Stepping Stones to Further Jewish-Christian Relations* (New York: Paulist, 1977).

Cullman, O., *Christ and Time* (Philadelphia: Westminster, 1950).

Dahl, N. A., 'The Atonement – an Adequate Reward for the Akedah? (Rom 8:32),' *Neotestamentica et Semitica: Studies in Honor of Matthew Black* (eds E. E. Ellis and M. Wilcox; Edinburgh: T&T Clark: 1969) 15–29. Also in Dahl, *Jesus the Christ* (Minneapolis: Fortress, 1991) 137–151.

——, 'Contradictions in Scripture,' *Studies in Paul* (Minneapolis: Augsburg, 1977) 159–177.

——, *Das Volk Gottes* (Darmstadt: Wissensshchaftliche Buchgesellschaft, 1963).

Dalbert, P., *Die Theologie der hellenistisch-jüduschen Missionsliteratur unter Ausschluss von Philo und Josephus* (Hamburg: Reich, 1954).

Daube, D., *The New Testament and Rabbinic Judaism* (London: Athlone, 1956).

Davies, W. D., 'A Note on *Josephus, Antiquities* 15.136,' *HTR* 47 (1954) 135–140.

—— and D. C. Allison, *A Critical and Exegetical Commentary on the Gospel of Saint Matthew* (Edinburgh: T&T Clark, 1988–1997).

De Boer, M. C., *The Defeat of Death* (Sheffield: JSOT, 1988).

——, *Johannine Perspectives on the Death of Jesus* (Kampen: Kok Pharos, 1996).

De Boer, M. C., 'Paul and Jewish Apocalyptic Eschatology,' *Apocalyptic and the New Testament: Essays in Honor of J. Louis Martyn* (eds J. Marcus and M. L. Soards; Sheffield: JSOT, 1989) 169–190.

De Jonge, M., *Jesus: Stranger from Heaven and Son of God* (Missoula: Scholars, 1977).

Delling, G., *'stoicheō,' TDNT* 7.666–687.

DeMaris, R. E., *The Colossian Controversy* (Sheffield: Sheffield Academic Press, 1993).

Dilthey, W., *Pattern and Meaning in History* (ed. H. P. Rickman; New York: Harper, 1961).

Dodd, C. H., *According to the Scriptures: The Sub-Structure of New Testament Theology* (New York: Scribner's, 1953).

Donaldson, T. L., 'The Law That Hangs (Matthew 22:40): Rabbinic Formulations and Matthean Social World,' *CBQ* 57 (1995) 689–709.

Donfried, K. P., 'Justification and Last Judgment in Paul,' *ZNW* 67 (1967) 90–110.

——, 'Paul and Judaism: 1 Thess 2:13–16 as a Test Case,' *Int* 38 (1984) 242–253.

—— (ed.), *The Romans Debate* (rev. ed.; Peabody: Hendrickson, 1991).

Downing, F. G., 'A Cynic Preparation for Paul's Gospel for Jew and Greek, Slave and Free, Male and Female,' *NTS* 42 (1996) 454–462.

Duff, N. J., *Humanization and the Politics of God: The Koinonia Ethics of Paul Lehmann* (Grand Rapids: Eerdmans, 1992).

Dunn, J. D. G., *The Epistle to the Galatians* (London: Black, 1993).

——, 'Jesus Tradition in Paul,' *Studying the Historical Jesus: Evaluations of the State of Current Research* (eds B. Chilton and C. A. Evans; Leiden: Brill, 1994) 155–178.

——, 'The New Perspective on Paul,' *BJRL* 65 (1983) 95–122.

——, 'Once More, *Pistis Christou*,' *SBL Seminar Papers 30* (Atlanta: Scholars, 1991) 730–744.

——, *The Partings of the Ways Between Christianity and Judaism and Their Significance for the Character of Christianity* (Philadelphia: Trinity, 1991).

——, *Romans* (2 vols; Dallas: Word, 1988).

——, 'The Theology of Galatians,' *Pauline Theology, Volume I* (ed. J. Bassler; Minneapolis: Fortress, 1991) 125–146.

——, *Unity and Diversity in the New Testament* (Philadelphia: Westminster, 1977).

Dunn, J. D. G., 'Works of the Law and the Curse of the Law (Galatians 3:10–14),' *NTS* 31 (1985) 523–542.

Eckstein, H. J., *Verheissung und Gesetz* (Tübingen: Mohr/Siebeck, 1996).

Erasmus, D., *Paraphrases on Romans and Galatians* in *The Collected Works of Erasmus* (vol. 42; ed. R. D. Sider; Toronto: University of Toronto Press, 1984).

Feldman, L. H., 'Abraham the Greek Philosopher in Josephus,' *TAPA* 99 (1968) 143–156.

——, *Jew and Gentile in the Ancient World* (Princeton: Princeton University Press, 1993).

——, 'Josephus,' *ABD*.

Fishbane, M., *Biblical Interpretation in Ancient Israel* (Oxford: Clarendon, 1985).

Fitzgerald, J. T., 'The Catalogue in Ancient Greek Literature,' *The Rhetorical Analysis of Scripture: Essays from the 1995 London Conference* (eds S. E. Porter and T. H. Olbricht; Sheffield: Sheffield Academic Press, 1996).

——, *Cracks in an Earthen Vessel: An Examination of the Catalogues of Hardships in the Corinthian Correspondence* (Atlanta: Scholars, 1988).

——, 'Virtue/Vice Lists,' *ABD*.

Fitzmyer, J. A., *The Gospel According to Luke* (2 vols; AB; Garden City: Doubleday, 1985).

——, *Romans* (AB; New York: Doubleday, 1993).

Foerster, W., *Gnosis* (Oxford: Clarendon, 1972).

Fortna, R. T., *The Fourth Gospel and Its Predecessor* (Philadelphia: Fortress, 1988).

Freeman, K., *Ancilla to the Presocratic Philosophers* (Cambridge, Mass.: Harvard University Press, 1948).

Friedrich, J., et al. (eds), *Rechtfertigung: Festschrift für Ernst Käsemann* (Tübingen: Mohr/Siebeck, 1976).

Furnish, V. P., *II Corinthians* (AB; Garden City: Doubleday, 1984).

——, *Jesus According to Paul* (Cambridge: Cambridge University Press, 1993).

——, *The Love Command in the New Testament* (Nashville: Abingdon, 1972).

——, *The Moral Teaching of Paul* (Nashville: Abingdon, 1985).

——, *Theology and Ethics in Paul* (Nashville: Abingdon, 1968).

Gadamer, H. G., *Wahrheit und Methode* (Tübingen: Mohr/Siebeck, 1972).

Gager, J., *The Origins of Anti-Semitism* (Oxford: Oxford University Press, 1985).

Gasparro, G. S., *Soteriological and Mystical Aspects in the Cults of Cybele and Attis* (Leiden: Brill, 1985).

Gaston, L., 'Israel's Enemies in Pauline Theology,' *NTS* 28 (1982) 400–423.

——, *Paul and the Torah* (Vancouver: University of British Columbia Press, 1987).

Gaventa, B. R., *From Darkness to Light; Aspects of Conversion in the New Testament* (Philadelphia: Fortress, 1986).

Georgi, D., *Die Gegner des Paulus im 2. Korintherbrief* (Neukirchen, 1964) = *The Opponents of Paul in Second Corinthians* (Philadelphia: Fortress, 1986).

——, *Remembering the Poor: the History of Paul's Collection for Jerusalem* (Nashville: Abingdon, 1991).

——, 'Weisheit Salomos,' *JSHRZ.*

Gnilka, J., *Der Philipperbrief* (Freiburg: Herder, 1976).

Goldin, J., *The Fathers According to Rabbi Nathan* (New Haven: Yale University Press, 1955).

Goodenough, E. R., *By Light Light* (New Haven: Yale University Press, 1935).

Goodman, M., 'Jewish Proselytizing in the First Century,' *The Jews Among Pagans and Christians in the Roman Empire* (eds J. Lieu, J. North, T. Rajak; London: Routledge, 1992) 53–78.

Grässer, E., *Der Alte Bund im Neuen: Exegetische Studies zur Israelfrage im Neuen Testament* (Tübingen: Mohr/Siebeck, 1985).

Grant, R. (ed.), *Gnosticism* (New York: Harper, 1961).

Haacker, K., 'Der Holocaust als Datum der Theologiegeschichte,' *Augapfel* (eds Brocke and Seim) 137–145.

Hafemann, S., *Paul, Moses and the History of Israel* (Tübingen: Mohr/Siebeck, 1995).

Hahn, F., 'Taufe und Rechtfertigung,' *Rechtfertigung: Festschrift für Ernst Käsemann* (eds J. Friedrich et al.; Tübingen: Mohr/Siebeck, 1976) 95–124.

Hall, B. B., 'All Things to All People: A Study of 1 Corinthians 9:19–23,' *The Conversation Continues: Studies in Paul and John in Honor of J. Louis Martyn* (eds R. T. Fortna and B. R. Gaventa; Nashville: Abingdon, 1990) 137–157.

Hamerton-Kelly, R. G., *Sacred Violence: Paul's Hermeneutic of the Cross* (Minneapolis: Fortress, 1992).

Hansen, G. W., *Abraham in Galatians: Epistolary and Rhetorical Contexts* (Sheffield: JSOT Press, 1989).

Harnack, A., 'Das Alte Testament in den Paulinischen Briefen und in den Paulinischen Gemeinden,' Sitzangsberichte der Preussischen Akademie der Wissenschaften (1928) 124–141.

——, *Marcion: Das Evangelium vom fremden Gott* (2nd ed.; Leipzig: Hinrichs, 1924).

——, *The Mission and Expansion of Christianity* (2 vols; London: Williams & Norgate, 1908).

——, *What Is Christianity?* (New York: Harper, 1957); *Das Wesen des Christentums* (Leipzig: Hinrichs, 1905).

Hawkins, J. G., 'The Opponents of Paul in Galatia' (Dissertation, Yale University, 1971).

Hay, D. M. and E. E. Johnson (eds), *Pauline Theology, Volume IV* (Atlanta: Scholars, 1997).

Hays, R. B., *Echoes of Scripture in the Letters of Paul* (New Haven: Yale University Press, 1989).

——, *The Faith of Jesus Christ: An Investigation of the Narrative Substructure of Galatians 3:1–4:11* (Chico: Scholars, 1983).

——, 'Justification,' *ABD*.

——, *The Moral Vision of the New Testament: Community, Cross, New Creation* (San Francisco: HarperSanFrancisco, 1996).

——, 'The Role of Scripture in Paul's Ethics,' *Theology and Ethics in Paul and His Modern Interpreters: Essays in Honor of Victor Paul Furnish* (eds. E. H. Lovering, Jr. and J. L. Sumney; Nashville: Abingdon, 1996) 30–47.

——, '*Pistis* and Pauline Theology: What is at stake?' *Pauline Theology, Vol. IV* (eds D. M. Hay and E. E. Johnson; Atlanta: Scholars, 1997).

Hock, R. F., *The Social Context of Paul's Ministry: Tentmaking and Apostleship* (Philadelphia: Fortress, 1980).

Hoffmann, R. J., *Marcion: On the Restitution of Christianity* (Chico: Scholars, 1984).

Hofmann, J. C. K., *Weissagung und Erfüllung* (2 vols; Nordlingen, 1841–1844).

Hofius, O., '"All Israel Will be Saved:" Divine Salvation and Israel's Deliverance in Romans 9–11,' *Princeton Seminary Bulletin*, Supplementary Issue 1 (1990) 19–39.

Holladay, C. R., 'Aristobulos (OT Pseudepigrapha),' *ABD*.

Holtz, T., *Der erste Brief an die Thessalonicher* (Zürich: Benzinger, 1986).

Holtzmann, H. J., *Einleitung in das Neue Testament* (Freiburg: Mohr, 1886).

Howard, G., 'The Faith of Christ,' *ExpTim* 85 (1974) 212–215.

——, 'Notes and Observations on the "Faith of Christ",' *HTR* 60 (1967) 459–465.

Hübner, H., *Das Gesetz bei Paulus* (Göttingen: Vandenhoeck & Ruprecht, 1978); *Law in Paul's Thought* (Edinburgh: T&T Clark, 1984).

Jacob, W., *Christianity through Jewish Eyes* (New York: Hebrew Union College Press, 1974).

Jansen, H., 'Allegorie van slavernij en vrijheid,' T. Baarda, H. Jansen, S. J. Noorda, J. S. Vos, *Paulus en de andere joden* (Delft: Meinema, 1984) 75–113.

——, *Christelijke theologie na Auschwitz* (den Haag: Boeken-centrum, 1984).

Jervell, J., 'The Letter to Jerusalem,' *The Romans Debate* (rev. ed.; ed. K. P. Donfried; Peabody: Hendrickson, 1991) 53–64.

Jewett, R., 'Ecumenical Theology for the Sake of Mission: Romans 1:1–17 + 15:14–16:24,' *Pauline Theology, Volume III: Romans* (eds D. M. Hay and E. E. Johnson; Minneapolis: Fortress, 1995) 89–108.

——, *Paul's Anthropological Terms* (Leiden: Brill, 1971).

Johnson, E. E., *The Function of Apocalyptic and Wisdom Traditions in Romans 9–11* (Atlanta: Scholars, 1989).

——, see D. M. Hay.

Johnson, L. T., *The Letter of James* (AB; Garden City: Doubleday, 1995).

Jones, F. S., *An Ancient Jewish Christian Source on the History of Christianity: Pseudo Clementine Recognitions 1.27–71* (Atlanta: Scholars, 1995).

Juel, D., *Messianic Exegesis* (Philadelphia: Fortress, 1988).

Jüngel, E., *Paulus und Jesus* (Tübingen: Mohr/Siebeck, 1964).

Käsemann, E., 'The Beginnings of Christian Theology,' *New Testament Questions of Today*, 82–107.

——, *Essays on New Testament Themes* (London: SCM, 1964).

——, 'Die Legitimität des Apostels,' *ZNW* 41 (1942) 33–71 = *Das Paulusbild in der neueren deutschen Forschung* (ed. K. H. Rnengstorf; Darmstadt: Wissenschaftliche Buchgesellschaft, 1964) 475–521 (references are to these pages).

Käsemann, E., 'Das Motiv der Leiblichkeit bei Paulus,' (unpublished paper).

——, *New Testament Questions of Today* (London: SCM, 1969).

——, 'On the Subject of Primitive Christian Apocalyptic,' *New Testament Questions of Today*, 108–137.

——, 'Paul and Israel,' *Questions*, 183–197.

——, *Perspectives on Paul* (London: SCM, 1969).

——, 'Principles of the Interpretation of Romans 13,' *New Testament Questions of Today*, 196–215.

——, '"The Righteousness of God" in Paul,' *New Testament Questions of Today*, 168–182.

——, *Romans* (Grand Rapids: Eerdmans, 1980).

——, 'The Spirit and the Letter,' *Perspectives on Paul*, 138–166.

——, *The Testament of Jesus* (Philadelphia: Fortress, 1968).

——, 'Worship in Everyday Life,' *New Testament Questions of Today*, 188–195.

Kamlah, E., *Die Form der katalogischen Paränese im Neuen Testament* (Tübingen: Mohr/Siebeck, 1964).

Kaufmann, W. (ed.), *Judaism and Christianity: Essays by Leo Baeck* (New York: Atheneum, 1981).

Keck, L. E., 'Searchable Judgments and Scrutable Ways: A Response to Paul J. Achtemeier,' *Pauline Theology, Volume IV* (eds D. M. Hay and E. E. Johnson; Atlanta: Scholars, 1997).

——, *Paul and His Letters* (Philadelphia: Fortress, 1988).

Kemmer, E., *Die Polare Ausdrucksweise in der Griechischen Literatur* Würzburg: Stuber, 1903.

Kennedy, G. A., *New Testament Interpretation through Rhetorical Criticism* (Chapel Hill: University of North Carolina Press, 1984).

Kertelge, K., '*Rechtfertigung' bei Paulus* (Münster: Aschendorff, 1966).

King, M. L., *Letter From Birmingham City Jail* (Philadelphia: American Friends Service Committee, 1963).

——, *Stride Toward Freedom: The Montgomery Story* (New York: Harper, 1958).

Kirk, G. S. and J. E. Raven, *The Presocratic Philosophers* (Cambridge: Cambridge University Press, 1960).

Klappert, B., 'Brücken zwischen Judentum und Christentum: L. Baecks kritische Fragen an das Christentum. Nachwort zur 3. Auflage des Leo-Baeck-Buches von A. H. Friedlander,' A. H. Friedlander, *Leo Baeck: Leben und Lehre* (3rd ed.; München: Kaiser, 1990) 285–328.

Klappert, B. and H. Starck (eds), *Umkehr und Erneuerung* (Neukirchen: Neukirchener, 1980).

Klausner, J., *From Jesus to Paul* (Boston: Beacon, 1939).

Klein, G., *Rekonstruktion und Interpretation* (München, Kaiser, 1969).

Klijn, A. F. J. and G. J. Reinink, *Patristic Evidence for Jewish-Christian Sects* (Leiden: Brill, 1973).

Knox, J., *Chapters in a Life of Paul* (Nashville, Abingdon,1950; rev. ed. Macon: Mercer, 1987).

Knox, W. L., 'Abraham and the Quest for God,' *HTR* 28 (1935) 55–60.

Kober, A., 'Die Hochschulen für die Rabbinerausbildung in Dautschland,' *Worte des Gedenkens für Leo Baeck* (ed. E. G. Reichmann; Heidelberg: Lambert Schneider, 1959) 19–28.

Koch, D. A., *Die Schrift als Zeuge des Evangeliums: Untersuchungen zur Verwendung und zum Verständnis der Schrift bei Paulus* (Tübingen: Mohr/Siebeck, 1986).

Koch, K., *The Rediscovery of Apocalyptic* (London: SCM, 1972).

Koester, H., *History, Culture, and Religion in the Hellenistic Age* (Philadelphia: Fortress, 1980).

——, 'Paul and Hellenism,' *The Bible in Modern Scholarship* (ed. J. P. Hyatt: Nashville, Abingdon, 1965) 187–95.

Kolenkow, A. B., 'Paul and His Opponents in 2 Cor 10–13: THEIOI ANDRES and Spiritual Guides,' *Religious Propaganda and Missionary Competition in the New Testament World: Essays Honoring Dieter Georgi* (eds L. Bormann et al.; Leiden: Brill, 1994) 351–374.

Kovacs, J. L., 'The Archons, the Spirit, and the Death of Christ: Do We Need the Hypothesis of Gnostic Opponents to Explain 1 Corinthians 2.6–16?' *Apocalyptic and the New Testament: Essays in Honor of J. Louis Martyn* (eds J. Marcus and M. L. Soards; Sheffield: JSOT, 1989) 217–236.

Kuhn, K. G., '*prosēlytos,*' *TDNT* 6.727–744.

Kümmel, W. G., *Das Neue Testament: Geschichte der Erforschung seiner Probleme* (Freiburg: Alber, 1958).

Lapide, P. and P. Stuhlmacher, *Paul. Rabbi and Apostle* (Minneapolis: Augsburg, 1984).

Léon-Dufour, X., 'Bulletin D'Exégèse du Nouveau Testament,' *RSR* 59 (1971) 583–618

Liebers, R., *Studien zu einer besonderen Art frühchristlichen Schriftbezugen* (Berlin: de Gruyter, 1993).

Lietzmann, H., *An die Korinther* I.II (revised by W. G. Kümmel; Tübingen: Mohr/Siebeck, 1949).

Lieu, J. M., 'Circumcision, Women and Salvation,' *NTS* 40 (1994) 358–370.

Lightfoot, J. B., *The Epistle of St. Paul to the Galatians* (original 1865; Grand Rapids: Zondervan, 1957).

Lindemann, A., 'Die biblischen Toragebote und die paulinische Ethik,' *Studien zum Text und zur Ethik des Neuen Testaments: Festschrift Greeven* (ed. W. Schrage; Berlin: de Gruyter, 1986) 242–265.

Lloyd, G. E. R., *Polarity and Analogy* (Cambridge: Cambridge University Press, 1966).

Longenecker, B. W., '*Pistis* in Rom 3:25: Neglected Evidence for The Faithfulness of Christ,' *NTS* 39 (1993), 478–480.

Longenecker, R. N., *Galatians* (Dallas: Word, 1990).

Luedemann, G., *Paulus, der Heidenapostel* (vol. 2; Göttingen: Vandenhoeck & Ruprecht, 1983).

Lührmann, D., 'Christologie und Rechtfertigung,' *Rechtfertigung: Festschrift für Ernst Käsemann* (eds J. Friedrich et al. Tübingen: Mohr/Siebeck, 1976) 351–363.

——, *Der Brief an die Galater* (Zürich: Theologischer Verlag, 1978); *Galatians* (Minneapolis: Fortress, 1992).

——, '*Tage*, Monate, Jehreszeiten, Jahre (Gal 4,10),' *Werden und Wirken des Alten Testaments* (eds R. Albertz et al.; Göttingen: Vandenhoeck & Ruprecht, 1980) 428–445.

Lütgert, W., *Freiheitspredigt und Schwarmgeister in Korinth* (Gütersloh: Bertelsmann, 1908).

Luther, M., *Lectures on Galatians – 1535 – Chapters 1–4 and Lectures on Galatians – 1535 – Chapters 5–6; 1519 – Chapters 1–6* (*Luther's Works*; 55 vols.; ed. J. Pelikan; Saint Louis: Concordia, 1955–1976) vols. 26 and 27.

Luz, U., 'Der alte und der neue Bund bei Paulus und im Hebräerbrief,' *EvT* 27 (1967) 318–336.

——, *Das Geschichtsverständnis des Paulus* (München: Kaiser, 1968).

——, *Matthew 1–7: A Commentary* (Edinburgh: T&T Clark, 1989).

——, *The Theology of the Gospel of Matthew* (Cambridge: Cambridge University Press, 1995).

Maccoby, H., *The Mythmaker. Paul and the Invention of Christianity* (New York: Harper & Row, 1986).

Malherbe, A. J., *Moral Exhortation: A Greco-Roman Sourcebook* (Philadelphia: Westminster, 1986).

——, *Paul and The Thessalonians* (Philadelphia: Fortress, 1987).

Marcus, J., 'The Circumcision and the Uncircumcision in Rome,' *NTS* 35 (1989) 67–81.

——, 'The Evil Inclination in the Epistle of James,' *CBQ* 44 (1982) 606–621.

——, 'The Evil Inclination in the Letters of Paul,' *IBS* 8 (1986) 8–21.

——, *The Way of the Lord: Christological Exegesis of the Old Testament in the Gospel of Mark* (Louisville: Westminster/John Knox, 1992).

Marshall, P., *Enmity in Corinth. Social Conventions in Paul's Relations with the Corinthians* (Tübingen: Mohr/Siebeck, 1987).

Martyn D. W., 'A Child and Adam: A Parable of the Two Ages,' *Apocalyptic and the New Testament: Essays in Honor of J. Louis Martyn* (eds J. Marcus and M. L. Soards; Sheffield: JSOT, 1989) 317–333.

Martyn, J. L., 'Apocalyptic Antinomies in Paul's Letter to the Galatians,' *NTS* 31 (1985) 410–424.

——, 'Clementine Recognitions 1,33–71, Jewish Christianity, and the Fourth Gospel,' *God's Christ and His People: Studies in Honor of Nils Alstrup Dahl* (eds. J. Jervell and W. A. Meeks; Oslo: Universitetsforlaget, 1977) 265–295; cf. Martyn, *The Gospel of John in Christian History*, 55–89.

——, 'The Covenants of Hagar and Sarah,' *Faith and History: Essays in Honor of Paul W. Meyer* (eds J. T. Carroll et al.; Atlanta: Scholars, 1990) 160–192.

——, 'Events in Galatia,' *Pauline Theology, Volume I* (ed. J. Bassler; Minneapolis: Fortress, 1991) 160–179.

——, *Galatians* (AB; New York: Doubleday, 1997).

——, 'A Gentile Mission that Replaced an Earlier Jewish Mission?' *Exploring the Gospel of John in Honor of D. Moody Smith* (eds R. A. Culpepper and C. C. Black; Louisville: Westminster/John Knox, 1996) 124–144.

——, *The Gospel of John in Christian History* (New York: Paulist, 1978).

——, *History and Theology in the Fourth Gospel* (2nd ed.; Abingdon: Nashville, 1979).

——, 'A Law-Observant Mission to Gentiles: The Background of Galatians,' *SJT* 38 (1985) 307–324.

Mayer, R., *Christentum und Judentum in der Schau Leo Baecks* (Stuttgart: Kohlhammer, 1961).

McKnight, S., A *Light Among the Gentiles: Jewish Missionary Activity in the Second Temple Period* (Minneapolis: Fortress, 1991).

Meeks, W. A., *The First Urban Christians* (New Haven: Yale University Press, 1983).

——, 'The Man from Heaven in Johannine Sectarianism,' *The Interpretation of John* (ed. J. Ashton; Philadelphia: Fortress, 1986) 141–173.

——, 'On Trusting an Unpredictable God: A Hermeneutical Meditation on Romans 9–11,' *Faith and History: Essays in Honor of Paul W. Meyer* (eds J. T. Carroll et al.; Atlanta: Scholars, 1990) 105–124.

——, *The Origins of Christian Morality* (New Haven: Yale University Press, 1993).

——, *The Prophet-King* (Leiden: Brill, 1967).

Meeks, W. A. (ed.), *The Writings of St. Paul* (New York: Norton, 1972).

Metzger, B. M., *A Textual Commentary on the Greek New Testament* (London: United Bible Societies, 1971).

Meyer, P. W., '"The Father": The Presentation of God in the Fourth Gospel,' *Exploring the Gospel of John: In Honor of D. Moody Smith* (eds R. A. Culpepper and C. C. Black; Louisville: Westminster/John Knox, 1996) 255–273.

——, 'Pauline Theology: A Proposal for a Pause in Its Pursuit,' *Pauline Theology, Volume IV* (eds D. M. Hay and E. E. Johnson; Atlanta: Scholars, 1997).

——, 'Romans,' *Harper's Bible Commentary* (ed. J. L. Mays; San Francisco: Harper & Row, 1988) 1130–1167.

——, 'The "This-Worldliness" of the New Testament,' *Princeton Seminary Bulletin* 2 (1979) 219–231.

——, 'The Worm at the Core of the Apple,' *The Conversation Continues; Studies in Paul and John in Honor of J. Louis Martyn* (eds R. T. Fortna and B. R. Gaventa; Nashville: Abingdon, 1990) 62–84.

Michel, O., *Der Brief an die Römer* (5th ed.; Göttingen: Vandenhoeck & Ruprecht, 1978).

Minear, P. S., 'The Crucified World: The Enigma of Galatians 6,14,' *Theologia Crucis – Signum Crucis* (eds C. Andersen and G. Klein; Tübingen: Mohr, 1979) 395–407.

——, *The Golgotha Earthquake* (Cleveland: Pilgrim Press, 1995).

Mitchell, M., *Paul and the Rhetoric of Reconciliation: An Exegetical Investigation of the Language and Composition of 1 Corinthians* (Louisville: Westminster/John Knox, 1991).

Moltmann, J., *Theology of Hope* (London: SCM, 1967).

Moore, G. F., 'Christian Writers on Judaism,' *HTR* 14 (1921) 197–254.

Moore-Crispin, D. R., 'Galatians 4:1–9: The Use and Abuse of Parallels,' *Evangelical Quarterly* 60 (1989) 203–223.

Morse, C. L., 'Bonhoeffer's Dialogue with America,' paper at AAR, November, 1995.

——, *The Logic of Promise in Moltmann's Theology* (Philadelphia: Fortress, 1979).

Moule, C. F. D., 'Fulfillment Words in the New Testament: Use and Abuse,' *NTS* 14 (1967) 293–320.

Munck, J., *Paul and the Salvation of Mankind* (Richmond: Knox, 1959).

Murphy-O'Connor, J., 'An Essene *Missionary* Document? CD II.14-VI.1,' *RB* 77 (1970) 201–209.

Mussner, F., *Der Galaterbrief* (Freiburg: Herder & Herder, 1974).

Nanos, M. D., *The Mystery of Romans: the Jewish Context of Paul's Letter* (Minneapolis: Fortress, 1996).

Neusner, J., 'Was Rabbinic Judaism Really "Ethnic"?' *CBQ* 57 (1995) 281–305.

Nock, A. D., *Conversion: The Old and New in Religion from Alexander the Great to Augustine of Hippo* (London: Oxford University Press, 1933).

O'Connor, F., 'Revelation,' *Everything That Rises Must Converge* (New York: Farrar, Straus, Giroux, 1965) 191–218.

——, *The Habit of Being* (ed. S. Fitzgerald; New York: Farrar, Straus, Giroux, 1979).

——, *Mystery and Manners* (New York: Farrar, Straus, Giroux, 1969).

——, 'Some Aspects of the Grotesque in Southern Fiction,' *Mystery and Manners*, 36–50.

Oepke, A., 'Irrwege in der neueren Paulusforschung,' *TLZ* 77 (1952), 449–458.

O'Neill, J. C., 'The Holy Spirit and the Human Spirit in Gal 5:17,' *ETL* 71 [1995] 107–120.

Pearson, B., '1 Thessalonians 2:13–16: A Deutero-Pauline Interpolation,' *HTR* 64 (1971) 74–94.

Perelman, C. and L. Olbrechts-Tyteca, *The New Rhetoric: A Treatise on Argumentation* (Notre Dame: University of Notre Dame Press, 1971).

Plummer, A., *The Second Epistle of St Paul to the Corinthians* (ICC; Edinburgh: T&T Clark, 1915).

Pluta, A., *Gottes Bundestreue: Ein Schlüsselbegriff in Röm 3,25a* (Stuttgart: Katholisches Bibelwerk, 1969).

Pohlenz, M. *Die Stoa* (Vol 1; Göttingen: Vandenhoeck & Ruprecht, 1948).

Räisänen, H., 'Galatians 2:16 and Paul's Break with Judaism,' *NTS* 31 (1985) 543–553.

Reicke, B., 'The Law and This World According to Paul,' *JBL* 70 (1951) 259–276.

Reitzenstein, R., *Die hellenistischen Mysterienreligionen* (Leipzig: Tuebner, 1910).

Rendtorff, R. and E. Stegemann (eds), *Auschwitz – Krise der Christlichen Theologie* (München, Kaiser, 1980)

Reumann, J., *Righteousness in the New Testament* (with J. A. Fitzmyer and J. D. Quinn; Philadelphia: Fortress, 1982).

Riches, J. K., *A Century of New Testament Study* (Cambridge: Lutterworth, 1993).

Ridderbos, H., *Paul. An Outline of His Theology* (Grand Rapids: Eerdmans, 1975).

Roetzel, C. J., 'No "Race of Israel" in Paul,' *Putting Body and Soul Together* (eds V. Wiles, A. Brown, G. F. Snyder; Valley Forge: Trinity Press, 1997) 230–244.

Rosner, B. S., *Paul, Scripture and Ethics: A Study of 1 Corinthians 5–7* (Leiden: Brill, 1994).

Rothschild, F. A. (ed.), *Jewish Perspectives on Christianity* (New York: Continuum, 1996).

Rusam, D., 'Neue Belege zu dem *stoicheia tou kosmou* (Gal 4,3.9; Kol 2,8.20),' *ZNW* 83 (1992) 119–125.

Sänger, D., *Die Verkündigung des Gekreuzigten und Israel* (Tübingen: Mohr/Siebeck, 1994).

Sampley, J. P., 'Romans in a Different Light,' *Pauline Theology, Volume III: Romans* (eds D. M. Hay and E. E. Johnson; Minneapolis: Fortress, 1995) 109–129.

——, *Walking Between the Times: Paul's Moral Reasoning* (Minneapolis: Fortress, 1991).

Sanders, E. P., 'Jewish Association with Gentiles and Gal 2:11–14,' *The Conversation Continues: Studies in Paul and John in Honor of J. Louis Martyn* (eds R. T. Fortna and B. R. Gaventa; Nashville: Abingdon, 1990) 170–188.

Sanders, E. P., *Paul and Palestinian Judaism* (Philadelphia: Fortress, 1977).

——, *Paul, the Law and the Jewish People* (Philadelphia: Fortress, 1983).

Sandmel, S., *The Genius of Paul* (New York: Schocken, 1970).

Schlier, H., *Der Brief an die Galater* (Göttingen: Vandenhoeck & Ruprecht, 1961).

Schlueter, C. H., *Filling Up the Measure. Polemical Hyperbole in 1 Thessalonians 2.14–16* (Sheffield: JSOT, 1994).

Schmithals, W., 'Zwei gnostische Glossen im zweiten Korintherbrief,' *EvT* 18 (1958), 552–573.

——, *Die Gnosis in Korinth* (Göttingen: Vandenhoeck & Ruprecht, 1956).

Schneider, G., 'Die Idee der Neuschopfung beim Apostel Paulus und ihr religionsgeschichtlicher Hintergrund,' *TTZ* 68 (1959) 257–270.

Schneider, N., *Die rhetorische Eigenart der paulinischen Antithese* (Tübingen: Mohr/Siebeck, 1970).

Schnelle, U., *Gerechtigkeit und Christusgegenwart* (Göttingen: Vandenhoeck & Ruprecht, 1983).

Schoeps, H. J., *Paul; The Theology of the Apostle in the Light of Jewish Religious History* (London: Lutterworth, 1961).

Schrage, W., *Der erste Brief an die Korinther* (3 vols; Zürich: Benziger, 1991–).

——, *Die knokreten Einzelgebote in der paulinischen Paränese* (Gütersloh: Mohn, 1961).

——, *The Ethics of the New Testament* (Philadelphia: Fortress, 1988).

——, 'Israel nach dem Fleische,' *Wenn nicht jetzt, wann dann?* (Festschrift H. J. Kraus; ed. H. G. Gewyer, et al.; Neukirchen: Neukirchener, 1983) 143–151.

——, '". . . den Juden ein Skandalon"? Der Anstoss des Kreuzes nach 1 Kor 1,23,' *Gottes Augapfel* (eds E. Brocke and J. Seim; Neukirchen-Vluyn: Neukirchener Verlag, 1988) 59–76.

——, 'Probleme paulinischer Ethik anhand von Gal 3,25–6,10,' paper for Colloquium Paulinum in Rome, 1995 (to be edited by A. Vanhoye).

Schubert, P., 'New Testament Study and Theology,' *Religion in Life* 14 (1945) 556–574.

Schubert, P., 'The Structure and Significance of Luke 24,' *Neutestamentliche Studien für Rudolf Bultmann* (ed. W. Eltester; Berlin: Töpelmann, 1957).

Schultz, S., 'Die Decke des Moses,' *ZNW* 49 (1958), 1–30.

Schweizer, E., '*sarx*,' *TDNT* 7.98–151.

———, 'Slaves of the Elements and Worshipers of Angels: Gal 4:3, 9 and Col 2:8, 18, 20,' *JBL* 107 (1988) 455–468.

Scroggs, R., *The Text and the Times* (Minneapolis, Fortress, 1993).

Segal, A. F., *Paul the Convert: The Apostolate and Apostasy of Saul the Pharisee* (New Haven: Yale University Press, 1990).

Sider, R. D. (ed.), *Collected Works of Erasmus: Paraphrases on Romans and Galatians* (vol. 42; Toronto: University of Toronto Press, 1984).

Siegert, F., *Argumentation bei Paulus* (Tübingen: Mohr/Siebeck, 1985).

———, *Philon von Alexamdrien: Uber die Gottesbezeichnung 'wohltätig verzehrendes Feuer' (De Deo)* (Tübingen: Mohr/Siebeck, 1988).

Smit, J., 'The Letter of Paul to the Galatians: A Deliberative Speech,' *NTS* 35 [1989] 1–26.

Smith, D. M., *The Theology of the Gospel of John* (Cambridge: Cambridge University Press, 1995).

Stanley, C. D., *Paul and the Language of Scripture* (Cambridge: Cambridge University Press, 1992).

Stanton, G., 'The Law of Moses and the Law of Christ; Galatians 3.1–6.2,' *Paul and the Mosaic Law* (ed. J. D. G. Dunn; Tübingen: Mohr/Siebeck, 1996) 99–116.

Stegemann, E. W., 'Introduction [to Martin Buber],' *Jewish Perspectives on Christianity* (ed. F. A. Rothschild) 111–121.

Stowers, S. K., *Letter Writing in Greco-Roman Antiquity* (Philadelphia: Westminster, 1986).

Strecker, G., 'Befreiung und Rechtfegtigung,' *Rechtfertigung: Festschrift E. Käsemann* (eds J. Friedrich et al.; Tübingen: Mohr/Siebeck, 1976) 479–508.

———, *Das Judenchristentum in den Pseudoklementinen* (2nd ed.; Berlin: Akademie, 1981).

———, 'The Kerygmata Petrou,' *HS* 2.102–127.

Stuhlmacher, P., 'Erwägungen zum ontologischen Charakter der *kaine ktisis* bei Paulus,' *EvT* 27 (1967) 1–35.

———, *Gerechtigkeit Gottes bei Paulus* (Göttingen: Vandenhoeck & Ruprecht, 1965).

Sumney, J. L., *Identifying Paul's Opponents: The Question of Method in 2 Corinthians* (Sheffield: JSOT, 1990).

Taubes, J., *Die politische Theologie des Paulus* (München: Fink, 1993).

Theissen, G., *The Social Setting of Pauline Christianity* (ed. J. H. Schütz; Philadelphia: Fortress, 1982).

Thrall, M. E., *A Critical and Exegetical Commentary on the Second Epistle to the Corinthians* (vol. 1; Edinburgh: T&T Clark, 1994).

Tillich, P., *Systematic Theology* (Chicago: Chicago University Press, 1951).

Trobisch, D., *Paul's Letter Collection* (Minneapolis: Fortress, 1994).

Urbach, E. E., *The Sages* (2 vols.; Jerusalem: Magnes, 1979).

Van Buren, P. M., *A Theology of the Jewish-Christian Reality* (Parts 1–3; San Francisco: Harper & Row, 1980, 1983, 1988).

Van Voorst, R. E., *The Ascents of James* (Atlanta: Scholars, 1989).

Verhoef, E., *Er Staat Geschreven . . . De Oud-Testamentische Citaten in de Brief aan de Galaten* (Meppel: Krips Repro, 1979).

Vermaseren, M. J., *Cybele and Attis: The Myth and the Cult* (London: Thames & Hudson, 1977).

Vermes, G., *The Dead Sea Scrolls in English* (3rd ed.; London: Penguin, 1987).

Vielhauer, P., *Geschichte der urchristlichen Literatur* (Berlin: de Gruyter, 1975).

——, 'Gesetzesdienst und Stoicheiadienst im Galaterbrief,' *Rechtfertigung: Festschrift für Ernst Käsemann* (ed J. Friedrich et al.; Tübingen: Mohr/Siebeck, 1976) 543–555.

——, 'Introduction [to Apocalypses and Related Subjects],' *New Testament Apocrypha* (eds E. Hennecke and W. Schneemelcher; 2 vols; Philadelphia: Westminster, 1963–1965) 2.581–607.

——, *Oikodomē. Aufsätze zum Neuen Testament* (vol. 1; Munich: Kaiser, 1979).

——, 'Paulus und das Alte Testament,' *Studien zur Geschichte und Theologie der Reformation* (ed. L. Abramowski, et al.; Neukirchen-Vluyn: Neukirchner, 1969) 33–62.

Von Arnim, J., *Stoicorum Veterum Fragmenta* (4 vols; Stuttgart: Teubner, 1964).

Vos, J., 'Antijudaismus/Antisemitismus im Theologischen Wörterbuch zum Neuen Testament,' *NedTTs* 38 (1984) 89–110.

——, 'Die hermeneutische Antinomie bei Paulus (Gal 3.11–12; Röm 10.5–10,' *NTS* 38 (1992) 254–270.

Vos, J., 'Inleiding: Leo Baeck en het Duitse jodendom,' *Leo Baeck: Een licht breekt door* (ed. J. S. Vos; Kampen: Kok, 1986) 9–41.

——, '*Legem statuimus*; Rhetorische Aspekte der Gesetzesdebatte zwischen Juden und Christen,' *Juden und Christen in der Antike* (eds J. van Amersfoort and J. van Oort: Kampen; Kok, 1990), 44–60.

——, *Traditionsgeschichtliche Untersuchungen zur Paulinischen Pneumatologie* (Assen: Van Gorcum, 1973).

Vouga, F., 'Der Galaterbrief: kein Brief an die Galater? Essay über den literarischen Charakter des letzten grossen Paulusbriefes,' *Schrift und Tradition: Festschrift Josef Ernst* (eds K. Backhaus and G. Untergassmair: Paderborn: Schöningh, 1996) 243–258.

Walter, N., 'Christusglaube und Heidnische Religiosität in Paulinischen Gemeinden,' *NTS* 25 (1979) 422–442.

——, 'Hellenistische Diaspora-Juden an der Wiege des Urchristentums,' *The New Testament and Hellenistic Judaism* (eds P. Borgen and S. Giversen; Aarhus: Aarhus University Press, 1995) 37–58.

——, 'Zur Interpretation von Römer 9–11,' *ZTK* 81 (1984) 172–195.

——, 'Paulus und die Gegner des Christusevangeliums in Galatien,' *L'Apôtre Paul* (ed. A. Vanhoye; Leuven: Leuven University Press, 1986) 351–356.

——, *Der Thoraausleger Aristobulos* (Berlin: Akademie, 1964).

Way, D., *The Lordship of Christ: Ernst Käsemann's Interpretation of Paul's Theology* (Oxford: Clarendon, 1991).

Wegenast, K., *Das Verständnis der Tradition bei Paulus und in den Deuteropaulinen* (Neukirchen, 1962).

Werblowsky, R. J. Zwi, 'Trennendes und Gemeinsames,' *Zur Erneurung.* 29–43.

Widengren, G., 'Leitende Ideen und Quellen der iranischen Apokalyptik,' *Apocalypticism in the Mediterranian World and the Near East* (ed. D. Hellholm; Tübingen: Mohr/Siebeck, 1983) 77–162.

Wilckens, U., *Der Brief an die Römer* (3 vols; Zürich: Benziger, 1978–1982).

——, *Weisheit und Torheit* (Tübingen: Mohr/Siebeck, 1959).

Wimsatt, W. and M. Beardsley, 'The Intentional Fallacy,' *The Verbal Icon: Studies in the Meaning of Poetry* (Lexington: University of Kentucky Press, 1954).

Windisch, H., *Der zweite Korintherbrief* (Göttingen: Vandenhoeck & Ruprecht, 1924).

Winger, M., *By What Law? The Meaning of Nomos in the Letters of Paul* (Atlanta: Scholars, 1992).

Winston, D., 'Solomon, Wisdom of,' *ABD*.

Winter, B. W. and A. D. Clark (eds), *The Book of Acts in Its Ancient Literary Setting* (6 vols; Grand Rapids: Eerdmans, 1993–).

Winter, M., *Pneumatiker und Psychiker in Korinth* (Marburg: Elwert, 1975).

Winter, P., *On The Trial of Jesus* (Berlin: de Gruyter, 1961).

Witherington, B., *Paul's Narrative Thought World* (Louisville: Westminster/John Knox, 1994).

Wright, N. T., *The Climax of the Covenant: Christ and the Law in Pauline Theology* (Edinburgh: T&T Clark, 1991).

Zahl, P. F. M., *Rechtfertigungslehre Ernst Käsemanns* (Stuttgart: Calwer, 1996).

Zur Erneuerung des Verhältnisses von Christen und Juden (Mülheim [Ruhr], 1980).

Index of Selected Scripture References

Index of Authors

(*medieval and modern*)

Index of Subjects

(including some ancient names)